13

Jews and Judaism in
the Middle Ages

Jews and Judaism in the Middle Ages

Theodore L. Steinberg

Praeger Series on the Middle Ages
Jane Chance, Series Editor

Westport, Connecticut
London

Library of Congress Cataloging-in-Publication Data

Steinberg, Theodore L. (Theodore Louis), 1947-
  Jews and Judaism in the Middle Ages / Theodore L. Steinberg.
     p. cm. — (Praeger series on the Middle Ages, ISSN 1939-2508)
  Includes bibliographical references and index.
  ISBN 978-0-275-98588-2 (alk. paper)
  1. Judaism—History—Medieval and early modern period, 425-1789. 2.
Jews—History—70-1789. 3. Jews—Intellectual life—History—To 1500. I. Title.
  BM180.S74 2008
  296.09'02—dc22   2007036479

British Library Cataloguing in Publication Data is available.

Library of Congress Catalog Card Number: 2007036479

ISBN: 978-0-275-98588-2
ISSN: 1939-2508

First published in 2008

Praeger Publishers, 88 Post Road West, Westport, CT 06881
An imprint of Greenwood Publishing Group, Inc.
www.praeger.com

Printed in the United States of America

The paper used in this book complies with the
Permanent Paper Standard issued by the National
Information Standards Organization (Z39.48–1984).

10 9 8 7 6 5 4 3 2 1

Every reasonable effort has been made to trace the owners of copyrighted materials in this
book, but in some instances this has proven impossible. The author and publisher will be
glad to receive information leading to more complete acknowledgments in subsequent print-
ings of the book and in the meantime extend their apologies for any omissions.

To the martyrs—
And the survivors.

Contents

A photo essay follows page 160

Copyright Acknowledgments

Preface

There are already many fine books on the history of the Jews in the Middle Ages; I need only mention the works of such scholars as Robert Chazan, Cecil Roth, and Kenneth Stow as examples. Furthermore, there are excellent detailed studies of virtually every topic that will be covered in the following pages. So the question arises, why is this book necessary? After all, Ecclesiastes says that "The making of many books is without limit" (12:12), so an author ought to have a pretty good reason for writing another one. Here is mine.

All of those other studies, as excellent as they are, presume a certain degree of knowledge on the part of the reader—knowledge about Judaism, knowledge about the Torah and the Talmud, knowledge of Jewish customs and traditions and beliefs, as well as a general knowledge about the Middle Ages. Certainly most readers of those books, since they already have some interest in the topic, do have that knowledge, which means that they can read and understand those sophisticated studies with little difficulty. But what of people who lack that knowledge? They might well have trouble entering the scholarly conversation, not only because they do not know what preceded their arrival but because they do not even know the subject of the conversation. For example, I am convinced, after many years of unscientific observation, that people generally do not know what Judaism is. I am not talking here about the vexed question of "Who is a Jew?," a subject that has been brought before the Supreme Court of Israel; I am referring only to a definition of Judaism. What does Judaism mean, and what does it therefore mean to say that someone is a Jew? As we will see, the word "Jew" was used frequently in the Middle Ages to mean anyone who was not a Christian, and the term was used frequently in places like Anglo-Saxon England where there were no actual Jews at all.

Of course, there still exists a notion that Jews are simply people who do not believe that Jesus was the messiah. While Jews do not, in fact, believe that Jesus was the messiah, neither do Muslims or Hindus or Buddhists—only Christians believe that Jesus was the messiah. Thus, non-belief in the messiahship of Jesus defines "non-Christian," but it does not mean Jewish, though in the earlier part of the Middle Ages, when Jews were the only non-Christians in most of Europe, it was possible to make that equation. Still, we need to know the positive attributes of Judaism so that we can know what it is rather than what it is not. What constitutes Judaism? What makes someone Jewish? Is there such a thing as Jewish belief? These and other questions require answers and will guide the development of the following chapters.

Numerous problems confront us in this task, but at this point I will mention only one, the common phrase, often used with the best of ecumenical intentions: the "Judeo-Christian tradition." For Christians this phrase can be quite meaningful, as it demonstrates the link that Christians see between their religion and the system that gave birth to it. For Jews, however, to whom Christianity is an alien belief system, the phrase is not only meaningless but a distortion, as Arthur Cohen illustrates in *The Myth of the Judeo-Christian Tradition*. For Jews there is Judaism. Except that so many Jews live in predominantly Christian societies and therefore interact frequently with Christians and Christian customs (the post office, for instance, is closed on Christmas), Christianity has no official influence on Judaism. When people ask me what Jesus' role is in Judaism, they are frequently astounded to learn that he plays no role. Surely, they argue, even if Jews do not believe that Jesus was the messiah, they must regard him as a prophet. Well, no, Jesus plays no official role in Judaism except to the extent that he was a Jew whose later title (Christ, anointed one, messiah) was applied to a religion that has interacted in many different ways with Judaism. (Many scholars, among the most recent being Israel Yuval, make the point that some aspects of Judaism developed as reactions to or under the influence of Christianity, but acknowledging that phenomenon is not the same as saying that Jesus has played any role in Judaism.)

The problem of the Judeo-Christian tradition can be seen even in the terminology that we apply to Sacred Scriptures. Jews and Christians may use the same word, Bible, which simply comes from the Greek word for "book," but Jews and Christians mean different things by that word. Christians mean what they call the Old and New Testaments, but because Jews do not include the New Testament as part of the Bible, they do not use the term "Old Testament." For Jews, the Christian "Old Testament" *is* the Bible. Consequently, in the pages that follow I will use the terms "Bible," "Old Testament," and "New Testament" when I refer to Christian concepts, but I will use the modern Hebrew "Tanakh," which is an acronym for the three sections of the Hebrew Scriptures, Torah (the Five Books of Moses), Nevi'im ("prophets"), and Ketuvim ("the other writings"), and the Hebrew word "Torah" when I refer to Jewish concepts.

Many writers on various aspects of the Middle Ages mention the Jews, though as Gavin Langmuir has shown in the first chapter of *Toward a Definition of Antisemitism,* such references have not always been so common. Nevertheless, it is not always clear that those writers are so well-informed about what they are saying, as I found in reading two recent books written by established scholars and published by major presses. In *The Formation of Christianity,* Judith Herrin writes, "Like Christianity, [Islam] broke from the primitive, tribal claims of the Israelites."[1] What does this statement actually mean? What does it mean to say that the Israelites were primitive and tribal in either the first century, when Christianity developed, or the seventh, when Islam appeared? Does it mean that they were backward and exclusivist? Their alleged backwardness is disproved by the culture they developed, but the charge of exclusivism has followed the Jews throughout their history, as though every other culture has been ecumenical and welcoming to outsiders, as though Christianity has not condemned non-Christians to everlasting perdition, and as though Islam did not have the concept of the dhimmi (the non-Muslim on whom additional burdens and restrictions could be placed), or as though there were no jokes today (unfair though they may be) of what conditions are like for tourists in France. People have tended to feel comfortable with other people like themselves, though of course the world would be a better place if we recognized how much we all have in common. And, as we will see, the Jews were bound together by religious restrictions such as Sabbath and holiday observances and dietary laws. But were they more "tribal" than the Romans with their notion of citizenship or than the medieval Franks?

In another recent book, *Medieval Foundations of the Western Intellectual Tradition,* Marcia Colish writes, "The commentaries on the moral and religious law known as Talmud and the commentaries on the Talmud

known as Mishnah, became increasingly important as a basis for religious identity for Jews after the destruction of the second temple of
Jerusalm in A.D. 70 and the diaspora."[2] Again, in an otherwise excellent
book that focuses on Christianity, this statement is startling. Conceivably,
the Talmud could be described as a commentary "on the moral and religious law," though that description is much like saying that a seven-
course banquet at a four-star restaurant provides sustenance. The statement is true, but it omits the flavor. But the Mishnah is certainly not a
commentary on the Talmud. It is the first stage of the written Talmud,
compiled and written down around the year 200 by Rabbi Yehuda ha-
Nasi (Rabbi Judah the Prince). Before that process, the Mishnah (the
Oral Law) existed orally. The other part of the Talmud, the Gemara,
was completed some time after 500. All of this material will be covered
in detail in the second chapter. My point here is simply that scholars
who write quite competently about the Western tradition may be at a
loss when dealing with the Judaic part of that tradition. Perhaps this
volume will be of some help to them.

The first two chapters, then, will examine the meanings of "Jew" and
"Judaism" and the development of rabbinic literature. While neither topic
is, strictly speaking, medieval, together they will provide the background
that readers need for understanding medieval developments. In the third
chapter, we consider theological problems among the three major faiths
of the medieval world—Judaism, Christianity, and Islam. The better we
understand the complex relationships among these faiths, the better we
can understand our topic and its complications, which we will reach in the
fourth chapter, an overview of medieval Jewish history. Among the complications of that history is that during the Middle Ages, Jews existed
within a number of different civilizations. The major areas that we will
consider, using terms that were first used in the tenth century, will be the
Sephardic world (Spain and Southern France), and the Ashkenazic world
(Northern France, England, and Germany), but we will also have to mention the Jews of Italy, of North Africa, of the Middle East, and even of
China and India. All of these Jews, depending on who their neighbors
were and on a variety of historical conditions, had different fates during
the Middle Ages. In the fifth chapter, we will look at the everyday lives of
medieval Jews, including such topics as education, prayer, messianic
expectations, and the role of women in Jewish life.

It is worth emphasizing here, and throughout this volume, that
despite popular misconceptions, Jewish life in the Middle Ages was not
merely a succession of horrors. There were horrors aplenty (massacres,

oppression, absurd accusations, expulsions) but Judaism during the Middle Ages must not be defined by those horrors. Certainly they should not be forgotten or overlooked, but they cannot be allowed to control our sense of history. The survival of the Jews in the face of those horrors is, on one level, miraculous; but on another level, mere survival may not in itself be so significant. What is more significant is that in the face of those horrors, the Jews created a vibrant culture. Salo Baron wrote that throughout his life he struggled "against the hitherto dominant 'lachrymose conception of Jewish History' ... because I have felt that an overemphasis on Jewish sufferings distorted the total picture of the Jewish historic evolution."[3] Taking Baron's words to heart, I will describe those sufferings, but I will try to focus more heavily on the culture that the Jews created.

That they did so in the face of such persecution is particularly remarkable, and before we begin to study those achievements, we will examine the causes of the persecution. In the Sephardic world, where Jewish culture flourished alongside its Muslim counterpart, Jews and Muslims often managed to live together in relative peace, though there were also periods of terror for the Jews. Even more startling was the relationship between Judaism and Christianity in Christian Europe, where Jews, as the only religious minority, became, in the words of Kenneth Stow, an alienated minority. The Middle Ages was not a time of inclusiveness and acceptance of difference, and for a variety of reasons, the Jews were perceived as a threat on both social and religious grounds. We will examine Jewish-Christian relations in some detail.

But we will also examine, in the concluding chapters, the achievements of medieval Jews in a number of areas, particularly in the fields of literature, philosophy, and religion. The sixth chapter, then, will focus on medieval Jewish biblical commentaries and their relationships to contemporary Christian approaches to the Bible. The seventh chapter will consider medieval Hebrew poetry. Challenging and beautiful though that poetry may be, it remains largely unknown in the poetry-loving world, although collections in translation are available and a few poems have begun to appear in world literature anthologies. We will look at both liturgical and non-liturgical poems from the whole of the Middle Ages. And the eighth chapter will consider medieval Jewish philosophy and mysticism. In the field of philosophy, the Jews played several important roles. First, the Jews were instrumental in bringing Greek thought from the Muslim world to the Christian, both as translators and as conveyors of books. But there were also, particularly in the Sephardic world, a number of Jewish philosophers whose works made a profound impact on both Jewish and non-Jewish philosophers, as they combined philosophical thought with religious belief.

In the Middle Ages, of course, philosophy and religion were often intertwined, but in the field of strictly religious studies, Jews also made significant contributions. In the field of biblical studies, they had the advantage of being able to read the Tanach in the original Hebrew and Aramaic. They also had a long history of literal interpretations of the Tanach, as well as more fanciful and imaginative interpretations. By the twelfth century, a number of Christian scholars in France, particularly at the Abbey of St. Victor in Paris, recognized the value of those literal interpretations and began to consult Jewish scholars and to learn a little Hebrew themselves.

Perhaps the greatest accomplishment of medieval Jewry, however, and a theme traced throughout this study, was the creation, transmission, and development of rabbinic Judaism. This process began much earlier, but the work of generations of medieval Jews contributed to a gradual evolution of religious thought and the establishment of a religious framework that allowed a people to pursue its vision of the world. And even though Judaism continued to develop after the Middle Ages, that medieval construct continues to exercise a powerful influence on modern Judaism. The modern study of the Tanach and of the Talmud is unthinkable without the work done by Rashi, Abraham ibn Ezra, Nachmanides, David and Yosef Kimchi, the Tosafists, and others whom we will encounter. Modern editions of these sacred books are still printed with the medieval commentaries, not just because of tradition but because those commentaries are still essential for understanding the texts.

This study, then, covers many aspects of medieval Jewish life, not as historical curiosities but as living history. It follows two major themes—the survival and accomplishments of Judaism in a world that became increasingly hostile and the solidification of rabbinic Judaism—but it also attempts to capture what life might have been like for Jewish men and women as they went about their ordinary activities. We have difficulty imagining what everyday life must have been like in the Middle Ages, despite the existence of well-researched books on the topic, such as Paul B. Newman's *Daily Life in the Middle Ages*. It is difficult for us to imagine the sounds and smells of the Middle Ages or to conceive of life without indoor plumbing or instant communications or heating and air-conditioning, even though many people around the globe still live that way. It is even harder for us to imagine living productive lives under those conditions in an often hostile and threatening social environment. My hope is that this study helps readers to understand and to internalize that way of life.

Readers should understand, however, that this book is highly selective. Eight volumes of Salo Baron's *Social and Religious History of the Jewish People* do not cover everything, so a single volume like this can provide only the briefest sketch of the subject. Also, because this volume is intended largely for readers who have little experience with the subject, I have confined myself to sources written in English. There are volumes and volumes of material in French, German, Spanish, Hebrew, and other languages, but every source that I cite is available in English so that readers can pursue the subjects that I cover in more depth.

Of course, all of the Jewish names that I cite must be transliterated from Hebrew. I do use the Hebrew forms (such as Moshe and Yehuda rather than the English Moses and Judah). A full list of Hebrew names with their English equivalents can be found in the first appendix. Also, I distinguish between the Hebrew letter כ, which is transliterated as *kh* and the Hebrew letter ח, which is transliterated as ḥ, though they are pronounced identically.

Passages from the Tanach are quoted from the Jewish Publication Society translations of the *Torah* (1962), the *Prophets* (1978), and *The Writings* (1982). Passages from the New Testament are quoted from the Douay Rheims Version.

Because this book deals so intimately with Judaism and Christianity, it refers frequently to God. God, of course, is incorporeal and is therefore neither male nor female. Nevertheless, English requires pronouns. In keeping with medieval views about God, I refer to God with male pronouns. To do otherwise would be to give a less accurate picture of medieval religion.

And one final point: There is a saying that where there are two Jews, there are three (or four or seven) opinions. The same point can be made about scholars. No area that I will examine in the following pages has not already been the subject of scholarly controversy. People who know far more than I do have taken equally strong stands on different sides of every issue. This is not a bad thing. In fact, it is a good thing. In fact, it is, as we will see, quite Talmudic. Through disagreement and resolution, we learn. Given the limited state of so much of our information and the paucity of our records, disagreement is inevitable.

But no one will disagree that while the writing of a book is largely a solitary occupation, its final appearance involves a community. I have many people to thank for their help as I worked on this project. Jane Chance, the editor of this series, and Elizabeth Demers and Elizabeth Potenza of Greenwood Publishing have been of incalculable help and have been a pleasure to work with. Minda Rae Amiran, Benjamin Gampel, and Rabbi Shalom Carmy have read either all or parts of the manuscript and made invaluable comments. My grandchildren, Akiva and Gavriel Davis, and Ida Steinberg (who all arrived as this project was in progress), helped to sustain me as I wrote. And most of all, as always, I owe so much to my wife Phyllis, who not only read the manuscript but listened to a lot of kvetching while the work was under way.

PART I

BACKGROUNDS

Jews and Judaism:
What Are They?

In 2004, Andrew P. Scheil published his study *The Footsteps of Israel: Understanding Jews in Anglo-Saxon England.* At first glance, this title is puzzling, because there were no Jews in Anglo-Saxon England. Either the book must be very brief or Scheil means something different than we might think. Scheil's focus, actually, is on the ways in which Anglo-Saxon writers portrayed Jews, despite their absence from the country and despite the writers' probably never having seen a real Jew. Similarly, there are numerous studies of Chaucer's blatantly anti-Semitic Prioress' Tale that seek to discover whether Chaucer was anti-Semitic or whether he was portraying his Prioress as being so. Again, however, the curious point is that the Jews had been expelled from England a century earlier, in 1290, so that when Chaucer wrote, there were effectively no Jews in England. Chaucer had traveled to the Continent, so he might have encountered Jews there, but why did Chaucer, like his Anglo-Saxon predecessors, describe Jews with such contempt if not outright hatred? A simple answer is that medieval Christians believed, based on the New Testament, on sermons they heard in church, and on images in popular culture, that the Jews were allegedly the killers of Jesus, were enemies of Christianity, and were allies of Satan. Thus, even if there were no Jews in Anglo-Saxon England or in Chaucer's England, they remained a threat in people's imaginations. Real Jews may have been absent, but "virtual Jews," a phrase that Sylvia Tomasch uses, were always there.

The reality of these "virtual Jews" was often greater than the reality of real Jews. For instance, as Cecil Roth points out, even in the late fifth-century Roman Empire the word "Jew" came to mean an opponent, someone with whom one disagreed. Thus Arianism, the Christian heresy against which early Christian theologians argued so vehemently, with its strong emphasis on God and on Jesus' inferiority, was described as a "Jewish" movement simply because it struck the theologians as un-Christian.[1] The negative connotations of the term "Jew" even then overwhelmed the denotations, as is the case in modern times. In the *Oxford English Dictionary*, the definition of "Jew" as a verb reads: "To cheat or overreach, in the way attributed to Jewish traders or usurers. Also, to drive a hard bargain ... to haggle. Phr. *To jew down*, to beat down in price." The 1989 edition of the dictionary adds, "These uses are now considered to be offensive," but the dictionary is quite correct in noting how the word has been and continues to be used.

Until recently there was no Hebrew term for the word "Judaism." Non-Jews may have referred to Judaism, but Jews did not. Shaye J. D. Cohen's *The Beginnings of Jewishness* examines the development of Jewish identity in antiquity, from both Jewish and non-Jewish perspectives. As he notes, the Greek word "Ioudaios," which is often translated as "Jew," more precisely means "Judean." That is, the word had national and geographic rather than religious meaning: it meant someone from Judea, one of the major provinces of ancient Israel. It was not until the time of Josephus that "Ioudaios" referred to someone who held particular beliefs, who worshipped "the God whose temple is in Jerusalem and who follows the way of life of the Jew."[2] Since the Greeks arrived in Israel in the late fourth century B.C.E. and Josephus wrote in the late first century C.E., the idea of Jewishness took a long time to reach even this stage; but outside of the land of Israel, the word that we understand as Jew meant someone who had come from Israel, and it was easy for Jews in the Diaspora to deny their Jewish identity simply by fitting into the surrounding cultures. The word "Ioudaismos," which we might translate as "Judaism," first appears in the Apocryphal Second Maccabees, where it means "the aggregate of all those characteristics that make Judaeans Judaean ...," though again, those characteristics are not specified.[3]

It was only after the destruction of the Second Temple in 70 C.E. and the subsequent developments of both Christianity and rabbinic Judaism that Judaism began to take on a more familiar shape. We can see in some famous Roman writers that Jews were well known in Rome. Even before the destruction, the Roman poet Horace, writing in the first century B.C.E., has one of his characters attempt to avoid an obligation by claiming, "Today is the thirtieth Sabbath. Would you affront the circumcised Jews?" (Horace, *Satires, Epistles, and Ars Poetica* I.ix.69–69). No one is quite sure what Horace meant by "the thirtieth Sabbath," and the likelihood is that Horace has his character speaking gibberish, but the reference to circumcision resonates. Circumcision, a central Jewish ritual, had been a major issue in the second-century B.C.E. Hasmonean rebellion when Hellenized Jews tried to abandon circumcision or undo the effects of circumcisions that had already been performed. The Romans, too, regarded circumcision as a peculiar custom associated with the Jews.

Elsewhere, Horace writes about an absurd idea that "Apella, the Jew, may believe it, not I" (*Satires* I.v.100), a line which is often taken as a reference to Jewish gullibility. And why should Jews be considered more gullible than anyone else? One possibility is that Horace refers to what he understood of Jewish belief, which seemed to many Romans like a new form of superstition. For instance, another Roman satirist, Juvenal, writing more than a century later, refers critically to Jewish worship of a deity who cannot be represented by an idol. The Romans were very fond of their statuary, their idols, and Juvenal undoubtedly knew that major incidents had been precipitated in Israel by the Roman insistence that various statues be placed in the precincts of the Temple.

Juvenal also refers to other Jewish customs, such as Sabbath observance, refraining from eating pork, and circumcision. He claims that Jews are clannish and they flout the laws of Rome while following those of Moses. While he was probably correct in the latter claim, his accusation of clannishness, a common accusation against the Jews, requires some explanation. Because of various Jewish customs, Jews have tended to stay together. Of course, it has been normal throughout history for people to be closest to those most like them, but traditions like dietary laws and Sabbath observance have necessitated a special closeness (or, in negative terms, clannishness) among Jews.

When we discuss Horace and Juvenal, we must remember that they were both satirists and that the satirist's job is to level humorous criticism, so it is hard to know how seriously we should take what some think is their anti-Semitism. Juvenal, in particular, seems not to have liked Jews, but Juvenal did not seem to like anyone but other Romans— and not all of them, either. At the same time, it is fascinating to see Juvenal refer to Jews with their baskets and hay, a reference that may appear odd until we understand that Jews were not allowed to cook on the Sabbath but were allowed to cover hot food with materials that would help them retain their heat. Although this regulation is recorded in the Mishnah (Shabbat 2:7), the Mishnah was not compiled until about 200 C.E., so Juvenal's criticism helps us to see a pre-Mishnaic application of the law.

If Horace and Juvenal were satirists, Tacitus considered himself a historian, though his account of the Jews, written around the beginning of the second century C.E., is hardly historical. After giving an account of Jewish history that is so garbled as to be nonsensical, he notes that "the Jews regard as profane all that we hold sacred; on the other hand, they permit all that we abhor." Like Juvenal, he refers to the practice of circumcision and to abstention from pork, a custom he mysteriously attributes to the memorialization of a plague. He also mentions the Sabbath and even the sabbatical year, but he shows no understanding of those institutions: "They say that they first chose to rest on the seventh day because that day ended their toils; but after a time they were led by the charms of indolence to give over the seventh year as well to inactivity. Others say this is done in honor of Saturn ..." He goes on to characterize other Jewish rituals as "base and abominable," signs of Jewish depravity, and he seems particularly upset that the Jews regard the common Roman practice of infanticide as criminal (*The Histories,* V.4–5).

Clearly Tacitus does not like Jews, but equally as clear, he has little idea of what he is talking about. Perhaps some of his hostility has its roots in the fact that the Jews—that is, the Judeans—gave the Romans a hard time during the Great Revolt (68–73 C.E.). To us, Tacitus appears, like Horace and Juvenal, to be attacking a religious minority, but, like the satirists, he is actually attacking members of a foreign minority who live in Rome and who follow a number of customs that Romans find unusual and absurd. These writers mock or attack Judeans, rather than Jews in the modern sense.

It was only with the rise of Christianity that Jews were defined, and defined themselves, as a religious group, and even then that designation is somewhat suspect. Because Christianity developed out of a Jewish background, early Christians had to determine and even exaggerate the differences between themselves and Jews, as we see already in the epistles of Paul, which were written in the 50's of the first century. As Christianity continued to grow and was transformed from a Jewish sect into a new religion, those differences, despite the existence of many similarities, continued to receive most of people's attention. When the Second

Temple was destroyed in 70 C.E., and Judaism had to find a way to maintain its continuity, the gulf between Judaism and Christianity widened further. By the time that the Roman Empire adopted Christianity as its official religion in 312, the enmity that had grown up during almost three centuries also became public policy. During those centuries, as Christianity defined itself (the Council of Nicea, where the Nicean Creed originated, was held in 325), and as Judaism was transformed from a cult centered on the Temple to a universal system, adherents of both systems began to see the world in terms of "us" and "them," as Cohen and many others have recognized. Christianity, with its proselytizing impulse (Matthew 28:19 reads, "Going therefore, teach ye all nations; baptizing them in the name of the Father, and of the Son, and of the Holy Ghost."), wanted everyone to be part of "us." Judaism, which had been and continued to be subject to persecutions, had a stronger sense that the differences between "us" and "them" were irreconcilable.

But all of this discussion does little to tell us what that Jewish "us" is. What does it mean to be Jewish? Cohen, as we have seen, says that "A Jew is someone who venerates the God of the Judaeans, the God whose temple is in Jerusalem." The Temple had been the center of Jewish worship for a millennium, even requiring long pilgrimages for those who lived in the Diaspora, and the destruction of the temple by the Romans in 70 C.E. was a cataclysmic event for the Jews. If Judaism could not accept a messiah who had been killed, it also could not define itself according to a temple that had been destroyed, even if it posited that the Temple had been destroyed as punishment for the sins of the people. The question for Judaism was how to define itself after the Temple had been destroyed.

Several answers suggested themselves. A prominent early answer was that the Temple would be rebuilt yet again. After all, the First Temple had been destroyed by the Babylonians in 586 B.C.E. and work on rebuilding it had begun only decades later when the Persians conquered the Babylonians and allowed the Jewish exiles to return to Israel. Many Jews, therefore, hoped that the Temple would be rebuilt yet again. Even as late as the 360's, when the emperor Julian (known to Christians as Julian the Apostate) tried to stop the spread of Christianity, hopes for the rebuilding of the Temple rose. Julian gave the Jews permission to begin the project, but work stopped almost as soon as it started and hopes for a rebuilt temple became tied to the coming of the Messiah.

So again the question arises, if there is no temple, what is a Jew? Clearly the Temple has not existed for nearly two thousand years and

yet the Jews continue to exist. What are they? One answer is that Jews
are people who believe in and follow the teaching of the Tanakh, particularly those in the Torah, the Five Books of Moses. Of course, many of
those teachings (those related to the sacrificial system of the Temple)
can no longer be followed, but many can. Let us take the Ten Commandments as an example:

6. You shall not murder	1. I the Lord am your God
7. You shall not commit adultery	2. You shall not make for your-self ... image[s]
8. You shall not steal	3. You shall not swear falsely by the name of ... God
9. You shall not bear false witness	4. Remember the Sabbath day and keep it holy
10. You shall not covet	5. Honor your father and your mother

In Judaism, the Ten Commandments are often depicted on the two
Tablets of the Law, and because Hebrew is written from right to left, the
columns also go from right to left. Also, different religious traditions
enumerate the Ten Commandments in different ways. This list represents the Jewish approach, in which the First Commandment, "I the
Lord am your God," hardly sounds like a commandment.

Even a quick look at the two columns indicates that the two sets of
five differ significantly: The first five relate to a human-divine relationship, how people should behave toward God, while the second five
describe human-human relationships ("Honor your father and your
mother" serves as a transition, since God is often regarded in the role
of a parent). What is particularly important here is that these two sets of
commandments are inseparable. People do not have the option of
choosing between them, of choosing to serve God, for instance, but
treating other people badly. In fact, it is this attitude that the biblical
prophets so often castigate, accusing the people of bringing sacrifices to
God while simultaneously abusing the poor. Such behavior is unacceptable. Our divine and human obligations intertwine. In the Gospel
According to Matthew, Jesus shows his Jewish awareness of this issue
when he is asked a silly question: Which is the greatest of the commandments? He answers by quoting Deuteronomy 6:5, "Thou shalt love the
Lord thy God with thy whole heart ..." But then he says, "And the second is like to this: Thou shalt love thy neighbor as thyself" (Matthew

22:37–40). Jesus, as a Jew, knows about the inseparability of those realms.

By treating the commandments in this way, however, we have not only treated them literally but we have also created at least one additional responsibility, the responsibility to see that the ritual and moral laws are inseparable. And we have not even begun to examine what the commandments themselves mean. For instance, the sixth commandment is often listed as "You shall not kill," even though the Torah prescribes capital punishment for a number of offenses. This seeming contradiction is simply the result of a mistranslation: the Hebrew actually says, "You shall not murder." But what about "Honor your father and mother?" What does that mean? Does it mean one should love one's parents? Does it mean that one should show honor to one's parents without considering love? Does it mean that one should do what one's father demands, even if that demand involves doing something immoral or illegal? Perhaps even more puzzling is the fourth commandment: "Remember the Sabbath day and keep it holy. Six days you shall labor and do all your work, but the seventh day is a Sabbath of the lord your God: you shall not do any work ..." (Exodus 20:8–10). The first question we have to ask here is what do some of the key words (like "holy" and "work") mean? Then we must decide how this commandment can be put into practice. As we will see in the next chapter, these are the kinds of questions that the Talmud considers.

At least for ancient and medieval times, Jews were people who uniformly believed that the Torah was given by God to Moses on Mt. Sinai and that they were obligated to follow the rules of that Torah as closely as possible. This definition requires refining, but it offers a starting point. It also requires some explanation.

For instance, a common question is whether Jews comprise a race, an ethnic group, a religion, a nation, or some other entity. The answer, as is so often the case, is yes and no. Part of the problem depends again on how we define those terms, all of which have, and have had, a variety of technical meanings. Nevertheless, during the Middle Ages, and well into the modern era, Jews have been considered a race, a nation, and a religious group. Race is the easiest of the concepts to dismiss. Jews have been called a race as a way of further alienating them from the rest of society, but there is nothing racial about Judaism. Jews can belong to any race, although the concept of race has itself been challenged in recent times.

Jews have also been referred to as a nation, again sometimes as a way of showing their difference from the rest of the society. If Jews are a nation and they live within the borders of another nation, like France or Germany, then their loyalty to that host nation is suspect. Many times throughout history, Jews have been accused of aiding the enemies of the places where they lived. At one time, as we have seen, the word Jew (or Ioudaios) did indeed refer to nationhood, but when Israel ceased to be a nation in 70 c.e., Jews ceased to be citizens of that nation. Today Israel is a nation, but Jews live in many other nations as well. A problem here, though, is that Jews have often referred to themselves as a nation, perhaps because they once were and have looked forward to being so again, but since the destruction of the Temple, they have been scattered among other nations.

As for religion, that term also raises problems. We are accustomed to thinking that Judaism is a religion, a faith, like Christianity or Islam, but when Jewish scholars as different as Daniel Boyarin and Adin Steinsaltz agree that Judaism is not a religion in the usual sense of the term, we must pay attention. Actually, their reservations about calling Judaism a religion are based on similar grounds: Judaism is not a "faith" in the same way that Christianity and Islam are; Judaism does not seek to be universal, and Judaism is linked specifically to the Jewish people. Let us briefly examine each of these points.

As the New Testament shows, Christianity clearly depends on faith. One of the perennial questions that confronts Christian thinkers involves the relationship between faith and works. Of course, in one place we read that "faith without works is dead" (James 2:26), but elsewhere, particularly in the Pauline epistles, the point is repeatedly made that faith in the divinity of Jesus has replaced the necessity of following the laws of the Torah. Thus, the third-century churchman Tertullian could say about his Christianity, "I believe because it is absurd," meaning that a full understanding of divine salvation is beyond human understanding and therefore we are required to suspend our understanding and rely on faith alone. As the Middle Ages progressed, this position underwent many changes, but in the twelfth century, the clash between Abelard and Bernard of Clairvaux over the primacy of faith or reason represented similar concerns and, incidentally, had a profound effect on the lives of the Jews. The Council of Nicea in 325 approved the Nicean Creed, a statement of what a true Christian must believe. "Creed" comes from the Latin "credo," which means "I believe," a phrase that is repeated often in the creed: "We believe in the one holy catholic and apostolic church. We acknowledge one baptism for the forgiveness of sins."

Islam also has a statement of faith, the Shahada, which says that "there is no God but Allah and Mohammed is his prophet," a statement that devout Muslims reaffirm five times each day. From this statement follow several other beliefs, as well as a number of required deeds, such as prayer, pilgrimage, and the observance of the holy month of Ramadan.

The question of faith in Judaism, however, is somewhat more complicated. From some perspectives, Judaism seems to have no particular credo. That is, there is no single statement that sums up Jewish beliefs. The closest that Judaism comes to such a statement is Deuteronomy 6:4, which can be translated in subtly different ways: "Hear, O Israel! The Lord is our God, the Lord alone," or "Hear, O Israel! The Lord our God, the Lord is one." A devout Jew repeats this statement several times a day in prayer, and ideally these are the last words that one says before death. All that this verse affirms is the unity of God, but everything else in Judaism flows from that idea. At the same time, that "everything else" is not always terribly well defined, especially in the field of beliefs. Jews are often asked, "What do Jews believe?" about a variety of topics, questions that are difficult to answer because Jewish beliefs are not always clearly spelled out. As Steinsaltz says, the effort "to determine the basic principles of Judaism … has never been able to get very far, not only because the number of such basic principles is so great that they no longer serve to define anything, but also because an abstraction of Judaism cannot demonstrate its singularity"; or as Boyarin puts it, Judaism cannot be separated from the Jewish people.[4] The Talmud, which was to play so large a role in medieval Jewish life, contains hardly anything that we would consider theological. Rather, it is a vast work that tells us what to do in order to sanctify our lives. It presupposes certain beliefs (that God exists, that God gave the Written and Oral Laws to Moses on Sinai, and others), but it hardly inquires into those matters. Instead it tells us how to observe the Sabbath, or what we should do when we find a lost article, or whether we can eat an egg under certain conditions, matters that at first glance may seem mundane but that as a totality combine to create a profound view of the world and of the role of human beings. Later on, under influence from Christians and Muslims, medieval Jewish thinkers like Maimonides tried to develop a list of basic Jewish beliefs, but those lists were controversial even in their own times.

Nor does Judaism claim to be universal. Christianity asserts that it is *the* way for everyone. Islam, too, seeks universality, which was at least part of the motivation for the Muslim armies that swept through the Middle East, across North Africa, and into Spain in the years after Mohammed's death. Judaism, of course, also feels that its teachings are true, but it never says that everyone should be Jewish. Isaiah's vision is that everyone will worship at God's holy mountain (2:2), but he does not say that everyone will be Jewish.

We can look at the ways several modern scholars approach Jews and Judaism in order to grasp what that medieval understanding might have been:

- "The Jews were a nation, a people, a family, bound together by a covenant with God; they were not a communion of true believers."
- "They are not really a religion or a nation; they are a family."
- "Judaism might be described as the way of understanding proper to one large family of people.... To be a Jew is, in large measure, to belong to this great, sprawling family."
- "By 'Judaism' I mean a world view and way of life formed by a group of people; who regard themselves, and are properly regarded by others, as Israelites, in which the life of the group is both defined and explained within the framework of Israel's holiness."[5]

Three of these four quotations use the word "family," and the fourth seems to imply the concept. We might see the Jews of the Middle Ages as a large family, bound together by the belief that they were, in fact, a family and by the belief that they had a special relationship, a covenant, with God. Much of their behavior, then, was symbolic of those two beliefs. There were, naturally, family quarrels, but there was also great solidarity and the adherence to an enormous number of "family traditions," all of which they saw as part of the covenant that had been made with God by the Patriarchs, by the Israelites at Mount Sinai, and by the Jewish people in the time of Mordecai and Esther.

It is particularly interesting, then, to look at two typical definitions of a Jew from the Middle Ages, one Christian and one Jewish. In Christian Spain from the thirteenth century, *Las siete partidas*, the Seven-Part Code of Alfonso X of Castile, instructs that a "party who believes in, and adheres to the laws of Moses is called a Jew, according to the strict signification of the term, as well as one who is circumcised, and observes the other precepts commanded by his religion."[6] In the thirteenth century, Rabbi Moshe of Coucy said that the three "identifying marks of the medieval Jew were Sabbath observance, male circumcision, and the wearing of tefillin."[7] These two statements demonstrate a significant point: the emphasis on ritual activities, for Judaism does make many demands on its adherents, and often those demands either set Jews apart from their non-Jewish neighbors or created active enmity.

Ultimately the source of the rituals is the Torah. According to the traditional Jewish count, the Torah contains six hundred thirteen commandments (*mitzvoth* in Hebrew), of which two hundred forty-eight are positive ("thou shalt" do something) and three hundred sixty-five are negative ("thou shalt not" do something), but because many of the commandments are quite complex, they involve what seem like many more commandments. To non-Jews (and even to Jews), the system may seem bewildering, but it does make sense.

Judaism makes no distinction between ritual law and moral law. The laws are all important, but while all religions teach similar morals (though the interpretations of those morals may differ), rituals vary. For example, both *Las siete partidas* and Rabbi Moses of Coucy refer to circumcision. For Jews, circumcision is a central ritual that originated in God's commandment to Abraham. While people do not usually invite family and friends to surgery, Jews do invite people to the circumcisions of their sons on the eighth day after birth. The ceremony is called, in Hebrew, the *b'rith* (or *b'ris*) *milah*, which literally means "covenant of circumcision" and marks the initiation of the child into the covenantal relationship that is Judaism. Christianity, under the influence of Paul, regarded circumcision not only as unnecessary but as a sign of weakness, of lack of faith. Numerous times, starting before the advent of Christianity, the enemies of the Jews tried to destroy Judaism by forbidding the practice of circumcision.

The wearing of tefillin, which Rabbi Moshe of Coucy mentions, is another important ritual. Tefillin are small boxes that contain pieces of parchment on which are written verses from the Torah, such as the *Shema* (Hear, O Israel). These boxes are attached to leather straps and are worn by men for morning prayers on weekdays, in accordance with Deuteronomy 6:8 ("bind them as a sign on your hand and let them serve as a symbol on your forehead").

The third ritual to which Rabbi Moshe of Coucy referred is Sabbath observance. As we saw, Juvenal and Tacitus thought that the Jewish practice of setting aside a day of complete rest was a sign of laziness. We will look more closely at Sabbath observance in our examination of the Talmud, but here we need only mention that the Sabbath, from just before sundown on Friday until after sundown on Saturday, was indeed a day of complete rest—no work could be done, no food cooked, no business transacted. The Sabbath, celebrated in imitation of God's rest after the six days of creation, was a monument in time, a foretaste of the World to Come. The Sabbath, one of the most important of Jewish holidays, occurs every week.

There were, however, other holidays. The Jewish New Year, Rosh Hashanah, occurs in the fall and is followed ten days later by the Day of Atonement, Yom Kippur. Rosh Hashanah is a solemn time when people consider their actions over the previous year and resolve to do better in the coming year, a process that extends until Yom Kippur, when people fast (eating and drinking nothing at all) from sundown to sundown as they atone for their sins.

Other holidays that were important for medieval Jews are the three Pilgrimage Festivals (so called because Jews were supposed to make the pilgrimage to the Temple): Sukkoth (Booths, commemorating the period of wandering in the wilderness after the Exodus from Egypt); Pesach (Passover, commemorating the Exodus); and Shavuoth (Weeks, or Pentecost, commemorating the giving of the Ten Commandments). While all of these holidays are significant, the latter two were particularly important for medieval Jews. Passover is intimately connected with the Christian holiday of Easter, since the events associated with Easter occurred during Passover. Furthermore, the date of Easter each year is determined according to the lunar calendar, so that the two holidays almost always coincide. To medieval Christians, it may well have seemed that the two holidays, one of which they regarded as an Old Testament throwback, were in competition. Furthermore, since medieval Christians considered the Jews guilty of killing Jesus, they often regarded Passover as a particularly good time to attack Jews and avenge the death of their messiah. Thus Passover, which is ordinarily a joyous holiday, was often transformed into a time of fear and suffering. Shavuoth corresponds to the Christian holiday of Pentecost, described in Acts 2, with the giving of the Ten Commandments corresponding to the descent of the Holy Spirit.

Several other holidays also marked the Jewish year. Purim and Chanukah did not play a large role in the Middle Ages, but the Ninth of Av did. Av, the Jewish month that falls in July and August, was traditionally the day on which both the First and Second Temples were destroyed, the First by the Babylonians in 586 B.C.E. and the Second by the Romans in 70 C.E.. Rabbinic teaching had decreed that the Ninth of Av, in Hebrew *Tisha B'Av*, be observed as a day of deep mourning marked by solemnity and fasting. Although the Ninth of Av has no biblical mandate, it indicates the central role that the Temples, those that had been destroyed and the one whose building was keenly anticipated, played in Jewish life.

But holidays, as important as they may be, are isolated events, whereas Jewish practice controls virtually every aspect of Jewish life, from eating to dressing to procreation. Human beings eat because we are animals, so in a basic way, eating is a sign of our bestial natures. Table manners, a cultural construction, attempt to elevate eating above a merely animal level. Judaism has taken that process a step further by making eating a potentially sacred act. This sanctification of eating begins with the dietary laws, which are described at length in Leviticus 11. These laws recognize that human beings eat other creatures, but they limit which creatures may be eaten. Thus, for an animal to be kosher, a word that literally means "proper," it must chew its cud and have cloven hoofs. A kosher fish must have both fins and scales. There is a popular notion that "kosher" simply means "blessed by a rabbi," which is totally incorrect. "Kosher" means that an item meets the dietary regulations as they are set out in the Torah and explained in the Talmud. With regard to food, "kosher" pertains primarily to meat and fish and to wine. Vegetables are all kosher. When people speak about things like "kosher" pickles, they are referring to a style of pickling rather than to the actual dietary laws. The Torah also says that we should not "boil a kid in its mother's milk" (Exodus 23:19 and 34:21; Deuteronomy 14:21), a commandment that is interpreted to mean that we should not mix milk and meat products together or eat them at the same time.

Why do Jews continue to follow these laws? Many explanations have been suggested (they were for hygiene, for instance, or they reflect ancient taboos), but the real reason that people followed and continue to follow them is because the Torah says to. We may try to understand the ideas behind them, which indicate that people must control their appetites when they consume other creatures and teach us compassion, but the only reason for doing them is that they are divinely ordained. The Talmud supplies yet other restrictions, including detailed instructions for how an animal must be slaughtered in order to be kosher, at which point the ritual slaughterer does indeed recite a blessing. These instructions, too, are intended to extend humane treatment to the animals. Some people even think that the dietary laws lead the way to vegetarianism, which may be the case, but in the Middle Ages, given the limitations on people's diets, vegetarianism was probably not an option. One final point is that Jews do not eat meat from the hindquarters of an animal unless certain veins are removed, which is usually not done. The explanation for this prohibition is not so clear, but it is related in Genesis 32 to the story of Jacob's limp after his wrestling episode.

These dietary laws have always played a large role in Jewish life, and they affected the relationships between Jews and non-Jews, leading to accusations of clannishness. One reason for that apparent clannishness is that Jews who follow the dietary laws simply cannot eat conveniently with non-Jews who do not. Not only will the non-Jews serve non-kosher foods, but they will serve them on dishes that have come in contact with such foods, which renders them non-kosher as well. Consequently, Jews in the Middle Ages, who adhered strictly to these laws, would not dine with non-Jews and could not have accepted their invitations, even if such invitations had been forthcoming. Because eating together has always been a sign of fellowship, the Jews' refusal to dine together was interpreted as a sign of clannishness.

For the Jewish community, this enforced separation was regarded positively because it meant fewer chances for Jews to be seduced by Christianity, but interestingly, Christians also interpreted it positively because it meant fewer chances for Christians to be attracted to Judaism. In fact, from its early centuries, Christianity attempted to restrict the ability of Jews and Christians to eat together. Furthermore, Christians were often insulted by the effects of the dietary laws. After all, if Jews could not eat their food, the implication arose that their food was not good enough, an implication that was reinforced by the Jewish restriction on eating the hindquarters. That is, when an animal had been slaughtered by a Jewish ritual slaughterer, Jews would buy the meat from the forequarters. The hindquarters, however, would be sold to a non-Jewish butcher who would sell the meat to non-Jews. For those who understand, the system seems perfect: people get meat and nothing is wasted. Unfortunately, such understanding was rare, and Christian writers often complained that they were getting the Jews' leftovers. Thus, Pope Innocent III, no friend of the Jews in any case, wrote on January 17, 1208, "While they [the Jews] themselves shrink from eating, as unclean, the meat of animals killed by Christians, yet they obtain it as a privilege ... to give the slaughtering of animals over to such who slaughter the animals according to the Jewish rite, and then take of them as much as they desire, and offer the leavings to the Christians."[8]

Dress is another area that affected relations between the Jews and the people among whom they lived. People like to express their individuality in the way they dress, but they almost always do so within the styles of their own times. We seldom see people wearing eighteenth-century breeches or stove-pipe hats (although modern Hasidic Jews, like the Amish, do indeed favor eighteenth-century styles for religious reasons). During the Middle Ages, Jews, like other people, enjoyed being in style. Again, however, this custom had important implications. For all three of the major religions that concern us, the distinction between "us" and "them" had fundamental importance. Not only are "we" different from "them," but those differences are inherent. In modern terms, we might say they are genetic rather than cultural. This attitude lay behind the fact that when people converted from one religion to another, they were often regarded with suspicion, and their transitions into their new lives could be quite difficult. A major problem, however, was that if people dressed alike, their religious identities became indistinguishable. A Christian and a Jew wearing the same outfits looked the same. Consequently, both Muslim and Christian countries created laws that required Jews to wear some distinguishing mark on their clothing. In Muslim countries, the mark might be an odd belt, while in Christian countries it might be a badge or a certain kind of hat. Although these laws were often ignored or the Jews were allowed to pay for the privilege of not following them, they were frequently enforced, particularly in certain European countries after the Fourth Lateran Council in 1215. In March of 1219, Pope Honorius III responded to a report that the Jews of Castile were moving elsewhere because the Lateran Council decree was being so strongly enforced there. Because the king of Castile, whose monetary income came largely from the Jews, was losing money, the pope suspended the decree for Castile.

There were, however, some religious restrictions on what Jews could wear. One major principle requires modest dress, especially for women. The problem, of course, is that what one person sees as modest may appear risqué to someone else. More specifically, men were required, according to Numbers 15: 37–41, to wear fringes on the corners of garments that had four corners. These fringes, *tzitzit*, are tied together in a prescribed way, and as the Torah says, their function is to serve as reminders of all the other commandments. Apparently the Jews found ways to follow this commandment without being ostentatious, for if those fringes had been obvious, belts and badges would have been unnecessary.

A more difficult problem concerns head coverings. Today, traditional Jewish men keep their heads covered at all times, but that custom seems to have begun in the later Middle Ages. From earlier times, however, men did keep their heads covered when they ate, studied, and prayed. Of course, local custom also had a great deal to do with what people wore, but when we look at manuscript illuminations that depict Jews, the major difference between Jewish and Christian garb involves the Jewish badge or a particular kind of hat that Jews were required to wear. Interestingly, there seem to have been no special requirements for women's clothing, except for the Jewish badge in those periods when the badge was required.

Another area of religious interest concerns sex and procreation. For official Christianity, sexual pleasure was a sign of the fall of mankind, and Paul, in his first letter to the Corinthians, urges everyone, if possible, to remain celibate. Because Paul believed that the end of the world was imminent, maintaining and replacing the population was not an issue. When the end of the world proved not to be imminent, however, and most people proved to be incapable of celibacy, Christianity had to come to terms with sexual activity, though virginity was always viewed as the highest sexual state, followed by celibacy. Thus, Margery Kempe in the fourteenth and fifteenth centuries could decide that she no longer wanted to have sexual relations as part of her marriage, a decision that her husband may not have liked but that he was coerced into. In Judaism the case was quite different. Jews held to a high level of sexual morality, but that meant that sexual activity should be carried on, according to certain rules, within marriage, where it was regarded most positively. The very first of the six hundred thirteen commandments in the Torah was to "be fertile and increase" (Genesis 2:28), and Jews were expected to comply. As was the case with all the commandments, there was a great deal of discussion about precisely what this one meant. One opinion was that a couple who had produced a male and a female child had fulfilled their duty. Of course, without birth control, with a high level of child mortality, and with the small number of Jews, procreation was a necessity. In cases when a husband or wife decided, for whatever reason, to withdraw from a sexual relationship, the rabbis would try to restore that relationship. They regarded sexual activity as a normal part of life, not to be abused but not be scorned.

Dietary laws and the wearing of fringes are clearly ritual requirements, while proper sexual behavior combines the ritual and the moral; but there are many purely moral laws as well. People who do not follow the ritual laws may think that they are difficult and burdensome, but in many ways they are easier to follow than the moral laws. Obeying the dietary laws becomes automatic (a traditional Jew would never consider *not* following them), but loving one's neighbor as oneself, which the Talmudic sage Rabbi Akiva said was the greatest of the commandments, never becomes automatic. It always requires effort. Nevertheless, many laws exist that govern moral behavior. For instance, the Torah tells us that if a poor man borrows money and uses his coat as collateral, the coat must be returned before nightfall lest the poor man freeze. Economically, such a law makes no sense, but socially and morally it makes a great deal of sense. The Talmud takes such laws from the Torah and elaborates on them, thereby creating a whole system of ethical behavior. This development has led to the notion that Judaism is ethical monotheism, but as this discussion has indicated, Judaism can hardly be defined in such concrete terms, partially correct though they may be. Moral behavior *is* religious behavior, for, like the rituals, moral behavior sanctifies life and is required by the Torah. People may often fail in their ritual and moral duties, which explains the necessity of atonement. When the Temple still stood, atonement was achieved through certain kinds of sacrifices. According to an early rabbinic work, *The Fathers According to Rabbi Nathan*, after the destruction of the Temple, a group of rabbis were walking through the ruins when one of them started crying because the place where people had come to make atonement through sacrifices had been destroyed. Another rabbi responded that those sacrifices had to be replaced, not by other sacrifices but by deeds of lovingkindness. As Yitzhak Baer wrote, and as this story indicates, Judaism's historical, legal, ethical, and theological aspects are inseparable, all united by Torah,[9] though Torah itself is open to interpretation.

And who controls the interpretation? Judaism has no central human authority figure. The last such person who might have been considered a central authority was Rav Hai Gaon, who died in the eleventh century. Since then, Judaism has had no individual or group who were recognized as authoritative by all Jews. In fact, though united by the various facets of Judaism, the Jews have had a knack for fitting into the societies in which they have lived. Jews have taken on the flavor of the people among whom they have lived while maintaining their own identity, and in most cases, they have added significantly to those societies. For example, Obadiah Bertinoro (fifteenth century) says that in Moslem countries, Jews remove their shoes before entering a synagogue or house. No Jewish law required them to do so, but because the Muslims who surrounded them removed their shoes, the Jews picked up the custom.[10] Such adaptability helped the Jews to survive in what were often hostile and dangerous environments.

Even so, the thing that held the Jews together, that defined them as Jews, was Torah, by which they meant both the Written and Oral Laws, the Five Books of Moses and the Talmud. Therefore, in order to understand Jews and Judaism in the Middle Ages, we need to understand what the Talmud was. Because medieval Christians did not understand this long and complex work, they feared it, so much that in 1242 copies of the Talmud that had been seized in France were burned at the stake. What was this work that Christian prelates and monarchs thought was so dangerous?

Talmud and Midrash

On June 9, 1239, Pope Gregory IX wrote to the archbishops of France

> If what is said about the Jews of France and of the other lands is true, no punishment would be sufficiently great or sufficiently worthy of this crime. For they, so we have heard, are not content with the Old Law, which God gave to Moses in writing: they even ignore it completely, and affirm that God gave another Law which is called 'Talmud,' that is 'Teaching,' handed down to Moses orally.... In this is contained matter so abusive and so unspeakable that it arouses shame in those who mention it and horror in those who hear it.[1]

The pope goes on to urge the archbishops to seize this allegedly pernicious text, and less than two weeks later he wrote again, telling them to burn these volumes at the stake.

Several points in this astounding letter require discussion, the first of which is how odd it seems that the pope, in 1239, has only just heard of the Talmud, a work that had been central to Judaism for some seven centuries. The Church's new awareness of the Talmud in the thirteenth century both resulted from and contributed to the growing hostility toward the Jews in that period. Also noteworthy are the pope's misperceptions that the Jews ignore the "Old Law" in favor of the Talmud and that the Talmud contains matter that is both "abusive" and "unspeakable," attitudes that had grave implications for the Jews of Europe.

The Talmud—What Is It?

To begin, we must make a crucial distinction between two approaches to the study of the Talmud, a distinction that applies as well to many areas of religious study. That is, we must distinguish between a religious approach and an historical approach. For example, according to the account in Exodus, Moses received the Torah from God on Mount Sinai, and according to Maimonides, based on a talmudic discussion in the tractate Bava Batra, Moses then wrote thirteen copies of the text in the weeks before his death. That account is part of the religious tradition. According to scholars, however, the Torah achieved its present form in the late sixth century B.C.E. when the Jewish people were allowed to return from Babylonia to Israel. Those two accounts are obviously incompatible, and yet they can coexist as the mythos of a people and as the historical record of the same people. We must make the same distinction in considering the development of the Talmud.

The simplest way to explain the Talmud is to say that it is a vast and complex commentary on and explanation of the Torah. But why does the Torah require explanation? The ability to use spoken language, as far as we know, makes human beings unique, but language is not perfect. It always requires interpretation. A person who reads the instructions for assembling a bicycle must interpret those instructions. So, too, with a more difficult text, like the Torah. For instance, as Maimonides points out, the Torah says in Leviticus 23:42, "You shall live in *succoth* seven days …" That statement expresses the biblical law, but the law remains unclear. What are *succoth*? What does the text mean by "live"? Who should live in *succoth*? (*Introduction to the Talmud* 36–7). And even if we know that a *succah* (singular of *succoth*) is a booth, the questions remain. As Maimonides explains, the answers to those questions can be found in that tractate of the Talmud known as *Succah*, where we learn, among other things, that only males are required to dwell in *succoth*, that men who are ill are exempted from the requirement, and that "live" means to eat, drink, and sleep in the *succah*. We also learn many other requirements about how a *succah* should be constructed, what materials should be used, and how big it ought to be. All those details make it possible for Jews to carry out the biblical laws. Without those details, the religion would be chaotic. Everyone would have to make up his or her own interpretation of the laws, and *succoth* would take any number of forms. We in the twenty-first century might like the individualism that such a system (or lack of system) would encourage, but such lack of standardization would quickly result in the dissolution of the religion. Furthermore—and herein lies the key concept—the command to dwell in *succoth* comes from God, and Jews must therefore do their absolute best to fulfill God's commandment, which requires that they understand that commandment.

Thus, as we saw earlier, the fourth of the Ten Commandments prescribes that "You shall remember the Sabbath day and keep it holy," and it orders that no work be done on that day. But what constitutes work? For a farmer, working in the fields clearly constitutes work, but for a gardener, working in the fields would be a pleasure, a means of relaxation. Must a farmer desist from such work on the Sabbath? Can a gardener engage in her hobby on the Sabbath? Again, the commandment requires clarification or the religion will descend into chaos, so the rabbis had to define work. They did so by noticing that one of the passages commanding the observance of the Sabbath (Exodus 35:1–3) followed the description of the building of the Tabernacle in the wilderness (in Exodus 31). Because the Israelites were forbidden to work on the Tabernacle on the Sabbath, the rabbis derived their definition of work from the kind of work that the Tabernacle required.[2] According to their calculations, thirty-nine major kinds of work were forbidden, including such activities as sowing, reaping, baking, dyeing, tying or untying a knot, sewing, lighting a fire, or moving things from what they called one domain to another (Mishnah Shabbat 7:2). Each of these main types of work subsumes other types. Thus, sowing includes planting a tree, and reaping includes plucking anything where it is growing (which means that the gardener cannot garden on the Sabbath and which, incidentally, gave rise to a controversy described in the New Testament when Jesus allowed his disciples to pluck grain on the Sabbath). But even with this explanation of what constitutes work, questions remain. For instance, what is a "domain"? Or what does it mean to bake on the Sabbath? Obviously a person could not make dough and put it in the oven, but what if that person made the dough and put it into the oven before the Sabbath began and then allowed the baking process to take its course? In such a case, the person is not actively baking. Would that procedure be permissible?

As should be apparent by now, virtually all of the six hundred thirteen commandments of the Torah require explanations and elucidations, which then give rise to associated rules, which then demand their own explanations and elucidations. This whole vast structure forms a large part of the Talmud. We might think in terms of the Constitution of the

United States, an eighteenth-century, Age-of-Enlightenment document that is, on the one hand, admirable in its clarity, and on the other, the subject of innumerable debates and interpretive battles. And while it is the job of the Supreme Court to interpret the Constitution, the Supreme Court can overturn the rulings of previous Supreme Courts in determining the law of the land. Unlike the Constitution, however, the Torah was conceived of as divine in origin and not subject to amendment. If people do not like something in the Constitution, they can change it—though, quite properly, with great difficulty. The Torah cannot be changed. Such a status could potentially lead to stultification, but the interpretive work of the Talmud showed how the Torah could be maintained as a living document. It taught not only what the Torah said but how the Torah could be read.

And as confusing as Supreme Court decisions may be, the Talmud is frequently not even that clear. Actually it is quite difficult, and this brief introduction to it will not prepare anyone to study Talmud, but it will perhaps capture the spirit of the Talmud and allow readers to understand why the Talmud was so important for medieval Jews (and why it retains that importance today). As Irving Agus says, the Talmud functioned as the "constitution" of the medieval Jewish community, whether or not its compilers intended that use.[3] Whatever their intentions may have been, their accomplishment was remarkable.

The Origins of the Talmud

As we explore the origins of the Talmud, we must keep in mind the religious and the historical approaches, for they differ significantly and they express quite different ideologies. Nevertheless, they are not incompatible and they both result in a text that profoundly affected the course of Judaism, just as the works of Augustine of Hippo, written toward the end of the talmudic era, profoundly affected the development of Christianity. One problem with tracing the history of the Talmud is that there is so little in the way of sources. There are no talmudic *Federalist Papers* and no letters from one Talmudic rabbi to another.

The Talmud itself provides an explanation of its origins at the beginning of the section called *Pirkei Avot, Ethics of the Fathers* (literally *Chapters of the Fathers*): "Moses received the Torah at Sinai and passed it on to Joshua, and Joshua to the elders and the elders to the prophets, and the prophets transmitted it to the Men of the Great Assembly." What does this statement have to do with the Talmud? When people use the word

Torah, they generally mean either the Five Books of Moses or the scroll containing those books, but in Judaism there are actually two Torahs, the Written one and the *Torah she-be'al peh*, the Oral Torah. According to this notion, when Moses ascended Sinai, he received both the written text of the Torah and all the explanations of the many commandments. Those explanations were meant to remain oral, and we must remember that in ancient times, oral cultures predominated. The Greek epic the *Iliad* was composed orally over several centuries and was only finally written down probably in the eighth century B.C.E.. Thus there would be nothing unusual in the oral preservation of a huge mass of material. The statement quoted above, then, sounds plausible as it traces the path of transmission of the Oral Law from Moses to the Men of the Great Assembly, who were the predecessors of the talmudic rabbis.

But there are also problems with that scheme. The Talmud is much more than a list of rules clarifying other rules, but even when it fulfills that function, when it explains the concept of a *succah* or of the Sabbath, it contains more arguments than it does rules. What we see are discussions that involve rabbis from several centuries who try to develop and clarify the rules. If Moses received the Oral Law on Sinai, what necessitates all these discussions? Sherira Gaon, who was one of the last great leaders of Babylonian Jewry, wrote a long letter in 986 C.E. in which he explained this apparent inconsistency. According to Sherira, the earliest of the rabbis all agreed about every interpretation of every law, but eventually, as the result of war and disorder in Israel, "there were many disciples who never studied long enough with their teachers. Hence controversies arose among them." Furthermore, he explains, various rabbis used different words to make the same point and those words were later interpreted in different ways, leading to the impression that the explanations themselves differed. Consequently, in around the year 200, Rabbi Yehuda ha-Nasi, with divine and human help, "arranged and wrote down" the ancient rulings so that "all the rabbis would use the same phraseology and no longer teach each in his own phrasing." The work of Rabbi Yehuda, like the work of Moses, was "a sign and a miracle."[4]

Later on, in the twelfth century, Maimonides gave a slightly different explanation, tracing the time of controversy back to Joshua, Moses' successor. According to Maimonides' account, Moses taught the Oral Law to the people and to their representatives; when a question arose, he could provide the answer. But when Moses died, no one was there who could definitively resolve controversies. In either case, Yehuda ha-Nasi is always acknowledged as the person responsible for first writing down the Oral Law.

Rabbi Yehuda's accomplishment cannot be overestimated, though modern scholars may argue that he only organized and codified the Oral Law and that the writing down part came later. Whichever actually happened, Rabbi Yehuda and his colleagues, on the basis of on the work of their predecessors, created the first part of the Talmud, which is called the Mishnah, around the year 200. Neither their activity nor the date is accidental. In the 60's of the first century, the Roman Empire controlled Israel. The Romans were harsh overlords, not just in Israel but throughout their empire. In Israel, however, they encountered more opposition than they were used to, especially from a people who did not have a strong martial tradition. The Romans' problem was that they had no interest in understanding the Jewish religious practices, practices about which the Jews could not compromise. For example, when the Romans conquered a polytheistic nation and insisted on adding their gods to those of the vanquished, there was no great problem. A people who worshipped many gods would have little trouble adding to their number, but the Jews were monotheistic and could not add more gods. Similarly, nations that used idols in their worship could add more idols to their temples (statues of Roman eagles or of emperors), but the Jews, who allowed no representational art in their Temple, could make no exceptions. These matters, and others, created strains between the Romans and the Jews and led to sometimes violent confrontations.

In the early decades of the first century there were four major religious-political groups in Israel. (A fifth group, larger than the other four, consisted of farmers and laborers who could not afford the time or the money to be involved in the current controversies.) These four groups were:

- Sadducees: strongly associated with the functioning of the Temple, willing to work with the Romans, relying only on the written Torah
- Pharisees: more representative of the common people (though hardly populist), willing to accommodate themselves to the Romans as long as the Romans did not interfere with religious obligations, heavily dependent on oral traditions
- Essenes: ascetics who opposed the Sadducees' control of the Temple while not allying themselves with the Pharisees
- Zealots: violently opposed to the Roman occupation, trusting that God would aid them in their fight against the far more powerful Roman army

In the year 66, war broke out between the Romans and the Jews, resulting in the destruction of the Temple in 70, an event that was crucial for both Judaism and Christianity. After this devastating defeat, Judaism faced a major crisis: could it survive the loss of its central sanctuary? Judaism had faced such a crisis earlier, in 586 B.C.E., when the First Temple was destroyed by the Babylonians, and this time certain circumstances made the question of survival a bit less traumatic. First, the Jews knew that their ancestors had indeed survived the earlier destruction, so they knew survival was possible; and second, there were more Jewish communities in the Diaspora (in Babylonia, in Egypt, in Rome, and elsewhere) who did very well without the Temple in their midst. Still, the Temple and its ceremonies had provided a focus for Judaism. What would replace it?

According to rabbinic sources, during the Roman siege of Jerusalem, one of the rabbis, Yoḥanan ben Zakkai, managed to escape from the city and appealed to the Roman general Vespasian for permission to open an academy in the town of Yavneh, mentioning that Vespasian was destined to become the emperor. Vespasian, who understandably liked that news, allowed him to open the academy, which, after the destruction of the Temple, became a gathering place for the rabbis as they struggled to accommodate Judaism to the new historical situation. With the Temple gone, the Sadducees had become less of a force; and with the revolt defeated, the Zealots either had been killed or had gone underground. The Essenes had never been among the major players in the country. Only the Pharisees were left, but by this time they had become (though we cannot reconstruct the process) the rabbis, who were now the dominant force in reconstructing Jewish life. They did so by trying to find, or create, elements of continuity between Temple and post-Temple times and then by retrojection, that is, by projecting into the past the traditions they were transforming. Such retrojection enabled them to see themselves as the heirs of the traditions that Moses had received orally from God on Mount Sinai. They were most definitely not deceiving themselves or dishonestly manipulating their positions. They were simply interpreting their situation according to their ideology, as everyone does. Without question, they saved Judaism by transforming it from the religion of the Temple to the religion of the Talmud, though the process took many centuries.

After the Temple's destruction in 70, conditions in Israel were relatively quiet, if not happy, until another revolt broke out in 132 under the leadership of a charismatic leader known as Shimon bar Kokhba.

Although this revolt lasted three years, it ended in another devastating defeat, showing once again the futility of military solutions. The failed revolt led to further hardships for the Jews of Israel, just as Jewish uprisings in the Diaspora, in Alexandria for instance, made life more difficult for Jews outside of Israel. In these chaotic conditions, Yehuda ha-Nasi evidently feared that the Oral Law would be lost if it were not organized and given an official status. So, on the basis of the work of his predecessors, he undertook that labor and created the Mishnah in about the year 200.

The Mishnah is beautiful in its clarity and organization. Written in a Hebrew style that is concise and eloquent, it consists of a long listing of laws, many of which are derived directly from the Torah while others are based on implications from the Torah and still others reflect current practices. Yet others create what the rabbis called "fences" around the Torah. These fences create additional space around the commandments in order to ensure that they not be broken. For example, from the Torah verse forbidding cooking a kid in the milk of its mother, the rabbis derived the law forbidding the combination of milk and meat. But what about poultry? Chickens do not produce milk, so can poultry be eaten with dairy products? Their answer was that it cannot, lest someone confuse poultry with meat and think that the forbidden combination is permissible.

One might think that the codification of the Mishnah, a monumental accomplishment, would have brought the "constitutional" process to an end. After all, the Mishnah seemed to include everything. It was divided into six orders dealing with agriculture, festivals, women's concerns, civil law, sacrifices, and purification, and those six orders were subdivided into sixty-three tractates. However, as Lawrence Shiffman argues, Rabbi Yehuda did not intend to create a code of laws. "He intended to create a curriculum for the study of Jewish law."[5] Consequently, the Mishnah forms only the first part of the Talmud. The other part, known today as the Gemara, consists of discussions of the Mishnah that lasted from about 200 until about 500, with some additions that may come from as late as the sixth century.

To make a confusing situation even more confusing, the Gemara in the Middle Ages was referred to as the Talmud, which means that that term was used both for the whole work and for that part that comments at great length on the Mishnah. Furthermore, there are actually two Talmuds, two collections of discussions on the Mishnah. The first is the Palestinian Talmud (also called the Jerusalem Talmud). This work records discussions that took place in Israel, and, because of the unsettled conditions there, it was constructed hastily in the fifth century. The other Talmud, which was far more influential in the Middle Ages, was the Babylonian Talmud, the Bavli, whose discussions are more extensive and include discussions that took place in the Babylonian schools. There was considerable competition between the sages in Israel and those in Babylonia over who would have primacy in the Jewish world. Both Talmuds are written in Aramaic, though in different dialects of that language.

Why were all of these discussions necessary? There are several reasons. First, just as the Mishnah interprets the Torah text, so the Gemara interprets the Mishnah. It tries to explain not only what the rabbis meant by what they said but why they said it. During the Middle Ages, Christians tended to think of Judaism as legalistic, as based on an unending series of laws that were followed blindly, and misguidedly. One reason for this view was Paul's reference to the Torah as "the Law," but Torah does not mean "Law." It means "Teaching," and teaching is meant to be understood. Thus, the Mishnah attempts not only to list the laws but to understand them, and the Gemara continues that process. If Rabbi Akiva said something, *why* did he say it? Thus, in one of its aspects the Talmud is a gigantic attempt to understand why things are as they are. At the same time, the Talmud acknowledges in *Pirkei Avot* that we can never fully understand, that the process is eternal, and that we cannot refuse to take part in the process: "You are not called upon to complete the work, yet you are not free to evade it" (2:21). Furthermore, discussions were necessary because conditions kept changing. The rabbis of the Talmud had to show not only how to interpret the laws but how to adapt them to modern times. For instance, many of the laws in the Torah apply to an agricultural society engaged in Temple sacrificial ceremonies. As society became somewhat less agriculturally centered, and in the absence of the Temple, how could those laws be applied?

The rabbis' solutions were often brilliant. Thus, in the absence of a formal priesthood, they made everyone equivalent to a priest. For example, the Torah spells out in detail how the priests were to accomplish the sacrifices at the altar of the Temple. The rabbis applied those rituals to meals. The table becomes an altar and the diners become priests. Before eating, the diners wash their hands and say a blessing. Then they say a blessing over the food they are about to eat (prepared, of course, according to the dietary laws), and after the meal they say a long grace.

The Temple may have been destroyed, but it lives on in these traditions. Furthermore, these traditions transform the animal act of eating into something holy. Like so many of the laws and traditions, they sanctify the everyday aspects of human life.

Today we may easily see the beauty of such customs, but other Talmudic discussions may seem terribly irrelevant. For instance, the tractate called "Betzah" ("Egg") begins with the question of whether an egg laid on the day of a festival can be eaten on that day. At first glance, the question seems silly. What difference does it make? And if one is uncertain about what to do, wait until the next day when the festival is over and eat it. No one needs an egg in an emergency. The Mishnah, however, tells us that there was a dispute over whether such an egg can be eaten on that day, and the Gemara discusses the issue for fourteen pages. (Since the eighteenth century, volumes of the Talmud have been printed with standard pagination, so that if one refers to Betzah 7a, one is always referring to the first, or recto, side of page 7 in the Tractate Betzah. This particular discussion, therefore, takes up fourteen pages in every modern edition of the Talmud.) Why? Because, as William Carlos Williams might have said, everything depends on that egg. The point itself may be minor, but the principle is not, nor is the need to understand. Things must be done properly, in a certain order, just as God created the world in a certain order.

Similarly, the tractate called Baba Metziah opens with a question about two men who claim to have found a cloak lying in the street at precisely the same moment. A long discussion ensues in which the rabbis try to figure out who should get the cloak. Again, the situation is somewhat absurd, but the precise situation is nearly irrelevant. The Talmud could not possibly consider every possible contingency, but by discussing a few, it can lay down the principles that should be followed in others.

Now for another confusing point. We have already seen that the Talmud consists of two parts, Mishnah and Gemara (or Talmud). We might expect to read part one and then part two, but that is not how the Talmud works. Instead it quotes a passage from the Mishnah and then the Germara that develops that Mishnah. But Talmudic logic can be quite difficult to follow. One difficulty arises because of the terseness of rabbinic expression. The reader must often work hard, must actually enter into the discussion, in order to follow the argumentation. In addition, the Talmud is not organized according to the kind of logic to which

Western readers are accustomed. Thus the first tractate in the Talmud is called Berakhot, Blessings. Had Aristotle written a book with that title, we would expect it to focus on blessings and to contain everything that Aristotle knew about the subject. Not so with the Talmud. Berakhot contains much material that has nothing to do with blessings, material that is arrived at by associative logic rather than deductive or inductive logic; and much material on blessings can be found elsewhere in the Talmud. The Talmud is indeed logical, but according to a special, Talmudic logic.

Mishnah and Gemara, then, are intertwined in the text, but there is also another division between two aspects of the Talmud: halakhah and aggadah. These, too, are intertwined. Halakhah, from the Hebrew root meaning "to go" or "to walk," tells us how we should "go," the rules for how we should conduct our lives—the laws of the Sabbath or the dietary laws, for instance. The aggadah, from the root for "telling," is more anecdotal, telling stories that illustrate the point that a speaker is making or providing stories about the rabbis themselves, though, oddly, the rabbis of the Mishnaic era seldom refer to the central events of their time, focusing instead on exegesis.

The Talmud is such a vast and difficult work that commentators like to refer to the "sea of the Talmud." Consequently, there is much about it that we do not know for certain. As we have seen, the Talmudic rabbis emphasized law in every aspect of human life. They took seriously the statement in the Torah that the people of Israel were to be for God "a kingdom of priests and a holy nation" (Exodus 19:6), which meant that every aspect of life was to be lived according to divine prescription. So halakhah, the way to "go," was central. At the same time, however, we cannot know what the editors of the Talmud, those who organized and wrote down the oral traditions, had in mind when they did so. We cannot tell if they intended to create a book of rules or if they were doing something else, but we can say that if they intended to create a book of rules, they could have done a more efficient job.[6] The Mishnah tends to lay down rules, but the Gemara often disputes and even occasionally dismisses those rules. At the same time, many of the extended discussions end inconclusively, with no clear decision on what the rule is in specific cases. Later medieval writers, most notably Maimonides, did codify the Talmud, creating a consistent, though controversial, list of rules with clearly organized topics. Surely the rabbis of the Talmud would have done so, had that been their goal; clearly it was not.

Studying the Talmud

How did the rabbis arrive at their decisions about halakhah? To begin to answer this question, we must first emphasize the central role of study in Judaism. As important as prayer is, in the early years after the destruction of the Temple, controversy arose over whether the Temple rituals would be replaced by prayer or study. In many ways, the controversy ended in a draw—prayer is incorporated in study, and study is incorporated in prayer. And what is study? It involves both the Written and the Oral Laws—not simply memorizing them but examining them and gleaning their implications.

In the uncertain conditions that prevailed in the decades and centuries after the destruction, with Jews scattered in different areas, and lacking central leadership, the Talmud, and the rabbis of the Talmud, formed the leadership. Those rabbis, who were held in the highest regard, are divided into several chronological groups: the Tanna'im (literally "Reciters," first-third centuries C.E.), the Amora'im ("Sayers," third-fifth centuries C.E.), and the Savora'im ("Opiners"), and each of these groups is divided into generations.[7] Each generation and each category were regarded with awe by their successors, and what they said was held to be correct, though there might well be dispute over the interpretation of what they said. These rabbis based their activities on biblical verses such as Joshua 1:8: "Let not this Book of the Teaching cease from your lips, but recite it day and night, so that you may observe faithfully all that is written in it."[8] Through the Middle Ages and into modern times, these rabbis became the heroes of the Jewish people, the models to be emulated. Military leaders such as Joshua, Judah Maccabee, or Shimon bar Kokhba received scant attention. They had, at best, brought temporary reprieves from oppression, and sometimes their activities had made conditions worse, but the rabbis had shown the way in which life should be lived, the way in which the Jewish people could serve God and survive.

But that way was not simple, as many of the Talmudic stories indicate. For instance, the Talmud might appear at first to be a book of endless and sometimes pointless arguments, and those arguments occasionally take on a note of bitterness. Nevertheless, the Mishnah says, "Any dispute that is for the sake of Heaven [that is, that tries to determine the divine will] will have a constructive outcome; but one that is not for the sake of Heaven will not have a constructive outcome" (*Pirkei Avot*, 5:20). In other words, the point of these disputes should not simply be to win. They are not debating contests. They are, rather, attempts to get at the truth. But the rabbis also knew that human intelligence, with its profound limitations, cannot achieve the truth, so they would discuss until they could discuss no more and then, following the instructions of the Torah, they would vote on the issue. Interestingly, however, the Talmud records all sides of the discussions so that we can reconstruct the reasoning behind the decisions, in order to see how even the greatest of the rabbis disagreed among themselves, just as we receive majority and minority opinions from the Supreme Court.

This technique stands in sharp contrast to what was happening in Christianity during the same centuries as the Church attempted to solidify its teachings. Many disagreements arose in the Church, but in most cases we know of them primarily through the refutations of the winning side. Augustine of Hippo, for instance, argued against many positions that were declared to be heresies, such as Pelagianism (the doctrine that salvation could be achieved through good works), but we know about Pelagianism largely through Augustine's writings. We have no works by Pelagius himself, because losing arguments were obliterated. Not so in the Talmud. But that technique had sometimes dire consequences, for when medieval Christians learned the contents of the Talmud, they came across occasionally troublesome passages that Jews knew had been rejected but that the Christians assumed represented "official" Jewish positions simply because they were recorded in this important text.

The Talmud, then, records winning and losing arguments and even calls the winning arguments into question. In one famous story, several rabbis were arguing over a very technical point concerning whether a certain kind of oven was ritually pure. Rabbi Eliezer, having been overruled by his companions, remained so certain that he was correct that he called on a nearby tree to prove his point and, miraculously, the tree moved a hundred feet from where it stood, to which his companions replied, "We don't bring proof from a carob tree." So Rabbi Eliezer called on a stream for support, but when the stream reversed its course, another miracle, his companions said, "We don't bring proof from a stream of water." So Rabbi Eliezer said, "Let the walls of the Study House prove it," at which point the walls of the Study House began to fall in, until another rabbi called on them not to interfere. Finally Rabbi Eliezer called on a heavenly voice to support his position, and the heavenly voice indeed proclaimed that Rabbi Eliezer was correct. To us, the heavenly voice might have seemed conclusive, but the other rabbis continued to declare Rabbi Eliezer's opinion incorrect, because once the Torah had been given to human beings, the rule set down by the Torah itself was that the majority decided on the interpretation. Later on, the story continues, one of the rabbis encountered the prophet Elijah (who was wandering the earth) and asked, "What did the Holy One, Blessed Be He, do at that point?" to which Elijah responded, "He laughed and said, 'My children have defeated me, my children have defeated me'" (Baba Metzia, 59a).[9]

This is a strange and profound story, and, clearly, anyone unfamiliar with the talmudic idiom might find it offensive to think that human beings had somehow defeated God. The story, however, makes several vital points:

- God has set forth a strict set of laws that the Jewish people are bound to follow.
- Because of the limitations of human intelligence, we may not always understand those laws the way God intended them.
- The interpretation of those laws therefore depends on cooperation among human beings and an agreement to follow the rule of the majority, thereby creating a working human community.
- The successful operation of that community is more important than the carrying out of the divine intent, so long as human beings make honest efforts to understand the laws.
- The attempt to understand correctly is more important than coming up with the "right" answer.
- God, in at least one of His many aspects, is benevolent and indulgent toward those who study His law.

In connection with this story, we should also note that God is portrayed in the Talmud as engaged in the study of Torah, as are the patriarchs Abraham, Isaac, and Jacob, even though the Torah was not given to Moses until hundreds of years after their deaths. The rabbis devised explanations for this anachronism, but those explanations are beside the point. The rabbis made Torah study, which meant Torah and Talmud study, into one of the highest virtues, along with good deeds, and therefore the Patriarchs, and even God, must have studied. And the rabbis themselves, by studying, continued to preserve the chain of tradition and became the true heroes of Israel, which explains why at the beginning of *Pirkei Avot* they present themselves as the heirs of Moses, Joshua, the prophets, and the men of the Great Assembly.

The Rabbi as Hero

Both the halakhah and the aggadah played vital roles in the history of the Jews in the Middle Ages. We will spend more time with halakhah later, but now let us consider the function of the aggadah, those stories that punctuate lengthy discussions of law. The first point that must be made is that these stories are neither history nor biography in the modern sense of those terms. This point must be stressed because until relatively recently they were regarded as historically and biographically accurate. Thus, Louis Finkelstein's 1936 biography of Rabbi Akiva is based almost entirely on the tales told about him in the rabbinic writings. Unfortunately, we have no material from outside the rabbinic writings to support those stories. The rabbis, as part of their work, tried to establish what it meant to be part of this rabbinic culture, and they used stories to illustrate what they meant. We can read the stories and feel that we know the sages as individual human beings, but there is no evidence that any of those stories are historically true in our sense of historical truth, and there is much evidence that they are not.

To offer an analogy, we know that some kind of war occurred at Troy at the time the Trojan War was supposed to have occurred. It may have been only a minor trade war, but it offers the historical core of the later legends and of the *Iliad*. Since the Gemara, which contains the aggadah, was written down in about 500 and based on three centuries of oral tradition, the analogy with the *Iliad* is appropriate. There must have been a historical core for the rabbinic legends, but the contents of that core are impossible for us to determine. We are left, then, with wonderful stories about the sages, but we must consider why these stories are there and what they mean.

Over the centuries, the halakhic sections of the Talmud have understandably received most of the attention of Talmudists; given their historical circumstances, Jewish communities needed guidance on how to preserve their lives as Jews, and that guidance would be found by analyzing the legal discussions and extracting laws. As for the stories, they tended to be taken at face value. They were neither read as allegories nor culled for moral lessons. In some ways, they were like the saints' lives that Christians were creating at around the same time, stories that were used as examples of virtuous behavior. Just as no one would argue for the historical accuracy of Sulpicius Severus' "Life" of St. Martin, so we need not argue for the accuracy of the Talmud's accounts of Rabbi Akiva or Rabbi Yohanan ben Zakkai in order to see the value of those accounts.

It would be a mistake to make a simple equation between saints' lives and sage stories, because they developed quite differently, but the impulses behind them were similar. Like the saints' lives, the stories of the aggadah were recorded to honor their subjects, the sages, whose legends had been transmitted over the centuries, and to explain the significance of the sage and his life. The early saints' lives were stories of martyrdom, and they were often written near in time to when the martyrdoms had occurred. They gave hope to a suffering community. After Constantine's conversion to Christianity, however, the cult of martyrdom largely ended and the pattern of the saints' lives shifted to focus on the saints' interior lives. The question for Christians became not how to be a Christian in a secular world but how to be a Christian in a Christian world. As the saint became a quester, the writers of saints' lives adapted the elements of Greek romances, the adventures and the exploration of motives, for Christian religious purposes. It is possible that by the twelfth century, those saints' lives had evolved into the chivalric romances.

What about the sage-stories? Many of them contain elements similar to those in saints' lives. For example, we have the story of Shimon bar Yohai, who criticized Rome and was sentenced to death. Eventually he and his son fled to a cave, where "a miracle occurred and a carob-tree and a water well were created for them. They would strip their garments and sit up to their necks in sand. The whole day they studied; when it was time for prayers they robed, covered themselves, prayed, and then put off their garments again, so they should not wear out" (*Shabbat*, 33b). Finally, with the help of Elijah, they were allowed to leave the cave after thirteen years. While this story is not exactly the same as a saint's life, it is certainly similar. So, too, are the stories in the Christian *Vita Abrahae* (*The Life of Abraham*) and the Jewish story of Rabbi Meir, in both of which holy men are called upon to rescue young women from brothels and are required to go through a certain amount of sexual pretense to accomplish their missions.

Why were these stories composed and preserved? In Babylonia, the rabbis played important public roles in the Jewish communal structure, and people expected them to be like the holy men of the cultures in which they lived.[10] Therefore the editors of the Talmud depicted their forerunners in this way. As the centuries passed, these sage-stories were studied by generation after generation, but because of the circumstances under which the Jews lived, these stories never developed as they might have, as the saints' lives did for Christians, into full-blown romances. Nevertheless, they continued to hold the attention of Jews.

One of the greatest of the sages was Rabbi Akiva, about whom there are so many stories, aside from his many legal rulings, that we could conceivably refer to the "matter of Akiva," just as we refer to the "matter of Charlemagne" or the "matter of Arthur." Here is one story that shows the elements of romance combined with Jewish ideals:

> Rabbi Akiva was the shepherd of Ben Kalba Savu'a. His daughter saw [in] him that he was modest and outstanding. She said to him: "If I become betrothed to you, will you go to the Academy?" He said to her: "Yes." She became betrothed to him in secret and she sent him away. Her father heard [and] banished her from his house [and] forbade her with a vow from [deriving any] benefit from his property. He went [and] sat [for] twelve years in the Academy. When he came [back], he brought with him twelve thousand disciples. He heard an old man saying to her: "For how long will you behave like a widow during [her husband's] lifetime?" She said to him: "If he would listen to me, he would [sit] there twelve more years." He said: "I am acting with permission." He went back and sat twelve more years in the Academy. When he came [back], he brought with him twenty-four thousand disciples. His wife heard [and] went out to [greet] him. The neighbors said to her: "Borrow something to wear and dress yourself!" She said to them: "A righteous man knows the life of his beast." When she reached him, she fell on her face, [and] she kissed his feet. His attendants were pushing her away, [but] he said to them: "Leave her. What is mine and what is yours is hers." Her father heard that a great man had come to town, [and] he said: "I will go to him. Perhaps he will invalidate my vow." He came to him, [and Rabbi Akiva] said to him: "Would you have vowed had you known … [that he would be] a great man?" He said to him: "Even one chapter, and even one law." He said to him: "I am he." He fell on his face and kissed his feet, and gave him half of his money. (*Ketubot*, 62b–63a)

This story has all the elements of romance: love, a woman of valor, a forbidden marriage, a father who finally recognizes the truth. Other stories about Rabbi Akiva are equally fascinating, culminating in his death as a martyr with the words of the Shema, Hear, O Israel, on his lips.

In fact, these sage-stories are rather like the raw material around which the Arthurian romances later developed. The sages form a society, the Haverim (literally Friends, as they referred to themselves), with definite goals. There are internal conflicts, like the rebellion against Gamaliel II or the expulsion of Eliezer ben Hyrcanus; there are tales of heroism; there are extensive family connections with sages marrying the daughters or sisters of other sages; there are encounters with the generals and emperors of Rome (in which those potentates often acknowledge the superiority of the sages).

Of course, the heroism of the sages differs significantly from that of Arthurian knights. It focuses on study (on Rabbi Akiva's twenty-four years in the Academy and his twenty-four thousand disciples) rather than on knights and ladies, dragons and giants. It focuses on the Jewish people's seeming to have been vanquished by Rome and yet actually having triumphed, on the Jews' ability to maintain their identity and integrity as a people despite almost unrelieved hostility. The rabbis were the model of what Jewish men should be, and although women played a far smaller role in the world of the Talmud, the wives of Rabbi Akiva and Rabbi Meir, among others, also served as models.

The Talmud in the Middle Ages

All of this background has been necessary because the Torah, both Written and Oral, was so central to Jewish life in the Middle Ages and eventually became a focus for the persecutors of Jews in the later Middle Ages. For the Jews themselves, the halakhic sections of the Talmud became most important, as they offered guidance on virtually every aspect of life. Whether or not the compilers of the Talmud had intended their work as a rule book, it rather quickly took on that role. How that transformation occurred is subject to debate. Jeffrey Rubenstein, for instance, theorizes that we can see the process in the Talmud itself, that for the Amoraim of the Gemara, Torah study, prayer, and the pursuit of moral perfection were the highest goals, but for the actual compilers, study alone had taken that place.[11] As proof, he points to a number of stories in the aggadah that depict the academy almost as a battlefield where the sages are indeed concerned with winning their arguments.[12] While Rubenstein may be overstating the case somewhat, he accurately portrays the rabbis' extensive use of dialectic to create new kinds of analysis and to expand the body of traditions and of laws. Jacob Neusner sums up the activities of the rabbis by saying, "The Gemara put forth for holy Israel a source of reasoned community that for all time would make of holy Israel a preserve of contentious argument in a world of inarticulate force. Its dialectic civilized Israel, the holy community, and, the theologians would add, Israel then conformed to the model and the image of God who created all things through reasoned speech."[13] The Talmudic academies may have become battlegrounds, but they were battlegrounds based on logic and reason, which made them far superior to more traditional battlegrounds.

We must recall at this point that the Palestinian Talmud had been compiled hastily, due to the hardships of Jewish life in Palestine. In

Babylonia, there were also periods of hardship, but the academies continued to operate. The historical records concerning the closing of the Talmud are scanty, but we do know certain things: that after the closing of the Talmud, discussions continued; that the Jewish community in Babylonia (modern-day Iraq) remained for many centuries the central, authoritative Jewish community in the world; and most important, that the Babylonian Talmud was transformed "from a literary corpus to a legal 'code,' which ... could serve as an authoritative guide to religious practice."[14] Halakhah, regarding both ritual and moral behavior, became the central concern of Judaism, as reflected in a saying of Rabbi Ḥiyya ben Ami in the name of 'Ulla: "Since the day that the Temple was destroyed, the Holy One, Blessed Be He, has nothing in the world but the four cubits of Halacha alone" (*Berakhot*, 8a). Halakhah, that is, has completely replaced the Temple as God's place in the world. If Rabbi Ḥiyya is correct, then halakhah must be understood and carried out as accurately as possible, and the guide to halakhah is the Talmud, now regarded as a guide to the rules.

We should note that the rabbis themselves occasionally comment on the artificiality of some laws: "Rab said: The precepts were given only in order that man might be refined by them. For what does the Holy One, blessed be He, care whether a man kills an animal by the throat or by the nape of the neck?" (*Genesis Rabbah*, 44:1). Nevertheless, whatever its meaning or function, the halakhah had to be followed, no matter how tenuous its relationship to the Written Torah. Thus, the famous passage in Exodus 21 that calls for retribution (an eye for an eye) was interpreted by the rabbis as calling for monetary compensation for injuries, although there is no support in the Torah for that interpretation. Even so, that is what the passage came to mean.

A major problem, however, was that the Talmud was intended for an intellectually elite readership.[15] Furthermore, when we deal with these early periods and with the transition from oral to written texts, we must always keep in mind how scarce and expensive writing materials were. Thus, the text is extremely difficult to read; it is written without vowels or punctuation, in Hebrew and Aramaic, in a terse and gnomic style. If we look back to the story about Rabbi Akiva and his wife, we can see how many words have to be supplied in brackets so that the story will make sense. The Talmud, then, is not the kind of work that one can read on his own. ("His" is intentional. Talmudic study was not generally in the purview for women.) A man needed a teacher and he needed time to study this difficult text, which meant that he also needed financial support. Consequently, the Babylonian academies became centers of Talmud study. Jews from all countries would write to the Babylonian academies or to their leaders, the Gaonim (literally "Eminences"), with questions of both theoretical and practical significance, and the Gaonim, after consultation with the scholars, would respond based on their interpretation of the Talmud. As the Babylonian academies declined in importance, however, and as Jewish communities elsewhere gained importance, talmudic interpretation became the work of local authorities, which created a need for people who were capable of reading and interpreting the text, a text which, with the passage of time, seemed to become even more obscure, as both its methodology and its vocabulary became increasingly alien.

Fortunately, in the late eleventh century there was a revival of talmudic study in both the Sephardic and Ashkenazic spheres. In the Sephardic world, a major figure was Yitzhak Alfasi (Rif),[16] who studied in Babylonia and lived in several localities, dying in Spain. He was an early codifier; in his *Sefer ha-Halakhot* (*Book of Laws*), he presented an early list of those laws that still applied in his day, omitting those that applied only in the land of Israel when the Temple still existed, such as laws relating to sacrifices. In this way he made the Talmud more accessible, more, as we might say, user friendly. His work differed from the approach taken by his Ashkenazic contemporary Rabbi Shlomo ben Yitzhak (Rashi), whose work we will examine in some depth later. Rashi had studied at some of the most famous schools in the German Rhine Valley before returning to his home in the French city of Troyes, where, according to some authorities, he was engaged in the business of grape farming, which would surely have taken a great deal of his time. Even so, Rashi wrote commentaries on every book of the Tanakh and on most of the Talmud. The importance of Rashi's commentaries cannot be overstated. By explaining clearly the meanings of words and phrases and by cross-referencing a variety of rabbinic writings, he made the Talmud comprehensible to a wider audience and sparked a renewal of talmudic study after the time of the First Crusade, a particularly dark period in Jewish history. As central as the Talmud had been to Jewish life until Rashi's time, afterwards it gained even more prominence, so that Rashi's grandson, Rabbi Ya'akov Tam (known as Rabbeinu Tam), thought that a person should not study the Bible or the Mishnah as separate subjects but should focus on the Talmud, which cites both sources.[17] One way of looking at medieval Jewish history focuses on the establishment and development of the Talmud as the central document of Judaism.

If the talmudic rabbis saw themselves as the direct heirs of Moses, the medieval talmudists accepted that portrait. In the twelfth century, Moshe ibn Ezra, like Maimonides, argued for the superiority of the sage over the prophet, because the prophet delivers messages given by God, but the sage delivers what he learned from the prophets, combined with what he learned elsewhere, refined by his own reason.[18] Avraham ibn Daud in the twelfth century wrote his *Sefer ha-Qabbalah* (*Book of Tradition*) to prove that the rabbinic tradition was the fulfillment of Scriptural revelation.[19] He did so partially to counter the opponents of rabbinic Judaism, but his own statement of intention indicates a deeper goal:

> The purpose of the Book of Tradition is to provide students with evidence that all the teachings of our rabbis of blessed memory, namely the sages of the Mishna and Talmud, have been transmitted…. Never did the sages of the Talmud, and certainly not the sages of the Mishna, teach anything, however trivial, of their own invention, except for the enactments which were made by universal agreement in order to make a hedge [or fence] around the Torah. (*Book of Tradition*, 3)

The Talmudic sages passed on the Oral Law, which went back to Moses and ultimately to God. Therefore the Talmud, no matter what anyone says about it, is of divine origin and therefore should be exempt from criticism. This attitude, which was shared by all Jews, helped to preserve the Jewish people during the persecutions of the Middle Ages. While Christian misunderstandings of the Talmud contributed to those persecutions, the long-standing traditions and the concept of their divine origin had a beneficial effect on the Jewish people. Without a homeland of their own, without the Temple, the Jewish people depended on the Talmud to provide a center for their lives.

Karaites

Of course, not everyone accepted the Talmud as authoritative. Islam and Christianity certainly rejected it, particularly Christianity, as we saw in the comments of Pope Gregory IX at the beginning of this chapter and in the fact that the Talmud was burned at the stake in Paris in 1242, in keeping with its "heretical" status. But another group who rejected the Talmud were the Karaites, a sect that claimed to be the true heirs of Judaism, as opposed to the corruptions of rabbinic Judaism. The origin of the Karaites remains a mystery, though they appear somehow to have adopted the position of the ancient Sadducees, who believed in the strict literal interpretation of the Torah. The basic stance of the Karaites toward the Rabbanites was, "Who put you in charge? Who said that your fanciful interpretations of the Torah take precedence?" The Rabbanites, who were far more numerous and powerful, responded that the Karaites were akin to Korah, who had rebelled against Moses on similar grounds (Numbers 16).

The ostensible founder of the Karaites in the eighth century was Anan ben David, though it seems more likely that late ninth- or early tenth-century Karaites, in search of a founder, chose him.[20] Other important Karaite leaders were Ya'qûb al-Qirqisani (tenth century), Levi ben Japheth (eleventh century), Yehudah Hadassi (twelfth century), and Aaron ben Elijah (fourteenth century).[21] Although these Karaite leaders were probably driven by sincere attachment to the Torah, they were vehemently attacked by their Rabbanite opponents. Anan ben David, for example, was accused of rebelling against rabbinic Judaism as a result of having been passed over for a promotion, a story that is almost certainly without foundation.

We might be tempted to see in this Karaite-Rabbanite opposition a case of power politics, with each side seeking to gain advantage, but that explanation would be too simple. First, the amount of power involved would be negligible, especially because the Karaites preached a doctrine of asceticism and self-denial. For instance, the Torah forbids the lighting of a fire on the Sabbath, which would seem to preclude cooking or having heat on a cold day. In the Talmud, the rabbis clarified these matters. Food could be put up to cook before the Sabbath to be eaten on the Sabbath, as long as the fire itself was not stoked or otherwise tended to on the holy day. Similarly a fire could be started before the Sabbath and then used for heat or light. The Karaites, however, felt otherwise, that fire could not be used on the Sabbath at all, so they chose to spend the holy day in darkness and cold.

While the Karaites did disturb the unity of rabbinic Judaism, they also had a positive effect on that institution, for their disagreement prompted rabbinic Jews to defend their positions, which meant that they had to consider the assumptions that they had begun to take for granted. The Karaites' insistence on what they considered the literal interpretation of the Torah and their rejection of traditional rabbinic prayer in favor of the recitation of biblical verses meant that they, and their rabbinic opponents, began to take a closer look at literal meanings, which meant, as well, that they began to consider the grammar and structure of Hebrew; and the result was a greater understanding of how that language worked.

It is difficult for us to know just how much of a threat the Karaites were to rabbinic Judaism. We know that Karaites flourished more at some times than at others. One high point came in tenth-century Iraq, when Qirqisani wrote his *Book of Lights and Watchtowers* and *Book of Gardens and Parks*, but these books were apparently not translated from Arabic into Hebrew and therefore had little impact on the non-Arabic-speaking world.[22] Nonetheless, Saadiah Gaon (882–942), the greatest of the early Jewish philosophers, campaigned against them, as did Avraham ibn Daud and others. At the same time, we must put this conflict into context. In the early sixteenth century, when Martin Luther and others rebelled against the authority of the Catholic Church, the result was a major split characterized by bitter hatred and violence. Although the Karaites, like the early Protestants, insisted on the validity of individual interpretation of Scripture, the conflict between Karaites and Rabbanites did not explode into violence. Their disagreements may have been stated in the most vehement terms (disputes of any kind in the Middle Ages were not characterized by moderation), but we have evidence that close relationships, including marriages, often existed between members of the two groups.[23] While the Karaites and Rabbanites were bound to disagree over certain fundamental points, they also held much in common, including a burning desire for the coming of the messiah and the redemption of Israel and a strong feeling for social justice.[24]

The Talmud as a Lens

Morton Bloomfield wrote, in a memorable phrase, that people in the Middle Ages spoke "Bible."[25] They knew the Bible so well that they could quote it with ease, and if they heard a word, they could identify its source in that vast text and probably quote other uses of the word. Of course, even today no one can approach the Bible impartially, and in the Middle Ages no one would have pretended to. Christians saw it as they saw everything else, through the lens of Christian theology. As Avraham Grossman says, medieval Jews saw the Bible through the lens of the Talmud.[26] We can go even further and say that medieval Jews saw their whole world through that lens. Furthermore, the level of literacy was extremely high among Jewish men (less so among women, though we have ample evidence of literate women), which means that Jewish men had direct contact with biblical and talmudic texts. When they went to the study halls, they probably imagined that their environment was like that of the ancient rabbis, as they studied the same texts and pondered the same questions that the rabbis had.

Of course, while much was indeed the same, much was different as well, and talmudic thought had to be adjusted on occasion to allow for new circumstances. For example, one tractate of the Talmud, Avodah Zara, concentrates on making separations between Jews and non-Jews, by which it means idolaters. We must remember that in Palestine when the Mishnah was compiled, Christians were not a major threat to Jews, and in Babylonia when the Gemara was compiled, Christianity barely existed. The strictures of Avodah Zara, therefore, cannot be directed at Christians. For medieval European Jews, however, Christianity was a major issue. For instance, a pressing question was whether or not Christianity was idolatrous. To Jews, sculptures and paintings of the Crucifixion, of the Virgin Mary, and of the saints certainly seemed like idols, though many Jewish writers argued that they were not. What, then, was the relationship between Jews and Christians?

Jews and Christians often lived together in relative peace. There were no ghettoes until relatively late in the Middle Ages, and even those areas of cities known as "Jewries" were not entirely inhabited by Jews. Jews and Christians could not eat together because of the dietary laws, but there were other areas that were problematic as well. For instance, the Mishnah forbids trading with gentiles for three days before their festivals lest what they buy be used for idolatrous practices. The rabbis wanted to prevent Jews from taking part even indirectly in such practices. However, in northern France, Jewish merchants depended heavily on the fairs as places to conduct business, and those fairs were held on Christian holidays (which were far more plentiful than just Christmas and Easter). Could the Jews trade with Christians on those days? If they did, they might, according to some interpretations, be contributing to idolatrous practices. If they did not, they might be reduced to poverty. The rabbinic leaders of the time had to find a way to allow such trade without violating the spirit of the Talmud. Other similar problems involved the hiring of Gentile wet-nurses, entering into partnerships with non-Jews, and teaching Hebrew to non-Jews.[27] For people who believed so strongly in the Talmud as a guide, these were pressing questions.

Such questions led to considerable tension between what the talmudic rabbis taught and the necessities of everyday life. After all, the Talmud had been compiled in about the sixth century, but the economic, political, and social situations of the Jews had changed. As Talmud study developed, particularly among the twelfth-century successors of Rashi known as the Tosafists, the Talmud in many ways became adapted to modern life, just as the Constitution of the United States has in many ways become adapted to life in modern America. But if the interpretations of the halakhah changed, what always remained was the focus on trying to understand and carry out the will of God, and every human activity was directed toward that end. The Talmud enabled the people to live Jewish lives.

Of course, all that has been said so far represents an ideal. On the level of everyday life, we may well wonder how strict the people were in carrying out the minutiae of the laws, many of which are quite detailed and often difficult. Furthermore, we know that in the Catholic Church, with its central power in the papacy, customs often differed on the local level. Judaism, with no central power, must have had even more local variation in following the law. In fact, we know that there were local variations on observance, and the Talmud even notes that, within certain limits, local tradition takes precedence over the law. As for observance, our knowledge about everyday life in the Middle Ages is limited. It would appear that levels of observance changed during the Middle Ages, depending often on the levels of persecution or interest. We also know that after Maimonides' philosophical reflections on the laws, some of his followers allowed their level of observance to decline. On the other hand, we also have evidence that people really did try to fulfill their religious obligations. Probably the best answer to this problem is that there was so much individual variation that no simple answer is possible. What we know is that the Jewish people, living in the most difficult of circumstances, survived largely through their adherence to the teachings of the Talmud and that when we talk about medieval Judaism, we are talking about religious beliefs and practices that were shaped and dominated by the Talmud. Medieval Judaism was somewhat fluid, since it was subject to the ways in which the Talmud was interpreted, but the Talmud itself was revered and honored as the oral Law delivered to Moses on Mount Sinai.

The Midrash

But the Talmud, as long and as difficult as it is, represented only one kind of rabbinic writing. Another was the Midrash. There are several kinds of Midrash, including a form known as halakhic Midrash, but what they all have in common is a particular approach to the biblical text, an approach that is often fanciful and surprising. The midrashic writings originated in sermons that were later written down and combined. They are Palestinian in origin rather than Babylonian and were compiled through several centuries, well into the Middle Ages. Midrashic reading seeks to move beyond the text of the Tanakh, to explain things that have been omitted or to illustrate the meaning of one part of the Tanakh by citing verses from other books, a technique that was used also by Christian commentators. We may today regard the Bible as an anthology of separate books that were written over many centuries, but ancient and medieval commentators regarded them as a unified whole, the word of God transmitted through human beings. Midrash gave the ancient rabbis tremendous freedom in biblical interpretation as they attempted to find the deeper meanings of the text, often, as is the case in sermons, for the purpose of teaching moral lessons. For example, commenting on Genesis 1:27—Male and female He created them—the Midrash Rabbah explains that God created Adam with four angelic attributes and four bestial attributes:

> [The four attributes of] the higher beings are: he stands upright, like the ministering angels; he speaks, like the ministering angels; he understands, like the ministering angels; and he sees, like the ministering angels [the point being that like angels, and unlike animals, human beings have peripheral visions—a nice piece of unnatural natural history]. He has four attributes of the lower beings: he eats and drinks, like an animal; procreates, like an animal; excretes, like an animal; and dies, like an animal.... Said the Holy One, blessed be He: 'Behold, I will create him [man] in [My] image and likeness, [so that he will partake] of the [character of the] celestial beings, while he will procreate, [after the nature] of the terrestrial beings.... If I create him of the celestial elements he will live [forever] and not die, and if I create him of the terrestrial elements, he will die and not live [in a future life]. Therefore I will create him of the upper and of the lower elements: if he sins he will die; while if he does not sin he will live.'" (Genesis Rabbah 8:11)

As Pico della Mirandola would say in his fifteenth-century "Oration on the Dignity of Man," human beings are composites of the spiritual and the earthly, and we must choose which we will emphasize. The rabbis of the Midrash make the question one of who will inherit eternal life and who will not, but there is no basis for their reading in the biblical text itself.

The Midrash also looks at questions raised by the Bible, often using the answers to support moral opinions. For instance, when they discuss the Tree of Life in Genesis Rabbah, "R. Meir said: It was wheat, for when a person lacks knowledge, people say, 'That man has never eaten bread of wheat.'" (Another rabbi does point out that wheat does not grow on trees.) Other rabbis argue, for equally cogent reasons, that the fruit was grapes, the citron, or figs, while Rabbi Yehudah ben Rabbi Shimon points out, quite literally, that the text does not tell us what kind of fruit it was (XV.7). Thus, to guess that the fruit was a citron or a fig is fanciful, while to guess that it was wheat or grapes, neither of which grows on a tree, is, in literal terms, outlandish. However, in terms of the lessons that the rabbis found in naming those fruits, those guesses make perfectly good sense.

Similarly, the Midrash, like the Talmud, is full of word play. The rabbis interpret and reinterpret passage after passage by rearranging the letters of words, by changing the vowels in words, and by dividing and connecting words to create new words. These techniques may make us smile, since we think of puns and such as a kind of humor, but because the rabbis believed that God had created the world through the medium of the Hebrew language, the same language in which the Torah was written, they believed that Hebrew offered a universe of relationships both within and between the created world and the world of the Torah. Thus, if the rabbis smiled at their discoveries of puns or anagrams, their smiles were directed not at their own cleverness but reflected, rather, the shock of recognition, for they had discovered another connection between words or between things, more evidence of the wisdom and the unity of God's creation. We will see the Hebrew poets of the Middle Ages using language in very similar ways.

On the other hand, midrashic interpretations can be so literal that they focus on a single letter; why, the rabbis ask, was the world created (that is, why does the Torah begin) with the letter *beth*, the second letter of the Hebrew alphabet? "Just as the *beth* [ב] is closed at the sides but open in front, so you are not permitted to investigate what is above and what is below, what is before and what is behind.... You may speculate from the day that days were created, but you may not speculate on what was before that" (Genesis Rabbah 1:10). This warning against metaphysical speculation was not always heeded, but it illustrates how closely the rabbis looked at the Tanakh.

One final point that we must consider is that the rabbis, quite naturally, interpreted the Bible according to the ideology that they brought to the task, just as Christians did. We read, on the basis of scriptural verses, that God himself carries out the commandments of the Torah, indicating that God is "Jewish." The rabbis' approach here is like that of the Christians, who approached biblical interpretation through a Christological ideology. The ideologies are certainly different, but they share the power to direct the interpreters' understanding of the text.

We can see another example when God addresses Abraham concerning the *mitzvah*, the good deed, of circumcision. Abraham asked:

> "If circumcision is so precious, why was it not given to Adam?" Said the Holy One, blessed be He, to him: "Let it suffice thee that thou and I are in the world. If thou wilt not undergo circumcision, it is enough for My world to have existed until now, and it is enough for uncircumcision to have existed until now...." Said he: "Before I circumcised myself, men came and joined me [in my new faith]. Will they come and join me when I am circumcised?" "Abraham," said God to him, "let it suffice thee that I am thy God; let it suffice thee that I am thy Patron." (Genesis Rabbah 46:3)

This passage operates on a number of different levels. First, it recalls the covenant between God and Abraham, which means between God and the Jewish people. Secondly, it reinforces circumcision as the sign of that covenant and therefore supports the continuation of that rite. Third, it counters Christian antagonism toward that rite, as expressed in the Pauline epistles and in the Church Fathers. And fourth, it makes the point that even if potential converts are put off by the requirement of circumcision (the reason that Paul abolished the requirement for Gentile Christians), it is sufficient if only the Jews remain faithful to it, for God will always be their Patron.

While the Midrash did not receive the same attention in the Middle Ages as the Talmud, it was still an important source of Jewish learning. It is cited often by Rashi and other commentators; and midrashic texts, those focusing on specific books of the Bible (Genesis Rabbah, Exodus Rabbah, Song of Songs Rabbah) or having another focus (*Pirkei de Rabbi Eliezer, The Fathers According to Rabbi Nathan*), were foundational to Jewish life in the Middle Ages. Together the Talmud and the Midrash helped to define Judaism and sustained the Jews through difficult times.

Jews, Christians, Muslims

Because the Jews formed a minority (usually a very small minority) wherever they lived during the Middle Ages, they were largely dependent on the Christians or Muslims among whom they lived. Even in the twenty-first century, people are only beginning to achieve tolerance for others whose religious beliefs differ from their own. During the Middle Ages, such an attempt could hardly be contemplated. People often put up with those who differed, but they did so in varying degrees and in the full knowledge that those who differed from them were simply wrong, whether through ignorance, willful perversity, or in the service of the forces of evil. Even at the best of times, like the period known as the Golden Age of Spanish Jewry, suspicion and mistrust abounded. In worse times, conditions were unthinkable.

It would be easy for us to list atrocities and condemn the perpetrators. Indeed we should, but we also must remind ourselves that the Middle Ages were not like modern times, that such violent behavior was often, though not always, considered normal and acceptable. And to put the Middle Ages in perspective, we should also remember that the greatest mass slaughter in the history of the world took place in the twentieth century. Our task, therefore, is not simply to condemn but to try to understand. At the same time, understanding can be difficult, because the matters with which we are dealing are seldom rational. Medieval people did not adopt their religions based on rational considerations of all the possibilities any more than modern people do. They were born into their religions, felt that those religions taught them truth, and then defended them. They were not seeking truth; they were defending their beliefs. Consequently, if we try to devise a simple explanation for religious enmity, we are bound to fail. People began with distrust or dislike or hatred and then justified it, and we will examine many of their justifications, knowing that the animosity usually preceded the reasons for the animosity. We find evidence of anti-Semitism in places like Anglo-Saxon England, where there were no Jews. In the ninth century, John Scotus Eriugena wrote, "There is an ancient house of death and deepest night—the heart of the Jew—a whirlpool filled with vice, ever a broad estate of fraud and envy, rejecting with rage the rays of hated light. Their faithless hypocrisy rules unrivaled; it stinks to high heaven and corrupts with its foulness the hearts of a carnal race ignorant of truth."[1] Such sentiments can have no rational basis, particularly from a man who probably never met a Jew in his life. But we can try to understand where these sentiments originated.

Before we begin, however, we must keep several points in mind. One is that in what follows we devote far more attention to Jewish-Christian than to Jewish-Muslim relations, because the former were more complicated than the latter. In both cases, though, we need to remember that the antagonisms we see do not represent a simple religious division. Those antagonisms are between "conflicting exponents of the same tradition."[2] Throughout the Middle Ages, the Jews were subject to, and often caught between, two religions that were offshoots of Judaism. Consequently, the quarrels among them are in the nature of family disputes, and family disputes are often the most rancorous kind. We never hear of Jewish-Hindu or Jewish-Confucian disputes, but the three Abrahamic religions, like members of a family, competed for superiority. Both Christianity and Islam felt the need to prove their superiority to their parent and to each other. As Cecil Roth points out, Jews were not compelled to account for the Qu'ran or the New Testament, but Christians and Muslims did have to deal with Jewish interpretations of the Old Testament.[3]

Yet another problem, particularly between Judaism and Christianity, is that people of the two faiths spoke different languages, even though they used the same language. What does this paradox mean? Jews tended to learn the languages of the places where they lived. A few, we know, even learned Latin. They knew Hebrew as well, but Hebrew was reserved primarily for study and prayer. So they used the same words as their Christian neighbors, but those words often meant different things. As Menachem Kellner says, the word "faith" means different things to Jews and Christians: for Jews it tends to mean "faith in" (as in the Hebrew *emunah*), while for Christians it tends to mean "faith that." The difference may seem trivial, but it is not. Jews had faith in God, as indeed Christians did, but Christians, with their more elaborate theology, had faith that their belief had particular implications. They believed in God, but they also had well-defined beliefs about God and about the process of salvation.[4] In fact, "salvation" was another term that Jews and Christians used differently, as were others like "messiah," "heaven," and many more. Furthermore, as we will see, Jews and Christians, while sharing many books in the Bible, interpreted them quite differently. The difference between the Old Testament and the Tanakh is more than a difference of names, and Jews and Christians would often cite the very same verses to support their own positions, with neither side quite able to understand how the other side could interpret so badly. Even the order of the books differs. The Tanakh, for instance, ends with Second Chronicles, which concludes:

> Thus said King Cyrus of Persia: The Lord God of Heaven has given me all the kingdoms of the earth, and has charged me with building Him a House in Jerusalem, which is in Judah. Anyone of you of all His people, the Lord His God be with him and let him go up. (II Chronicles 36:23)

The Persian monarch Cyrus, having defeated the Babylonians, here encourages the exiled Jews to return to Jerusalem, where they will be able to rebuild their destroyed temple, which they subsequently did. This rebuilding, with its messianic implications, makes the Tanakh open-ended: the Jewish people, again in exile, again await the opportunity to return to Jerusalem, after the coming of the messiah, when they will build the Third Temple. The Christian Old Testament, however, ends with the prophet Malachi:

> Lo, I will send the prophet Elijah to you before the coming of the awesome, fearful day of the Lord. He shall reconcile fathers with sons and sons with their fathers, so that, when I come, I do not strike the whole land with utter destruction. (Malachi 3:23–24)

Here we have a foreshadowing of the coming of the messiah, whose coming will be announced by Elijah, immediately before the opening of Matthew, in which, for Christians, that prophecy is fulfilled. Jews, then, who await the coming of the messiah, look forward to his arrival, while Christians celebrate his having already appeared. If such basic differences exist merely in the order of the books, we can expect that the words themselves will show profound conflicts. To paraphrase Winston Churchill, Jews and Christians were divided by a common text.

Finally, once again we must emphasize the role that ideologies play in biblical interpretation. Augustine of Hippo, in his treatise on how to read, *On Christian Doctrine*, points out that the "text of the prophet Isaias reads: 'If you will not believe, you shall not understand,' and in another translation: 'If you will not believe, you shall not continue.' Which of these is to be followed is uncertain unless the text is read in the original language." Augustine, who knew no Hebrew, wrote before a standard Latin translation of the Bible existed, and here he is confronted with two different translations of the same passage. A modern reader, facing this discrepancy, might try to find someone who could read the passage in the original language and explain which translation, if either, is correct. But that is not the response of Augustine, who continues, "But both of them nevertheless contain something of great value for the discerning reader" (*On Christian Doctrine*, 45). Augustine does not particularly care which translation is correct (in our sense of "correctness"); he cares that both translations present a doctrine with which he agrees. The doctrine controls what the words say rather than the other way around: "Whoever ... thinks that he understands the divine Scriptures or any part of them so that it does not build the double love of God and of our neighbor does not understand it at all. Whoever finds a lesson there useful to the building of charity, even though he has not said what the author may be shown to have intended in that place, has not been deceived ..." (*On Christian Doctrine*, 30). Augustine knows Christian doctrine, and the biblical text must support what he knows, regardless of what the words actually say. Jewish commentators occasionally fell into this way of thinking as well, but because they were not trying to demonstrate that all of the Tanakh foreshadows the New Testament, and because they did read the Tanakh in its original language, they were not driven to the same kinds of interpretive gymnastics.

Robert Chazan illustrates this point in his examination of medieval Jewish and Christian interpretations of Psalms 2 and 110, which Christians, of course, read Christologically and Jews did not. As Chazan demonstrates, the beliefs of the interpreters preceded and therefore dictated the interpretations.[5] What we see here is the practice of eisegesis (reading interpretations into texts) rather than exegesis (getting meaning from the text). And neither side could understand the others. What Jews, Christians, and Muslims thought about each other's religious beliefs was virtually always incorrect and derogatory.

Jews and Christians: The Beginnings of the Split

How did Judaism and Christianity, which share so many similarities, become so divided? What in particular lay behind the Christian animosity toward Judaism that resulted, in the Middle Ages, in discrimination, persecution, forced conversion, expulsion, and murder? The Jews formed such a minuscule part of the population that their importance as victims far outweighs their numbers. Why did the Christian majority simply not ignore them? There is no single or simple answer to these questions. There are, rather, a number of answers, and they go back to the story of Christian origins.

When Jesus was born, ancient Israel was under the control of the Roman Empire. While Renaissance humanists may have extolled the virtues of the Romans, the Romans were in reality cruel rulers who sought to dominate and extract wealth from the peoples they had conquered. The Romans' cavalier attitude toward Jewish religious practices led to armed uprisings by the Jews, and the Roman response was vicious. Their favorite form of punishment for rebels was crucifixion, a terrible torture, and there are reports of roads lined with crucified rebels meant to serve as a warning to those who would challenge Rome's might. Many Jewish leaders urged the people to be patient and live as best they could, because the Romans would eventually disappear, as had the Assyrians, the Babylonians, and the Seleucids, earlier oppressors of the Jews. Others, however, urged active opposition to the Romans, opposition that ultimately brought about the destruction of the Temple.

It was in this context that Jesus lived. Scholars and Christian believers differ about Jesus' role in these conflicts, but apparently the Romans considered him to be a political threat, because they killed him by crucifixion. In Jesus' time, just as before and after, there were many people who proclaimed themselves the messiah. Literally, in Hebrew, the messiah means someone who has been anointed, with the implication that such a person will be a political leader and will rescue the Jewish people from oppression by driving away their enemies. In the 130's, Rabbi Akiva and others thought that Bar Kokhba was the messiah, though they were proven wrong when he was defeated by Roman forces. Jesus' followers thought that Jesus was the messiah, and the political implications of that term may have dictated his form of execution. Ordinarily the death of someone who was thought to be the messiah put an end to that claim, but Jesus' followers continued to believe.

At first, Christians were also Jews. They, like Jesus, followed Jewish teaching and formed a subset of Judaism, like numerous others at the same time. In the 50's, however, Saul of Tarsus appeared and changed everything by transforming the belief in Jesus as the messiah from a Jewish to a gentile movement. Few Jews were willing to believe in a messiah who had been executed in such a demeaning way. To Jewish belief, the concept of a messiah who had died verged on the oxymoronic. After all, how could a dead messiah lead the people to political independence? Saul, who was now Paul, reconceived the idea of the messiah and of Jewish law. For Paul, the messiah's task was to lead to personal rather than national salvation, and salvation meant not the defeat of the oppressor but the attainment of heaven. Furthermore, people could only attain heaven by believing in the messiahhood of Jesus, not by following the religious rituals (not that anyone had ever said that following those rituals would lead to heaven). This position allowed him to challenge the "Christian establishment" of his time, which consisted largely of people who had actually known Jesus and who insisted that a follower of Jesus had to be Jewish, which meant that gentiles who wanted to be followers of Jesus had to undergo conversion. Since conversion for males requires circumcision, recruitment was slow. By convincing the establishment that non-Jews could be followers of Jesus (in Acts 15), Paul allowed for a huge increase in the Christian population, but he also began the split between Judaism and Christianity. No longer could one be a Jewish-Christian. One was either a Jew, who followed Jewish teaching, or a Christian, who believed that Jesus was the messiah. Under his leadership, "at Antioch the disciples were first named Christians" (Acts 11:26).

As Paul's thought developed, he became increasingly hostile to the Jewish rituals, seeing them, particularly circumcision, as obstacles to true belief. As we have seen, there are many commandments, and they can be difficult to carry out. Paul felt that they were impossible to carry out, that therefore everyone was sinful and condemned to punishment. The only escape was belief in Jesus. To explain why God had given these laws to the Jews, Paul said that the laws had been preparatory, but they were no longer necessary. They prefigured the Incarnation, but now that that event had taken place, they had outlived their usefulness. Faith in Jesus had replaced them, with the implication that those who continued to follow the laws were deficient in their faith. For Paul and his followers, the true course of Judaism led to faith in Jesus, and so those who followed him were the true Jews, while those who followed traditional Judaism and its laws were engaged in falsehoods. Jews were no longer Jews. Christians were the new Jews, a concept that was repeated often in the Middle Ages.

Here we find the root of one source of the Jewish-Christian conflict in the Middle Ages, the question of who constituted true Judaism, with Christians claiming that they had superseded the Jews, had taken the right course while the Jews insisted on following laws that were no longer valid (except for the few that Paul himself had chosen). But there were other reasons for the conflict as well. Paul, as anyone who reads his letters can see, was a man of strong emotions. He believed that he had a wonderful message for the Jews, and when the Jews rejected that message, he reacted bitterly (a pattern that was followed a millennium and a half later by Martin Luther). In Galatians, for example, he reinterprets the story of Hagar and Sarah as an allegory. In Genesis, Sarah is the wife of Abraham and bears him Isaac. Hagar, her handmaid, bears Ishmael. Both Isaac and Ishmael are heirs to Abraham, but Isaac, one of the Jewish patriarchs, is primary, while Ishmael, about whom God says, "I will make a great nation of him" (Genesis 21:18), is secondary. Much later, the Islamic version of the story will reverse those roles, but Paul alters them completely, seeing the two mothers as representing "two testaments. The one from mount Sina, engendering unto bondage; which is Agar. For Sina is a mountain in Arabia, which hath affinity to that Jerusalem which now is, and is in bondage with her children. But that Jerusalem, which is above, is free: which is our mother.... Now we, brethren, as Isaac was, are the children of promise" (Galatians 4:24–28). In his version of the story, which was to have dire consequences for the Jews of the Middle Ages, Paul completely rewrites it. In Genesis, the half-brothers Isaac and Ishmael are both destined to be the ancestors of great nations, but in Paul's version, there is no sense of brotherhood. There is "them" and "us." "They" are slaves while "we" are free; "they" are Jews while "we" are Christians. From almost its very beginning, Christianity saw itself as apart from and superior to Judaism.

But of course virtually every nation (or religion or gender or group of baseball fans) has seen itself as superior to others. Jews certainly did. In this case, however, historical events intervened. When the Second Temple was destroyed in 70, Judaism seemed to have lost its foundation. It could easily have disappeared had it not been rescued by the rabbis who created Rabbinic Judaism based on, but independent of, the Temple rites. But the destruction of the Temple was also read as God's punishment on the Jews. In the Talmud it is seen as punishment for the sin of "causeless hatred," but the new Christian church developed the notion that it was divine punishment for the Jews' refusal to acknowledge Jesus. If Paul's opening of Christianity to the gentiles began the split between the two religions, reactions to the Temple's destruction made the split permanent. Both Rabbinic Judaism and Christianity are reactions to that disaster, reactions that sent the two religions in completely different directions.

A number of scholars, such as Israel Yuval and Annette Reed, make the important point that Judaism and Christianity continued to influence each other. While we must not overlook this point, we must also remember that those influences were almost always unconscious and unacknowledged and that both Jews and Christians would have denied their existence. Thus, by the time the Gospels were written down, probably between about 70 for Mark and 100 for John, ideologies were hardening. In Matthew 25, Jesus addresses the scribes and Pharisees in the most bitter and condemnatory terms: "You serpents, generation of vipers, how will you flee from the judgment of hell?" (23:33), even though Jesus shared many of his teachings with the Pharisees. And, Matthew reports, when Pilate asked the Jews what he should do with Jesus, "They say all: Let him be crucified" (27:22). Historically this scene is virtually impossible. We know that Pontius Pilate was so cruel and so hated by the Jews that even the Romans, for whom cruelty could be a virtue, removed him from office, so the Jews were not likely to cooperate with him. Furthermore, crucifixion, because it is a terrible torture, would have violated several Jewish laws regarding capital punishment, the very kinds of law that Paul condemned, so that the people who were described as following that law so closely were unlikely to demand that it be violated. Furthermore, the Jews despised the Romans and would not likely have cooperated with them in the execution of someone who was accused of being a rebel. What we see here, then, is the consequence of Paul's thought. For him, the Jews were the other; now they are becoming the enemy, a process that continues in John, where it is no longer the Pharisees who are cursed and condemned but the Jews as a whole and where the Jews assume even more of the responsibility for the crucifixion. Possibly those early Christian writers, seeing the Jews out of favor with the Romans, tried to court their rulers' favor by showing that together they had, in the Jews, a common enemy. Furthermore, it is unlikely that a Roman audience (or a medieval Christian audience) had much of an idea of what a Pharisee was. "Pharisee" simply became another term for "Jew," losing the meaning that we saw in the previous chapter, and it is probably no accident that the apostle who allegedly betrayed Jesus was Judas, whose name is so like "Judea."

In short, the New Testament helped to lay the basis for medieval anti-Semitism. Such a statement is difficult to make and may strike some readers as offensive, but there are passages in the Tanakh and in other religious Scriptures that are also offensive. We do nothing to strengthen our religions if we ignore or try to explain away their problematical aspects. We asked earlier why the Jews were regarded with such horror and hatred in Anglo-Saxon England when no Jews had ever lived there, when most Englishmen of the time had never met a Jew. One answer is that in fact they *had* met Jews—they had met them in the New Testament, in the writings of the Church Fathers, and in the sermons of their priests. From those sources they knew that Jews were guilty of deicide, that Jews were in league with the devil, and that Jews sought to do harm to Christians. Jews had become a mythical standard of evil.

There were, it is true, anti-Christian passages in the Talmud, though a reader would have trouble finding them today, largely because they were edited out, under Christian pressure, during the Middle Ages. The fragments that have survived show Jewish doubts about Jesus as messiah and about the whole New Testament story. Two passages in the siddur, the prayer book, should be considered. One major prayer, recited three times each day is the *Shemonah Esreh*, literally "the Eighteen," because originally it consisted of eighteen benedictions. During Talmudic times, a nineteenth was added, which reads, "May the slanderers have no hope; may all wickedness perish instantly; may all thy enemies be soon cut down" (Birnbaum, *Daily Prayer Book,* 88). Who the targets of this prayer were is a matter of dispute. Some think that it refers to all sectarians who refused to acknowledge the authority of the rabbis, others think that it refers to a particular unidentified group, and others think that it refers specifically to the new group of Christians who were beginning to be troublesome for the Jews. We have no clear evidence to support any of these positions, but we do know that during the Middle Ages, the Church found the passage to be offensive. Similarly, the Aleinu prayer includes a statement that reads, "For they bow to vanity and emptiness and they pray to a god that does not save" (Birnbaum 136), the latter part of which is a quotation from Isaiah 45:20. The Church also found this passage offensive and actually banned it from the prayerbook. Even today, most prayerbooks omit the line, though it probably originally had nothing to do with Christianity, first because it is a direct quotation from the Bible, but primarily because the prayer was most likely composed in Babylonia, where Christianity was not an issue for the Jews. (At the same time, it is possible that medieval Jews did in fact regard this line as a reference to Christianity.)

Even if all of these passages were directed against Christianity, they never begin to approach the virulence of the Christian attack on Judaism. The fourth-century John Chrysostom equates the synagogue with the dwelling place of the devil and says in his "Homilies against the Jews," "You Jews did crucify him. But after he died on the cross, he then destroyed your city ... it was then that he scattered your nation over the face of the earth. In doing this, he teaches us that he is risen, alive, and in heaven."[6] Ambrose, the mentor of Augustine, learned that a mob, led by a bishop, had burned a synagogue and that the emperor had punished the bishop. Ambrose responded by refusing the sacrament to the emperor until he withdrew the punishment.[7] Jerome wrote in one of his letters, "I will not weep with Jacob and David for sons who died under the Law, but with Christ I will welcome those who rise again under the Gospel dispensation. The Jew's mourning is the Christian's joy" (Letter 60). Given the history of Jewish persecution during the Middle Ages, that last sentence could almost serve as a motto.

Jerome, incidentally, also influenced the medieval Christian attitude toward Jews and Judaism through his translation of the Bible into Latin. Since every translation is also an interpretation, we can hardly fault him for producing a Christian translation, though some of his word choices change the biblical text, as when he translates the Hebrew for "young woman" as "virgin" in the verse, "A young woman will conceive," thereby transforming an ordinary occurrence into a miracle. More damaging, however, is what he did to Moses: according to Exodus, when Moses descended the second time from Mount Sinai, his face was shining, so much so that he had to cover his face with a veil whenever he spoke to human beings; but in his translation, Jerome transformed the rays of light from Moses' face into horns, and since, as everyone knew, the devil had horns, Moses, the Hebrew law, and the Jewish people all came to have demonic associations. (Those "horns" can clearly be seen on Michelangelo's monumental sculpture of Moses.) Jerome, then, though he learned Hebrew from the Jews, used the Hebrew Bible in ways that were to prove detrimental to that people.

Jerome's translation of the Bible was a major influence on medieval thought. So, too, was the work of his contemporary, Augustine. In many ways, Augustine helped to shape medieval thought, and his influence on medieval views of Jews and Judaism was profound. Augustine wrote voluminously, but we need only look at his masterpiece, *The City of God*, to get the essence of his ideas about Judaism. He tells his readers, for instance, that when the Jews "do not believe in our Scriptures, their own

Scriptures, to which they are blind when they read, are fulfilled in them" (18:46). Augustine laments that the Jews do not believe in the New Testament, and he criticizes them for not reading their Scriptures as the Christians do, that is, Christologically, seeing everything in the Old Testament as a foreshadowing of the New. And Augustine goes on:

> So God has shown the church the grace of his mercy in the case of her enemies the Jews, since, as the Apostle says: "Their sin is the salvation of the Gentiles" [Romans 11:11]. For this reason he did not slay them ... lest through forgetting the law of God they should bear no effective witness on this point that we are concerned with. So it was not enough for him to say: "You are not to slay them, lest they some day forget your law," without also adding: "Scatter them" [a rough translation of Psalm 59:11]. For if they dwelt with that testimony of their Scriptures in their own land only, and not everywhere, then the church, which is everywhere, could not have them at hand among all the Gentiles as witnesses to those prophecies that were given in advance concerning Christ. (18:46)

Because this passage directed the course of Jewish-Christian relations through much of the Middle Ages, it deserves a close examination. First, Augustine clearly states that the Jews are the enemies of Christians and of their church. Nothing could be plainer. Thus, whatever relationships between Jews and Christians may have developed later, Jews were always considered the enemy. Even if there were no Jews, they still represented the enemy. The normal thing to do with enemies in the Middle Ages was to kill them, but Augustine, basing himself on the translation that he had of Psalm 59, forbids such action. The Jews, having been dispersed throughout the world by the Romans, should be allowed to exist because they, through their Scripture and through what Augustine considers their lack of true belief in that Scripture, bear witness to the truth of Christianity.

This logic, twisted though it may seem to us, actually helped to preserve the Jews, for official Church doctrine took a similar position: the Jews were the enemy, but they were not to be killed. Thus, throughout the Middle Ages, even when the Church took harsh positions regarding the Jews, it also tended to preserve their lives. On many occasions it stopped, or tried to stop, massacres of Jews. At the same time, however, there was a corollary to Augustine's positions. Yes, the Jews should be preserved for propaganda purposes, as proof of the truth of Christianity; but if the Jews seemed to prosper in the world, if they lived happy lives, their existence would be a challenge to Christianity. How could people living in blindness and error be happy? Therefore, while the Jews could live, their lives should be made miserable so that they could serve as an example of what happens to people who deny Christianity. Obviously this position required a kind of balance that was impossible to maintain, as the history of Jews in medieval Christian lands illustrates. Sometimes there was relative peace; often their lives were made miserable; and too often, they were called on to give up their lives for the sake of their Judaism.

Of course, by Augustine's time the Roman Empire had already been officially Christian for many decades, a factor that complicated the lives of Jews, for the Empire had not favored Jews even before the conversion of Constantine in 312. Peter Brown says that the "conversion of a Roman emperor to Christianity ... might not have happened—or, if it had, it would have taken on a totally different meaning—if it had not been preceded, for two generations, by the conversion of Christianity to the culture and ideals of the Roman world."[8] Christianity, as it gained adherents and power, adapted to the Roman world by adopting Roman ways of thinking. For example, a great deal of what we think of as Christian imagery originated with Rome; the image of the Virgin Mary suckling Jesus descends from images of Isis suckling Horus, which had become Roman through Hellenistic syncretism.[9] Similarly, as the Western Roman Empire declined, the Church increasingly replaced it as "the origin and symbol of law," giving a theological basis to law and making obedience to the law a religious duty.[10] All such developments were bound to be bad for Jews, who were now "enemies" on political and theological grounds. As Wolfgang Seiferth indicates, there is a significant difference between Jesus' "Father, forgive them for they know not what they do" and Augustine's words to a personified Synagogue, "Go away from me, you accursed ones, into the eternal fire."[11]

Constantine's adoption of Christianity for himself and for Rome, then, had a deleterious effect on the Jews, who continued to exist in the Empire as a barely tolerated minority, a situation that continued when the Empire split into eastern and western divisions. In the western half, Jews were harassed and subjected to forced baptisms. In 598, amid complaints about the Jews' religious celebrations, the locations of synagogues, and Jewish ownership of Christian slaves, Pope Gregory the Great wrote in a letter, "Just as one ought not to grant any freedom to the Jews in their synagogues beyond that permitted by law, so should the Jews in no way suffer in those things already conceded to them."[12] Why did those complaints arise, and what effect did Gregory's pronouncement have?

Jewish religious ceremonies, while often lacking the decorum of Christian ceremonies, are not particularly raucous, and yet often in the Middle Ages we hear complaints about noise coming from synagogues. The likelihood here is that the synagogues were not overly noisy but that to some Christians, who thought that Jews should be downtrodden and silent, any sound of celebration was too much. Similarly, they were probably offended by the mere existence of synagogues, so wherever they were would have been considered a bad location. As for slavery, the issue is complicated. We, of course, condemn any kind of slavery as well as those who profit from it, but slavery was perfectly acceptable through much of the Middle Ages. In Gregory's time, slaves would have been captives largely from Slavic countries (hence the etymology of "slave"), and Christians as well as Jews bought and sold them. Christian concern over the Jews' role had nothing to do with compassion or with objections to slavery. Their fear was only that Jews might try to proselytize among the slaves and convert them to Judaism.[13] Christians were therefore content if the Jews acted only as temporary owners of the slaves until they could sell them, thereby forestalling Jewish proselytization but allowing the slave trade to benefit Christian countries.[14]

Forced baptisms were yet another problem. Ordinarily it might seem that a person baptized against his or her will, through either force or coercion, should not be considered baptized, that religious conversion should be something that the person desires. But baptism, whether forced or otherwise, was considered irrevocable. If one had gone through the ritual, in whatever manner, one was baptized, and there were severe penalties, including death, for anyone who tried to go back. At various times in the Middle Ages (after the Crusade massacres, for instance) these penalties were ignored, but in both Jewish and Christian writing we can see the religious authorities struggling with the issues. Back in the sixth century, Gregory tried to discourage the policy of forced baptism because he recognized that it was counterproductive in the case of Jews. It was acceptable for pagans, he said, but Jews should be converted by preaching and other inducements.

Growing Oppositions—The Twelfth Century

Gregory urged that the Jews be treated humanely, that they should not be given special privileges, but neither should their rights be taken away, a position that was often repeated throughout the Middle Ages. On September 15, 1199, Pope Innocent III wrote:

> Although the Jewish perfidy is in every way worthy of condemnation, nevertheless, because through them the truth of our own Faith is proved, they are not to be severely oppressed by the faithful. Therefore, just as license ought not to be granted the Jews to presume to do in their synagogues more than the law permits them, just so ought they not to suffer curtailment in those (privileges) which have been conceded them.[15]

At first glance, Innocent seems to say that no matter how terrible the Jews may be, their rights should be preserved, but when we realize that Innocent, writing six hundred years after Gregory, was only one of several popes who made such statements, we must ask why such constant repetition was necessary. The answer is clearly because many people disregarded such statements. And it was the same Innocent III who wrote two years later:

> One who is drawn to Christianity by violence, through fear and through torture, and receives the sacrament of Baptism in order to avoid loss, he (like one who comes to Baptism in dissimulation) does receive the impress of Christianity, and may be forced to observe the Christian Faith as one who expressed a conditional willingness though, absolutely speaking, he was unwilling.[16]

This is the same Innocent III who in March, 1204, defended the seizure of a synagogue and its transformation into a church and who objected in January, 1205 to Jews being given more credence in trials when they have documents supporting their case than are the Christian witnesses who deny what the documents say.[17] And it was Innocent III, at the Fourth Lateran Council in 1215, who instituted in Christendom the order that Jews wear an identifying badge on their clothing to distinguish them from Christians, a practice that was adopted by the Nazis in the 1930's. These attitudes are largely summed up in a poem by Gautier de Coinci (c.1177–1236): "The Holy Spirit hates them a lot and I do too. And God hates them and I hate them and the whole world must hate them because they do not wish to desist from their errors."[18]

As we will see, this hatred manifested itself in many ways throughout the Middle Ages. There were many reasons for this antipathy, all of them irrational, but they appealed to different people at different times. One of its major sources, as we have seen, was the accusation that the Jews were the killers of Jesus, an accusation to which the Jews responded only with great difficulty. For many Jews, the accusation seemed like an absurdity, something to which one could not respond rationally, or even respond at all. How could they be accused of killing God, since, from their perspective, God could not be killed? For others, the charge was absurd on other grounds. After a Holy Week riot in 1452, Yosef ibn Shem Tov delivered a sermon in which he said:

> And now, my brothers and friends, look, and you will see how this tragedy has come upon us. You know, of course, that our hands did not shed the blood of that man in whose name our enemies in every generation have risen against us to destroy us. Rather, our righteous ancestors, basing themselves upon the Torah and justice, hanged him on a tree.[19]

Joseph does not deny that Jews killed Jesus, but he denies the possibility of vicarious guilt. After all, Jews do not have a concept of original sin. Each person is responsible for his or her own sins and repentance. Therefore, even if our ancestors did execute Jesus, *we* are not guilty. In fact, as Marc Saperstein notes in commenting on this sermon, medieval Jews did not deny Jewish involvement in the crucifixion, though they denied that they should suffer for it. And as Yosef ibn Shem Tov points out in the same sermon, Jews also suffered in Moslem lands, where the crucifixion was not an issue.

What we must recognize, as Yitzhak Baer says, is that "the rivalry between Judaism and Christianity … took the form of a contest between two divergent conceptions of human history and two conflicting approaches to the problem of salvation."[20] We might juxtapose the assumption of Mishnah Sanhedrin 10:1, that all Israel is righteous and deserves a place in the world to come, with Augustine's assumption that everyone is stained by original sin and therefore no one deserves a place in the world to come.[21] These two views can hardly coexist. It has become a cliché that the God of the Tanakh is a God of wrath and the God of the New Testament is a God of love, but that cliché severely oversimplifies the case. In the New Testament, Jesus makes nearly impossible demands on human beings. One of the Ten Commandments says, "You shall not commit adultery," but in Matthew Jesus says that anyone who looks at a woman lustfully has in fact committed adultery (Matthew 5:27). Which view is more demanding? Christian theology also spells out the penalty for non-compliance: eternal damnation. The ideal is practically unreachable, and the penalty for medieval Christians was both real and severe. Similarly, when someone asked Jesus, " 'Good master, what good shall I do that I may have life everlasting?' Jesus' ultimate answer is, 'If thou wilt be perfect, go sell what thou hast, and give to the poor'.... And when the young man had heard this word, he went away sad" (Matthew 19:16–22). How many people could follow that command, with its implication that not following it would bar one from heaven? Not many. So Christians, with all their power and surface confidence, must have felt a great sense of insecurity—for which the Jews suffered. First, the Jews denied the validity of the New Testament and so were not held to those standards. Second, because of Paul, Christians believed that the Jews thought they could achieve heaven by following ritual laws, which, for all their difficulty, are easier to do than selling all of one's possessions. Thus, the Jews undermined Christianity by their very existence.

Furthermore, this relationship played into another aspect of Christianity, its emphasis on martyrdom. Early Christians, unfortunately, were often called upon to give their lives for their faith, and stories of martyrdom became great favorites. When Christianity became the dominant religion, however, it was one of the most powerful forces in the world. Although actual martyrdom became a thing of the past, the memory of martyrdom as an ideal persevered, and the Jews, who refused to accept Christianity's teaching and challenged its accepted truths, were construed now as the persecutors of Christians.

As the Middle Ages progressed, this situation became even more complex. The twelfth century was a remarkable time, a renaissance in some ways more important than the period we usually call the Renaissance. One reason for this development was the arrival in Europe of the works of Aristotle, particularly his works on natural philosophy and some of his work on logic. Some of those logical works had been available in Boethius' Latin translations earlier, but they became most influential in the twelfth century. These books had been translated from Greek into Arabic and then, sometimes through the agency of Jews, from Arabic into Latin. In twelfth-century Europe, they produced a revolution in thought, as men such as Peter Abelard began to use reason and logic to examine Christian doctrine. For many years attempts were made to limit such examinations, but they continued and culminated in Thomas Aquinas' *Summa Theologica* and the subsequent history of scholasticism. But they also complicated Christian thought and belief.

Gavin Langmuir argues that during the twelfth century, some Christian thinkers, having used Aristotelian tools, raised doubts about such difficult Christian doctrines as the relationship between Jesus' divine and human natures or transubstantiation. These doctrines, which were based on faith rather than reason, required Christians to suppress their rationality because they simply could not be understood rationally, and this suppression of rationality then appeared elsewhere, in charges against the Jews of ritual murder and other heinous infractions. Anna Sapir Abulafia takes a different approach to the question. According to her interpretation, twelfth-century thinkers used reason to show that Christian doctrines were indeed reasonable. Consequently Christians could not understand why Jews would not accept such a reasonable religion, and they concluded that Jews were therefore unreasonable.[22]

Langmuir and Abulafia are probably both correct for different groups of thinkers. Certainly the result for the Jews was the same—an increased level of hostility—though we can argue that the Jews themselves were only a convenient target. David Berger, in his study of Christian anti-Jewish polemics, says that it is difficult to tell when a polemic is actually directed against the Jews and when it shows a Christian author trying to work out his own uncertainties and defend his beliefs. Berger adds that the number of anti-Jewish polemics "seems disproportionate to the threat that Jews could have posed."[23] Was Judaism itself, then, the threat? In many cases the real threat was Christian doubt, which was transferred to the Jews and concretized on such matters as usury. Such doubt appears in the famous disputation held in Barcelona in 1263, when the leading Christian speaker said that "even the angels and the heavenly forces do not comprehend" the Trinity, a position that may not have strengthened his argument that the Jews were unreasonable.[24] Similarly, in the eleventh century, Lanfranc said about the Eucharist, "What we receive is the very body which was born of the Virgin, and yet it is not. It *is*, in respect of its being and the characteristics and power of its true nature; it *is not*, if you look at the outward appearance of the bread and wine."[25] Lanfranc here makes an important point, but to ordinary Christians, his statement might well appear self-contradictory. How can the bread and wine both be and not be the body of Jesus? Christians who accused Jews of host desecration, of obtaining sanctified wafers and stabbing or burning them in order to re-enact the tortures of Jesus, had no doubt that the bread was the body of Jesus. They even assumed that Jews believed it was the body of Jesus, which of course they did not, but that accusation provided Christians with a means of expunging their own doubts about transubstantiation. The basic problem was that Christian theology defied logic; we today might say that there is no reason that religious belief should be logical, but under the influence of Aristotle, many medieval thinkers tried to demonstrate the logic of Christianity. Either way, the Jews lost—either they were simply non-believers, or they were irrational, which indicates again that dislike of the Jews came first and the rationalizations for that dislike came later.

Among those rationalizations, one that stands out concerns how Christians and Jews read the Bible. This aspect of Jewish-Christian relations is particularly fascinating because it involves two groups of people, both of whom regard the Bible as the word of God, interpreting the same text in drastically different ways, although they also share some similarities. For example, modern scholars often regard the Song of Songs as a collection of often sensual wedding songs that were gathered together in the centuries after King Solomon; but earlier, the book was regarded as the work of Solomon himself, who, with his seven hundred wives and three hundred concubines, was assumed to know something about love. Although Jewish tradition valued love and sexuality within marriage, Rabbi Akiva declared that the Song of Songs must not be read as a poem about human love. It should be seen, instead, as an allegory of God's love for Israel. In some communities it is recited on Friday evenings at the beginning of the Sabbath because it is also regarded as an allegory of Israel's love for the Sabbath, which is conceived of as a bride. Not by coincidence, married sexual love is also encouraged on Friday evenings as a laudatory Sabbath activity. Christianity, with its emphasis on chastity, also declared that the Song of Songs should be read as an allegory, but of Jesus' love for the Church. Thus Jewish and Christian commentators both declare it an allegory, but they differ dramatically on what the allegory is.

Another example of these alternate readings involves Jacob and Esau, Isaac and Rebecca's twin sons. Although Esau was born first, Jacob was born immediately after, holding on to his older brother's heel. When Rebecca was pregnant, she was told she would bear twins and "the older shall serve the younger" (Genesis 25:23). As the story progresses, Jacob becomes Isaac's heir (not, it should be emphasized, through trickery, as is often asserted, but by having Esau reveal how little he cares about his birthright), so that the elder, Esau, indeed becomes subservient to the younger, Jacob. For Jews, this story at first had a simple meaning: Esau was the ancestor of the Edomites, who were conquered by the Jews, thereby making the elder serve the younger. During early talmudic times, when Israel was dominated by Rome, the rabbis used the names Esau and Edom as code words for Rome, which helps to explain why rabbinic commentary makes Esau so much more villainous than the biblical text does. The rabbis were actually talking about the hated Romans. Even later, when the Roman Empire became dominated by Christianity, Esau and Edom stood for Christianity (just as Ishmael, the ancestor of the Arabs, stood for Islam). But no matter whom Esau represents, the biblical prophecy is that the elder shall serve the younger, that Jacob, Israel, will triumph.

It should come as no surprise that Christian commentators approached the story differently. As Augustine says in *The City of God*, "As to the statement, 'the elder shall serve the younger,' however, scarcely anyone among us has understood it to mean anything else than that the older people of the Jews should serve the younger Christian people" (16:35). For the Jews, then, Jacob represents the Jews and Esau represents first Rome and then Christianity, while for the Christians, Jacob represents the Christians and Esau represents the Jews.[26] This is not a disagreement that can be resolved. Jews and Christians are on opposite sides in both interpretations. During the Middle Ages, Christians pointed to their actual dominance as proof that their reading was correct, while Jews had confidence that the prophecy given so long ago to Rebecca would yet come true.

This particular disagreement hinges on both Jewish and Christian tendencies to allegorize the biblical text. Christians were more likely to engage in that kind of allegorical interpretation, while Jews, who also had the advantage of reading the Tanakh in Hebrew, tended to be more literal. Thus, Christian interpreters used an interpretive method known as typology, in which everything in the Old Testament foreshadows something in the New: Noah's Ark foreshadows the Church, which rescues people from destruction; the burning bush, which burned and was not consumed, foreshadows the Virgin Mary, who could bear a child and remain a virgin; the Akedah, the binding of Isaac, foreshadows the Crucifixion. For Jews, these stories were history that taught lessons. For Christians they were history that pointed to the future. In Genesis we learn that "Leah had weak eyes; Rachel was shapely and beautiful" (29:17), about which Isidore of Seville says, "Leah embraces the figure of Synagoga, who could not perceive God's secrets with the weak eyes of her heart. Rachel, on the other hand, with her clear vision represents the type of Ecclesia [Church]—with sharp eyes she comprehended the secrets of God."[27] In medieval sculpture and painting, we often see two women, one of whom is blindfolded and represents Synagoga, the Jews, while the one without a blindfold represents the Church. Isidore applies this image to Leah and Rachel.

Christian commentators also applied this method of interpretation to the commandments. Jews read the dietary laws of Leviticus 11 in the most literal terms: a Jew should not eat the meat of an animal that does not have cloven hoofs and chew its cud, and the most popular example of forbidden animals is the pig. To Jews, that commandment seems clear enough; but for Christians, who no longer followed the dietary laws, it seems nonsensical. Gilbert Crispin, in the eleventh century, said that while Jews claim to follow all these laws, they cannot, because there are so many and because they are so complicated. Instead, he argues, Christians actually do follow all the laws, because Christians see the allegorical meaning behind them. Thus, when the Bible says that pigs are unclean, it does not mean not to eat them. It means to avoid moral uncleanness.[28] This reading relies on the common stereotype that Jews are materialistic while Christians are spiritual, as does Ralph of Flaix's comment on the biblical notion that dead bodies create ritual uncleanness. Ralph, living in a Christian society that venerated such relics as the bones of saints, cannot possibly accept such a notion, so he allegorizes the idea and says that "dead bodies" do not mean dead bodies. They mean sin, which creates uncleanness.[29]

We today may cherish multiple ways of reading texts, but in the competition between Judaism and Christianity during the Middle Ages, no one cherished the other side's approach. There was right and there was wrong, and the other side was not only wrong but also often incomprehensible. Especially from the Jewish perspective, Christians were making texts say things they plainly did not say while ignoring their clear meanings; and from a twenty-first century perspective we can say that they did so in order to justify their own beliefs and to obliterate, as far as possible, the Jewish roots of Christianity. While Christianity claimed for itself the title of "true Israel," it also regarded anything Jewish with some horror. In the twelfth century, when Christian scholars at the Abbey of St. Victor in Paris decided that Christians should learn the literal meaning of the Bible and consulted Jewish scholars, they were accused of "Judaizing," a serious charge that manifested itself numerous times throughout the Middle Ages.

There are thus several probable sources for the massive hatred of Jews, all of which were undoubtedly true for different people at different times: genuine hatred for the people who had allegedly killed Jesus, fear of those who are different, the need to preserve a sense of martyrdom, and insecurity about Christian beliefs (which became a serious issue in the twelfth century). If logic took on new significance and if Christian beliefs did not seem totally logical, perhaps they would become subject to doubt. This possibility troubled Church leaders.

Again, then, the twelfth century becomes pivotal, for just as Aristotelian logic struck some people as a revolutionary tool for arriving at Truth, others saw it as a threat to true belief. Peter Abelard, an early advocate of Aristotelian logic, wrote *A Dialogue of a Philosopher with a Christian and a Jew*, in which, of course, the Christian triumphs but which presents a rational and civil discussion; but Abelard was opposed by one of the monumental figures of the twelfth century, Bernard of Clairvaux, a man who was both politically and theologically influential and who succeeded in having Abelard discredited. The twelfth century opened with the First Crusade, during which the crusaders slaughtered large numbers of Jews in the Rhineland, an event that traumatized the Jews of Europe and that marked the beginning of the decline of medieval European Jewry. When the Second Crusade began to be organized, then, the Jews became understandably nervous, but Bernard of Clairvaux took steps to see that, so long as they cooperated with the crusaders, they would not be harmed, and he largely succeeded, thereby earning the gratitude of the Jews. In taking this action, Bernard stands in contrast to his contemporary, Peter the Venerable, who claimed that the Jews lacked the ability to read the Bible correctly and who tried to stir up anti-Jewish activity. Bernard did not encourage such action, content, in good medieval tradition, to see the Jews merely degraded; but Bernard's own comments on the Jews were so inflammatory that at times they led to actual violence.[30]

By the thirteenth century, conditions had gotten even worse. We should note, however, that none of this narrative forms an actual continuum. Sometimes things were better and sometimes worse, but overall there was a decline in the fortunes of European Jews. The thirteenth century helps to illustrate this history. The thirteenth century is the century of Thomas Aquinas and his monumental *Summa Theologica*, that vast and brilliant work constructed on the basis of Aristotelian logic; but with regard to the Jews, that century reveals more irrational attitudes, as we saw in the case of the burning of the Talmud. A contributing factor was the rise of the mendicant orders, the friars, who, with the cooperation of the papacy, led an attack on the Jews. Perhaps the general attitude can be summed up in the ruling of a Church synod in 1284 that a Christian man should not have sexual relations "with a Jewess, a Muslim woman, and a brute animal."[31]

As we saw at the beginning of Chapter 2, one of the targets of Christian wrath in the thirteenth century was the Talmud. Pope Innocent III, in 1244, said that the Jews should be grateful that they are allowed to live in Christian lands, but instead they "throw away and despise the Law of Moses and the prophets, and follow some tradition of their elders ... called 'Talmud' in Hebrew.... In it are found blasphemies against God and His Christ, and obviously entangled fables about the Blessed Virgin ..."[32] We have already seen how difficult the Talmud is, and the popes certainly knew neither Hebrew nor Aramaic, so how did they claim to know what the Talmud says? In a number of cases, their purported knowledge came from Jewish converts to Christianity. In fact, some of the greatest damage to Jews in the Middle Ages came from such converts. Earlier in Spain, the convert Peter Alfonsi had spread lies about Judaism and worked to undermine the religion of his birth, and in the 1230's and 1240's, Nicholas Donin performed the same function. Donin advised officials of the Church about Judaism, using his pernicious imagination to paint a frightening and false picture of what the Talmud said, but he was so effective that in 1239, Pope Gregory IX issued an order to the archbishops of France "that on the first Saturday of the Lent to come, in the morning, while the Jews are gathered in the synagogues, you shall, by our order, seize all the books of the Jews who live in your districts, and have these books carefully guarded in the possession of the Dominican and Franciscan Friars."[33] Eventually these books were declared heretical and were burned.

The motivations of Peter Alfonsi, Nicholas Donin, Pablo Christiani, and others not only to abandon Judaism but to become its enemies and to lead the attack on it are not always obvious. It is hard to avoid the suspicion that they were somehow getting even with the Jewish communities that had rejected them. Whatever the cause, though, their efforts made life even more difficult for the Jews. Gilbert Dahan says, "The discovery of a Judaism other than biblical stunned the Christian world, which defined the Jews precisely as contemporaries of Christ, practicing the laws of the Old Testament."[34] The Church had been willing to put up with the Jews because the Jews, living embodiments of the time of Jesus, proved to them the truth of Christianity. Now, however, it turned out that Jews were not such living embodiments, that they practiced a different kind of Judaism, based on the Talmud. If that was the case, perhaps they no longer merited the protection of the Church. The Jews, of course, would have denied this whole conception. As far as they were concerned, they were practicing the religion that had been given to Moses on Mount Sinai.

This whole discussion of Jewish-Christian relations in the Middle Ages must seem fairly messy, largely because the subject itself is so messy. The official Church doctrine, that the Jews should be allowed to exist in Christian society but should be despised and made miserable, was basically untenable, as untenable as Paul's formulation in Romans: "As concerning the gospel, indeed they are enemies for your sake: but as touching the election, they are most dear for the sake of the fathers" (11:28).

Jews and Christians lived in the same neighborhoods, dressed alike, spoke the same languages, had their churches and synagogues near each other, and often formed business relationships and personal friendships. Ariel Toaff describes one particularly interesting example of Jewish-Christian cooperation. In fifteenth-century Italy, Abramo di Ventura da Roma headed a Jewish-Christian criminal organization that specialized in kidnapping and extortion, which proves, perhaps, that people can get along when they want to.[35] The problem for us is that we would like to see order and get a sense of rational behavior, neither of which played much of a role in Jewish-Christian relations in the Middle Ages. There was official doctrine, which was untenable, and there were the ways in which people actually behaved, which are, on doctrinal grounds, inexplicable, though on economic and political grounds, which so often rely on matters of self-interest, relations are often less puzzling.

For example, in the earlier part of the Middle Ages, Jews and Christians often held friendly discussions on their religious differences. Some Latin works, like those of Boethius, were translated into Hebrew, and Christians occasionally showed interest in Hebrew scholarship.[36] There were friendly religious discussions between a Jewish physician and Wazo, the future archbishop of Liège in the early 1030's and more serious discussions between Elezar (formerly Bodo, a convert to Judaism) and Paulo Alvaro (a Christian of Jewish descent) in the ninth century.[37] In the late eleventh century, Gilbert Crispin wrote his *Disputation of a Jew and a Christian*, which probably reflects actual conversations between himself and a Jew.[38] But things were not always so friendly, and during the twelfth and thirteenth centuries they got worse. Thus, Christian interest in Hebrew scholarship became a way for Christians to use rabbinic literature against the Jews.[39] Nicholas Donin in the 1230's had depicted the Talmud as totally inimical to Christianity, full of lies, distortions, and heresies; but in the 1240's, records from the Barcelona disputation indicate that Pablo Christiani tried to argue that the Talmud itself recognized that Jesus was the messiah and that only the blindness or perversity of contemporary Jews prevented them from agreeing. Nachmanides, who wrote an account of the disputation, was forced to argue that the halakhic sections of the Talmud are binding but that the aggadic sections are not, an argument that Jews could readily accept but that would seem contradictory to the Christians, because Jews focused on the laws while Christians focused on doctrine.

So far we have been considering the more learned classes (churchmen and rulers), but the thirteenth century also saw changes in popular anti-Semitism. Earlier times had certainly seen violence done to the Jews for a variety of alleged causes, but the thirteenth century saw two new allegations, that of the blood libel and that of host desecration, both of which rely on the characterization of the Jews as the killers of Jesus. While this accusation lacked historical validity, it played a powerful role throughout the Middle Ages and later. In fact, medieval interpreters even intensified the gospel accounts. A good example is the episode of Jesus being given vinegar to drink. "Vinegar" was probably soldier slang for wine, and the man who offered it to Jesus was probably a kindly soldier, but the medieval interpretation that said it was actual vinegar made the image of the allegedly Jewish tormenters worse.[40] And when we look at medieval paintings or illuminations of the Crucifixion, we can see that Jesus' tormenters are often given stereotypically Jewish features, as are other biblical villains; in depictions of the Cain and Abel story, Cain, the murderer, often has stereotypically Jewish features.

The Jews' supposed association with the Crucifixion story led to a variety of medieval customs, often during Holy Week or coinciding with other Christian holidays. Palm Sunday in Béziers, in France, was a time of street brawls, with the bishop encouraging the crowd to stone the Jews. In Toulouse and elsewhere, a ceremony known as the *calafus judeorum* consisted of having the local ruler publicly slap the Jewish community leaders on the face.[41] On Easter itself, the Jews were well-advised (and often required) to stay in their homes with the shutters closed as crowds would gather to thrown stones at them.

In 1144, we find the first accusation of ritual murder in connection with the death of a young boy, William of Norwich, who supposedly was crucified by the Jews during Passover. William was buried in the cathedral and his grave was said to be the site of miracles. At least one leader of the Jewish community was murdered, allegedly in retaliation for William's death, though the murderer was a follower of a knight who owed money to the Jew.[42]

In the middle of the thirteenth century, these stories and customs took another step, as the theory arose that one of the major ingredients of the matzah used for Passover was the blood of a Christian. Matzah, to be sure, is made only of flour and water, but the proximity of Passover to Easter made the association with Christian blood and the Passion almost automatic. Thus, when a young boy, Hugh of Lincoln, went missing and then was found dead in 1255, the accusation quickly arose that the Jews had killed him. According to one account, the Jews had circumcised him, beaten him, cut off his nose and lip, broken his teeth, crowned him with thorns, given him poison, crucified him, and stabbed him; but little Hugh, playing the role of a martyr, never complained. Nineteen Jews were executed for their roles in this alleged outrage.[43] One possible explanation for the Hugh of Lincoln story is that local authorities were eager to have a martyr in their midst, because the presence of a martyr brought pilgrims, who were good for local prestige and for the economy. The story of Hugh gained great currency in England and was recounted for many centuries. It forms the basis of Chaucer's Prioress' Tale, and it is also the distant ancestor of Bernard Malamud's novel *The Fixer*, which is based on an accusation of ritual murder in twentieth-century Russia.

Accusations of ritual murder (or the blood libel) continued to arise during the Middle Ages, making Passover a time of dread rather than a celebration. If a Christian child disappeared or died near the time of Passover, the Jews knew that they faced grave dangers. But other calumnies were still to come.

The ritual murder accusation first appeared in the mid-thirteenth century, while the host desecration accusation appeared at the end of that century. The basic form of this accusation is that a Jew, or a group of Jews, somehow comes into possession of a consecrated host, that is, a communion wafer that has become the body of Jesus. In a re-enactment of the Crucifixion, the Jew abuses the host in a variety of ways, by stabbing it, by boiling it, by trying to burn it. The host, of course, resists these attacks. Somehow the Jews' deeds are revealed, and they are severely punished, often through a divine agency. Additionally, Jewish witnesses to these stories invariably are persuaded of the truth of Christianity and convert. A further refinement of the story is that the Jews obtain the host as a result of moneylending: someone owes them money and they are willing to take the host as payment so that they can torture it. As Miri Rubin points out, the host desecration story obviously relies on the premise that Jews shared the Christian belief that the host had become Jesus, which they certainly would not have done. But those who delighted in such stories were not terribly concerned with their lack of logic. As was the case with the ritual murder accusation, Jews were actually killed on the basis of these stories.[44]

Even in 1272, however, Pope Gregory X wrote that ritual murder charges ought not to be believed, that the "Bible prohibits Jews from using the blood of even cloven-hoofed animals, let alone drinking human blood," and he ordered that Jews who were imprisoned on ritual murder charges should be set free. Two years later, he even went so far as to say that "when a dead body is found, it is thrown into the Jews' midst, and, without proper trial, they are despoiled of their property, imprisoned, afflicted with all sorts of penalties, and shamefully executed," and he required Church officials to prevent such behavior.[45] Obviously he knew how anti-Semitism functioned.

A third such accusation arose in the middle of the fourteenth century, with the arrival in Europe of bubonic plague, the Black Death. It is difficult for us today to imagine what the Black Death was like. Even if we face epidemics, we have some knowledge of viruses and bacteria, and we harbor the hope that we can find cures or develop preventive measures. The medievals had no such knowledge or hope. All they knew was that the Black Death struck suddenly, killed quickly, and wiped out a large part of the population. One explanation for the plague was that God was punishing the people, an understandable position that required people to accept responsibility for sinfulness, although the particular sins were not identified. The other explanation, in places where there were Jews (unlike England, where the Jews had already been expelled), was that the Jews were poisoning the wells. Again, this explanation lacked a certain cogency: Jews, like Christians, died from the disease, and the plague raged in places where there were no Jews. Nonetheless, to people who lived in fear and panic, this explanation made sense: God was not responsible, they were not responsible, and the Jews were their enemies. The result, once more, was that Jews came under attack. According to one chronicle, in Strasbourg, despite the efforts of authorities to protect the Jews, about two thousand were burned. Even if we make allowances for the medieval tendency to inflate numbers, clearly many Jews died at the hands of mobs.

Other Causes of Anti-Semitism

In this long discussion, we have focused on theological differences between Judaism and Christianity, but those differences cannot totally explain the enmity that Christians felt for Jews or the harsh measures they used against them. In cases like ritual murder, host desecration, and well poisoning, the accusations clearly arose out of pre-existing enmity.

We have already touched on the powerful motif of the Jews as killers of Jesus, which surely had a profound effect, but there were other, more practical sources of Jew hatred as well. One that we have also mentioned was Christian insecurity about Christian doctrine, to which the existence of the Jews presented an additional challenge. But we must not overlook the normal human reaction to the existence of a perceived enemy in our midst. We need think only of what happened to Japanese-Americans during the Second World War, to Asians during Vietnam, or to Muslims during the Gulf War. The Jews, though they spoke the same language and dressed the same way as other people, were still different; and because they were the only obvious minority in Christian Europe, and because they bore the burden of New Testament criticism, they received attention far beyond what their numbers might dictate, attention that was almost entirely negative.

Jews differed from their Christian neighbors in a number of ways. Their religious observances differed considerably from those of Christians, with different holidays, dietary laws, and a variety of other customs. In addition, there was the matter of literacy. Many Jewish boys, and some girls as well, learned to read, whereas among Christians through much of the Middle Ages, reading was the province of an elite class. Furthermore, Jewish religious leaders, rabbis, and cantors were encouraged, or required, to marry and have children, whom they taught to read, whereas Catholic priests, the most educated segment of Christian society, were forbidden to have children.

Jewish literacy did more than simply distinguish Jews from Christians. It had other consequences as well. Jews, like other people, had to earn a living. They practiced a number of professions, but at most times and in most places throughout the Middle Ages, Jews were not allowed to work the land. Consequently, they could not be part of the large percentage of the population that was involved in growing crops. Nor could they belong to guilds, which required their members to swear a Christian religious oath. Thus they were shut out of most professions. But their high level of literacy did open for them the possibility of being merchants and conducting business, professions that required the ability to read and to keep records. In the early part of the Middle Ages, then, Jews formed a majority of the middle class in the places where they dwelled.

However, as the Middle Ages progressed, economic conditions changed. Cities developed, the Christian middle class increased, literacy among Christians grew, and Christians became merchants and businessmen. When Jews were the only merchants, people accused them of charging too much or of being too demanding about payments, and when Christians became merchants, things got worse for the Jews, because now they were perceived as alien competitors. Because the Christian middle class was becoming more powerful, it was able to put restrictions on those competitors, a factor that brings us to one of the biggest problems of the Jewish Middle Ages, usury, moneylending.

Why did the Jews become moneylenders? Why is the most famous Jew in literature, Shakespeare's Shylock, a moneylender? Why did Jews continue to practice this profession when it so obviously made them objects of hatred? Jews did not begin as moneylenders. In fact, according to halakhah, lending money at interest, whether to Jews or gentiles, was forbidden; but, as the medieval economy developed and people needed capital, and as, simultaneously, the Jews were excluded from other professions, moneylending became an economic necessity.[46] Christians, too, were forbidden, by Church law, from lending at interest, and though some did, most did not; but credit was as necessary then as it is now. The situation, then, was that Jews were largely forced into the profession of moneylending but then were reviled for being moneylenders. Jews as moneylenders also served as a distraction. The kings of England in the twelfth and thirteenth centuries did not want their people to focus on royal profligacy and so used the Jews as a foil. For example, Richard the Lionhearted spent six months of his ten-year reign in England, which he regarded as a source of funding for his military adventures. He was much happier having his people's attention focused on the Jews' financial dealings rather than on his own. A century later, in 1290, when Edward I had borrowed as much as he could from the Jews of England, he avoided paying them back by expelling them from the country, to which they did not formally return until the seventeenth century. We should also note that many of these rulers profited handsomely from usury by taxing the Jews heavily and by occasionally seizing their assets, on the pretext that they were outraged by usurious practices. Philip Augustus, who had expelled the Jews from his domain in France early in his reign in the late twelfth century, eventually allowed them to return and to remain there because they were so convenient and easy to exploit. He could hardly afford not to have them there.[47]

In France, too, the Jews were denounced as moneylenders, though not as early as in England. Their role as moneylenders was often cited during the various expulsions from France that took place during the thirteenth century, though it is interesting to note that moneylending had become a societal necessity, so that the expelled Jewish moneylenders were replaced by Christian moneylenders, who were often seen as even more demanding! In 1204, Philip Augustus promised the merchants of Caen that their moneylending activities would remain legal as long as the interest rate remained under one hundred percent.[48] Many Christians were quite properly upset when churchmen used Church vestments or ornaments to secure their loans, leaving Christian ritual objects in the control of Jews, but their wrath tended to be directed against the Jews rather than against the offending churchmen.

Thus, through both normal commerce and moneylending, the Jews became associated with monetary activities. While there were Jews who became quite rich (most famously, Aaron of Lincoln), most did not. Nevertheless, the image of the rich Jew, usually in league with demonic forces, became a powerful part of the popular imagination. The result was that many of the anti-Jewish outrages that we examined earlier actually had economic roots. The chronicle that records the two thousand Jews burned at the stake in Strasbourg during the plague notes, "The money was indeed the thing that killed the Jews. If they had been poor and if the feudal lords had not been in debt to them, they would not have been burnt."[49] Those feudal lords aroused the populace, leading to a mob action that in effect cancelled their debts by eliminating their creditors. Similarly in the late fifteenth century in Italy, Abramo di Isacco of Bevagna's sons "were arrested on charges of having crucified a local child: after a difficult trial they were sentenced to a heavy fine and banished from Bevagna."[50] Again it looks as though financial considerations formed the basis for the accusation, since it strains credulity that a fine would suffice as punishment for crucifying a child. After the deaths of the Jews of York (an episode that will be discussed in the next chapter), the mob, under the influence of men who were in debt to the Jews, moved on to York Minster, where they burned the financial records, thereby canceling their debts. Accusations of ritual murder and host desecration often also had financial bases; accusations could easily be directed against one's creditors in the hope that their deaths would eliminate one's bills.

A Way Out: Conversion

This history should not be construed to mean that the Jews were all good or that they were all innocent victims, nor that Christians were all villainous persecutors. We have a great deal of evidence that Jews could be as venal and dishonest as anyone else and that some Christians, both inside and outside of the Church, intervened on behalf of Jews. Even so, there can be no denying that the tiny population of Jews in medieval Europe were frequently the victims of persecutions that were carried out in the name of Christianity. That Jews survived is something of a miracle. Many died, and many others succumbed to the temptation of conversion. To people who lived under constant threats, whose lives and livelihoods were frequently in danger, conversion seemed to offer a way out.

Often, however, conversion was imposed on Jews. In the tenth century, a story spread through southern Italy, which was still under Byzantine control, that a group of Jews had claimed victory in a religious disputation in Jerusalem and that this blasphemy had caused an earthquake that damaged the Church of the Holy Sepulcher. Although no part of this story had any factual basis, it outraged the population and resulted in forcible baptisms.[51] In the 930's, Pope Leo VII wrote a letter in which he said that Jews should be preached to, and if they still refused to convert, they should be expelled.[52] This letter offered a choice, but not a good one. Somewhat earlier, the anti-Jewish archbishop of Lyons, Agobard, convinced fifty-three Jewish children that they should be baptized, and when their parents protested to King Louis the Pious, the king forced Agobard to return the children to their families because such conversions were prohibited.[53]

We can hardly imagine the kinds of conversionary pressures that were exerted even in the earlier part of the Middle Ages. One of the outstanding rabbis of the tenth century was Rabbeinu Gershom Me'or ha-Golah, the Light of the Exile. Rabbeinu Gershom's son was forced to convert to Christianity and then died before he could renounce his apostasy (which also would have been dangerous). Such cases were fairly common, and rabbis were frequently consulted by people who wanted to know how they should behave toward apostates. Some three centuries after Rabbeinu Gershom's tragedy, Rabbi Meir of Rothenburg was asked whether one should mourn for an apostate, that is, whether one should regard an apostate as one who has died. He said no: "Although Rabbeinu Gershom mourned his son for two weeks, this is not the halakhah. He did so out of his intensely bitter grief."[54] One further example will make the point: in Wrocław, Poland, in 1453, a group of Jews was accused of host desecration. Those who were found guilty were tortured to death. Those who were not found guilty were given a choice: death by being burned at the stake or baptism. Twenty chose baptism; the rest chose death.[55]

Beginning in the twelfth century, conversionary pressures on the Jews increased, and in the thirteenth century the growing influence of the friars made them even stronger. In England, in the late 1200's, Jews were required to hear conversion sermons delivered by Dominican friars, a pattern that existed elsewhere as well. While we have no definitive records of the number of converts, we know that at certain times and places, depending on the levels of persecution, they were numerous, though many stories also exist about wives in particular who prevented their husbands from converting or who refused to accompany them into apostasy.[56]

Strangely enough, however, while the Church encouraged Jews to convert, it did little to support those Jews who complied. Such people were generally cut off from their families and were often left without livelihoods, and yet the Church made no provision for them. They were frequently regarded with suspicion by Christians. In 1232, the English king Henry III founded the Domus Conversorum (House of Converts) in London to offer support and Christian instruction to converts, but that institution, though it lasted a long time, was not terribly successful.[57] Even so, conversion was apparently a viable option for many people, either out of sincere religious belief or to escape the pressures that came with being a Jew.

As we have seen, a number of converts to Christianity became persecutors of the Jews, but one particularly interesting case of conversion is that of "Herman-Judah," who is known by both his Christian and Hebrew names. Herman, who lived in the twelfth century, has left us an autobiographical record of his conversion, somewhat like Abelard's *Historia Calamitatum* but with a happier ending, though there is some doubt about whether this record is historically accurate or is a piece of fiction. At one point, Herman says that the Jews considered him a "scribe learned in the Law" (94), even though he was only twenty years old at the time and seems not to have known a lot about Judaism. Later in the text he calls himself "I, as a Jew of the Jews" (104), a clear reference to Paul, who was addressing gentiles rather than Jewish audiences. That Herman was doing the same is shown by his use of Latin, a language that few Jews knew. Herman's audience, then, must have been Christian, so that the point of his book was not to encourage Jewish conversion but to confirm Christian belief, which he does by contrasting literal Jewish and allegorical Christian interpretations of the Bible. For example, he mentions a priest who shows that laws such as " 'Thou shalt not plow with an ox and an ass together; thou shalt not seethe a kid in its mother's milk' [Deuteronomy 22:10; Exodus 23:19] were fatuous according to the letter. Nevertheless, through a most beautiful way of reasoning, he translated [these precepts] into allegorical meanings. Using this kind of distinction, he adverted to the example of the Jews, like some beasts of burden, content with the letter of the precepts alone ..." (79). Similarly, his whole narrative is framed by a dream he has, which is given a literal interpretation by a Jew and then the "correct" spiritual interpretation by a Christian (77, 110).

Much of what Herman tells us is quite revealing. At one point he is urged to "cast off the burdensome yoke of the Mosaic law and to shoulder the easy one of Christ" (80), a clear reference to the alleged burdens of the biblical commandments but also an acknowledgement that Jesus' very demanding prescriptions were not well understood. Thus Herman cites the Jewish understanding of Leviticus 19:18—"Love your neighbor as yourself"—as "Love your friend and hold your enemy in hatred," which he contrasts with Matthew 5:44—"Love your enemies" (84). But then when his chaperone dies, an older man who had reported Herman's activities to his parents, Herman confidently reports that he went "into the eternal torments of hell." God, he says, showed both mercy and truth: truth "by repaying him with punishments rightly due him and mercy, on the other hand, by freeing me from his assaults and accusations" (91). This statement does not embody the concept of loving one's enemy, but it does indicate a level of hostility that was on the increase.

Of course, Jewish conversion represented a problem for the Church as well as for the Jews. It was true that the continued existence of the Jews represented a threat to the truths of Christianity as the Church conceived of them, a theme that runs throughout the Middle Ages, but at the same time there was a fear about Jewish conversion. Because Christian thought had associated the conversion of the Jews with the Second Coming, conversion seemed desirable, but the possibility existed that if the Jews did convert, the Second Coming might not take place, as it had not taken place after other indications that it was imminent. If that scenario were to occur, Christianity would face a real challenge.[58]

Perhaps this section on anti-Semitism should conclude with a comment made by Caesarius of Heisterbach in the thirteenth century. Caesarius has an apostate woman say, as a group of Jews approaches her, "I do not know whence it comes, but an odor of Jews is troubling me."[59] This reference to the *Foetor Judaicus*, the Jewish Stink, reveals much. First, in a time when everyone must have smelled in ways that we can barely imagine, there is something odd in mentioning that certain people have a bad odor. And second, it indicates that Jews were thought to have, merely by their existence as Jews, defects that could only be eliminated through baptism. This former Jewess obviously no longer has the odor, but having been baptized, she can now smell it on others. It may not sound like much, but it sums up the irrationality and hatefulness of prejudice.

Jewish Reactions

It would be fascinating to know how Jews reacted to the circumstances in which they lived during the Middle Ages. Unfortunately, our resources in this area are somewhat limited, for several reasons. First, Jews obviously had to be careful about what they said. If they were caught criticizing Christianity, they might well find themselves in even more danger. Twenty-four cartloads of Talmud volumes were burned in Paris in 1244, partially on the allegation that they contained such criticism. For this and other reasons, written criticism of the persecutions might have been destroyed, if they ever existed. As a result of increasing persecutions, Jews began not merely to separate themselves but to isolate themselves from Christians.[60] Nevertheless, we do have some examples of Jewish reactions.

Unless they were forced to respond to Christian arguments in public disputations or to defend themselves against specific charges, Jewish reactions were aimed at a Jewish audience, as we can tell by the fact that they were written in Hebrew. While they attack Christian beliefs, their primary intention is to strengthen the Jewish audience by showing where the Christians are mistaken and how their often seductive arguments can be countered.[61] They are also intended to help settle Jewish doubts. For example, one common Christian argument in favor of Christian superiority, especially after the initial successes of the Crusades, was that Christianity was flourishing while Judaism lagged far behind. The evidence for this assertion was plain to see and caused Jews considerable discomfort. After all, they were supposed to be "the chosen people," and whatever that problematic phrase might mean, it was supposed to mean something positive, not "chosen" for suffering and degradation. So Ashkenazic Jewry transformed suffering and degradation into martyrdom and "developed the theory that one reason for its suffering was that it was chosen because of its unique qualities to sanctify the divine name through martyrdom."[62] This interpretation dignified and gave meaning to their suffering, as can be seen in stories that were popular among medieval Jews. One popular work was the fifth-century Midrash Lamentations Rabbah, which appropriately contains numerous stories of martyrdom. There is the story, taken from Second Maccabees, of Miriam and her seven sons, each of whom is martyred before her eyes by the cruel emperor (I.16.50—in the medieval Hebrew history *Yosippon* she is called Hannah), and the story of three shiploads of captives being sent by Vespasian to serve in Roman brothels. Knowing their fates, they refused to undertake such impure behaviors and threw themselves into the sea, quoting, from Psalm 44, "Surely we had not forgotten the name of our God, or spread forth our hands to a strange god. Nay, but for Thy sake we are killed all the day …," to which God responds, "For these things I weep" (I.45).

One story needs to be quoted at length:

> A Jew passed in front of Hadrian and greeted him. The king asked, "Who are you?" He answered, "I am a Jew." He exclaimed, "Dare a Jew pass in front of Hadrian and greet him!" He ordered, "Take him and cut off his head." Another Jew passed, and seeing what had happened to the first man, did not greet him. The king asked, "Who are you?" He answered, "A Jew." He exclaimed, "Dare a Jew pass in front of Hadrian without giving greeting!" He ordered, "Take him and cut off his head." His senators said to him, "We cannot understand your actions. He who greeted you was killed and he who did not greet you was killed!" He replied to them, "Do you seek to advise me how I wish to kill those I hate!" (III.58–64.9)

Clearly this story conveys an essential understanding about the Jews' plight and about the nature of their persecution: the hatred preceded the rationalizations. Hadrian and his modern counterparts wanted the Jews eliminated, and they made up the reasons to fit the circumstances. Similarly, another story tells of Trajan's wife, who had a baby on the Ninth of Ab, the day when Jews mourn the destruction of the Temples. The child died on Chanukah, when the Jews light candles. She was told that the Jews had mourned when the baby was born and lit lights to celebrate its death. She complained to Trajan, and he brought his army and slaughtered them (IV.18–10.22). In other words, the Jews' religious customs were misinterpreted, intentionally or not, and then used as weapons against them.

Significantly, Lamentation Rabbah interprets passages from the biblical book of Lamentations as referring to both the Babylonians and the Romans, so that the medieval audience would have been fully justified in seeing their own lives reflected there as well. Such is the case also in the narrative of *"Eleh Ezkerah"* ("These I remember"), one version of the story that narrates the martyrdom of a group of rabbis by the Romans, on the absurd pretext that they are being punished for what the biblical Joseph's brothers did to him. This story, which still forms part of the Yom Kippur liturgy, is historically impossible, because the rabbis involved lived at different times, but the story explains and even glorifies martyrdom—not that one should seek martyrdom but that one should accept it, as the ninety-year-old Rabbi Akiva, having his skin scraped from his body, says the "Hear, O Israel" in order to prove that he really does love God with all his heart, with all his soul, and with all his might. We can only imagine the conditions under which the Jews lived that would require them to write such a narrative, and we might wonder as well whether Akiva's martyrdom is somehow related to the martyrdom of Jesus.

Occasionally, however, there are stories of divine intervention that frustrate the oppressors. In the eleventh-century *Chronicle of Ahimaaz*, Rabbi Hananeel and the archbishop both calculate the time of the appearance of the new moon, but Rabbi Hananeel's calculation is mistaken, though he does not see the mistake. The two men make a bet on the outcome, and Rabbi Hananeel says that if he loses he will convert. When he redoes his calculations and finds his error, he prays to God. That night, dense clouds obscure the moon, so no one can tell who was correct. The archbishop gives Rabbi Hananeel three hundred pieces of gold, which the rabbi gives to the poor (*Chronicle of Ahimaaz*, 79–80). Unhappily, few such stories end so well.

During the twelfth and thirteenth centuries, Jews began to write specific defenses of Judaism, which naturally included criticisms of Christianity, partially, at least, as a result of the increased pressures they felt, as Robert Chazan illustrates throughout *Fashioning Jewish Identity in Medieval Western Christendom*. Jews could be as intemperate as Christians, and we often find what we should consider intolerable invective in these works: churches are called "houses of idolatry," Christians are called "uncircumcised ones" or "unclean ones," and Jesus is called "the hanged one."[63] This appellation undoubtedly originated in images of the Crucifixion that Jews frequently saw. Joseph Kimhi, who fled from Spain and settled in southern France in the mid-twelfth century, wrote *The Book of the Covenant*, generally a relatively temperate and reasoned rejection of Christian beliefs, but at one point his Jewish speaker says, "How shall I believe that this great inaccessible [God] needlessly entered the womb of a woman, the filthy, foul bowels of a female, compelling the living God to be born of a woman, a child without knowledge or understanding, senseless, unable to distinguish between his right hand and his left, defecating and urinating …?" (36). On one level, Kimḥi is expressing an accurate Jewish point of view, that Jews simply cannot imagine the divine having become human, having gone through the birth process, having to have his diaper changed. On another level, however, Kimḥi's question not only denies the divinity of Jesus, but it also insults the Virgin Mary, who, in the twelfth century, was becoming increasingly a figure of veneration. While such intemperance frequently characterizes medieval argumentation, it also illustrates the gulf that separated Jewish and Christian belief, a gulf that was wide from the beginning and that increased in scope through the Middle Ages.

There are a number of works of Jewish apologetics that have been examined by scholars such as David Berger, Robert Chazan, and Daniel Lasker, but we can focus on one, the *Nizzaḥon Vetus* (a Hebrew-Latin title that translates as *The Old Book of Polemics* or *The Ancient Triumph*). In this late thirteenth- or fourteenth-century work, the author looks seriously at Christian interpretations of the Bible and then counters them. For example, when Moses came down from Mt. Sinai, his face shone, and Exodus 34:33 tells us that he therefore wore a veil over his face. Christianity allegorized this veil as a curtain that prevents the Jews from seeing the true meaning of the Bible, to which the *Nizzaḥon Vetus* responds that the veil indicates that one should not believe in the divinity of Jesus, for if Moses' face glowed from only seeing God, then Jesus, whom the Christians claim is divine, should have glowed even brighter. Therefore, he is not divine.

Like almost every other work of Jewish and Christian apologetics, the *Nizzaḥon Vetus* attempts to explain one of the most puzzling verses in the Bible, Genesis 49:10, a passage that is difficult to quote in English because the translation is so uncertain. Jacob, as he is dying, addresses each of his sons, sometimes chastising them and sometimes predicting their future. Genesis 49:10 is addressed to Judah, the founder of the tribe from which David and Jesus were to come, and refers to the scepter of rulership. Christian exegetes interpreted this verse as saying that the Jews would rule until the coming of Jesus, at which point Christianity would take over. Jewish commentators, naturally, rejected that interpretation and saw the verse as a prediction of a future Jewish domination. This was an argument that neither side could win, since the biblical verse itself was so unclear and since they translated it in such starkly different ways. Nevertheless, both sides tended to glory in their own interpretations, acting as though their arguments had triumphed, another indication of how little communication was actually possible. The *Nizzahon Vetus* asks,

> How can one maintain that the kingdom of Judah did not cease until Jesus? There was, after all, no king in Israel from the time of Zedekiah, for even in the days of the Second Temple there was no king in Israel but only governors subordinate to the kings of Media, Persia, or Rome. Now, a long time passed between Zedekiah and the birth of Jesus [over five hundred years], and so how can the verse say that the kingdom would not depart from Judah until Jesus comes? Furthermore, what relationship is there between "Shiloh" and Jesus' name? (60)

To a Jewish audience, this argument undoubtedly seemed conclusive, but to a Christian audience, the Christian interpretation undoubtedly seemed equally conclusive. A less complex but equally important point that Berger makes throughout his edition of the *Nizzahon Vetus* is that Jews objected to the Christian practice of applying positive biblical statements about Israel to themselves and negative statements to the Jews.

The major textual battleground for Jews and Christians was naturally the Tanakh, since it was recognized by both religions and because it was written in Hebrew. Jews simply dismissed the New Testament and seem seldom to have learned Latin, although beginning in 1170 with Jacob ben Reuben's *Milhamot HaShem* (*Wars of God*), we do find some Jewish familiarity with the Christian Bible. As Berger points out, the two religions were learning more about each other, even if what they learned was frequently incorrect or superficial, and Jewish attacks on the New Testament correspond to Christian attacks on the Talmud.[64] Again, though, in most written work, both Christian and Jewish attacks on the other side were directed not at conversion but at reinforcing the belief of one's coreligionists. It was in the sermons that Jews were forced to attend or in the disputations in which they were forced to take part that conversionary pressures were brought to bear; and those pressures, along with economic and psychological pressures, must have been powerful indeed.

Another point of Jewish criticism of Christianity focused on the Christian failure to live up to Christian ideals. Joseph Kimhi, for instance, cites several such failures:

- "There are no murderers or adulterers among [Jews]. Oppression and theft are not as widespread among Jews as among Christians who rob people on the highways and hang them and sometimes gouge out their eyes" (32).

- "The Jews keep their Sabbaths and festivals conscientiously, while the Christians do all manner of work and travel about even on Sunday which is their holy [day]" (33).
- Christians practice usury, lending money to both Jews and Christians, while Jews do not lend to Jews (38).
- "It is well known that your priests and bishops, who do not marry, are fornicators" (35).

More subtle is the argument of Rabbi Meir bar Simon (early thirteenth century), who responds to Christian charges that Jews are materialists (based on their literal interpretations of the Bible) by pointing out that the Eucharist itself symbolizes materialism, being both made by men and serving as a material representation of God.[65]

Rather less subtle was another manifestation of Jewish feelings toward Christianity, a short work that reads like a parody of the gospels. In the *Toldoth Yeshu*, Yeshu (Jesus) is the illegitimate son of Miriam and a Roman soldier who raped her. As a learned young man, Yeshu is disrespectful toward his teachers and eventually announces that he is the messiah. Yeshu, having learned God's secret name, uses that name to perform miracles but is eventually defeated and executed as an impostor, after which his body is hidden so that his disciples cannot claim that he ascended to heaven. While the disciples still claim him as the messiah, the Jews declare him a false prophet.

Had this scurrilous work been well known to Christians, it would surely have called forth their wrath, but we have no way of determining how well known it was even to Jews. If it is indeed a parody of the gospels, it is rather crudely done. At the same time, given the constant opposition between Judaism and Christianity and the deterioration of conditions in the later Middle Ages, we can hardly be surprised at the existence of such a work.

We can conclude this discussion of Jewish reactions to Christianity and the Christian treatment of Judaism by citing several Jews who had relatively little contact with Christianity, men who lived primarily under Islamic rule. Saadiah Gaon in his *Book of Facts and Opinions* argues against the concepts of the trinity and the incarnation, against the Christian dismissal of the laws, and against the notion that the messiah has already arrived.[66] Yehuda Halevi, who did have contact with Christians early in his life, writes briefly about their religion in his *Kuzari*. But most interesting are the words of Maimonides in his *Mishneh Torah*, in a passage that was often censored during the Middle Ages:

> All the prophets affirmed that the Messiah would redeem Israel, save them, gather their dispersed, and confirm the commandments. But [Jesus] caused Israel to be destroyed by the sword, their remnant to be destroyed and humiliated. He was instrumental in changing the Torah and causing the world to err and serve another besides God.
>
> But it is beyond the human mind to fathom the designs of the Creator; for our ways are not His ways, neither are our thoughts His thought. All these matters relating to Jesus of Nazareth and the Ishmaelite (Mohammed) who came after him only seemed to clear the way for King Messiah, to prepare the whole world to worship God with one accord ... (*Maimonides Reader,* 226)

Maimonides' point is that although he rejects Christianity and Islam, those religions keep alive religious discussion and a focus on the commandments, even if they reject those commandments. Consequently, when the true messiah does come, Christians and Muslims will be prepared to receive him.

Maimonides' position certainly does not fit into what we might think of as twenty-first-century ecumenicism. Nevertheless, compared to the positions we have seen articulated by both Jews and Christians, it appears to represent the height of tolerance, as does the position of one of his followers, Rabbi Menahem Ha-Me'iri, a fourteenth-century rabbi from Provence, who, like others, rejected Islam and Christianity but acknowledged that both were monotheistic faiths and did not constitute idolatry. Again, it may not be much, but it was far superior to the denigration of other faiths that so often characterized medieval discussions.

Judaism and Islam

Judaism and Islam shared a much different relationship than did Judaism and Christianity in the Middle Ages, or than Judaism and Islam do today. In fact, the time during which Judaism and Islam coexisted in Spain is often referred to as a Golden Age. That designation, however, needs to be understood loosely, for several reasons: although conditions were "golden" in contrast to conditions in other times and places, they were certainly not ideal; there were periods when conditions were even worse and the Jews were forced to flee elsewhere; even in the best of times, Jews and Muslims were never considered to be equals. Of course, even today, when discrimination is routinely condemned, it continues to exist; during the Middle Ages, there was no such condemnation, and everyone looked down on people of other nations, other religions, and other beliefs. What we consider prejudice was the norm, so that what surprises us about Muslim-Jewish relations during the Middle Ages is how good they often were, despite the normal prejudices of the time.

When Mohammed, the prophet of Islam, preached his message in seventh-century Arabia, Jewish tribes were among his neighbors and influenced his message. We must remember, however, that the Judaism that Mohammed knew differed from modern Judaism, since it had not yet come fully under the sway of Talmudic teaching. What it consisted of is hard for us to say, but Mohammed, like Paul before him and like Martin Luther after him, expected that once the Jews had heard his message, they would readily accept it, an expectation in which he was largely disappointed.[67] In the Qu'ran, we can see him arguing with Jewish positions and actions, and his words do not always convey a sense of reconciliation:

> Believers, take neither Jews nor Christians for your friends. They are friends with one another. Whoever of you seeks their friendship shall become one of their number. Allah does not guide the wrongdoers. (393)

> The Jews say: "Allah's hand is chained." May their own hands be chained! May they be cursed for what they say! (394)

> Many of the People of the Book [Jews and Christians] wish, through envy, to lead you back to unbelief, now that you have embraced the faith.... Forgive them and bear with them until Allah makes known His will. (343)

> Abraham was neither Jew nor Christian. He was an upright man, one who had surrendered himself to Allah. (413)

These and other verses like them certainly strike modern readers as confrontational, but as is always the case with Scriptures, so much depends on how verses are interpreted. Mohammed clearly had differences with Jews and Christians, though his knowledge about those religions may have been questionable. He says, for instance, that the "Jews say Ezra is the son of Allah" (323), though no such doctrine exists in Judaism. Still, his assertion that Abraham belonged to Islam rather than to Judaism or Christianity constitutes a forthright statement that Islam is the true path, that Abraham had established a path from which both subsequent Jews and Christians had wandered. However, unlike

Christianity, which had rejected Judaism, Mohammed does not simply reject the two earlier Abrahamic faiths. Jews and Christians were the "People of the Book," quite different from the pagan Arabs to whom he brought the teachings of Islam. Bernard Lewis cites sura 109 as a verse that was used in medieval Islam to justify religious coexistence: "You have your own religion, and I have mine."[68]

Even when Islam, in the seventh and eighth centuries, had spread through the Middle East, across North Africa, and into Spain, Jews and Christians retained a special status: they were *dhimmis.* As such, they lacked many of the rights of Muslims and were subject to specific restrictions. Their clothing was to differ from the clothing of Muslims, they were not to ride horses or other animals, and they were not to build new houses of worship. Although Christians seemed to find these restrictions more galling than the Jews did, the restrictions were often not enforced, frequently as a result of bribes paid to local officials. The one restriction that was always enforced, however, was the payment of high taxes, particularly the *jizya,* a tax that was imposed specifically on dhimmis and that guaranteed them freedom of worship.[69] Not only was the *jizya* financially oppressive, but perhaps even more significantly, it was regarded as a sign of humiliation imposed on non-Muslims in accordance with sura 2:61, which Lewis translates, "They were consigned to humiliation and wretchedness ..."[70] Even so, this practice differs significantly from practices in Christian Europe. As Lewis says, "The Muslim attitude toward non-Muslims is one not of hate or fear but simply of contempt."[71] Still, Rabbi Shlomo ben Adreth in thirteenth-century Christian Spain lists among the extra expenses imposed on Jews the poll tax, the tax on possessions, the cost of billeting soldiers, the tax for maintaining clergy, and more for bribes and communal expenses.[72] Being a Jew was expensive.

An interesting side effect of these taxes had to do with conversion. In Christian states, as we saw, Christians tried, for theological reasons, to convince Jews to convert, for the conversion of the Jews would not only affirm the truth of Christianity but would herald the second coming. In Islamic states, there was much less conversionary pressure, not only for theological reasons, but because when dhimmis converted, as they often did, the state's income declined. For most Muslims, then, the continuing existence of the dhimmis was just fine. An ironic effect of dhimmi status was that in Islamic territories, Christians were subjected to restrictions similar to those that were imposed on Jews in Christian territories. Obadiah Bertinoro (c. 1450–c.1516), for instance, noted that in Alexandria, at night and during mosque time on Fridays, Christians were confined to their houses, just as Jews were on Easter and other religious occasions in Christian lands. Equally ironic, perhaps, is that because Islam imposed restrictions on banking and moneylending in Islamic lands, financial matters were left to Jews and Christians.[73] The fact remains, however, that Jews who lived under Muslim domination usually fared no worse than those who lived under Christian domination and often fared better, as can be demonstrated by a single episode: after the original Muslim conquest of Jerusalem from the Christians in the eighth century, the Muslims discovered that the Temple mount, the holiest site in Judaism, had been used as a garbage dump to reinforce the Christian belief that the old covenant had ended. The victorious Muslims cleaned up the site and, according to the stories that have been handed down, they were helped even by their leader, Umar.[74]

Even so, relations were often difficult. For example, non-Muslim funeral processions in Spain might be pelted with stones and garbage, and dhimmis who were caught without an identifying patch and the thick vest that was supposed to set them apart were supposed to be "flogged, displayed in the Jewish or Christian neighborhood, and imprisoned." And even if these laws were frequently not enforced, they continued to exist and threaten the dhimmis.[75] Furthermore, there were occasionally outbursts of violence against Jews. Some of these were relatively minor, but others had greater effects. In considering Jewish life in Spain, we must always remember that the Jews were caught between the Muslims and Christians, who fought for domination over the Iberian Peninsula.[76] Occasionally it was hard to tell who was on which side. Thus, in the eleventh century, Rodrigo Diaz de Vivar, El Cid, led armies for both the Christians and the Muslims. Late in that century, when the Christians seemed to be doing particularly well, Muslim leaders invited to Spain the Almoravides, Berbers from North Africa, who were much less accommodating to the dhimmis than their predecessors had been, resulting in the flight of many Jews to Christian territories.[77] Later, in the middle of the twelfth century, the Almohades, a fanatical Muslim sect, arrived in Spain and outlawed Judaism, resulting in even more flight to Christian or other Muslim areas.[78] At the same time, however, the Almohades also attacked other Muslims who refused to accept their version of Islam.

Another instance of anti-Jewish violence involves Joseph ibn Nagrela, the son of Shmuel ha-Nagid, who took on the role of vizier in Granada after his father's death. Joseph was killed and there was a massacre in the Jewish community, but this seems to have been a fairly isolated event, as opposed to the frequent attacks in Christian Europe.[79]

Jewish-Muslim relations, then, were fairly complex, ranging from hospitable to hostile. Generally, however, they were better than Jewish-Christian relations, perhaps largely because of the absence of serious theological disagreements. Christianity saw itself in opposition to Judaism and accused Jews of deicide. Islam naturally regarded itself as superseding Judaism, but it made no accusation of deicide. Actually Islam and Judaism shared many characteristics, such as the rejection of Jesus as the messiah and a rejection of visual images of religious figures. In Christian countries, Jews were separated from the Christian population in a number of ways, but in Muslim countries like Spain, Jews were largely allowed to become part of the general population, with the result that Jews had to become conscious of making their own distinctions, lest they become too assimilated. As we saw earlier, Jews in Spain tended to remove their shoes before they entered synagogues, just as Muslims removed theirs before entering mosques. Many Jews also regarded it as permissible for Jewish men to take non-Jewish concubines, which may not have been a great lesson.[80] We can find polemical comments made by Jews about Islam, but there are no Jewish works devoted entirely to refuting Islam as there were on the subject of Christianity.

In fact, a fascinating aspect of this subject concerns forced conversions, which, as we saw, were quite common in Christian lands, where conversion, whether forced or not, was considered permanent. Occasionally in Islamic lands, conversions were also forced on the Jews, though usually the Jews were later allowed to resume their own religion. Significantly, however, medieval scholars often regarded the two kinds of conversion rather differently. In Christian lands, Jews were encouraged to accept martyrdom rather than conversion (if at all possible), whereas in Islamic lands, Jews were allowed to accept conversion, as long as they continued to practice their Judaism in secret and to revert to Judaism at the first opportunity. This difference resulted from the perception, whether accurate or not, that Islam upheld strict monotheism but that agreeing to the divine nature of Jesus constituted idolatry, and Jews were required to accept death before idolatry.

The story of Yitzhak, the son of the poet and commentator Abraham ibn Ezra and the son-in-law of the poet and philosopher Yehuda Halevi, illustrates important aspects of Jewish life in Moslem countries. Born in Spain, Yitzhak converted to Islam of his own accord. Then, when he decided to return to Judaism, he could not, because such a reversion was a capital crime. In order to reassume his Judaism, therefore, he went to a Christian country where his story was not known, but there he died "away from the comforts of civilization."[81] This peculiar story illustrates aspects of life in the Muslim world, especially in Spain. Yitzḥak was tempted to accept Islam, and his death was attributed to his having left a civilized country. Spain under the Muslims was indeed more civilized than was Christian Europe, and when European Christian armies arrived in Christian Byzantium at the time of the Crusades, the eastern Christians found their European coreligionists to be barbarians. As we saw, in Christian lands Jews and Christians occasionally engaged in informal discussions of religious questions, but formal discussions were always stage-managed to illustrate the superiority of Christianity. In Islamic lands, on the other hand, not only Jews and Muslims but also Christians, Zoroastrians, and others were concerned with matters of poetry, philosophy, science, medicine, and religion, all influenced by Arabic translations of Greek works and discussed openly. Islamic culture, particularly before the twelfth century, far outstripped that of Christian Europe. If we can rely on a generalization, before the twelfth century, the major subject of study in Christian Europe was Christianity, whereas in Islamic lands, study embraced not only religion but the science and culture of the ancient world. This difference affected the Jews: when we look at medieval Jewish poetry, we will see that the poetry produced in Christian Europe consisted largely of penitential hymns and poems reacting to a variety of massacres and outrages; the Jewish poetry from the Islamic world, however, while it often expresses the weariness of exile and a longing for redemption, also deals with a variety of other topics. And even the more strictly religious poetry is not nearly as gloomy as its European counterpart.

Immersion in the general culture proved to be quite important for the Jews. Politically it made them valuable to both Muslim and Christian rulers, since Jews knew the languages of both camps and could serve in diplomatic positions. Some Jews, like Shmuel ha-Nagid and his unfortunate son, even attained high governmental positions. In addition, Jews were also involved in the translation of classical works from the Arabic (into which they had been translated from the Greek) into Latin. In thirteenth-century Toledo, Alfonso X employed Jews, among others, for this purpose, so that Jews had a hand in the creation of the twelfth-century renaissance, as these new translations spread through the rest of Europe.[82] Furthermore, works by Jewish philosophers like Maimonides and ibn Gabirol influenced European Christian philosophers (though the *Fons Vitae* of ibn Gabirol was actually thought to have been written by a Christian).

Jewish life became increasingly difficult in all of western Europe beginning in the twelfth century, but it was generally less oppressive under Muslim rule, until the arrival of the Almoravids and the Almohades. These cruel fundamentalists brought death and change to Spain, but usually the Jews in Muslim lands did not live with the same fear as those in Christian lands. They still longed for their own homeland, as their poetry reveals, but for the most part they managed to live Jewish lives in Spain. It was only after the Reconquista, the Christian reconquest of Spain from the Muslims in the late fifteenth century, that the Jews of Spain, like those of England in the thirteenth century and those of France in the fourteenth, found themselves fleeing under an order of expulsion.

PART II

THE HISTORICAL RECORD

The Medieval Jewish Experience

Having examined what constitutes Judaism, the seminal works that contained and formed the ideologies of Judaism, and the outside forces that affected medieval Judaism, it is time now to examine how the Jewish people lived in the Middle Ages. This examination is divided into two parts: the first presents the events of medieval Jewish history—where the Jews lived, how they arrived there (to the extent that we know), and what happened to them there—while the second part examines the internal life of the Jews—how they lived their everyday lives, how they prayed, how women's lives differed from men's.

Exile

The overarching theme of Jewish life in the Middle Ages, as in so many eras, is exile. It was felt by those who dwelled in terrible conditions, and it was felt by those whose lives were relatively comfortable. Three times each day, during the daily prayers, one says, "Be pleased, Lord our God, with thy people Israel and with their prayer; restore the worship to thy most holy sanctuary.... May our eyes behold thy return in mercy to Zion" (Birnbaum 90–92). As we saw earlier, many of the daily rituals (like the ritual washing of the hands before eating) allowed Jews symbolically to bring the Temple with them, though always there were reminders that they were strangers in a land not their own and that they yearned to return to their homeland. That consciousness of exile, which pervaded their lives, became especially poignant at Passover, in the concluding words of the Seder, *l'shanah ha-ba'ah bi'y'rushalayim*, next year in Jerusalem. Jerusalem was the city of David and Solomon, of historical greatness. It represented independence; it was the place where the First and Second Temples had stood. It was the place to which Jews would return when the messiah finally arrived.

However, as is so often the case, the story is more complicated than it may seem at first. After the destruction of the First Temple in 586 B.C.E., much of the population of ancient Israel was exiled to Babylonia, and when, some fifty years later, the Persians defeated the Babylonians, the victors allowed the exiles to return home. But not all of them wanted to return. After all, during those fifty years they had established communities, businesses, and homes, so while many did return to Israel, many stayed in Babylonia, which is modern-day Iraq. And there were Jewish communities elsewhere as well. All of these communities regarded Jerusalem as the center of the Jewish people, and there was a good deal of traffic between Jerusalem and the cities of the Diaspora. After the Roman destruction of the Second Temple in 70 C.E. and, even more, after the Bar Kokhba rebellion in the early second century, Jews were forbidden to live in parts of their land, including Jerusalem, while others were deported as slaves. Consequently, the Romans, foes though they were to the Jews, actually helped to preserve Judaism by dispersing Jews throughout the Roman world. Had the Jews all been kept in one place, they might easily have been destroyed, but scattered throughout Europe and the Middle East, they were protected, for when oppression reigned in one place, relative peace often prevailed elsewhere.

A question that comes up over and over in considering medieval Jews and Judaism is how the people and the faith survived all of that oppression when it would have been so easy to give up and give in. One factor out of many that contributed to their preservation is the concept of exile, for if they were truly in exile, that exile was bound to end and they would eventually return to their land, where they could practice their religion openly and entirely—for many of the six hundred thirteen commandments can only be practiced in the land of Israel, and of those, many can only be practiced when the Temple is rebuilt. Toward the end of our period, in 1452, Yosef ibn Shem Tov delivered a sermon in Segovia in which he commented on a Talmudic story that Moses had a vision in which he saw Rabbi Akiva and the terrible suffering of his martyrdom. Moses was naturally disturbed, but, says Yosef, "eventually he understood that this was God's plan, that God's mode of governing is different from ours, and that the verdict was a true one even though we are ignorant of how it was reached ..."[1] And Yosef then goes on to apply this lesson to his own time, a time, in Spain, of suffering and confusion. Yes, there was suffering, but there was a reason for that suffering, though we may not be able to discern it. And surely it will end, though we may not know when

The Early Years

Two convenient markers define the thousand-year period that we call the Middle Ages: the fall of the Western Roman Empire (roughly in the year 500) and the Renaissance (very roughly in the year 1500). Jewish history, however, differs somewhat, although the Hebrew term for the period, *y'mei ha-baynayim*, translates literally as "days in the middle." But neither the fall of the Roman Empire nor the Renaissance is particularly significant as a marker in Jewish history. Much more significant as an ending point is the eighteenth century, when Jewish life began to feel the effects of the Enlightenment and the primacy of rabbinic Judaism confronted the challenge of modernity. Several modern varieties of Judaism can trace their origins to that period. As a starting date for the Jewish Middle Ages, Jacob Marcus suggests the reign of Constantine in the early fourth century, because Constantine, by adopting Christianity as the religion of his empire, combined secular and religious powers that both viewed Jews with suspicion and hostility. Now those powers were officially working together, so that from the reign of Constantine we have official prohibitions of marriage between Jews and Christians, prohibitions against Jews owning slaves, and prohibitions against Jews offering legal testimony against Christians.[2] We could, therefore, argue that the Jewish Middle Ages lasted from about 300 until almost 1800, a period of fifteen hundred years. If a millennium constitutes an unwieldy period, fifteen hundred years is half again as unwieldy. For purposes of this study, then, but not as an absolute definition of the era, the Jewish Middle Ages will extend from about 500, around the time when the Talmud was completed, until 1492, when the Jews were expelled from Spain.

Life in the later years of the Roman Empire, as already noted, was difficult for the Jews. After the western Empire finally collapsed, when there was no longer a central political power, Jews were subjected to local control, which could be harsh or lenient, depending on the whims of the rulers and the political conditions under which they operated. For example, it appears that Jews had been in Spain at least since the time of Jesus. Paul actually intended to go to Spain (Romans 15:24), though he never made the trip. Reccared, the Visigothic king of Spain from 586 to 601, converted to Catholicism in 587 and immediately adopted anti-Jewish policies.[3] In 613, Sisebut issued a decree calling for the forced baptism of all Jews in his territories, thereby inaugurating a century of martyrdom for the Jews.[4] In 636, Chintilla banned non-Catholics from living in Spain and, perhaps because that policy was unsuccessful, in 640 Chindaswith made circumcision a capital offense.[5] Slightly later, the persecutions increased in intensity: under Egica, Jewish children, beginning at the age of seven, were to be taken from their parents and raised by Christians. Cecil Roth blames some of these policies on Spanish fears of Muslim expansion, for in this time the Muslim armies were indeed spreading across North Africa and heading for Spain; and Roth, like many other historians, argues, despite a lack of concrete proof, that in the face of such persecutions, the Jews quite understandably aided the Muslim attackers when they finally did appear, just as, in the twelfth century, when the Almohades were persecuting the Jews, they aided the Christian cause.[6] Stow argues that the Jews of Spain, having heard about the Muslim slaughter of Jews in Medina in the previous century, were unlikely to aid the invaders, but it does not stretch credulity to imagine the persecuted Jews of Spain being willing to trade the horrors they knew for horrors that were only potential.[7] The Jews knew that their suffering under the Visigothic kings received encouragement from Church leaders like Isidore of Seville, and they might well have chosen to take their chances with the Muslim invaders.

Meanwhile, back in the east, in the Byzantine Empire, conditions were not much better. The sixth-century emperor Justinian adopted a harsh policy toward the Jews: he forbad the study of the Mishneh and forced Jews to use specific Greek translations of the Bible in an attempt to convince them to convert.[8] His policies continued after his death, as the whole Mediterranean area became a Christian society, so that Jews were considered "outlaws." All around the Mediterranean, Jews found themselves subjected to official persecution and to forced baptism.[9] In Israel, conditions were also deplorable, but in 615, Jerusalem was conquered by Persian armies, who killed many Christians, aided by Jews who took the opportunity to avenge themselves on their tormenters. By 629, however, the Persian king Chosroes expelled the Jews from Jerusalem; and when the Byzantines under Heraclius recaptured the area in the mid-seventh century, the Jews were ordered to be baptized and were subject to mass slaughters.[10] These years were indeed dark for the Jews, foreshadowing what would come later.

In these early centuries of our period, there were two major centers of Jewish authority, although Jews lived all around the Mediterranean and, probably in small numbers, further north in Europe. Those two centers were the ancestral homeland of Israel (usually called Palestine in this period) and Babylonia. Although there were times when Jewish life in Babylonia was difficult, conditions tended to be much worse in Palestine, where there were frequent wars and where Christian attitudes toward Jews complicated their lives.

Although there was frequent contact between these two centers, they differed in significant ways. For instance, while learning was central to both traditions, valued above almost any other activity, the subjects of learning diverged. In the Babylonian schools, study, until the ninth century, focused almost entirely on the Talmud, while in Palestine somewhat less attention was paid to the Talmud, and other subjects were studied as well. At the same time, Palestinian Jews were responsible for the creation of the Midrashim and other important works that focused less on halakhic matters.[11] Another difference involves prayer: in Babylonia, prayer consisted of the prayers that had been presented in the Talmud or that had been handed down for many generations, but in Palestinian synagogues, some of those prose prayers were replaced by liturgical poems called *piyyutim*. The Hebrew word actually comes from the Greek root *poiein*, which means "to make" and which is the root of the English word "poet." These *piyyutim*, some of which we will examine in a later chapter, could be very difficult poems, full of biblical allusions and cross-references, showing off the learning and the ingenuity of the poets (the *paytanim*), who were often also the cantors who performed their own works in the synagogues. Rabbis found the *piyyutim* objectionable, since they could easily call attention to themselves and distract worshippers from their primary duty. Nonetheless, they remained popular. The Babylonian and Palestinian communities even differed on the proper pronunciation of Hebrew.[12]

Another difference between the two communities concerned the reading of the Torah, which forms part of the Sabbath synagogue service. In Babylonian synagogues, every week a specific portion was read so that, beginning with Genesis in the fall, the whole of the Five Books of Moses would be completed by the following fall. In Palestine, however, the Torah was read on a triennial basis rather than an annual basis, so that the completion of the reading required three years. Even more significant were disputes over the calendar. Without getting into the intricacies of the Jewish lunar calendar, we need only understand that a new month begins at the time of the new moon in Jerusalem. In Palestine, the time of the new moon was determined by observation, even after the development of calculations that could arrive at the same determination, calculations that were employed in Babylonia. Because control of the calendar was so important (those who controlled the calendar also controlled when holidays were celebrated and therefore played a key role in the religious life of the Jews), disputes arose. We might choose to see those disputes as simple battles for power, but they were also motivated by sincere religious feeling. In 921, one such dispute arose from which the Babylonians emerged triumphant, thanks in large part to one of the outstanding Babylonian leaders, Saadiah Gaon.[13]

Actually Saadiah's Hebrew name was Saadiah ben Yosef. "Gaon" was his title, a word that means "Eminence" and that served as the honorific for the heads of the Jewish academies in Babylonia. There were two major academies in Babylonia. According to a historical sketch by Sherira Gaon, the academy of Sura was founded by the Palestinian sage Rav in the third century, while another sage, Samuel, founded the academy at Nehardea at about the same time, although the latter later moved to Pumbedita. By the end of the Geonic period, in the eleventh and twelfth centuries, both were located in Baghdad, which was the capital of the Muslim Abbasid Empire.[14] People being people—and Jews being Jews—there were also disputes between the two schools, with Sura tending more in the direction of Palestinian customs. The two schools developed different customs and laws and thereby provided ammunition to the anti-Rabbinical Karaites, who pointed out that rabbinic law could not be as traditional as had been claimed if there were such debates over it.[15] Even when Babylonian Jews left Iraq and moved to Palestine, they retained their Babylonian customs, so that there were Babylonian communities with Babylonian synagogues even in Palestine.

Nevertheless, those two schools played a vital role in the development of medieval (and therefore of modern) Judaism, for after the Babylonian Talmud had been completed, the work of those schools made it authoritative. After the Palestinian schools ceased playing a central role in Jewish life, the Babylonian schools, with their focus on the Talmud as the Oral Law and their devotion to its dissemination, made rabbinic Judaism definitive. They were helped by their location at the heart of the Abbasid Empire, which at the time was the great center of Islam, but it was their teaching more than anything else that made them so important.[16] The Geonim, whose work was important in itself, form a link between the talmudic era and the Middle Ages. In fact, the age of the Geonim marks the last time that Judaism had a physical center, a place and a group of leaders who were considered authoritative by all Jews. When the Geonic system ended, Judaism broke up into a collection of individual communities, but even then they were influenced by what the Geonim had accomplished. For instance, much of the imagery and many of the customs that Jews today associate with the Rosh Hashanah and Yom Kippur holidays originated with the Geonim, who developed them from biblical and talmudic sources.[17]

How did the Geonim become so influential? For one thing, they were at the heart of the Abassid Caliphate, and they benefited from its unifying power. Furthermore, Judaism has always emphasized study—the talmudic rabbis imagined that the patriarch Jacob had studied Torah in the academy of Shem, despite the fact that the Torah had not yet been revealed, since the rabbis could barely imagine a world in which Torah study did not play a central role in men's lives. Consequently, students came from all over the Jewish world to study in the Babylonian academies. But of course, these students, however influential they might have been, constituted a small minority of Jews, so the Geonim employed another method of spreading their influence. Whenever a question arose in a Jewish community, whether on moral or ritual issues, local authorities would attempt to answer it; but when they could not, or if someone were dissatisfied with the answer, they would write a letter to one of the academies stating the issue and requesting a resolution. The questions (and there were many of them) would be discussed by members of the academy, and the head of the academy would then devise an answer that, once approved by the members, would be sent to the questioner. This process might take a very long time indeed, for Jewish communities existed at great distances from Baghdad, and travel, whether on land or by ship, was both difficult and dangerous. Undoubtedly, many questions or responses never arrived at their destinations; but even so, and even with the inevitable disappearance of many early medieval documents, we have thousands of examples of such questions and answers. This system marked the development of the responsa literature, which had begun in talmudic times and which continued even after the academies had disappeared, when people would send their questions to famous rabbis, who would respond. Many, many thousands of such responsa still exist, and we will see some of them later in this chapter.

Those responsa are valuable in a number of ways. They show us the kinds of issues that people found important in their lives during these centuries. For other medieval cultures, which lacked such a system, our knowledge of everyday life is much less complete, but when people wrote to the academies or to the rabbis asking questions about holiday observances or dietary laws or financial matters or what should be done with forced converts who wish to return to Judaism, they provided us with a window into their lives. We may be amazed, as we read the responsa literature, at the kinds of esoteric questions that concerned people, but we can also see how like ourselves they often were, simultaneously petty and noble, trying to do the right thing but often hoping that the right thing is not too inconvenient.

And the responsa are valuable in yet another way. At one point, one of the Geonim, Amram, was asked about the proper order of prayers, and in response he created the first organized prayer book in Judaism. He relied on tradition, but his compilation of prayers became the model for prayer books until today. Another famous responsum we saw in chapter two: the letter of Sherira, which provides an early history of the Talmud and its sages. Many of the responsa have been translated into English, but unfortunately not all.

While the Geonim were theoretically the religious leaders of world Jewry, there were also political leaders, the Exilarchs. Because there was not always such a clear dichotomy between the political and the religious, there were frequent disputes between the political and religious leaders, the Exilarchs and the Geonim. According to the twelfth-century traveler Benjamin of Tudela, who visited Baghdad, every fifth day the Exilarch would be led to a throne opposite to that of the Caliph, not only as an honor but to demonstrate the truth of the biblical verse "The scepter shall not depart from Judah," a verse that, as we saw earlier, Christians viewed as a Christological prophecy. Whether or not Benjamin's description is historically accurate, it did serve to demonstrate the historical truth of the verse as opposed to the allegorical reading developed by Christianity. In fact, by Benjamin's time, the great centuries of Babylonian Jewry were almost over. Now the focus of Judaism moved to North Africa and Europe, where conditions were quite different.[18]

Nonetheless, the Babylonian academies, and the Palestinian, continued to be influential, though their influence varied in different places. The Jews of Rome were more strongly influenced by Palestinian traditions, and as Jews from Italy slowly moved north into other parts of Europe, those Palestinian traditions moved with them. At the same time,

Jews in North Africa and Spain, Islamic areas, were more strongly influenced by Babylonian traditions, which had developed at the heart of the Islamic Empire.[19] The result was that the Jewish people, unified as they were by so many practices and beliefs, were divided into two factions, the Ashkenazim (Jews in northern Europe) and the Sephardim (Jews in Spain). The area of Provence, in southern France, bordering on Spain, possessed its own unique culture and served as a kind of bridge between Sephardim and Ashkenazim.[20] We must not, however, think of Ashkenazim and Sephardim as rivals or enemies, the way Catholics and Protestants were during the Reformation. They respected each other's customs, even if they disagreed with them, and in times of danger came to each other's aid, insofar as anyone did. There were times when their perspectives came into conflict, as happened during the Maimonidean controversy, but those conflicts were exceptions. We can see the general level of competition from a report from Fustat in Egypt. Apparently the Babylonian and Palestinian synagogues, like synagogues (and churches) today, competed for members. The Babylonian synagogues bragged about the quality of their cantors, while the Palestinian synagogues boasted that their services were shorter (because the cantors were not showing off?) and their scrolls and carpets were more attractive.[21] However fierce the competition for members may have been, these issues are hardly substantive. More significantly, in the early fourteenth century, the Ashkenazic rabbi Ya'akov ben Asher ben Yehiel moved to Spain, where he became familiar with Sephardic traditions and brought them together with the Ashkenazic in his *Arba'ah Turim* (*Four Columns*), a major code of law that greatly influenced the most important code of laws, the sixteenth-century *Shulchan 'Aruch* (*The Set Table*).[22] Thus, by the end of the period, Ashkenazim and Sephardim, while still maintaining their distinctiveness, had their unity as Jews reaffirmed.

Ashkenazim

By the end of the fourteenth century, the Jews had been expelled from England, from France, and from parts of the Germanic territories, while the Sephardim were not expelled from Spain and Portugal until the end of the fifteenth century. As we review this history, we may recall Salo Baron's warning that we should not emphasize the "lachrymose" aspects of Jewish history, that we should focus instead on the positive aspects of that history, a warning that we should take seriously so that we do not regard Jewish history as a series of catastrophes. But we cannot ignore those catastrophes, the most prominent of which were:

1096–Crusade massacres
1190–York
1298–Rindfleisch massacres
1320–attacks in southern France
1336–beginning of host desecration accusations
1348–blame for causing the Black Death
1391–attacks in Spain

The list does not include the almost constant verbal attacks or the various expulsions that affected the Jews. While we must heed Baron, then, we must not bend too much in the other direction and forget the many hardships of medieval Jews.

While Jewish life was difficult throughout the Middle Ages, we can see clear turning points when conditions became worse. One of the anomalies of medieval Jewish history, however, involves Italy. We might think that Italy, and particularly Rome, the center of the Catholic Church, would have been a center of anti-Jewish activity, but in fact such was not the case. It is true, as we saw earlier, that the popes were frequently not fond of the Jews, but often during the Middle Ages, sometimes in the darkest days of the period, the papacy continued to protect them. Of course, we must be clear about what we mean by "protect." Generally, the Church adhered to the old Augustinian policy that the Jews should be allowed to survive as long as they lived in misery, thereby illustrating the superiority of Christianity. Consequently, the popes frequently protected the lives of the Jews, though they had few qualms about anti-Jewish activities that were not life-threatening. Thus the Jews who lived in Italy, in close proximity to the Vatican, tended to receive more protections than those who lived elsewhere. Furthermore, because Italy did not go through the same nationalistic process as France, England, or Spain, Italian Jews were never expelled from the whole country. It is true, of course, that Italian Jews were subjected to ritual stoning and their leaders were subjected to receiving the ritual slap at Easter, though later a monetary settlement replaced these degrading traditions.[23] That financial arrangement indicates that interest had shifted from a supposed religious motivation to an attempt to benefit from the Jewish presence; but even so, Jewish life in Italy, which had a very long history, was not so bad as it was elsewhere. It is fascinating to note, for instance, that in Dante's *Divine Comedy*, no contemporary Jews appear. There are biblical Jews (Rachel and Judas are prominent) but no contemporaries, almost as though they did not exist.

France offers a more complicated story. When we examine the history of the Jews in France, we might think at first that France had a huge Jewish population, but except for the largest cities, like Paris and Rouen, it did not. In many villages and smaller cities, there were so few Jews that for holidays people would have to gather in a central location in order to achieve a minyan, the ten men required to hold religious services. Nevertheless, there were great concerns about Jews.

Although we do not know for certain how Jews arrived in what we now call France, we do know that the Carolingian monarchs offered them protection. Norman Golb maintains that under the Carolingians, there was a *rex* or *magister Judaeorum* (a "king" or "master" of the Jews) who was responsible for governing the Jewish subjects.[24] Rabanus Maurus, an important Carolingian churchman, acknowledges receiving help with biblical passages and with information about the Jews from a rabbi. The educational reforms begun under Charlemagne may have benefited the Jews, and there may have been disputes between Jewish and Christian scholars. Even a rabid anti-Semite like Agobard of Lyons was forced to restrain himself a bit, though his writings are full of hatred.[25] In the ninth, tenth, and eleventh centuries, Jews were often invited, either individually or in groups, to participate in the development of cities and communities.

In the tenth century, however, another current arose simultaneously. Tenth-century Europe was threatened by Norsemen, by Saracens, and by Magyars. The anxiety caused by these threats prompted the people to turn on the nearest and most convenient enemy, that is, the Jews.[26] According to one account, in Le Mans in 992 a Jewish convert to Christianity put a wax figure in the ark in the synagogue, then led authorities to it and claimed that the Jews used it to work magic against the local ruler. Although the account breaks off in the middle of the story, it looks like no harm came of the incident, but between 1007 and 1012, the Jews of northern Europe were confronted with the choice of conversion, expulsion, or death. While most chose expulsion, some were killed.[27]

But this history, discouraging though it may seem, does nothing to prepare us for the horrors that developed at the end of the eleventh century. While the initial atrocities took place in German cities, they originated in France and had a strong effect on that country. What happened was the First Crusade, which was inaugurated by Pope Urban II in 1095. Steven Runciman has written that the Crusades can be viewed as "the most tremendous and most romantic of Christian adventures or as the last of the barbarian invasions, and critical opinion has indeed swung between those two poles."[28] For the Jews, there was no doubt: the Crusades were far worse in both Europe and in Palestine than any barbarian invasions. The Crusades were the worst collective experience for the Jews since the destruction of the Temple, for as the crusaders set out, whether they were booty-seeking adventurers, as some historians contend, or sincere religious warriors, as others maintain, a terrible thought occurred to them. That thought was paraphrased by Shlomo bar Shimshon in the history he wrote shortly after the events:

> Now it came to pass that as they passed through the towns where Jews dwelled, they said to one another: "Look now, we are going a long way to seek out the profane shrine [the Church of the Holy Sepulcher in Jerusalem] and to avenge ourselves on the Ishmaelites [the Muslims who controlled Jerusalem], when here, in our very midst, are the Jews—they whose forefathers murdered and crucified him for no reason. Let us first avenge ourselves on them and exterminate them from among the nations so that the name of Israel will no longer be remembered, or let them adopt our faith and acknowledge the offspring of promiscuity [as the Jews referred to Jesus]. (*Chronicle of Solomon* in Eidelberg 22)

Although these words are not the exact words of any crusader, since they use Jewish locutions, there was a report that one of the Crusade leaders, Godfrey of Bouillon, had vowed to avenge the death of Jesus on the Jews.[29] Because the crusader army was so huge, it moved across Europe in several streams, and those groups that made their way through the Rhineland, probably for a number of reasons but basically out of pure hatred, launched vicious attacks on the Jews in cities like Mainz, Worms, Cologne, Speyer, Trier, and many others. Sometimes local authorities or loyal neighbors tried to protect the Jews, but often they abandoned those efforts, either because they understandably feared for their own safety or because they decided to side with the oppressors. The Jews, at times, attempted to fight back, but they were basically powerless against the frenzied, well-armed mobs that attacked them.

The Jews appeared to have two options: they could abandon their religion and convert to Christianity, if the mobs would allow them; or they could die at the hands of their attackers, probably after suffering rape and torture. Remarkably, the Jews found another solution, one that bespeaks their desperation: they engaged in mass suicides. People killed themselves, or fathers and mothers killed their children and then themselves. The Jewish chronicles of these events abound with astounding descriptions. One man, Yitzhak, after having been forcibly converted, went home and locked the doors:

> The pious man then asked his children, "Do you wish me to offer you as a sacrifice to our God?" They replied, "Do as you will with us"…. Master Isaac the saint then took his two children—his son and his daughter—and led them … before the Holy Ark, and there he slaughtered them, in sanctification of the Great Name, to the Sublime and Lofty God, who has commanded us not to forsake pure fear of Him for any other belief, and to adhere to His Holy Torah with all our heart and soul. He sprinkled some of their blood on the pillars of the Holy Ark so as to evoke their memory before the One-and-Only Everlasting King. And he said: "May this blood expiate all my transgressions." (*Chronicle of Solomon* 40–41, in Eidelberg)

Yitzhak returned home and set fire to his house, while his mother was inside, then burned down the synagogue and died in the conflagration. How desperate people must have been to do such things, but we may understand their desperation when we read in Ekkehard of Aura that the troops of Emico "either utterly destroyed the execrable race of the Jews wherever they found them (being even in this matter zealously devoted to the Christian religion) or forced them into the bosom of the Church."[30] In other words, it was their religious duty to hate the Jews. Somewhat more sympathetic is the account of Albert of Aix, who says that the slaughter came "I know not whether by a judgment of the Lord, or by some error of mind." He also refers to the mass suicides and the killing of families, because the Jews preferred "to perish by their own hands rather than to be killed by the weapons of the uncircumcised."[31]

Still, there is more going on in those Jewish chronicle accounts than may at first be apparent, for however accurate they may be about the events they recount, the way they recount them is highly stylized. In all three of the First Crusade chronicles and in the only Second Crusade chronicle we have, the self-sacrifice of the Jews is described in biblical terms that would have been obvious to everyone. In the account of Yitzhak killing his children, for example, we read the apparently extraneous and revolting detail that he "sprinkled some of their blood on the pillars of the Holy Ark." We naturally recoil from such a description. How could he do such a thing? Actually, since he was alone with them and then died shortly thereafter, we have no way of knowing whether he sprinkled their blood, but an audience that knows the Torah and its laws regarding sacrifices would immediately recognize the ritual aspect of the description. Of course, human sacrifice is forbidden in the Torah, but Yitzhak had little choice, so he—or the chronicler—transformed his action into a sacred ritual: his children die as a sin offering, which makes sense since the Jews had to assume that if they were being tormented in this way, it must have been punishment for their sins. Thus several of the killings are described in sacrificial terms.

The other major image that is used in these descriptions recalls the Akedah, the Binding of Isaac, the test of Abraham that required him to sacrifice his son. Over and over, the chronicles and poems of the Crusades recall this episode, relying, as Shalom Spiegel points out in his masterful study *The Last Trial*, on traditional commentaries that say that Abraham actually did kill Isaac and that God miraculously revived him. Thus these children, also sacrificed by their own parents, might be revived, if not in this world then in the world to come. As Salo Baron says:

> In the mass hysteria, sanctified by the glow of religious martyrdom and compensated by the confident expectation of heavenly rewards, nothing seemed to matter but to end life before one fell into the hands of the implacable foe and had to face the inescapable alternative of death at the enemy's hands or conversion to Christianity.[32]

That hysteria may seem inexplicable to us, but nothing had prepared the Jews for crusader violence. They had lived in a kind of truce, however uneasy, with their Christian neighbors, when suddenly they were set upon by merciless hordes, some of whom were motivated by religious fanaticism while others lusted after booty.

While the Jewish chronicles of the Crusades depict grisly scenes of martyrdom, we know from other sources that during the tumult, as at other times of crisis, numbers of Jews actually did succumb to their fears and convert. Among our sources are responsa from rabbis who were asked how such converts should be treated when they desired to return to Judaism, as so many of them did. Naturally there are varieties of opinions, but generally such converts were dealt with leniently and were allowed to resume their Judaism after performing acts of repentance. Even Christians, for whom baptism was theoretically ineradicable, allowed such Jews to return to their religion.

Historians disagree about how the Crusades affected Jewish history. Some argue that aside from the most immediate effects—the deaths and disruption in the individual communities—not much changed after the massacres. Robert Chazan, for example, argues that twelfth-century Jews were secure and flourished and that the Crusades served as a warning of things to come. Jeremy Cohen doubts the veracity of the chronicles themselves, arguing that they were written by ideologically driven survivors who wanted to demonstrate that Jewish martyrdom was more genuine than Christian martyrdom and who wanted to justify the large number of Jews who converted and then reconverted.[33] On the other hand, some historians consider the Crusades a turning point in medieval Jewish history. As difficult as conditions had been before the Crusades, after the Crusades they deteriorated, at some times and in some places more quickly than others, until, by the end of the fifteenth century, the Jews had been expelled from most of western Europe.

John Van Engen, commenting on these two approaches to the Crusades, says that both are valid: after the Crusades, we can see both increasing persecution of the Jews and increasing interaction between Jews and Christians. As he points out, the two religious communities lived side by side. In Speyer, the synagogue was only a block away from the cathedral, and Mainz was a center of both Jewish and Christian authority. And if the two communities had not lived in such close proximity, there would have been no reason for the decree of the Fourth Lateran Council in 1215 that Jews should not wear the same clothing as Christians.[34] At the same time, the Jews still fulfilled an important economic function in the communities where they dwelled. Thus, Jews had little choice but to continue living in their Christian surroundings (where else could they go?); but a number of Christians, knowing that the crusader army led by Count Emico, who had been responsible for some of the worst atrocities, had collapsed shortly thereafter, attributed that collapse to divine punishment for the murder of the Jews.[35] At the same time, the Jews, knowing of Emico's failure (or perhaps thinking that none of the crusaders had gone all the way to Jerusalem), contrasted that failure with their own symbolic reconstruction of the Temple in Mainz through the sacrifices that they had made, a notion that seems grotesque to us, though we are not under attack and may not be qualified to judge.

In fact, though, we know that the crusaders eventually did make their way to Jerusalem, after great hardships to themselves and to those whom they encountered on their way. When they conquered Jerusalem, on July 15, 1099, another bloodbath ensued. They "violated their promise to the inhabitants that they would be left alive, and slaughtered some

20,000 to 30,000 people, a number which may be an exaggeration, although the Muslim sources speak of even 70,000." As for the Jews, many were killed, some when they were forced into a synagogue which was then set afire, while others were taken captive.[36]

The Crusades, then, may still have the aura of romance and adventure in the popular imagination; but in the history of the Jews, and the Muslims, they were a time of horror. Thomas Asbridge, in his recent history of the First Crusade, pictures the crusaders, covered with the blood of their enemies and carrying plunder, entering the Church of the Holy Sepulcher, and he warns us against the modern tendency to regard them as having "simply cloaked the expedition in a patina of spirituality and fervent piety so as to excuse and justify their actions. There was certainly nothing noble or praiseworthy about the Frankish sack of Jerusalem, but it demonstrates that many crusaders were driven on, not simply by bloodlust or greed, but also by an authentic and ecstatic sense of Christian devotion." If he is correct, the implications for what their Christianity meant are far from the ideals that Jesus proclaimed. But as he also points out, the crusading Roman Catholics also rejected eastern Christian sects, who "soon discovered that they had in fact been better off under Muslim rule than they were in a 'liberated Jerusalem.'"[37] Subsequent crusades were not quite so bad—Bernard of Clairvaux ended some of the anti-Jewish violence of the Second Crusade—but each of them resulted in some outrage to the Jews.

Whether the effects of the First Crusade were felt immediately or occurred over a longer span of time, the Crusade certainly seems to mark a turning point in the history of Ashkenazic Jewry. As the concept of the modern nation began to develop, and as those early modern nations began to develop a middle class that assumed many of the roles that the Jews had filled, the Jews increasingly began to feel and to be treated as outsiders, a status that the crusades had confirmed. Before the Crusade, the Jews had often been protected by kings and by archbishops (almost always for selfish reasons) but after the Crusade, some historians argue, that protection began to disappear.[38] Furthermore, as Stow notes, "The Crusaders' attack on the Jews [was] integral to the idealized quest for a pure Christian society which had been restated in the eleventh century."[39] If a "pure Christian society" were to exist, the Jews would have to be eliminated somehow, whether through conversion, expulsion, or slaughter.

Shmuel Shepkaru demonstrates how the Jewish Crusade chronicles ironically borrowed images of martyrdom from the crusaders themselves.

Jews and Christians were in competition, with each side claiming that it alone taught the truth. Thus each side claimed that its dead were martyrs, while the dead of the other side faced damnation. The result was that, by adopting similar views of what the martyr's heaven would be like, the two competitors made themselves more alike while simultaneously viewing each other as more different, more alien, and more deluded.[40] Over the centuries, these views would grow even stronger.

For the Jews of Ashkenaz, the centuries following the First Crusade must have seemed confusing. On the one hand, they were characterized by political and physical attacks and expulsions, while on the other hand, they produced biblical and talmudic commentaries that revolutionized the study of those texts and whose brilliance has never been surpassed. Historians speak of the renaissance of the twelfth century, a time when medieval thought became transformed, when the works of Aristotle were introduced into Europe, when Gothic architecture began, when vernacular literature gained a new brilliance. The Jews, living in Europe, still side-by-side with Christian neighbors, could hardly have been unaffected by these cultural developments, and we can see them reflected in Jewish cultural productions. In later chapters we will explore those biblical and talmudic commentaries, as well as the poetry that Ashkenazic Jews produced at the time of these developments. For now, however, we must look at the social and political developments that affected Jewish life.

One of the most important events occurred in the French city of Blois in 1171. According to an account left by Ephraim ben Yaakov, a contemporary, the Jews were accused of killing a Christian child and throwing the body into the river. The Jews were condemned to death, though with the proviso that they could save themselves by converting to Christianity. They refused (though a Christian account says that some did comply) and were burned at stakes. As the story relates, the flames burned the ropes that bound the Jews and the stakes to which they were bound, and the Jews emerged from the fire, claiming that they should therefore be freed. The Christians, disagreeing, killed the Jews with their swords and pushed the bodies back into the fire, but even then the bodies were not consumed, thus, in Ephraim's account, convincing the Christians that the Jews had been saints.[41]

As is so often the case, the story is more complicated than it may at first seem. Without minimizing the deaths of the thirty Jews who were executed, we must recognize that the incident in Blois marked the first time that a secular ruler, Thibaut, Count of Blois, had turned on the

Jews who were under his protection.[42] Before this time, rulers may have attacked Jews outside of their own territories, as they did during the Crusades, but they protected their own Jews, usually for at least one of two reasons. First, the Jews, through their business dealings and through the taxes that were imposed on them, added to their rulers' wealth. And second, because the rulers had undertaken to protect the Jews, an attack on the Jews was construed as an attack on the ruler and on his power. The Blois incident showed the weakness of these two propositions: the Jews were expendable. They were tools that Thibaut used in his own defense, in two ways. Thibaut, it seems, had had a Jewish mistress, Pucellina, which caused a great deal of resentment among his people, who accused him of showing favoritism to the Jews. By supporting the executions, he acquitted himself of that charge. Furthermore, Thibaut was involved in a conflict with the French king, Louis VII, and the trial of the Jews served as a direct challenge to the king. The Jews were simply caught in the middle of a quarrel between two rulers.[43] In some ways, the Blois incident, though far smaller in scale than the Crusade massacres, was more significant, for if the Crusades showed how vulnerable the Jews were to outside forces, the Blois incident indicated how little they could now trust their own supposed protectors.

The remaining history of the Jews in medieval France consists of a long history of declining fortunes until the final expulsion in the 1390's. This part of the story begins with the reign of Philip Augustus, who ruled from 1180 until 1223. A brief summary of his actions illustrates the fragility of Jewish life:

> 1180: Philip Augustus imprisoned the Jews in his lands until they paid a
> heavy ransom
> 1181: Philip Augustus annulled loans made by Jews to Christians, but he
> demanded twenty percent of the value of those loans for himself
> 1182: Philip Augustus confiscated Jewish property and drove the Jews out
> of his realm but then discovered how much he missed the income
> they generated
> 1198: Philip Augustus readmitted the Jews and regulated their moneylending
> so that he received a larger share[44]

In all fairness, we must recognize that although Philip Augustus was the king, through much of his reign he exercised actual control only over a relatively small area of France, including Paris. Because there were so many Jews in Paris, Philip Augustus apparently thought that the Jewish population of France was larger than it was, but his actions against the

Jews did help to improve his relations with the French clergy, who were already hostile to the Jews.[45]

If the twelfth century had started and ended badly for the Jews of Ashkenaz, the thirteenth was mostly bad. Through most of the century, French rulers tried to distance themselves from accusations of supporting Jewish usury. Their actions had both financial and religious motives. Jews no longer comprised the merchant and moneylending class and were therefore not so important to the country's welfare as they had once been, and the rulers, particularly Louis IX, desired to make France an exclusively Christian kingdom. As the royal power expanded throughout France during the thirteenth century, the life of the Jews became increasingly endangered. When the French crown annexed the south of France in 1223, for the Jews the new rulers replaced relative tolerance with greater oppression.[46] Prevented from entering the guilds, and therefore from entering the skilled professions, Jews were increasingly forced to fall back on commercial endeavors, particularly moneylending, which they were then forbidden to practice.

Louis IX, then, may have been Saint Louis to the French, but to the Jews he was a bitter persecutor, as he brought increasing hardship to their lives. Rabbi Meir ben Simeon of Narbonne listed the king's injustices to the Jews:

- He prevented the Jews from moving from one overlord to another (thereby allowing their lords to take advantage of them).
- He took their money.
- Despite taking their money, he insisted that they continue to pay heavy taxes.
- He prevented the nobility from enforcing the payment of debts to the Jews.
- But the Jews had to pay *their* debts to Christians.
- He forbad moneylending.[47]

Louis IX was also responsible for one of the terrible acts of the Middle Ages, the burning of the Talmud. As we saw earlier, he came under the influence of Nicholas Donin, a renegade Jew who made ludicrous accusations against Judaism and the Talmud. Under his influence, the Church ordered the seizure of Talmud volumes, and under his influence, Louis IX's France was the only country that obeyed. After the Talmud was put on trial in 1242, twenty-four cartloads of Talmud volumes were burned in Paris, not far from Notre Dame and the Sainte Chappelle, beautiful places that remind at least some tourists of the ugliness that happened there.

Perhaps the enormity of this book burning is not immediately apparent to non-medievalists. After all, the Talmud still exists, so this particular episode did not destroy Judaism's foundational literature. We must realize, however, that in the manuscript culture of the Middle Ages, when every book was copied by hand and when individual books represented not only the text that was being copied but the traditions of the scribe and of his locality, every book presented alternate readings of passages that might illuminate either the text itself or interpretive traditions that might help us in understanding the text. Among those twenty-four cartloads of books, there might also have been unique manuscripts of works that no longer exist. After all, masterpieces like *Beowulf* and *Sir Gawain and the Green Knight* have survived into our time on the basis of unique manuscripts. Who knows what treasures were lost as a result of this massive book burning undertaken by the sainted King Louis?

And the burning of the Talmud had yet another effect on French Jewry. In fact, Robert Chazan argues that the mid-thirteenth century marks a significant turning point for French Jews, who had managed to cope with occasional expulsions and attacks. In the face of such hardships, French Jewry had retained its vitality because of a series of great leaders whose religious authority gave them social standing as well. They were rabbis and teachers. But as Chazan points out, citing the work of Ephraim Urbach, the anti-Talmud legislation of the mid-thirteenth century put an end to the influx of students who would have studied with these rabbis and greatly affected talmudic study in general.[48] The Jews could survive oppression, but they could not flourish when deprived of their basic texts.

Looking back on the thirteenth and early fourteenth centuries, it is easy for us to discern a pattern, so that the final expulsion of the Jews from France seems all but inevitable. To the Jews of that time, however, that pattern was not so clear. Even today, with instantaneous communications and voluminous records, we can only guess at the pattern of developing history. Lacking our technology, their understanding was quite different. Most often it had a theological basis: God was punishing them for something. For Christians, the theological explanation was simple: the Jews were being punished for having rejected and killed the messiah. For Jews it was not so simple. They were doing their best to live according to their understanding of divine law, and yet conditions grew worse and worse. They searched for understanding and put their hopes into the future redemption that they believed was coming. Of course, from our perspective there were important economic and political factors as well. Because of developments in the Christian world, the Jews were no longer required to perform the duties of a middle class, and they became pawns in the conflicts between rulers. One ruler or another might have triumphed in those conflicts, but the Jews almost always lost.

Nevertheless, from the time of the Crusades in the very late eleventh and early twelfth centuries until the early fourteenth, we can see a decline in the fortunes of French Jewry. In the early thirteenth century, the French monarchy, along with the papacy, undertook a new kind of crusade, this one against the population of southern France who had adapted the so-called Albigensian heresy. This crusade was a strictly intra-Christian affair, as the Albigensians adapted a form of religious belief at odds with Catholic orthodoxy. The orthodox armies showed no more mercy to the Albigensians than the crusaders had shown to the Jews and the Muslims, but even this intra-Christian conflict affected the Jews. Although the Jews played no part in the development of the Albigensian heresy, one result of this crusade was stricter control on heretics and Jews.[49] And while the middle years of the century were difficult for the Jews, the end was worse. In 1288, Jews were accused of killing a Christian child in Troyes, and thirteen Jews were executed. In 1290, the charge of host desecration appeared in Paris, and although only one Jew was executed on that occasion, the implications for the future were profound.[50]

In 1306, the Jews were again expelled, though Frenchmen who owed money to the Jews were still required to pay their debts—not to the Jews, of course, but to the crown. In 1315, the Jews were allowed to return to France, because Louis X needed money. They paid for permission to return and then paid high taxes.[51] But in 1320, amid reports that a new crusade was forming, gangs of Frenchmen from the lowest classes, those classes that had been most harmed by royal policies, began attacking wealthy Christians and then turned against the Jews. While anti-Semitism may have played a role in these attacks, known as the Shepherd's Crusade, the attacks were actually aimed at the monarchy. Because the Jews lived under royal protection (such as it was), an attack on them constituted an attack on the king. Pope John XXII ordered an end to these outrages, but again, the damage had been done.[52] By 1396, the Jews were gone from France. With the actual Jews gone, the French could now more easily identify themselves as "Israel of the Spirit" or as the true Chosen People, an identification that the presence of real Jews had made rather awkward.[53]

Jews had lived in Germany possibly since the time of the Romans, but they had settled in the Rhine Valley in significant numbers during the tenth century. By the time of the Crusades in the late eleventh century, they considered themselves relatively safe, but the crusading armies, coupled with the behavior of their neighbors, destroyed that illusion. After the First Crusade, life appears to have returned to normal, though clearly, from the accounts we have and from poetry that still exists, the people bore deep psychological scars. Through the rest of the Middle Ages, there were occasional outbursts of violence against the Jews, as a result, for instance, of the blood libel or of accusations that the Jews had brought on the Black Death; but there was also tremendous creativity in the Jewish communities of the German lands, as we will see. One factor that seems to have helped the Jews was the lack of a strong central German government, so that when Jews ran into trouble in one area, they could flee to another, where the local ruler might be, at least temporarily, more sympathetic to them. Beginning after the Crusades, many Jews from German lands also fled further to the east, to Poland for instance, where they were initially welcomed because the rulers knew that the Jews would contribute to the country's prosperity. This movement of the Jewish population laid the groundwork for the important Eastern European communities that were so prominent until the Holocaust. It also resulted in the development of the Yiddish language, based on the Germanic dialect that the fleeing Jews brought with them. That German, which had been the everyday language of the Jews, was combined with Hebrew and with local languages to produce a new language whose full literary power flowered in the late nineteenth and early twentieth centuries.

Given this history of the Jews in France and Germany, we might well wonder again what sustained the people, what enabled them to survive attacks, expulsions, exploitation, and all the rest. Among the major factors was their adherence to their religious faith, to the promise that they would be redeemed, and to the texts that they studied so diligently, the Tanakh and the Talmud. In fact, despite their troubles, the Jews of the later Middle Ages developed new approaches to those texts that helped to keep them as vibrant and central to their lives as when they had been written centuries earlier.

The history of the Jews in England is depressingly similar, as is the history of Jews in other countries. Any account of medieval Jewish history must begin to seem repetitive or to sound like special pleading. The persecutions, however, were real and must be acknowledged. Then, as we examine the accomplishments of medieval Jewry, we can appreciate them more deeply, as we recognize that the Jews did more than just survive.

Jews play a prominent role in Old English literature, that is, in the literature that predates the Norman Conquest in 1066, even though no Jews lived in England before that date. The first Jews to arrive in England came in the wake of the Conquest, having been invited by the conquering forces because of their value to the society. Later in the eleventh century, after some anti-Semitic episodes in France, more Jews fled to England, where a number of Jewish communities were established in places like London, Lincoln, and York. As both Cecil Roth and Vivian Lipman have shown, Jews and Christians lived side by side without significant conflict.[54] Even after the Jews had been expelled from England in 1290, the *South English Legendary* describes a Jewish child playing with Christian children in his neighborhood "as children will" (I.227). We see no mention here of distinctive clothing or any other kind of separation.

At first, the Jews quickly rose in importance in England. The fact that they spoke French, the language of the new ruling class, initially worked in their favor, as it allied them with their rulers and allowed them to take an active role in the economic life of the kingdom.[55] At the same time, their Judaism made them aliens to the ruling class, while their Jewishness and their Frenchness made them doubly alien to the lower classes. Even later, when the rivalry between the native English and the French conquerors subsided, the Jews differed from other national rivals like the Irish and the Scots, because the Jews were aliens within England rather than at the borders.[56] Furthermore, the English kings, not noted for their thriftiness, borrowed more and more heavily from the Jews and then joined the lower classes in their resentment of the aliens among them. Theoretically the Jews were under the protection of the crown, but that protection was far from certain. Whenever the crown was threatened, the kings made the Jews their scapegoats.

As was the case elsewhere, Jews became prominent in economic affairs, particularly moneylending, largely because they were prohibited from entering other professions; and, as usual, moneylending brought resentment. But Jews were certainly not the only moneylenders. In the middle of the thirteenth century, Henry III imposed heavy taxes on the Jews and demanded immediate payment, forcing the Jews to sell their bonds to Christian moneylenders at a huge discount.[57] Those Christian moneylenders never suffered the same opprobrium as the Jews. Jewish moneylending is even mentioned in the Magna Carta (1215) as one of the grievances of the barons.

As in France, anti-Semitic outrages also took place in England. In the late 1270's, for instance, Jews were accused of coin clipping—that is, of shaving bits of precious metal from coins to lower the value of the currency and to enrich themselves—and hundreds of Jews were executed.[58] The punishment exceeded anything that was done to non-Jews for the same crime. More famous is the case of William of Norwich, the young boy allegedly killed by the Jews. Thomas of Monmouth, in 1173, in his *Life and Miracles of St. William of Norwich*, claimed to have heard from an apostate Jew that the Jews would not be able to get freedom or to return to their homeland without shedding human blood. "Hence it was laid down by them in ancient times that every year they must sacrifice a Christian in some part of the world to the Most High God in scorn and contempt of Christ, that so they might avenge their suffering on Him; inasmuch as it was because of Christ's death that they had been shut out from their own country in exile as slaves in a foreign land."[59] This charge of ritual murder had dire consequences for the Jews.

But the most striking episode in Anglo-Jewish history occurred at the very end of the twelfth century in York. The York Jewish community was one of the largest in England, and it appears that Jews and Christians in that city coexisted peacefully for many years. In 1189, the Jewish community of York, like many others, sent a delegation to Westminster for the coronation of Richard I; but there, apparently against Richard's commands, the Jews were attacked, several were killed, and a number of houses were burned down. Richard responded by at least making a show of trying to apprehend those who were responsible, who, after all, had challenged his royal authority. But Richard's plans for the Third Crusade and his absence from England for that purpose permitted further anti-Jewish uprisings throughout the country. In York, in 1190, a mob under the leadership of Richard Malebysse, a dissolute nobleman who had gotten himself deeply in debt, attacked the Jews, who were offered protection in the Norman castle. Through a tragic misunderstanding, the sheriff who had offered them protection thought that they were trying to take over the castle, and so he went from being their protector to being one of their besiegers. Inside, the Jews, under the leadership of their spiritual head, the religious poet Rabbi Yom Tov of Joigny, knew they were doomed and feared what would happen to them once the mob succeeded in entering the castle. Because of this fear, they engaged in an act of mass martyrdom; and the next day, when the mob did enter the castle, they found virtually everyone dead. These events happened, incidentally, on the night of Good Friday, the night before the beginning of Passover.[60] This story is very effectively told at the beginning of André Schwarz-Bart's novel of the Holocaust *The Last of the Just*.

What lay behind these tragic events? Perhaps attackers' motives rested on the usual anti-Semitic stereotypes, but as many historians point out, the motives actually had a complicated economic foundation. In 1186, the richest Jew in England, Aaron of York, had died. Henry II, father of Richard I, confiscated Aaron's estate, including about £75,000 in money that was owed to Aaron. Henry's attempts to collect that money, probably more vigorous than anything Aaron himself could have done, led to resentment against the crown, which then, naturally, was transferred to the Jews.[61] In addition, the leaders of the mob, men like Richard Malebysse, were indebted to other Jews, and it was entirely to their advantage to wipe out their creditors. In fact, after the mob discovered that the Jews in the castle were dead, they went immediately to the cathedral and destroyed the records of loans made by what the chronicler William of Newburgh called "royal Jewish usurers." Malebysse thus used the mob to cancel his own considerable debts. He operated not out of religious fervor but out of simple greed. William of Newburgh, who had no particular sympathy for the Jews, wrote that "Bold and greedy men thought that they were doing an act pleasing to God, while they robbed or destroyed rebels against Christ and carried out the work of their own cupidity with savage joy and without any, or only the slightest, scruple of conscience— God's justice, indeed, by no means approving such deeds ..." Even this Christian chronicler, who elsewhere refers to the Jews as "impious usurers," acknowledges the cruelty and the self-serving nature of the attackers.[62] Although William shared his society's animus toward the Jews, he could not condone the violence that was done to them at York—a kind of divided attitude that was fairly common.

Through the thirteenth century, life for the English Jews became more and more difficult because of hostility to moneylending, because the Jews refused to be converted, and because the Jews were increasingly viewed as aliens, strangers in a land not their own. Again, the hostility that the Jews aroused was out of proportion to their very small numbers. Finally, in 1290, King Edward I, having borrowed as much money as he could from them, expelled them from England. Theoretically, they were expelled because they were usurers, but actually the expulsion was part of a deal that allowed Edward to raise taxes; secondarily, the expulsion signified Christian frustration with the Jews' refusal to accept

Christianity. Yet another explanation is that English merchants wanted to be rid of Jewish competitors (though their efforts to eliminate other competitors, like Italian merchants, were not successful.)[63]

Whatever the reasons may have been for the expulsion, they were clearly more practical and economic than spiritual, and the result was that Jews were not officially permitted back into England until the mid-seventeenth century. Unofficially, however, a few Jews did remain. After the expulsion, Jews who had become Christians remained in England, where, never fully accepted as Christians, they existed as outcasts. Later, in the sixteenth century, a small number of Jewish refugees from Spain were allowed, unofficially, to settle in England for a time. But for over four centuries, England was largely devoid of Jews.

It is curious, then, that in the absence of real Jews, so many Jews appear in late medieval English literature. Sophia Menache makes an important distinction between "Israel of the flesh" (real Jews) and "Israel of the Spirit" (ancient, biblical Jews who formed the model for the modern English, the chosen people), and she argues that in England, as in France, the expulsion made it easier for the natives to ignore the real Jews while picturing themselves as the chosen people.[64] Like Old English literature, Middle English literature is full of references to Jews, though for the former, Jews had never been in England, while for the latter, they were only a memory. Part of the reason for the unflattering presence of Jews in Old English literature is that the Old English authors, having never seen an actual Jew, based their writings on the descriptions of Jews in the New Testament and in Christian commentaries. Of course, then, they were depicted as the killers of Jesus, as the allies of the devil, as a monstrous race.

But what about the Jews in Middle English literature after the expulsion? Many critics explain their role there as the result of anti-Semitism, but it is an odd kind of anti-Semitism that continued to flourish for over a hundred years after the Jews had disappeared. Certainly biblical stereotypes played a role, but other factors were involved as well. The twelfth-century French author Chrétien de Troyes writes:

> The Jews, in their wicked jealousy
> (They ought to be killed like dogs!)
> Setting him high on the Cross,
> Harmed themselves but helped us,
> For they were lost, and we
> Were saved. (*Perceval* ll. 6293–98)

Chrétien's words are certainly deplorable, but when he wrote, there were actual Jews in France against whom he might be depicting such hostility; when we read in the fourteenth-century English poem *Cleanness* the following lines, questions arise:

As ʒet is proued expresse in his [Daniel's] profecies,
Hov þe gentryse of Juise and Jherusalem þe ryche
Watz disstryed with distress, and drawen to þe erþe.
For þat folke in her faith watz founden vntrwe,
Þat haden hyʒe God to halde of Hym euer … (1157–61)
[As yet is clearly proved in Daniel's prophecies
How the Jewish people and Jerusalem the rich
Were destroyed with distress and razed to the ground.
For that people was found untrue in its faith,
Whom God had bidden to trust in him forever.]

This passage can hardly be considered anti-Semitic—part of it originates in the biblical book of Chronicles, and its like can be found almost everywhere in the prophets—but why does it appear in *Cleanness*, since it cannot be addressed to contemporary Jews? The poem as a whole is a moral homily addressed to the English, urging them to study the biblical examples and adopt cleanness, or purity. Consequently, this passage is addressed specifically to the English people as a warning that what befell the Jews as a consequence of their sins will befall the English unless their similar sins are eliminated. The English are like the Jews who, in the Christian conception, called on God to preserve them forever but were untrue in their faith. The biblical Jews, then, serve as a standard against whom the English can be judged. If the English, as Christians, claim to be the "true Israel," then they must look to ancient Israel as their model. They must compare themselves to the Jews of the Bible and guard themselves from committing the same sins lest they be subject to the same punishments. Being a "chosen people" is never easy.

If Jews in Old Testament contexts are treated without active hostility in Middle English texts, exactly the opposite is true of Jews in New Testament contexts. The most common such context, naturally, concerns the Passion. In the Townley Plays, for instance, the Jews accuse Jesus of being in league with the devil, and they beat him and spit on him, culminating in the cry, "Nayle him, nayle him to the crosse" (XVI.220). These are the kinds of passages that stick in our memories, just as, unhappily, they stuck in the memories of their earlier audiences. And what is worse, the plays, as popular entertainments, had larger audiences than much other literature. They were both reflections of and shapers of popular religion. Even in the absence of real Jews, the Jews' alleged role in the crucifixion had to be exaggerated rather than overlooked. There can be no doubt about the anti-Semitic nature of the Jews' portrayal, just as there can be no doubt about the effects such accusations would have had if there had been a Jewish community near the performance sites. Still, this scene seems like powerful rabble-rousing when the people against whom the rabble were roused were unavailable for attack. Surely the purpose here was not, as it was elsewhere in Europe, to provoke attacks on the Jews. It does nothing to minimize the anti-Semitism of such portrayals to say that their primary purpose was to deepen the people's sense of Jesus' suffering, which unfortunately was accomplished at the expense of the Jews.

We can see, then, that Jews were used in a number of ways in Middle English literature, and dismissing them all as simply anti-Semitic ignores the variations. They were certainly based on anti-Semitic stereotypes, and England excelled in its anti-Semitism. Except for the burning of the Talmud, England was quicker to accede to the anti-Semitic policies of the Church than any other European country. Nonetheless, at the time when Middle English literature flourished, in the late fourteenth century, the Jews had been long gone, so simple anti-Semitism cannot explain their frequent literary appearances. But the English tendency to think of the English people as the true heirs of ancient Israel often can, as we can see in this passage from William Langland's great fourteenth-century poem *Piers Plowman*:

> Iewes lyuen in þe law þat oure lord taughte
> Moises to be maister þerof till Messie come,
> And on þat lawe they leue and leten hit for þe beste. (C.XVII.297–99)
> (Jews live according to the law that our Lord taught
> Moses, who was to be responsible for it until the messiah comes;
> They believe in that law and hold it to be the best.)

Langland's sense here, in one of his many exhortations to his English audience, is that the Jews continue to believe in their religion even though, in the Christian view, that law has been superseded. But if Jews can be so loyal to their beliefs, even if those beliefs are outmoded, how much more should Christians be loyal to theirs? In a kind of fine irony, the Jews are praised for upholding their superseded beliefs while the Christians are upbraided for neglecting their true ones.

Similarly, elsewhere Langland writes:

A Iew wolde noȝt se a Iew go Ianglying for defaute
For alle þe mebles on þis moolde and he amende it myȝte.
Allas þat a cristene creature shal be vnkynde til anoþer! (B.IX.84–87)
[A Jew would not see a Jew go begging from need
For all the goods on this earth, if he could help.
Alas that one Christian should be unkind to another!]

And he goes on to ask why, if Jews, "whom we call Judas' fellows," help each other in times of trouble, do Christians not help each other. If we have to learn from the Jews, he says, "shame to us all." Langland's focus here, as always, is on the failings of his society, and the Jews, the perennial outsiders, offer him an opportunity to condemn the lack of Christian charity among his fellow Christians. Later, he says that the Jewish law is "*Dilige deum & proximum*," serve God and one's neighbor, a law that was given by God and to which the Jews remain faithful, with the implication that Christians ought to as well. Thus, the absent Jews serve as a contrast to Langland's contemporaries. They are the frequently despised non-Christians against whom Christians can be measured.

Of course, not all of Langland's references to the Jews are so benign. He refers often to Jews as usurers, and in the lengthy scene devoted to the crucifixion, the Jews play their usual, hateful, New Testament role. But whether he cites Jews positively or negatively, Langland probably never saw an actual living Jew. His contemporary, Geoffrey Chaucer, who traveled in France and Italy, probably did. Chaucer's attitude toward Jews is extremely difficult to discern, particularly because Chaucer wraps everything he says in so many layers of ambiguity and irony. We can see in some places that Chaucer uses the Jews in much the same way as Langland. In the Parson's Tale, which concludes the *Canterbury Tales*, the Parson denounces men who "sweren so horribly by his blessed name, that they despire moore booldely than dide the cursed Jewes, or elles the devel, that trembleth whan he heereth his name" (I.595–600—men who "swear so horribly by His blessed name, which they despise more boldly than did the accursed Jews or even the devil, who trembles when he hears His name.") Of course the Jews are "accursed" in this passage, and they are associated with the devil; but the purpose of this passage is not to raise havoc with the Jews. Its real import is an emphatic condemnation of the Parson's Christian contemporaries. If the Jews are "accursed" because of their attitude toward Jesus, how much more accursed are those Christians whose acts exceed those of both the Jews and the devil.

Similarly, in the Pardoner's Tale we read about riotous young people, whose behavior is equivalent to torturing Jesus. Apparently, "Hem thoughte that Jewes rente hym noght ynough" (C.475—"They thought that the Jews had not torn him enough"). If the Jews crucified Jesus in the past, such Christians continue to crucify him in the present. By saying that these young people behave worse than Jews, Chaucer certainly relies on an anti-Semitic misrepresentation of history; but he does so not to attack Jews. His target, or rather the target of the complex Pardoner, is contemporary Christians, and once more we see the Jews used as a standard against whom Christians can be judged.

But now we come to Chaucer's Prioress and her violently anti-Semitic tale. The major question about her tale in recent years is whether the tale is overtly anti-Semitic or whether its anti-Semitism functions as Chaucer's critique of the Prioress herself. Thus, before we can even look at the tale, we must consider its teller. Is that teller Chaucer, the author of the *Canterbury Tales*? Is it Geoffrey, Chaucer's alter ego who tells us what happened on the pilgrimage? Or is it the Prioress, a nun who thinks of herself as romance heroine, who uses her nun's habit to make a fashion statement, who violates the rules of her order by raising dogs that feast on "roasted flesh," and who thinks that she is glorifying the Virgin Mary by telling a story about the blood libel that involves the massacre of a Jewish community? (We need to remember that many stories glorifying the Virgin Mary did indeed end in such massacres.) If the tale is Chaucer's he was indeed a rabid anti-Semite, but throughout the *Canterbury Tales*, Chaucer tries to present tales that are appropriate to their tellers. The Prioress' spirituality, like her praise for the Virgin, is superficial and is undercut by factors that the Prioress cannot possibly understand. Nor can she see the viciousness inherent in her tale any more than she can the viciousness of her dogs, who eat their "roasted flesh" while the poor starve.

Chaucer need not have opposed anti-Semitism to recognize that the Prioress' Tale is repugnant, but he did, in fact, recognize that repugnance. His reliance in the tale on Old Testament Jewish types—Moses, and especially Rachel—indicates his recognition of the irony in the tale. Combined with the picture of the fastidious, self-preening, but heartless

Prioress in the General Prologue, and the general level of anti-clerical satire in the *Tales*, these references point to the tale as indeed an ironic attack on the Prioress. The glorification of the Virgin through such a bloody tale, told by such a teller, might have seemed incongruous to perceptive readers even in a brutal age like Chaucer's. But the issue is Christian behavior, not anti-Semitism.

The works of Langland and Chaucer stand in clear contrast to another roughly contemporaneous poem, *The Siege of Jerusalem*, which tells of the destruction of Jerusalem by Titus and Vespasian as retaliation for the crucifixion, a stance that severely distorts history but that feeds into popular anti-Semitism. Even as a picture of Jews in their customary New Testament role as crucifiers, *The Siege of Jerusalem* is gratuitously cruel and crude. In this work the Jews are simply villains, and the more they can be punished, the better.

It is worthwhile, however, to contrast a poem like *The Siege of Jerusalem* with the other works we have examined. Langland and Chaucer certainly based their comments about the Jews on anti-Semitic stereotypes that still had an audience in late medieval England, in a country that had driven the Jews out. It may be foolish to castigate medieval authors for relying on such stereotypes, but the continued existence of anti-Semitism in a country devoid of Jews, as evidenced by *The Siege of Jerusalem*, is a good indication of the perniciousness of anti-Semitism—indeed, all bigotry—which can thrive on any food that is supplied to it, however meager. And finally, we must note that even if the works of Chaucer and Langland are not consistently anti-Semitic, those works have certainly contributed to the history of anti-Semitism in England and elsewhere.

Sepharad

Nineteenth-century scholars called the period from the mid-tenth to the mid-twelfth centuries the Golden Age of Spanish Jewry, and they did so with good reason, though we might today be inclined to say that it was "golden" more in relation to Jewish life elsewhere than as an absolute standard. Of course, no age, for anyone, anywhere, has ever been truly "golden," except in various mythologies. According to rabbinical commentaries, even Adam and Eve spent only six hours in the Garden of Eden before things went bad, so we should not be overly critical of the life Jews led in Spain in those centuries. Nevertheless, as Yitzḥak Baer points out, the "golden age" was golden only because the authorities tended not to enforce oppressive strictures against the Jews.[65] The threat of the strictures was always there.

We should remember, again, to be careful in our use of the terms "Sepharad" and "Sephardim," which refer specifically to the Jews of Spain. There were still Jews living in other places in the Muslim world, in the Middle East of course, and in North Africa. These Jews often lived in difficult circumstances, but they, too, survived. However, when persecutions began in Spain, in the middle of the twelfth century, then reappeared periodically and culminated with the expulsion of 1492, many Sephardic Jews fled to those Muslim-controlled areas, bringing with them their customs and their language. Over time, as these different Jews mingled, so did those customs and languages, and it became easy to refer to anyone who was not Ashkenazic as Sephardic. Technically, though, that term should be applied to the Jews of Spain.

What made Spain so special, not only to Jews but to Muslims and even to Christians? Medieval Spanish history is quite complicated. In 711, Muslim armies crossed the Strait of Gibraltar and began a campaign in Spain that resulted in the Muslim conquest of large parts of the peninsula. The Muslims of Spain, however, particularly before the twelfth century, differed from the Muslims of the Middle East, and their distance from the central authority of the empire in Baghdad allowed them to govern their new territories in their own style. Much of the subsequent history of medieval Spain involves the conflict between Muslims and Christians for control of the country, though we must keep in mind that many warriors fought on whichever side offered them greater advantages. The Jews, as usual, were caught in the middle, and they, too, quite naturally favored the side that was most favorable to them, sometimes profiting from the conflict and at other times being harmed by it. Thus, at the time of the Muslim invasion, the Jews had been living under Visigothic Christian persecution, so it is hardly surprising that they regarded the Muslim invasion favorably and may even have helped the invaders. Later, when they suffered under Muslim persecution, many Jews fled to Christian territories. To behave otherwise would have been foolish, if not suicidal.

While we know that Jews had been in Spain long before the Muslims arrived, the twelfth-century writer Avraham ibn Daud tells a fanciful story about how Spain became a Jewish center. According to ibn Daud, a Muslim sea captain captured a boat in which four rabbinical scholars were traveling. Two he sold in Egypt, where they distinguished themselves as scholars and became heads of academies in the important Jewish centers of Fustat and Qairawan, and two he sold in Spain, where they likewise distinguished themselves (ibn Daud, 63ff.). Ibn Daud concludes, with some nationalistic pride, that the "mastery of the Talmud now rested in Spain," though he does acknowledge that there might also be great scholars in France (78, 88). Although ibn Daud tells a good story, we know that the basis for Jewish success in Spain was laid by two tenth-century rulers, the caliphs Abd-ar-Rahman III and Hakam II. One of the Jewish courtiers in Abd-ar-Rahman's powerful kingdom was Abu Yusuf Hasdai ibn Shaptrut, who served as court physician, translator, and diplomat, and was sent on diplomatic missions to negotiate with Christians in Leon and Pampona.[66] Hasdai was followed by other Jewish courtiers, probably the most famous of whom was Shmuel ibn Nagrela, also known as Shmuel ha-Nagid, Samuel the Prince. This extraordinary man was a general, a political leader, a scholar, and an important poet, whose work we will examine later. When he died in 1056, his position was taken over by his son, who developed many enemies, some on religious grounds, and who was assassinated in Grenada in 1066, along with a number of other Jews.

By the middle of the eleventh century, internal quarrels among the Muslims in Spain had weakened them enough to encourage Christians in their dreams of reconquest, but those dreams were postponed by the arrival of two fanatical Muslim sects, the Almoravides in the 1100's and the Almohades in the 1140's. Both of these sects attempted to establish stricter religious controls over Spain, and they attacked Muslims whom they thought were too lax in their observances as well as Jews. Thus, while the Jews of the Rhineland were suffering the attacks of the crusaders, the Jews of Spain were undergoing their own persecution. Many Jews, including Maimonides and his family, fled from Spain. Others were forced to convert, though in many cases they were eventually allowed to resume their Jewish identities.[67] These persecutions, particularly those wrought by the Almohades, brought to an end the "golden age," which had lasted about two hundred years. Those two centuries did indeed produce a succession of brilliant thinkers and poets, men like Hasdai, Shmuel ha-Nagid, Shlomo ibn Gabirol, Avraham ibn Daud, Moshe ibn Ezra, Avraham ibn Ezra, and others, but as we will see when we look more closely at the works they produced, they hardly thought of themselves as living in a golden age. After the mid-twelfth century, as the Christian reconquest progressed, conditions for the Jews grew worse; and though there were still times when the Jews lived in peace and even in prosperity, their history in Spain shows a gradual decline, with periods of respite, until the final expulsion in 1492.

Among the highlights (or more accurately, the low points) of those centuries is the famous Disputation in Barcelona in 1263. For Jews in Spain, the thirteenth century was a period of economic and political success, but, as we have already seen, in the thirteenth century the Church discovered that the Jews had a book called the Talmud. In order to cope with that book, the Church developed different strategies. The first and most obvious was to destroy it, a strategy that resulted in the burning of the Talmud in Paris. Another strategy, developed by the friars, was to use the Talmud itself to prove the "truths" of Christianity. The most famous confrontation employing this methodology was the Disputation at Barcelona, at which the Christian side was represented primarily by the friar Pablo Christiani, a convert from Judaism, and the Jewish side by Rabbi Moshe ben Nachman, better known as Nachmanides or by the acronym Ramban. The judge for the disputation was the king of Aragon, Jaime I, a Christian king and thus inclined to favor the Christian arguments, but more sympathetic to the Jews than we might expect. Once again, however, the Christian quarrel with the Jews amounted also to a quarrel among Christians, because the Church's attack on the Jews was also an attack on the secular power that had jurisdiction over the Jews, that is, the king. Furthermore, the king knew Nachmanides and allowed him to respond openly to Pablo Christiani's arguments.

Fortunately, we have accounts of the disputation from both the Jewish and Christian participants, and there are significant studies of these accounts by scholars such as Yitzhak Baer, Robert Chazan, and Jeremy Cohen. Nachmanides' account is particularly fascinating, for we know that after the disputation, the king gave him the sum of 300 dinars and sent him home, and Nachmanides says, "I parted from him in abounding love" (42). But we also know that shortly thereafter, Nachmanides fled to Israel, for what he had said in the disputation was dangerous indeed. When the friars demanded that Nachmanides be punished for his views, the king suggested a light punishment, and when the friars protested his suggestion, the king decided not to punish him at all. Jaime I was not about to destroy the Jewish community, which provided him with a good deal of income.[68]

In his account of the disputation, Nachmanides says that the two sides had agreed to discuss the subject of the messiah, "whether he had already come, which is the belief of the Christians, or was still to come, which is the belief of the Jews." Then they would discuss whether the messiah is divine or mortal and then whether "the Jews hold the true Torah, or whether the Christians fulfill it" (4). Clearly these were dangerous topics even in a free and open discussion, and this discussion could hardly be free or open. Its purpose, for the Christian organizers, was to demonstrate that Christianity was true and that Judaism was not, so the outcome was never in doubt. Nevertheless, the Jewish participants could not refuse to answer the Christian arguments, which means that they had publicly to deny the validity of Christian belief, a dangerous undertaking. If the Jews refused to argue, they would lose; and if they did argue, they would lose. Still, Nachmanides argued to the best of his ability, and, according to his account, he outargued Pablo Christiani from start to finish. (The Christian account, naturally, presents a somewhat different interpretation.) The Christian spokesman began by saying that he would prove from the Talmud that the messiah had already come, but Nachmanides responded that the talmudic sages could not have remained Jewish, let alone have established the laws of Judaism, had they believed that the messiah had already appeared.

Of course, Nachmanides' knowledge of the Talmud was far greater and deeper than that of his opponent, whose arguments he was able to refute, though he did have to take one dangerous step. As we saw earlier, the Talmud contains both halakhah, law, and aggadah, legend. Much of the Christian argument was based on very loose reading of the aggadah, to which Nachmanides responded by saying that while halakhah was binding on Jews—that is, Jews had to follow the laws—aggadah was not binding. Jews could accept or reject it. This argument was easily subject to misunderstanding. It seemed to say that a Jew was free to accept or reject whatever he chose from the tradition, which is certainly not the case. Nevertheless, the Christians were unable to refute Nachmanides' words.

In addition to denying that the messiah had come, Nachmanides also denied the doctrine of Original Sin and argued that the messiah will be a human rather than a divine figure: "the Messiah is but a king of flesh and blood" (18). "He will be born close to the time of the designated period of redemption. He will live normally for many years and die in honors, and he will bequeath his crown to his son. I have already stated that I believe in this view, and the only difference between the present world and the era of the Messiah is political subjugation" (30). And lest we think that these are Nachmanides' most inflammatory statements, he told the king that the king only believed in Christianity because that is what he had been taught for his whole life, but that really Christianity was irrational. It is no wonder that even if the king rewarded him for his part in the disputation, he had to flee. After the disputation, the Jews were forced to listen to conversionary sermons in the synagogue.

Fortunately, there was no overt violence in reaction to the disputation, but such was not the case later, when the Church roused popular ire against the Jews and the rulers were either unable or unwilling to protect their Jewish subjects.

Even before the Barcelona Disputation, the blood libel had made its first appearance in Spain, in 1250, and after the disputation, conditions continued to worsen. In 1320, the Shepherd's Crusade killed a number of Jews in the south of France and then in Spain; in 1321, the Jews of Toledo were accused of poisoning the wells; in 1328 there were anti-Jewish disturbances in Navarre; and after the arrival of the Black Death in Spain in 1348, there were numerous attacks on the Jews.[69] But the most serious attacks occurred in 1391. In that year, a century before the expulsion, there was widespread anti-Jewish rioting throughout Christian Spain, largely against the wishes of secular rulers, for until 1391, the Jews were still considered to be the property of the king, a theory that broke down in the aftermath of the bloodshed. For example, the king and queen of Aragon tried to stop the attacks on their Jews, but they also accepted their share of the wealth that had been confiscated from the Jews in the riots, thereby sending an impossibly mixed signal to both rioters and Jews.[70] Ultimately, however, the message was that the Jews were expendable. So Jews were killed, Jewish women and children were sold as slaves to Muslims, and synagogues were turned into churches.[71]

We can perhaps get a taste of the feelings created by these riots from a letter written by a prominent Jewish leader of the time, Hasdai Crescas:

> Many sanctified the Holy Name [that is, became martyrs], my only son among them, an innocent lamb; him have I offered up as a burnt offering. I shall vindicate God's judgment against me, and I shall be comforted with the goodliness of his portion and the sweetness of his fate. Many slaughtered themselves and some threw themselves from the tower ... and some went out and were martyred in the street ...[72]

What is not mentioned in these lines is another phenomenon that was to play a large role in the following century: the large number of Jews who either converted to Christianity or who pretended to convert. Some, perhaps, converted out of conviction. Having seen their people attacked once more, they decided that God must favor the other side. Of those, some simply lived quietly as Christians, but others, possibly to demonstrate their zeal, became oppressors of their former coreligionists.

(As we have seen, some of the worst enemies of the Jews, men like Nicholas Donin and Pablo Christiani, were converted Jews!) Other Jews, who had converted to save their lives, either continued to practice Judaism in secret or maintained secret ties to their old communities.[73] Even before 1391, the number of conversions appears to have been rising, as Jewish life became more and more unbearable, but afterward the number increased greatly. However, in Spain, as elsewhere, Jewish converts to Christianity were not always accepted by the Christian community, and when many of the "converts" were known to practice Judaism in secret, the problem became worse, for now the converts were perceived as undermining Christianity. Thus, while the proper name for converts should have been *conversos*, they were often called *marranos*, an insulting word that means "pigs."

In the fifteenth century, violence broke out between Old Christians and the *conversos*, and naturally the problem of the converts drew the attention of the Inquisition. In the middle of the fifteenth century, we see the first accusation that even truly converted Jews defiled the blood of pure Spaniards, that even baptism could not change the essential nature of Jews.[74] Such a charge meant that conversion of the Jews could no longer be the goal. They had to be gotten rid of, through either killing or expulsion. As Jeremy Cohen points out, if rabbinic Judaism had no place in Europe, according to the friars, neither did the Jews themselves.[75]

Throughout the fifteenth century, conditions for the Jews worsened. In 1413–1414, another major disputation was held, this time at Tortosa. As bad as the Barcelona Disputation of 1263 had been, the Disputation at Tortosa was worse, for the Christians had had a chance to sharpen their arguments, while the Jews, having suffered a century and a half of further humiliation and oppression, were less able to respond. Jews had been forced to listen to conversionary sermons, had been attacked as they were marched through the streets to hear those sermons, and were forced to respond to passages allegedly from the Talmud and Midrash that had actually been invented by the earlier Christian oppressor Raymond Martini.[76] At about the same time in Castile, Jews were required to wear distinctive clothing, Jewish physicians were no longer allowed to treat Christian patients, and Jewish merchants and artisans could not trade with Christians.[77] Finally, when the Christian reconquest of Spain had been completed under Ferdinand and Isabella, the Jews were expelled from Spain. A long and sometimes glorious history came to an end. The Jews fled wherever they could go, some to North Africa or the Middle East, some to whatever European countries might let them in. (Some apparently settled even in England, where they were not officially allowed.) Some fled to Portugal, hoping that the expulsion orders would be repealed, but they and the Portuguese Jews were expelled shortly thereafter. As subsequent history would show, neither the expulsion of the Jews nor the Inquisition was beneficial to Spain. For the Jews, even after a century of persecution, the expulsion was regarded as a tragedy, so much so that it has ever since been associated with the Ninth of Av, the day on which Jews mourn the destructions of the First and Second Temples.

Living as Jews in the Medieval World

Although interest in describing the everyday lives of people in the Middle Ages has been on the rise, the difficulty of such a task for medievalists stems from a lack of records. We have no diaries or newspapers, for instance, that we can study for clues. Fortunately for the study of medieval Jews and Judaism, however, some extraordinary resources exist. Some of these resources are like those available for Christian or Muslim societies, such as sermons, letters, literary works, deeds, contracts, and court records that reflect the societies of their authors, but there are other resources as well. One such resource consists of thousands of letters written by individuals and communities to well-known rabbis asking for guidance on a variety of issues, as well as the answers to those questions. As we saw earlier, this responsa literature covers all sorts of questions, particularly on religious and moral issues, and it gives us insights into the concerns and customs of Jews in a large variety of times and places. The other major resource is something unique to Judaism, the Cairo Genizah.

In Judaism, it is forbidden to destroy any paper (or parchment) that has the Hebrew name of God written on it. Such documents, whether they are copies of the Bible, prayer books, or any other kind of writing, have to be buried. Therefore, synagogues often have a special storeroom, called a genizah, in which such documents can be kept until there are enough to bury. One such storeroom belonged to the synagogue in

Fostat, or Old Cairo, in Egypt. Over the years, people put documents containing the name of God in the genizah, but also, because Hebrew was regarded as a sacred language, they also put in any documents in Hebrew script. Medieval Jews who lived in Arabic-speaking environments often wrote in Arabic but used Hebrew letters, so many documents in Arabic also ended up in the genizah.[1] But the documents in the Cairo Genizah were never buried. Instead, the storeroom was sealed up. In the nineteenth century, scholars began to examine these documents and discovered what a treasure they were. Some consist of only part of a single sheet while others consist of many sheets. There are letters, records of commercial transactions, poems, all sorts of writing. And they do not come only from Egypt. There are documents either from or about many other places. These documents have now been removed from the genizah and are scattered in museums and libraries around the world. Scholars are still trying to sort them out and read them all, a very difficult process, but they have already taught us a great deal. One of the most important products of the genizah is S. D. Goitein's five-volume study *A Mediterranean Society*, but there are many other works of genizah scholarship that help illuminate the daily lives of medieval Jews.

Everyday Life

Jews, as we have seen, constituted a small percentage of the population wherever they dwelled, and they often gravitated toward cities. Thus, as previously noted, Philip Augustus, seeing how many Jews lived in Paris, assumed that the Jewish population in the rest of France was larger than it was. In many smaller towns, the Jewish population was very small, sometimes consisting of only a few people or a few families, so that not only did they have trouble getting enough Jewish men for a minyan, but they had difficulty with other necessities of Jewish life. Jews required kosher meat, cemeteries, ritual baths, and other elements central to religious observance. Either they traveled to meet these needs (and travel in the Middle Ages could be quite difficult and dangerous) or they provided for themselves. Or they did without.

Their small numbers also raise another issue: how did Jews and non-Jews get along? We know, of course, what the Church and the state said officially, and we know that there were periodic outbreaks of popular violence against the Jews, but what was life like at other times? There were no official ghettoes during the Middle Ages—the ghetto was a

Renaissance invention—but at the same time, people often like to live near others with whom they have something in common. Furthermore, Jews gathered together so they could share religious requirements and celebrations and undoubtedly for protection. As Goitein says, men made friends on the basis of religion, because the usual gathering place was the church, mosque, or synagogue.[2] In fact, the Hebrew name for a synagogue actually means "house of assembly." In Ashkenaz, one way we know that synagogues were often built near Christian places of worship is from Christian complaints about the Jews' noisy praying. At the same time, in Muslim lands, during what Goitein calls "the good years of the High Middle Ages," Jews, Christians, and Muslims lived next to each other, and members of the same profession, whatever their religion, were possibly more closely allied than co-religionists.[3] During the Golden Age, and even after, Jews in Spain participated in the general culture, and such works as Yehuda Halevi's *Kuzari* and Maimonides' *Guide of the Perplexed* were written in Arabic (though Maimonides no longer lived in Spain when he wrote the *Guide*). In Ashkenaz, the Jews knew the vernaculars, but when they wrote, they used Hebrew.

Still, our knowledge about everyday life is limited, as we can see in the disagreement between two important scholars, Norman Golb and William Chester Jordan, over the designation "Street of the Jews" that so often appears in the cities and towns of Ashkenaz. In his study of the Jews of Normandy, Golb contends that this designation indicates the presence of Jews, while Jordan argues in his book on the Jews and the French monarchy that the designation does not necessarily indicate the presence of Jews, and, even if it does, it does not tell us when the Jews were there or how many there were. (Even today, in many places where Jews no longer live, we can still find a Rue des Juifs or a Judenstrasse.) Ongoing work in archives of medieval documents will undoubtedly help to clarify some issues.

If there are gaps in our knowledge of such factual information, however, the gaps in our knowledge of less concrete matters are even larger. Again, we know what the official positions of the religions were toward each other, and they were hardly ecumenical, but how actual people got along on a day-to-day basis is less clear. Undoubtedly there was much suspicion and distrust on both sides, and yet we know, even from those terrible Crusade chronicles, that at least some Christians tried to help their Jewish neighbors. We know from other records that when Dolce, the wife of Eleazar bar Yehuda of Worms, was murdered in 1196, Christian authorities captured and executed at least one of the murderers.[4] Ariel Toaff makes the point that the small number of Jews scattered in Christian society created many opportunities for interreligious contacts and often led to sexual relationships. In fact, there were numerous regulations regarding such relationships, though in practice such relationships usually resulted only in a fine, and probably there were far more cases than we know of. In 1418, at a meeting of representatives from Jewish communities in central Italy, attendees expressed their concern that the high number of illegitimate children resulting from liaisons between Jewish men and Christian women was weakening Jewish society.[5]

As Christian society developed during the Middle Ages, religious hostility toward the Jews was often accompanied by economic hostility. One cause of this development, naturally, was Jewish moneylending, but another had to do with the economic development of Europe, which involved Christians moving into professions that had previously been dominated by Jews and then viewing the Jews as competitors who had to be eliminated. And, of course, all of these factors combined and recombined in a variety of ways in different times and places, making it impossible for us to devise accurate generalizations about how the people got along in their daily lives. Perhaps the best example of the problem can be found in an example provided by Elisheva Baumgarten. It was a common, though often debated, practice among the Jews of Ashkenaz to hire Christian wet nurses for their children. (Jews were forbidden by Christian law to nurse Christian children.) On the one hand, this practice indicates a certain closeness between Jews and Christians. After all, a wet nurse would practically become part of the household in which she worked, and parents would have to have some amount of confidence in the women to whom they entrusted their children. At the same time, accusations were made by Christians that if a Christian wet nurse took communion, her Jewish employers would force her to discard her milk for three days, lest the Jewish child be polluted by the Christian ritual. Jewish sources make no mention of such a requirement, and it seems unlikely that such a requirement existed (what would the child eat during those three days?), but the mere existence of such an accusation regarding such an intimate relationship indicates the complexity of Jewish-Christian co-existence.[6] We do know that overt displays of Jewish religious life were often met with hostility. Most Jewish rituals take place at home or in the synagogue, but funerals, during which the cortège passed through the streets accompanied by the singing of dirges, could be particularly problematic, calling forth rude comments and stone-throwing by observers.[7]

To varying degrees during the Middle Ages, Jewish communities were allowed to govern themselves. They were, of course, bound by secular law, but they also had their own leaders and their own legal system and courts, based on the Talmud, which served as a guide to virtually every facet of life. In cases that brought individual Jews and Christians into conflict, recourse was made to secular courts, but when individual Jews were in conflict, they were enjoined to use Jewish courts, on the presumption that Jewish law came from God, while the secular law was created by human beings.[8] It did happen, however, that occasionally a Jew who was unhappy with the decision of the community leaders or with the verdict of a Jewish court—after all, someone is bound to be unhappy with almost any verdict—would then take the case to a Christian court. Such behavior was frowned upon, not only because of theological differences, but because the Jews did not want to reveal the workings and conflicts of their communities to the outside world. When Christian authorities did become involved, as they did in the Maimonides controversy, the results were often bad for the Jews.

At various times during the Middle Ages, Jews adopted a variety of professions. Often they were merchants, a profession that was supported by the almost universal literacy among Jewish men. But being a merchant did not mean simply opening a shop. Merchants often had to travel, either to sell their wares or to buy new merchandise for selling in their home areas. Travel, as we have already mentioned, was dangerous. Maimonides' brother David was only one of many mercantile travelers who lost their lives on such journeys. And travel was also time-consuming. Merchants from Spain who traveled to India and other distant nations could be gone for years at a time, leading to marital problems and to great hardships for families left at home. If someone became ill or died, either on a voyage or while waiting at home, it was often nearly impossible to convey the news.

Jews were often physicians, Maimonides and Yehuda Halevi being two of the best known, and pharmacists. Documents from the genizah also indicate that Jews worked as dyers, perfumers, and in the metal trades, dealing in iron, copper, gold, and silver.[9] And Jews occasionally worked as farmers, despite being forbidden to own land. One agricultural field in which they played a large role was the cultivation of grapes. Jewish law prohibited Jews from drinking wine that was manufactured by non-Jews. Because wine played a significant part in medieval life and was required for many Jewish and Christian rituals, Jews often became winemakers for the whole community. The great commentator, Rashi, whether correctly or not, has traditionally been thought of as a cultivator of grapes. One interesting difficulty that arose in relation to the wine trade was that Jewish winemakers who made wine for the Jewish and Christian communities made the wine that was used in churches for communion, a fact that occasionally produced complaints from Church leaders.

Another significant profession for Jewish men throughout the Middle Ages involved learning, and even those who were not professional scholars or religious leaders tended both to honor and to practice Jewish learning. A sermon by Jacob Anatoli, from the late-twelfth or early-thirteenth century, focuses on Proverbs 22:29, "See a man skilled at his work—He shall attend upon kings; He shall not attend upon obscure men." Jacob's comment on this verse is that "Solomon's subject ... is the supreme vocation: study of the Torah, philosophical wisdom, and the pursuit of prophecy."[10] Study was the "supreme vocation." What study meant may have been open to interpretation, but no one took very seriously the literal meaning of the biblical verse, "Much studying is a wearying of the flesh" (Ecclesiastes 12:12). Study was akin to worship. It was what Jews were called on to do, and medieval Jews saw evidence of the importance of study everywhere. According to the Talmud and to medieval commentators, Esau loved to hunt, but, as we have already seen, Jacob loved to study, and he studied Torah in the school of Noah's son, Shem. The historical impossibility of this activity was meaningless compared to the ideological importance the story gave to the value of study.

One troubling question that arose about the nature of study involved the subjects of study. Obviously the Torah, both the Written and Oral Torah, was primary. Other biblical books were also appropriate subjects, particularly since so many play a role in Jewish ritual. But there was considerable disagreement over the extent to which Jews should study secular subjects, which were seen by opponents as at least a distraction and at worst a lure away from the world of Judaism. The problem became particularly acute in the time of Maimonides, the twelfth century and after, because of the rising popularity of Greek, especially Aristotelian, philosophy. Aristotle's works, especially his works on logic and on natural history, prompted students to re-examine sacred texts, and frequently that re-examination led either to allegorizations of the text to deny its clear meaning and bring it into line with the requirements of logic or, even worse, to denials of the text's validity. If even one part of the Tanakh could be shown to be untrue or irrational, then the text could not have been divine in origin, and if it was not divine in origin, then there was no point in following all the laws that the Tanakh and the Talmud required. Thus, the result of secular learning could be, and sometimes was, apostasy.

On the other hand, many Jewish leaders understood the necessity of secular learning, both for daily life and for the purpose of elucidating the sacred texts. After all, many sections of the Tanakh cannot be understood without some secular knowledge. Avraham ibn Ezra's commentary on the Tanakh is full of references to Greek science and even to the Greek language, and Rashi, too, shows an awareness of secular subjects. The problem of secular learning has never been fully settled in the Jewish world. Today, too, there are Jewish leaders who deny the need for secular learning or who allow secular learning only to the extent that it is necessary for one's profession.

Regardless of what they were studying, however, learning was always a focus of Jewish life. One of Peter Abelard's students, in the twelfth century, wrote a letter in which he contrasted the Jewish emphasis on education, exemplified by the regularity with which Jews educated their sons, with the Christian failure to do so:

> If the Christians educated their sons, they do so not for God, but for gain, in order that the one brother, if he be a clerk [a cleric], may help his father and mother and his other brothers.... But the Jews, out of zeal for God and love of the law, put as many sons as they have to letters, that each may understand God's law ...[11]

Slightly later in the same letter, the writer notes that the Jew educates "not only his sons, but his daughters," a significant observation to which we will return. Another important point to consider in this matter of educating children concerns priestly celibacy. Jews were enjoined to be fruitful and multiply, as apparently they did, and they tended to educate their children. Christian clergy, however, were forbidden to procreate, so that while there were many brilliant scholars and theologians among them, they had no children whom they could influence (though they certainly had students and disciples). In a later chapter we will discuss the grandsons of Rashi and their influence on Jewish life; many other Jewish scholars, like Maimonides, had scholarly offspring. We never hear about the children of Bernard of Clairvaux or Thomas Aquinas because they had none.

Of course, educational practices differed from area to area. For example, in Spain the communities tended to support schools, whereas in the

Ashkenaz' community, schools were limited and individual families hired teachers. At higher levels, schools were identified with individual teachers rather than with the cities in which they were located.[12] Like Christian students, Jewish students often traveled from one school to another to soak up wisdom from a variety of teachers. In a comment on Song of Songs 5:16, Rashi says, "Like doves that wander from one dovecote to the second to seek their food, so they go from the school of one scholar to the school of another scholar to seek explanations ... for the Torah."[13] Such young men had learned the value and the sweetness of study from an early age, for when a young boy started school, he participated in a ceremony in which the new student was given letters made out of honey to eat. Because the words of the Torah are like honey, this symbolic meal indicated the joy of internalizing the words of the Torah.[14]

Since the major subjects of learning were the Jewish sacred texts, students also had to study languages. Jews spoke the languages of the places where they lived, but because they studied and prayed in Hebrew and Aramaic, students learned these languages and could examine the Tanakh and the Talmud in their original languages. Commentaries and poetry, both sacred and secular, were also written in Hebrew (though occasionally in other languages as well). During the twelfth century, as Beryl Smalley made clear in *The Study of the Bible in the Middle Ages*, many Christian scholars consulted Jews or studied Hebrew with them so that they, too, could read Scripture in its original language. These Christian scholars were occasionally accused of "judaizing," that is, of being too much like Jews, but their efforts to learn Hebrew demonstrate their recognition that the language of Scripture was important. Later Christian clerics also attempted to study the Talmud, but, as we saw, they did so in order to use the text to refute Jewish beliefs.

Prayer

As it was for Christians, prayer was central to Jewish life. A Jewish man is supposed to recite three prayer services every day, in the morning, afternoon, and evening; but he also prays when he awakens, when he retires, and when he eats, as well as at other times. Women, too, are required to say many of these prayers. Given how important prayer was, it is interesting how limited our knowledge of its origins remains. While we know that many biblical characters pray, Stefan Reif comments on how difficult it is to be definitive about medieval developments in prayer, since our sources are scanty and we cannot always tell whether they describe conditions as they were or as the authors thought they should be.[15] In fact, the problem of discussing Jewish prayer goes back to before the Middle Ages, to the Second Temple period. We know that synagogues existed concurrently with the Temple. Because sacrifices could only be performed in the Temple, however, we have to speculate about what went on in the synagogues. In 1913, I. Elbogen argued that people in the synagogues did pray, while more recently, Ezra Fleischer has countered that the synagogues predate prayer and were primarily used for public reading of Scripture. And Ruth Langer has complicated the situation by arguing that both Elbogen and Fleischer were influenced by their own ideologies of Judaism, with the former reflecting Reform thought and the latter Orthodox.[16] Furthermore, there is significant disagreement over whether prayers existed in a single original form or whether there were many different texts that were eventually standardized. By the year 200, Lawrence Hoffman contends, there was a fixed service.[17] We do know that the Talmud refers to and even quotes prayers, but we do not know how widely accepted, or even how widely known, they may have been at that time. The Mishnah (Tamid 5:1) cites biblical passages that were meant to be recited, while the Gemara (Berakhot 26b) refers to prayers that were composed at a later time, though they were attributed to the Patriarchs.[18] The first actual Jewish prayer book (in Hebrew *siddur*) appears in a responsum by Rav Amram Gaon, one of the leaders of Babylonian Judaism in the mid-ninth century. Although the geonim, like their talmudic predecessors, attributed the prayers to the Patriarchs (Rav Sherira Gaon claimed that the first synagogue in Babylonia was built in the sixth century B.C.E. from stones taken from the Temple, and Rav Amram Gaon explained that the prayers had originated in biblical times, had been forgotten, and had then been recovered by the talmudic rabbis), we can be certain that these prayers and the prayer services were standardized in Babylonia.[19]

A key factor in the development of Jewish prayer was the destruction of the Temple in 70. When sacrifices could no longer be brought to the Temple, prayer gradually emerged as a substitute for sacrifice. Certain biblical passages were retained, particularly the Shema (Hear, O Israel—Deuteronomy 6:4) and two other passages that accompanied it. Other prayers were composed, most significantly the Avodah. The Avodah is also known as the Amidah (which refers to the requirement that it be said while standing) or the Shemoneh Esreh, which means "eighteen" and refers to the eighteen blessings of which it was originally comprised.

The Avodah was viewed as the substitute for the sacrifice, so that on the Sabbath or on holidays, when additional sacrifices used to be offered, the Avodah is recited an additional time, with variations appropriate to the occasion. The reading of passages from the Torah that had been a feature of pre-destruction synagogue services was retained, and other prayers, like the Aleinu, were also added to the service.

As we have seen, Jewish tradition developed differently in the Babylonian and Palestinian centers. An important Palestinian development in the prayer service was the creation and use of *piyyutim*, poems based on and elaborating on already existing prayers. Although the rabbis tried to discourage the use of *piyyutim*, which they viewed as a distraction, we can still find many in modern prayer books, particularly for the holidays. Other differences between Babylonian and Palestinian rites can be seen in the prayer book of Saadiah Gaon, from the tenth century. Although Saadiah was a gaon in Babylonia, he was born in Egypt and had lived in Palestine, and his prayer book reflects some Palestinian customs as well as his concern with combating the threat of Karaism.[20]

While the prayer books of Rav Amram Gaon and of Saadiah Gaon helped to standardize prayer services, in an era before the printing press and when contact between various communities was limited, local customs frequently developed. Thus, within certain strict parameters—the absolute requirement that the Shema and the Avodah be recited, for instance—there were many local variations on the prayers. We can still see such variation today in synagogues around the world. (The same situation, incidentally, applied to Christianity, where local customs influenced the ways Mass was said and the holidays that were celebrated.)

When people pray, they seldom consider the origins of the prayers they are reciting, so Jewish worshipers might well be surprised at certain aspects of their prayers. For example, on Yom Kippur, the alphabetical acrostic *Ashamnu* ("We have sinned") is recited ten times. We should think such repetition is appropriate for the Day of Atonement, but we might also consider that those repetitions reflect the ten times that the High Priest asked for forgiveness by calling out the Divine Name on Yom Kippur in the Temple.[21] Or modern Jews who might think that *Kol nidre* is the quintessential Yom Kippur prayer should consider a letter written by Rav Natronai Gaon in the ninth century: "It is not customary in the academy nor anywhere to annul vows, neither on Rosh Hashanah nor on Yom Kippur. We have heard, however, that in other countries they say *Kol nidre*, but we have never heard or seen any record of it from our rabbis."[22] Other prayers in modern prayer books that people might think have been around forever also originated in the Middle Ages, or even later. *Adon olam* ("Master of the Universe") is possibly the work of Shlomo ibn Gabirol in the eleventh century; *Akdamuth* (which is recited on the holiday of Shavuoth) also dates from the eleventh century. The popular Passover songs *Echad mi yodayah* ("Who knows one") and *Had gadyah* ("One goat") first appear in the fifteenth and sixteenth centuries, while the Sabbath hymns *Lekhah dodi* ("Come, my beloved") and *Shalom aleichem* ("Peace be upon you") date from the sixteenth and seventeenth centuries.[23] As is so often the case, in both Jewish and non-Jewish matters, the Middle Ages was the time that gave birth to the modern world.

Two Twelfth-Century Developments: The Ḥasidei Ashkenaz and the Tosafists

For both European Judaism and European Christianity, the twelfth century was of enormous importance, as our references to the twelfth-century renaissance have indicated. Details about the Christian twelfth century (the arrival of Aristotelian works in Europe, the development of vernacular literature, the origins of modern notions about love) are available in a large variety of sources. Details about the Jewish twelfth century are harder to find. Two movements in particular will concern us in this section: the Ḥasidei Ashkenaz (the German Pietists) and the Tosafists.

Ivan Marcus points out that in the twelfth century, there were four types of sophisticated trends in Judaism: 1) the religious-philosophical; 2) the mystical; 3) the intellectualist-legal; and 4) the pietist.[24] The first two we will examine in a later chapter, but the third and fourth are represented by the Tosafists and the Ḥasidei Ashkenaz. The Ḥasidei Ashkenaz, who, as their name indicates, lived in Germany, may have developed as a reaction to the depredations of the Crusades in the very late-eleventh century. Our knowledge of the Ḥasidei Ashkenaz, as of so much else, is limited and subject to uncertainty and debate. Nevertheless, we are fortunate to have works written by the movement's leaders that help us to understand what the movement taught: "The central theological conception of the Pietists was that all of life is composed of suffering and trial, tribulations imposed by God so as continuously to test an individual's faithfulness."[25] The ultimate goal of life in this vale of tears they saw in otherworldly rewards, which would be achieved by rejecting worldly pleasures.[26] This belief sounds very much like the strict Christian belief, expressed by Saint Augustine and many others, that earthly life is a pilgrimage whose goal is heaven and that earthly pleasures distract us from that goal and threaten our eternal salvation. A major difference, of course, is that the Hasidei Ashkenaz were concerned not only with the general vicissitudes of life but focused specifically on Jewish suffering, which had been brought to the fore by the Crusades. Thus, Jacob Katz is certainly correct when he points to such Christian phenomena as the reform movement at Cluny and the development of the fraternal movement (the friars) as part of the general environment in which the Hasidei Ashkenaz operated, while Kenneth Stow is equally correct in pointing to the differences between the Franciscans, who often took extreme ascetic positions, and the Hasidei Ashkenaz, who were only mildly ascetic. What the Franciscans and Hasidei Ashkenaz shared was a desire for a separation between the two religions: the Franciscans persecuted the Jews, while the *Sefer Hasidim*, one of the major texts of the Pietists, urges that Jews have nothing to do with Christians.[27]

We know of three major figures among the Hasidei Ashkenaz: Rabbi Shmuel ben Qalonimos (Kalonymos), who was known as "the Pietist" and who lived in the mid-twelfth century; his son Rabbi Yehuda the Pietist, who died in 1217; and Rabbi Yehuda's relative, Rabbi Eliezer bar Yehudah of Worms, who modestly referred to himself as "the Insignificant" and who is also known as ha-Rokeah, the Perfumer.[28] While these three leaders agreed on the need for individuals to pursue personal otherworldly salvation, they disagreed about the social implications of their philosophy. The movement was rather short lived, though it made a deep impression on Judaism, and aspects of it have reappeared since the Middle Ages and exist today.

Interestingly, the Hasidei Ashkenaz opposed the method of the Tosafists and yet influenced some of the later Tosafists.[29] And who are the Tosafists? The answer begins with the history of the Talmud in medieval Europe and the role of Rashi at the end of the eleventh century. From the time of its final compilation, through the era of the Geonim and into the eleventh century, the status of the Talmud as central to Jewish life continued to grow. The Talmud was studied through the text itself and through oral commentaries that were handed down from one generation of scholars to the next. But there were also problems with Talmud study: as we saw earlier, the text of the Talmud is difficult to read and understand. Not only is the text extremely long, but it is written without punctuation or vowels, in Hebrew and Aramaic (languages that were no longer spoken by European Jews), its syntax is often confusing, and its logic is quite different from the logic to which we are accustomed. Consequently, the Talmud became increasingly difficult to study, until Rashi appeared. We will examine Rashi's career in the next chapter. Here we need only note that Rashi was, and remains to this day, the greatest Jewish commentator on the Tanakh. Just as important, however—or perhaps even more important—was his commentary on the Talmud, in which he explained the meanings of individual words and clarified the detailed and intricate arguments of the ancient sages. In his youth, Rashi studied in the famous schools of the Rhine Valley, and his commentaries preserve the traditions of those schools, traditions that might well have been lost after the massacres of the First Crusade, which occurred toward the end of Rashi's life. Rashi's commentaries brought new life to the study of the Talmud.

Rashi, who died in 1105, had many students, and though he had three daughters, he had no sons. According to the records we have, however, Rashi's daughters were learned, and two of them married great scholars. In the next generation, Rashi's grandchildren were also great scholars, who continued and furthered the work that Rashi had begun. They were the first of the Tosafists, and their work reflects developments in the Christian world as well. Rashi had clarified the talmudic text, had made it accessible. Now the Tosafists began to explore that text in even more detail. In doing so, they discovered logical inconsistencies and contradictions between authorities, problems that had largely been overlooked as the Talmud grew in status and importance. From a rationalist perspective, these inconsistencies and contradictions can be explained through an understanding of the way the Talmud was put together and by the fact that it represents more than five hundred years of discussions, but from a religious perspective, in which the Talmud represented the Oral Law transmitted by God to Moses on Mount. Sinai, those inconsistencies and contradictions had to be accounted for. Such was the work of the Tosafists.

It is important here to clarify some terms. When the Mishnah was compiled, numerous quotations from rabbinic authorities were omitted. They were later collected and given the title of the *Tosefta*. The *Tosefta* has nothing to do with the Tosafot. The Tosafot are dialectical discussions of talmudic passages written in the twelfth century and later. The authors of the Tosafot are the Tosafists. However, both "Tosefta" and "Tosafot" come from the same root, which means "addition."

Actually, the Tosafists represented a return to the origins of the Talmud. As we saw, the Talmud began as an argumentative text, but as it gradually became authoritative, the geonim and others used it as a guide to practical matters. The Tosafists returned to the original dialectical methodology that created the Talmud in the first place. When Tosafists analyze a talmudic passage, they use the same techniques that the sages of the Gemara used to analyze the Mishnah. Among the functions of the Tosafists are raising questions, arguing with other commentaries, deciding on correct readings (especially important in a manuscript culture), and deriving new understandings of the rules of Judaism.[30] They always begin with the assumption that what the Gemara says is correct and that the inconsistencies and contradictions are therefore only superficial and can be explained away.

Although the Tosafist commentaries appear in every standard edition of the Talmud, they have not been translated into English. Because they are written in Aramaic (a sign of how well their authors knew the Talmud), they are quite difficult to read. Furthermore, relatively little work has been done on them in English. The most important work about them, by E. E. Urbach, has also not been translated. Nevertheless, their importance, both for medieval Judaism and for the modern study of the Talmud, should not be underestimated. One of the most important aspects of the Tosafists is that their method is similar to the methods used by contemporary Christians, under the influence of the twelfth-century study of Aristotle's works in Europe, to study their own tradition. We can see here how intertwined Jews and Christians actually were at the time, for Jews played a major role in bringing those Aristotelian works from Muslim Spain into Christian Europe. The work of the Tosafists resembles, for instance, the work of Peter Abelard in the twelfth century. Abelard's *Sic et Non* examines the words of the Church Fathers and finds inconsistencies and contradictions in them; but Abelard's goal is not to discredit the Church Fathers. Like the Tosafists, he seeks to reconcile those inconsistencies and contradictions by finding logical explanations for them. Most assuredly, the Tosafists did not read Abelard or the other Scholastic philosophers, nor did Abelard read the Tosafists, but they all showed an interest in the new science of dialectic.[31]

Listing some of the most important Tosafists can be confusing because of the Hebrew style of abbreviating their names, which relies on the use of acronyms. Thus Rashi's name, as we saw earlier, was <u>R</u>abbi Solomon (<u>Sh</u>lomo, in Hebrew) son of <u>I</u>saac. Among the most famous of the Tosafists were his daughter Miriam's husband Yehuda ben Natan (Rivan), his daughter Jochebed's husband Rabbi Meir ben Shmuel, their sons Rabbeinu Shmuel (Rashbam), Rabbeinu Ya'akov (Rabbeinu Tam),

Rabbeinu Yitzḥak (Rivam), and other scholars like Rabbi Moshe of Coucy and Rabbi Yechiel of Paris. These scholars formed a potent force in Judaism in the twelfth and thirteenth centuries and helped to determine the course that Talmud study, and therefore Judaism itself, would take in subsequent centuries. At the same time, in Spain other developments were taking place, as we will see when we examine the career of Maimonides in a later chapter, though eventually the method of the Tosafists would come to influence Spanish Jewish study as well.

The Tosafists and the Ḥasidei Ashkenaz, then, represented different responses to the pressures of the twelfth century. The Tosafists relied for their world view on the analysis of texts, while the Ḥasidei Ashkenaz relied on custom for theirs.[32] Nevertheless, the Tosafists were pious, while the Ḥasidei Ashkenaz were learned. They signify not opposing but complementary points of view, both rooted in Jewish tradition and both with modern-day resonances.

Jewish Self-Government and Responsa

It may come as a surprise to realize how much control Jews had over their own lives during much of the Middle Ages. Of course they were always subject to their rulers, both Christian and Muslim. Those rulers, as we have seen, often took action against the Jews, and their subjects often took actions that even the rulers could not control; but generally, Jews were allowed to control their own affairs. One reason for this situation was that Jews simply did not fit into any of the normal feudal classes, and it was just easier to allow them a certain amount of self-government, with at least one major stipulation: the government told the Jewish communities how much it demanded in taxes, and the communities had to determine how they would raise the money.[33] Inevitably, such policies led to disputes among people who thought they were being taxed unfairly. It is true that the governments' demands were often outrageous, but almost no one in history has ever felt that taxes were fair.

Irving Agus has listed twelve functions that were performed by Jewish community governments:

1. Allowing or denying people permission to settle in the community
2. Taxation
3. Overseeing real estate transactions
4. Overseeing business practices
5. Enforcing order

  6. Regulating marriages and divorces
  7. Dealing with civil authorities
  8. Establishing courts
  9. Recovering lost property
  10. Looking after religious needs, like the maintenance of synagogues or the hiring of cantors
  11. Collecting and distributing charity
  12. Looking after orphans[34]

Obviously, these functions were essential for the community, but they could also be dangerous. Dealing with the civil authorities almost always involved risks, particularly if those authorities were bringing accusations against members of the community. But allowing strangers to settle in the community could be fraught with risks. As we have seen, Jews were occasionally compelled to undergo forced baptism, or felt that they had to be baptized in order to avoid death. Such people might flee their homes and seek to resettle elsewhere, resuming their lives as Jews; but doing so was often regarded as a capital crime, and allowing them to do so also involved severe penalties. Thus, the leaders of the Jewish communities operated under tremendous pressures. Their decisions could easily bring disaster to their communities, and the possibility also existed that giving people so much power over a community's activities could lead to abuses of that power.

Interestingly, the community leaders were often scholars, who had a thorough knowledge of Jewish laws. One such leader was Rabbi Meir of Rothenburg (1215–1293). Rabbi Meir was never elected or appointed to office. As the greatest scholar of his area, he was simply acknowledged as the leader.[35] Among Rabbi Meir's great accomplishments was the composition of hundreds of responsa. Rashi, too, wrote many responsa, but over ninety percent of Rashi's responsa deal with questions about ritual, with most of the others focusing on civil cases. More than a century later, most of Rabbi Meir's responsa concern civil cases, such as questions about marriage, community affairs, or business.[36]

Several examples will illustrate the kinds of concerns people had. There is a law that states that one who bakes bread should take a small portion of dough, called ḥallah (not to be confused with a loaf of twisted bread used today on the Sabbath), and throw it into the fire as a reminder of one of the ancient sacrifices. Rabbi Meir was asked whether one who bakes bread that is to be used to fatten geese should also take ḥallah. The question may seem silly to us, but to a society that wanted to operate according to their perception of divine commandments, it was not silly at all. Rabbi Meir's response was that talmudic authorities differ on the matter and therefore the solution would be to intend to eat some of the bread oneself, thereby necessitating the need to take ḥallah. In other words, change the situation from one in which there is doubt to one in which there is certainty. The second example might strike us as having more serious consequences. Someone informed Rabbi Meir that some Jews took an oath not to clip coins, but they made mental reservations about their oath and therefore felt justified in continuing their illegal activity. Rabbi Meir condemned them in the strongest terms, declaring that not only is stealing from Gentiles a clear crime, but it can have severe repercussions on the Jewish community.[37] Rabbi Meir does not tolerate hiding behind the technicalities of Jewish law in order to undermine or circumvent secular law.

The responsa literature, then, illustrates the kinds of questions that arose in everyday life, and it also illustrates the thought processes of the rabbis. For instance, Rabbi Nissim Girondi (fourteenth century) was asked about a man who marries in France, where polygamy was forbidden, and then moves to Spain, where it was allowed. Can that man take another wife? Rabbi Nissim's response is that the Talmud says that a person who moves must observe the law of the place where he came from and also the law of the place where he moves, though those laws may come into conflict. But, he says, if the first wife consents, then the man may take another wife, since the ban on polygamy was instituted for the woman's benefit and protection. But then he reconsiders: What if the ban was actually for the man's benefit? Then the ban cannot be lifted, so his final answer is that the man cannot take an additional wife.[38] We get not only Rabbi Nissim's answer but the reasoning behind the answer.

Responsa literature also shows us the hardships with which people struggled. Many questions are asked about kidnapping, indicating that this crime must have been fairly common, and there are a large number of questions concerning Jews who converted to other religions, whether through choice, intimidation, or physical force. How should such people be treated? What should be done if they want to rejoin the Jewish community? Rabbi Yitzhak ben Sheshet Perfet was asked about a couple who had been divorced: the husband, the wife, and the witnesses to the divorce were all forced converts. They have now moved to a new place and want to resume their lives as Jews. Are the witnesses acceptable—do they fulfill the requirements of Jewish law?—and is the couple therefore legally divorced? Rabbi Yitzhak's answer is affirmative, because, he reasons, people who have been forced to convert are still Jews.[39] In this example, and in hundreds of others, we can begin to sense the upheaval and confusion that outside pressures brought to Jewish communities.

The Messiah and the World to Come

As the above examples indicate, most Jewish concern focused on interpretations of the laws. We find many hypothetical situations in responsa literature, but even those situations revolve around the laws: what would one do in such-and-such a case? But Jews were also concerned about more metaphysical issues, such as questions about life after death. Menachem Kellner says:

> Classical Judaism ... includes the clear assumption that some of us, at least, will survive our deaths in one form or another and that after we die the righteous are in some way rewarded and the wicked in some way punished. Beyond that, there is very little agreement in Jewish tradition about how the world to come is constituted or what happens there.[40]

In the Middle Ages, this situation underwent a change, often in conjunction with historical developments. In the tenth century, Saadiah Gaon writes that the "righteous servant of God ... loves the life of this world merely because it serves as a stepladder by means of which he reaches and ascends to the next world, not for its own sake" (387), a fine Neoplatonic sentiment, but elsewhere he refuses to describe specific rewards and punishments in the hereafter, for they have "not been defined by God in this world of ours" (354). This lack of definition contrasts with Deuteronomy 11:13–21, part of the daily recitation of the Shema, that describes reward and punishment in terms of earthly matters: if the people are good, the rain will fall, and the consequences will be good; if they are wicked, the rain will not fall, and the consequences will be bad. As Shepkaru says, the world-to-come (in Hebrew, *olam ha-ba*) in earlier writing refers to an earthly realm with eschatological overtones; and in an early midrash on the story of the rabbis who were martyred by the Romans, there is no real mention of heavenly rewards for those revered martyrs. After the Crusades, however, a major change occurred, as the world-to-come increasingly came to be depicted, perhaps on the basis of the Christian model, as a heavenly dwelling place.[41]

Nevertheless, the concept of postmortem reward and punishment was never as well developed in Judaism as it became in Christianity, where it reached its incredible climax in the work of Dante. S. D. Goitein offers a good summary of the Jewish position when he notes that Jews shared a general belief that human behavior was either rewarded or punished but that Jews seem to have followed the talmudic advice not to speculate on how. The world to come could be good or it could involve the disappearance of the soul. There was little speculation on Gehinnom (or Gehenna, a Jewish term for a place of punishment) or on the tortures endured there because, as Goitein says, "Life on earth was hell enough."[42]

But another subject that did prompt speculation was the messiah, for obvious reasons: Christians believed that the messiah had come, and Jews did not. Messianic speculation constituted a major source of contestation between the two religions, as both tried to prove that they were right. Jews did so in large part by emphasizing that the messiah was yet to come and by describing what he would accomplish. Thus, many elements in the prayers that Jews recited at least three times a day (the end of oppression, the return of the Jews to Israel, the rebuilding of the Temple, and the establishment of an age of peace) became associated with the messianic era.[43] Some writers also thought that the coming of the messiah would herald the general resurrection of the dead.

While Jews always hoped for the coming of the messiah, that hope varied in intensity depending on outside events. In times of peace and relative security, it was not felt as strongly as during times of stress, a phenomenon we can see as well in the Christian expectation of the second coming, but it was always there. In the works of Avraham ibn Daud, Gerson Cohen finds a belief that the coming of the messiah was imminent and that it would take place in Spain.[44] Goitein argues that at the end of the "Golden Age" in Spain in the mid-twelfth century, the coming of the messiah "assumed an aura of urgency, as if redemption were around the corner, as if one had to do something to hasten its realization."[45] This feeling may help to explain why the poet and philosopher Yehuda Halevi decided to leave Spain and travel to Jerusalem, where, as he says in his poetry, the windows of heaven are more accessible.

Of course, messianic speculation, while it can be invigorating, also has a negative side, for when one's highest expectations remain unfulfilled, despair can easily follow. We can see this dichotomy in a sermon written by Shem Tov ibn Shem Tov in Spain in the 1480's, shortly before the expulsion:

> There are three modes of salvation that we anticipate; they are the foundation of our faith and the essential meaning of our Torah. The first

is physical: the coming of our Messiah. The second is spiritual: the life of the world to come. The third is a composite of both: the time of the resurrection.[46]

In these words we see the hope, but then Shem Tov goes on to say that the time of the coming of the messiah cannot be revealed, because if people realized that it would not be in their lifetimes, they might not remain Jewish. There are, then, high expectations, but the realization of these expectations must be indefinitely postponed. In the meantime, the people should continue to live their lives as Jews. It is almost as if this aspect of Jewish life followed the teaching of the talmudic rabbi Yohanan ben Zakkai, who is quoted in *The Fathers According to Rabbi Nathan* as saying that one who is planting a tree and hears that the messiah has come should finish planting the tree and then go to greet the messiah. We can see several points in this story. First, we should be wary of those who announce that the messiah has arrived. Rather, we should carry out our earthly duties and then go to investigate. Second, the arrival of the messiah will not be the kind of cataclysmic event that people think it will be. And third, the kingdom of the messiah will be an earthly kingdom.

Jewish Women

Much of the material that we have examined so far has related to the Jewish people as a whole, but much has also related more to men than to women. The reasons, naturally, are not hard to find: patriarchy and a shortage of writing by women themselves. Certainly women shared the lives of the men, but they also had other concerns peculiar to themselves, though those concerns also affected men. While Avraham Grossman is correct in saying that we have no written works by medieval Jewish women, we do have records that help us to understand women's lives to some extent; there are documents either written by or dictated by women in the Geniza records, and there are responsa questions both from and about women. Furthermore, two recent books have appeared in English that examine the lives of medieval Jewish women, one by Avraham Grossman himself, *Pious and Rebellious,* and one by Elisheva Baumgarten, *Mothers and Children.*[47]

As with so many topics in Judaism, the role of women should be examined first through the lenses of the Bible and the Talmud, which played a role in so much that came later. While there are many important women in the Tanakh (Sarah, Rebecca, Rachel, Leah, Miriam, Deborah, Esther), women are only mentioned when they play a significant role. We read the names of many sons, but of very few daughters. In Proverbs, we find warnings against women (Knowledge "will save you from the forbidden woman, From the alien woman whose talk is smooth"—2:16), but also words of praise ("What a rare find is a capable wife! Her worth is far beyond that of rubies. Her husband puts his confidence in her, And lacks no good thing"—31:10–11. This passage goes on in this way for another twenty verses; and though it begins by describing how rare such a wife is, traditionally on Friday evenings, at the beginning of the Sabbath, a husband sings this to his wife, indicating that she is indeed such a paragon.) The Talmud, too, presents, a confusing picture. In thousands of pages, the words of hundreds of sages are likely to show conflicts over attitudes towards women. For instance, in talmudic discussions, women are often classed with servants and minors ("Women, slaves, and minors are exempt from reciting the Shema"— Berakhot 20a.) Such language, clearly demeaning, shows that women were regarded as lesser than men. Of course, one would be hard put to find a society in talmudic times where women were not so regarded. At the same time, elsewhere we find a different attitude ("A man must love his wife like his own body and honor her more than his body"— Yebamot 62b).[48]

How did these attitudes affect medieval women? The important answer to this question is that there is not a single answer to the question. In different times and different places, both men and women adopted different approaches to questions involving gender, though some things remained constant. For example, during the Middle Ages (and in some places until relatively recently), wife beating was commonly regarded as an acceptable practice. There were rules governing it (how thick a stick a man could use to discipline his wife, for instance), but the act itself was not condemned. Rabbis, however, consistently condemned such behavior. We know from the responsa literature that there were indeed abusive husbands among the Jews, but Rabbi Meir of Rothenburg's comment on such men is typical:

A man must honor his wife more than he honors himself. If one strikes one's wife, one should be punished more severely than for striking another person.... If he persists in striking her, he should be excommunicated, lashed, and suffer the severest punishments, even to the extent of amputating his arm.[49]

So heinous is such behavior that the abusive husband should be cut off from his Judaism.

But women's lives were certainly not easy. Baumgarten cites a mishnaic passage that names laxity in three areas as the cause for death in childbirth, which was a common phenomenon. Those three areas are taking *hallah*, lighting the Sabbath candles, and *niddah*.[50] *Niddah* refers to the whole complex of regulations concerning menstruation. According to biblical and talmudic law, a menstruating woman is ritually unclean. During the time of her period and for many days after, she is not to come in contact with ritual objects or with her husband. Men, too, are not allowed to touch women at that time, but since men cannot tell when a woman is menstruating (and since it is impolite to ask), men are forbidden to touch any woman but their wives. Grossman argues throughout his study that the emphasis on menstrual separation became more stringent throughout the Middle Ages. We know that at the beginning of the era, men and women sat together in the synagogue and that separate seating was not fully established until the late-twelfth or early-thirteenth century.[51] Even after separate seating became the norm, women joined men in the male section of the synagogue for circumcision celebrations. A student of Rabbi Meir of Rothenburg, Samson ben Tzadok followed his teacher in opposing such customs, lest mixed seating lead to sinful thoughts.[52]

That notion of sinful thoughts played a large role in gender relations. In the *Sefer Hasidim,* a major work of the *Hasidei Ashkenaz,* we find that an unmarried man should not teach unmarried girls even if their father is present, "For even this will not avail if the teacher's sexual desire overcomes him or her desire is too much for her." And Maimonides says that a Jewish man must send away a female slave rather than remaining alone with her, because "it is the Torah's intent to curb our natural instincts."[53] Women, then, represented a temptation to men, but sex in itself was not regarded negatively. Not only was it not a sign of mankind's fallen nature, as it was often presented in the Christian tradition, but the command to be fruitful and multiply was celebrated as the very first commandment in the Torah. According to Rabbi Avraham ben David, "Appropriately directed sexuality, as the halakha says, leads to personal sanctity, or holiness."[54] Illicit sex could certainly be a temptation, but when sex was approached with the proper intentions and the proper attitude, it would also be a means to holiness.

All of these factors played a role in determining women's relations to religious rituals. In the Talmud, Rabbi Eliezer says, "Whoever teaches his daughter Torah, it is as though he teaches her lewdness" (Sotah 21a), and elsewhere we learn that "All affirmative precepts limited to time, men are liable and women are exempt" (Qiddushim 29a). The first passage came to be regarded as a prohibition against teaching girls, though there were many exceptions, including Rashi's daughters. This prohibition removed women from the activity that was considered central to Jewish life, Torah study. The second passage recognized a reality of women's lives, that if they were responsible for caring for children and running the household, they could not neglect those responsibilities in order to say prayers or undertake other ritual obligations at the required times. Idealistically it recognized the equality of men's and women's spheres of activity, but the practical outcome was that women's activities came to be devalued; because they were caring for children, they could not perform the rituals that were so important to the men.

There are other possible explanations for this division. Some say that women have an internal clock that controls the menstrual cycle and therefore have no need to be subject to time-bound rituals. Others say that the rituals are meant to tame our less-civilized tendencies and that men need such taming more than women do. Even if these explanations are accepted, however, women's exclusion from the rituals was regarded as a handicap. As Grossman notes, that exclusion damaged both their public image and their self-image.[55]

In the eleventh century, women began to take a greater part in religious life in some areas, probably because they demanded that right and the rabbis either could not or would not stop them. In the thirteenth century, possibly as a result of the pressure of increasing persecution of the Jews, restrictions were reinstated because it seemed to the authorities that the Jews were receiving divine punishment for their laxity. As Baumgarten notes, before the thirteenth century, young boys were allowed to fulfill a number of commandments, such as wearing tefillin (phylacteries), but in the thirteenth century, they were forced to wait until their thirteenth birthdays. Similarly, women's roles in ritual were reduced. Although Baumgarten points out similar changes in Christian society, those occurred because of conditions that were specific to Christian society.[56]

Despite the stricture of Rabbi Eliezer against teaching girls Torah, we have clear evidence that many Jewish women were literate. Both Grossman and Goitein offer much evidence that when Jewish merchants were traveling, often for long periods, their wives ran both the households and the businesses. At the same time, most women were not learned in the way men were, though exceptions existed: the daughter of Samuel ben Ali of Baghdad was learned enough to teach Tanakh and Talmud to males, though she had to do so from behind a window so that her pupils could not see her.[57] Typically a girl's education included basic religious training, for girls had to know the laws of kashruth, of holiday observance, and of their other domestic responsibilities, but clearly many women went beyond such rudimentary learning. Many could apparently read Hebrew prayers, even if they were not fluent in Hebrew.[58]

The daughters of Rashi, who were also the wives and mothers of scholars, were reputed to be well educated, and Rashi himself, throughout his commentaries, shows tremendous respect for women, while Maimonides took a much harsher stance toward women, arguing that a woman should only be allowed to leave her house a few times each month.[59] Although we know that women functioned as elementary teachers and in other professions, Maimonides, as a good Aristotelian, believed that women were not capable of learning. Women represented matter, while men represented form, which gives shape to matter. Theoretically, therefore, women could not undertake such male activities as learning, the fact that they actually did so notwithstanding. Perhaps, as Grossman argues, the role of women in Jewish communities reflected their roles in the larger communities around them, so that Rashi's attitude reflects attitudes in Ashkenaz, and Maimonides' attitude reflects those in the Islamic world.

Nevertheless, both communities extended special protections to women. We have already seen Jewish attitudes toward abuse, but there were other protections as well. In recent years, pre-nuptial agreements have become somewhat popular, but in Judaism, a major part of the marriage ceremony is the signing of the *ketuvah*, the marriage contract, which is essentially a prenuptial agreement. One of the most important parts of the *ketuvah* guarantees that the wife will receive a settlement in case of divorce. Beautifully decorated *ketuvoth* have again become an essential element at Jewish weddings, but the English "translations" of the Aramaic formulaic text are usually not translations at all, because the text is largely a legal contract. Instead, the "translations" present poetic passages about love and commitment, which are very nice but which have little to do with what the contract actually says. It may seem odd, if not utterly unromantic, to make plans for a divorce at a wedding, but without such plans, women would have been at an even greater disadvantage, for they would have lacked all resources if a divorce became necessary. Such provisions may not have been necessary in Christian society, where divorce was supposed to be rare; but in Jewish society, where there were any number of grounds for divorce, it was not uncommon. Maimonides ruled that a woman was entitled to a divorce (a *get* in Hebrew) if she found her husband disgusting, though other authorities disagreed with his ruling.[60]

Another problem arose concerning merchants, who were often away from home for years at a time. Occasionally such merchants, who had wives at home, would marry again in some distant foreign land, thereby creating problems for both wives (not to mention for themselves). Rabbinical authorities took steps to stop such practices or at least to make it possible for one of the wives to be released from the marriage. On the other hand, Goitein prints a letter written by a merchant to his wife that found its way into the Geniza:

> I swear by God, I do not believe that the heart of anyone traveling away from his wife has remained like mine, all the time and during all the years—from the moment of our separation to the very hour of writing this letter—so constantly thinking of you and yearning after you ...[61]

Students of medieval literature are accustomed to such professions of love, but they always typify the upper classes, who are, according to the conventions of the literature, blessed with the sensibility to appreciate the meaning of love. This letter, however, and others like it, indicate that ordinary people also experienced the deepest feelings of love.

One provision of marriage was that, even if a marriage was arranged, the bride had to approve of the groom. We can imagine that such approval might have been coerced by overbearing parents, especially since, under worsening social conditions, Jews tended to arrange marriages for their daughters at younger ages. Typically, girls were married at between twelve and sixteen years of age.[62] Nevertheless, it is obvious that even if a couple were not in love at the time of the marriage, love often developed after the ceremony. And if it did not, divorce was an option. It is hard to imagine that their system worked much worse than ours.

In addition to being wives, with all the work that that position required—cooking, sewing, raising children, and numerous other duties, including supervising servants—many women also had occupations. Some, of course, worked with their husbands in the family businesses. Geniza records indicate that women "provide medical services for other women while others specialized in wholesale dealing, in the sale of flour, in the teaching of embroidery, in book sales, or in the making of perfumes."[63] Women could also be copyists (another sign of literacy) and, surprisingly perhaps, could serve as circumcisers.[64] Two major occupations for women that are noted on surviving tombstones are midwife and prayer leader.[65] What was a prayer leader? When women occupied a different section of the synagogue than men, the prayer leader led the service in the women's section, a position of responsibility and honor.

There was yet another role played by Jewish women that we dare not forget: martyr. Our records, both chronicles and poems, contain the stories of many married and pregnant martyrs. Susan Einbinder argues that those portraits of female martyrs make a statement about the ideal Jewish woman, who had children and a full family life, as opposed to Christian saints, who are so often famed for both their chastity and their martyrdom.[66] The persecutors of the Jews showed no gallantry toward Jewish women. As the Crusade chronicles and numerous other texts demonstrate, Jewish women were in the forefront of standing up for their religion.

But we should conclude this very brief look at the roles of women in medieval Jewish life on a more positive note by recalling a peculiar Jewish custom regarding naming. Most of the men whom we have encountered so far have had biblical names—Avraham, Yitzhak, Ya'akov, Moshe, David. For men, the Tanakh was the most common source of names. For women, however, names were chosen from the local cultures. In twelfth-century Ashkenaz, for example, we find Jewish women bearing the names of romance heroines. We may not have a clear explanation for this custom, but it does indicate that Jews were indeed integrated into their surrounding cultures to some degree. And it may be further proof, as Baumgarten argues, that women, because of their household responsibilities, because they had to go to marketplaces and to tradesmen, had closer ties to those cultures than did many men.[67]

Photo Essay

Page from a modern printed edition of *Mikraoth Gedo-loth* showing two verses (Exodus 20:8–9, and two words from v.10) as well as the commentaries of Rashi (upper right), Ibn Ezra (upper left), and Nachmanides (lower two-thirds), the Aramaic translation, and the commentary of the sixteenth-century scholar Rabbi Ovadiah Sforno. (Courtesy

Page from an Italian Manuscript Bible (c. 1300), including not only vowels and end stops for each verse, but also indications for how the text should be chanted and references to related biblical verses.

Two pages from a Talmud volume (tractate Avodah Zara) written in 1290. (Courtesy of The Library of The Jewish Theological Seminary)

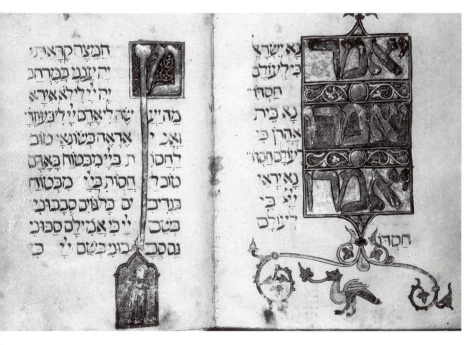

Like their Christian counterparts, Jewish scribes liked to decorate their manuscripts in a variety of ways, as seen in these pages from a fourteenth-century Catalonian Haggadah, the text of the Passover seder. (© British Library Board. All rights reserved Or. 2884 PL07119)

First page of the book of Job in a German manuscript from about 1300 showing the popular Jewish technique of micrography: the design at the top of the page consists entirely of tiny Hebrew writing. (Courtesy of The Library

Page from a modern printed Talmud (*Berakhot* 15a) showing the text of the Mishnah and Gemara in dark print in the middle surrounded by commentary. (Courtesy of The Library of The Jewish Theological

Letter sent by Moshe Maimonides in 1170, with Maimonides' name visible in the last line. (Courtesy of The Library of The Jewish Theological Seminary)

Petition from Rabbinites to a Karaite leader, written in Tripoli in the early eleventh century. (Courtesy of The Library of The Jewish Theological Seminary)

First page of Shlomo ibn Gabirol's long poem, *Keter Malkhut, The Kingly Crown*, in the Rothschild Mahzor, copied in Florence in 1492. (Courtesy of The Library

First page of *Pirke Avot, Chapters of the Fathers*, in the Rothschild Mahzor, copied in Florence in 1492. In accordance with the opening verse, we see Moses receiving the Ten Commandments on Mount Sinai. (Courtesy of

אשׁרי

הֹצדִק יְהוּדִים

עים'	כְּנְטֹי	בּ נם מְגדְלים	
עים'	מֵשׁ	ג וֹע תפֹאְרֹת	
עים'	דֹרֹד	ד בְקים חֲשׁוּקים	
עים'	וְנִשְׁמֹי	ה גוֹרֹם חֹגוֹנֹם	
עים'	מֵשֹׁב	ו תֹיּכֹם נְבֹחֹרֹם	
עים'	נִיד	ז רֹעֹם בֹמֹרֹם	
עים'		ח מוֹרֹם וֹבְמֹעֲשֹׁיּהֹם בּ	

(above left) Alphabetical acrostic and a collection of dragons from an early four-teenth-century German prayer book. (Courtesy of The Library of The Jewish Theological Seminary)

(above right) David, the "sweet singer of Israel," playing a medieval harp in a thir-teenth-century French Hebrew illumination. (© British Library Board. All rights reserved Add. 11639 PL07119)

Havdalah, the ceremony marking the end of a holiday, being recited by a father holding a cup of wine while the child holds the traditional braided candle. (© British Library Board. All rights reserved Add. 14761 PL07119)

(above) School scene showing a talmudic rabbi in the setting of a medieval school, with the two tablets of the Ten Commandments at the top. (© British Library Board. All rights reserved. Or. 2737 PL07119)

(facing page top) Prayers being recited in a synagogue in a scene from a fourteenth-century Catalonian manuscript. (© All rights reserved British Library Board Or. 2884 PL07119)

(facing page bottom) Late twelfth-century French illumination showing Aaron, the brother of Moses and the first high priest, adding oil to the menorah, in accordance with the commandments in Leviticus 24:1–4. (© British Library Board. All rights reserved Add. 11639 PL07119)

מעל הבית וגם בתוכו שעומדים בתוכה

Matzot, sheets of unleavened bread, being distributed for Passover in an early fourteenth-century Catalonian illumination. (© British Library Board. All rights reserved Add. 27210 PL07119)

Depiction of women playing a variety of medieval instruments from a fourteenth-century Haggadah representing the Song of Miriam after the crossing of the Red Sea. (© British Library Board. All rights reserved Add. 27210 PL07119)

Solomon, in the costume of a medieval monarch, judging the case of two women who claim to be the mother of the child on the right in a late twelfth-century French illumination. (© British Library Board. All rights reserved Add. 11639 PL07119)

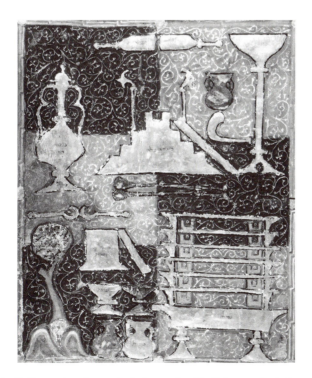

Reflecting both the past and messianic hopes for the future, a depiction of utensils that were used in the Temple and that will be used again when the Temple is rebuilt. (© British Library Board. All rights reserved Harley 1528 PL07119)

The Romanesque synagogue in the German city of Worms, in a photograph taken before the synagogue was destroyed in 1938 (and rebuilt in 1961). (Courtesy of The Library of The Jewish Theological Seminary)

Early photograph of the Altneuschul (the old-new Synagogue) in Prague, originally completed in 1275. (Courtesy of The Library of The Jewish Theological Seminary)

PART III

THE JEWISH CULTURAL LEGACY

Commentaries

We can see from the preceding pages that Jewish life in the Middle Ages was highly complex, as indeed life always is. The point is worth noting, however, because of the tendency in writers since the Middle Ages to focus on the negative, on the lachrymose aspects of Jewish experience. Undoubtedly, life during the Middle Ages was difficult for everyone, with no central heating or modern plumbing systems, with high rates of infant mortality and short life expectancies, with frequent famines and primitive medical facilities. Of course, for medieval people, these conditions seemed normal, since they lacked our experience with modern developments. If we were to go back to the Middle Ages, we would feel more deprived than actual medieval people felt.

Still, for medieval Jews, life was even more difficult, for they lived with persecutions and restrictions that we would find intolerable. But focusing on those persecutions and restrictions shortchanges medieval Jewry, for it takes the focus away from their many accomplishments. We have already considered some of those accomplishments in fields such as prayer and talmudic studies. The remainder of this study will look at other fields, at biblical commentary, at poetry, at philosophy, and at mysticism.

One area that will not receive much written comment but that is represented in the illustrations involves the visual arts. Jewish culture is often closely associated with writing. Mohammed referred to Jews as the people of the Book, and that designation continues to be influential, though music and art have both been important facets of Jewish culture. But the visual arts have suffered, particularly from ideas about the

Second Commandment, which declares, "You shall not make for yourself a sculptured image, or any likeness of what is in the heavens above, or on the earth below, or in the waters under the earth" (Exodus 20:4). This commandment is often understood as a prohibition against any kind of representational art. Thus, most synagogues, even today, have a minimal number of images in their decorative schemes. But a minimal number is not the same as none. Not only do synagogues generally have a representation of the tablets of the Ten Commandments, but Torah decorations invariably show the lion of Judah, which certainly constitutes an image of something that is "in the earth." When we look at medieval Hebrew manuscripts, we find pictures of birds and animals, of everyday objects, and of human figures, sometimes contemporaries and sometimes representations of biblical characters. (In some manuscripts, the human figures are given the heads of birds, perhaps to try to comply with an interpretation of the Second Commandment.) These images help historians learn about everyday life for the Jews, what they wore, what implements they used, what things they valued. Even if the illuminations were created by non-Jews, they frequently adorn Hebrew manuscripts. To the extent that medieval art is representational, then, some of those representations illustrate aspects of Jewish life.

Were the Jews who made or used such pictures violating the Second Commandment? It is difficult to imagine that a people who valued the Torah so highly that they suffered martyrdom for it and who went to such pains to observe other teachings, like the Sabbath laws, would then blithely violate a prohibition on the making of images. We know that early synagogues, from the mishnaic period on, had elaborate mosaic floors depicting birds, animals, fruits, the signs of the zodiac, and even a figure representing the sun. In fact, as Kalman Bland argues, the Second Commandment was understood not as forbidding the making of images but as forbidding idolatry, which, to the Jewish mind, was the worship of images. Bland finds support for this position in such medieval luminaries as Maimonides, Ya'akov ben Reuben, Profiat Duran, and Meir of Rothenburg.[1] Rabbi Meir, for instance, was asked how prayer books could be decorated with pictures of animals and birds in seeming contravention of the Second Commandment. He responded that he disapproved of such decorations if they were distracting, but he saw no prohibition against the creation of such two-dimensional representations and he even asserted that the Talmud allowed the creation of three-dimensional figures.[2] Thus we have prayer books, haggadahs, and other kinds of books with both marginal illustrations and elaborate illuminations, as well as ritual objects that depict natural objects, animals, and people without violating the commandment. We can only imagine how much such material has been lost or destroyed over the centuries.

Jewish Commentators

As was virtually always the case for medieval Jews, their attitude toward pictorial art depended on their understanding of Torah, by which, of course, we mean both the Written and Oral Torahs. But a major problem involved the proper understanding of those difficult texts. Because neither Hebrew nor Aramaic was a spoken language for the vast majority of Jews, their sacred texts were not immediately accessible to them. The text of the Tanakh had been established by the Masoretes beginning in the seventh century, but that statement requires explanation. If we examine the biblical sections of the Dead Sea Scrolls, which were copied some two thousand years ago and which were unknown in the Middle Ages, and compare them to modern texts, we find that they are nearly identical, indicating that these sacred texts were transmitted with a remarkable degree of accuracy. But the Dead Sea Scrolls, like modern Torah scrolls, contain no punctuation, no capital letters (which do not exist in Hebrew), and, most strangely to readers of other languages, no vowels (which is how Hebrew is often written). The Masoretes, based on tradition (the word itself comes from the root that means "tradition"), but also using their own judgment, in effect "punctuated" the text. They did so by indicating where verses ended and by adding cantillation symbols. These symbols, on the most basic level, indicate how the text should be chanted, but in doing so, they also indicate where major and minor pauses occur in each verse, thus serving the same role as punctuation marks like commas and semicolons. In addition, the Masoretes decided on the correct vocalization of words, that is, the correct placement of vowels. To give an elementary example, the Hebrew letters transliterated as *shmrt* could read *shamarta*, "you observed," masculine, or *shamart*, "you observed," feminine. In such a case, the correct reading is easily determined by seeing whether "you" refers to a male or a female, but many cases are more difficult, and the work of the Masoretes was essential for the standardization and clarification of the biblical text.

But even with the work of the Masoretes, that text was difficult. Large sections of it had been interpreted in the Talmud and in the various midrashim, and there were numerous oral interpretations as well, but for a person who wanted to understand the text, many difficulties remained. And because passages from the Torah and the Prophets are read regularly in the synagogue service, many people sought that understanding, while a number of commentators tried to provide it. We will look very briefly at three of them, Rashi, Ramban, and Avraham ibn Ezra, as we compare their commentaries on the book of Genesis.

The most famous of all Jewish commentators is Rashi. Rashi was born around 1040 and died in the French city of Troyes in 1105, so he lived through the horror of the First Crusade, although he was not directly involved. He had, however, studied during his youth in the academies that had been established along the Rhine, in those cities that would later be attacked. In particular he studied at the school of Rabbi Gershom in Mainz, and when he returned to Troyes, he brought with him the traditions of his teachers. When those Rhenish Jewish communities were devastated by the crusaders, Rashi's commentaries preserved their traditions.[3]

The importance of Rashi's commentary can be illustrated in a number of ways. First, his commentary is still often printed with the biblical text and is consulted by readers who want to understand that text. Second, Rashi's commentary was the first Hebrew book that was printed after the invention of the printing press. Third, Rashi's commentary was frequently cited by other commentators. And finally, Rashi (and his parents) became the subject of legends shortly after his death. For instance, one story tells how his mother, pregnant with him, was passing through a narrow street when a runaway horse came charging towards her. In her attempt to avoid the horse, she pressed against the wall, which bent in and created a niche to protect her.[4] Such stories are told only about the greatest of heroes, and in Jewish culture, Rashi is such a hero.

Before we look at Rashi's biblical commentary, we should note that he also wrote an extensive commentary on most of the Talmud. If the biblical text was difficult to understand in his time, the Talmud was almost impossible. It was, as we saw, written in Aramaic, which was less familiar than Hebrew, it lacked punctuation and vocalization, and the talmudic style of argumentation is often difficult and verges on obscurity. Rashi's commentary on the Talmud made this text accessible to a wider audience and contributed greatly to the developing interest in the Talmud in the twelfth century. Like his biblical commentary, Rashi's Talmud commentary is still printed with the text and is always consulted by Talmud students. Both the Bible and the Talmud commentaries are remarkable works that demonstrate Rashi's encyclopedic memory for cross-references and for talmudic and midrashic allusions, as well as his brilliance in using those cross-references and allusions to solve problems in the text. For many Jewish scholars today, it might seem easy to take Rashi's commentaries for granted simply because they are always printed with the texts being commented on, but when we consider the scope of that work and the conditions in which it was created, we can begin to sense how extraordinary it actually is. We might also contrast Rashi's commentary, as well as those of the other commentators we will consider, with medieval Christian commentaries. Those commentaries, whether by Church Fathers like Augustine, Gregory, or Jerome or by later giants like Thomas Aquinas, are seldom consulted by modern readers. Seminary students will take a course or two in medieval exegesis, but those commentaries are not nearly so central to modern Christian thought as the medieval Jewish commentaries are to modern Jewish commentators. In modern synagogues and religious writings, Rashi's comments are still frequently cited, more than those of any other commentator.

Throughout his biblical commentary, Rashi insists that his fundamental purpose is to explain the simple, literal meaning of the text, what in Hebrew is known as the *p'shat* (as opposed to the more fanciful interpretations that fall into the category known as *d'rash*, from which is derived the term "midrash"). Thus, in his comment on Genesis 3:8, "They heard," Rashi says, "There are many Midrashic explanations and our Teachers have already collected them in their appropriate places in Bereshith Rabbah [the great midrashic collection on Genesis] and in other Midrashim. I, however, am only concerned with the plain sense of Scripture [*lip'shuto*, with its *p'shat*] and with such Agadoth [homilies] that explain the words of Scripture in a manner that fits in with them," and on 3:24 he notes, "There are Agadic Midrashim, but I come only to explain it according to its plain sense [*lip'shuto*]."

An example of this simple meaning involves the fruit that Adam and Eve ate, a fruit that is specifically not named in the biblical text. In the Midrash, as we saw, the rabbis made suggestions about the kind of fruit it was, even venturing that it was a grape or wheat, neither of which grow on trees. Clearly these are fanciful suggestions that are advanced in order to make a homiletic point. (The more familiar notion that the fruit was an apple depends probably on a pun in the Latin translation of the Bible, where the word *malum*, evil, is also the Latin word for apple.) Rashi simply comments on the fact that Adam and Eve hide their nakedness with fig leaves by saying that the fruit must have been a fig so that "by the very thing through which their ruin had been caused was some improvement effected," a notion that he derived from a talmudic discussion.

Rashi's focus on the simple meaning of the text leads him frequently to discuss various grammatical issues, an interest that he shares with ibn Ezra, Nachmanides, and most other commentators. While the Hebrew Bible had been studied continuously, Hebrew grammar was a relatively new field in Rashi's time. Dunash ben Labrat and Menachem ben Joseph ibn Saruq were important grammarians in tenth-century Spain, but in Rashi's time—and long after—there were still many uncertainties about Hebrew grammar and therefore about how to translate and understand many biblical passages. The very first word of Genesis provides an example. We are accustomed to having that word, B'reshith, translated as "In the beginning," but grammatically that translation is impossible. To say "In the beginning," Rashi points out, the Hebrew would have to be "B'rishonah." To translate the verse "in its plain sense," he says, "explain it thus: At the beginning of the Creation of heaven and earth when the earth was without form and void and there was darkness, God said, 'Let there be light.'" From this correct translation, Rashi draws the conclusion that the "text does not intend to point out the order of the *acts* of Creation." The text rather establishes the fact of divine creation.

Many of Rashi's grammatical discussions would be very difficult to explain to readers who have no familiarity with Hebrew, but because they are important, we will try. Thus, one relatively simple grammatical comment concerns Genesis 9:23, "But Shem and Japheth took." At first, the sentence in Hebrew looks to be grammatically incorrect, for it has a compound subject (Shem and Japheth) but a verb in the singular (*va-yikah*, and *he* took). The verb should be *va-yikhu*, and *they* took, but of course the biblical text is sacred and could not therefore contain an elementary grammatical error, so Rashi explains that the singular form of the verb is used to illustrate that Shem "devoted himself to this duty with more eagerness than Japheth." That is, the brothers both did their duty, but Shem took it more seriously. Therefore, Rashi concludes, the descendants of Shem, specifically the Jews, have received a greater reward than the descendants of Japheth, the Christians around him, the privilege of obeying the commandments, though Japheth's descendants have also received a reward. In such ways, with both insight and concision, Rashi explains almost every verse in the Tanakh.

Often, however, Rashi finds it difficult to explain a concept in his usual Hebrew, and so he turns to his everyday language, which we know as Old French. This technique has helped French scholars understand Old French pronunciation in Rashi's time, for Rashi transliterates those French words, presenting them in Hebrew characters and indicating how they were pronounced.

Although Rashi intended to explain the plain, literal meaning of the biblical text, and for the most part remained true to that intention, the word "literal" can be understood in different ways. Rashi often cites midrashic explanations that he felt were literal and that we find more fanciful (a sense shared by Nachmanides, as well). And Rashi was certainly not free of ideological constraints, for no one can be. As we saw in the example of Shem and Japheth, Rashi consistently sees the Tanakh as containing special messages for the Jewish people. His very first comment on Genesis, for example, points to such a message, for Rashi begins by asking why the Torah begins with the story of Creation and then moves on to the Patriarchs. After all, if the Torah is exclusively the book of commandments for the Jews, as some felt that it was, it should begin with Exodus 12:1–2, which is the first commandment given to the Jews as a people. Rashi's response is that the stories of Creation and the Patriarchs all help to establish Jewish ownership of the Promised Land, for it was given to them by God. This comment is particularly interesting when we consider how few Jews lived in Israel during Rashi's time. Most Jews lived in exile in Europe, Asia, and North Africa. Nevertheless, they continued to believe in the promise that eventually they would be able to return to their homeland. Furthermore, although the First Crusade had not yet begun when Rashi wrote this commentary, the crusading spirit had begun, and Rashi's comment says that while the Christians and the Muslims may fight over the holy land, ultimately it will belong to the Jews.[5] As we know, this particular conflict has yet to be settled.

But Michael Signer takes Rashi's comment even further, as he argues that it reveals "the connection between the people Israel and its God, and how this bond is reflected in the unfolding chapters of the book of Genesis. The proposal that the Torah begin with Exodus 12:2 would mean that God's revelation had been limited exclusively to Law and commandment."[6] For Rashi, the Torah represents not a collection of laws, however treasured those laws might be. That those laws are indeed treasured we can see in his comment on Ruth 1:16, where he says that "our people is divided from all other peoples by the six hundred thirteen commandments." Even so, the Torah represents primarily the relationship between God and Israel, a relationship that was to be tested toward the end of Rashi's life, as the First Crusade passed through the Rhineland and then massacred the Jews of Jerusalem, a relationship that was to be tested many times in the future. Rashi's commentary, by making the Torah, the rest of the Tanakh, and the Talmud more accessible to the Jewish people, was to be one instrument in the preservation of that relationship.

Rashi's ideological bent is evident elsewhere in his commentaries. Fortunately for him, he was never called on to engage in public disputations and he never overtly attacks Christian beliefs, but we can see that he was familiar with, and rejected, those beliefs. For instance, Genesis 1:26 reads, "Let us make man in our image." Rashi explains that God here addresses his heavenly council, but only as a courtesy, for God Himself created man, as 1:27 states: "So God created man in His image." Rashi derives from this passage the lesson that leaders should consult their subordinates, that such behavior is beneficial. On one level, Rashi's comment explains the literal meaning of the verse, particularly the troublesome pronoun "we." Who is "we"? For Rashi, it is the heavenly council, though nowhere have we seen the creation of such a council. But Rashi is doing more than simply positing a heavenly council or deriving an important rule of leadership. He is, in fact, responding to Christian readings of that passage, in which the "we" is understood to be the persons of the Trinity. Rashi's comment refutes that reading, not to the satisfaction of Christians, certainly, but to the satisfaction of Jews.

Similarly, Rashi's comment on Genesis 34:14 is revealing. In this passage, when Jacob's sons demand that their sister Dinah's attacker, Shechem, must be circumcised before he can wed her, they say, "We cannot … give our sister to a man who is uncircumcised, for that is a disgrace among us …" Rashi comments, "Amongst us it [lack of circumcision] is somewhat of a blot on our pedigree, for if one wishes to revile another, he says to him: 'You are an uncircumcised person,' or 'the son of an uncircumcised person.'" Just as Christians viewed circumcision as a blot (Othello, just before killing himself, tells how in a fight he killed a Muslim opponent whom he calls "a circumcised dog"), so Jews viewed the lack of circumcision as a blot. In this comment, which, of course, Rashi never expected Christians to see, he expresses that Jewish view.

Rashi's explanations are often very clever, and they always make an important point, as we can see in his comments on the story of Esau's selling his birthright to Jacob. This story was important to Jews because it explained how the younger son became dominant, a theme that appears frequently in the Tanakh. But it was also important to Christians, who often interpreted it as an example of Jewish perfidy, as Jacob, in their view, tricked Esau and, in effect, stole the birthright. (Other Christian commentators followed the example of Augustine who in *The City of God* [16:37] described Jacob as a type of Jesus.) These divergent interpretations, explosive in themselves, were made even more dangerous by the Jewish tradition of referring first to the Romans and later to the Christians as "Esau," thus giving the conflict between the two brothers a contemporary meaning. The story of the birthright is told in Genesis 25, where Jacob is cooking pottage when Esau appears, says he is famished to the point of fainting, and asks for some of the red pottage. According to Genesis, this request explains why Esau was also called Edom, which means "red." Jacob gives him some of the pottage, but only in return for the birthright, even though Esau claims to be "dying" of hunger.

Clearly Esau is not "dying" of hunger, but Jacob's behavior has often been viewed as less than charitable. Rashi, however, offers another explanation: Jacob is making pottage out of lentils, because lentils are a sign of mourning. Mourning for whom? For his grandfather Abraham, who had died that morning. As Rashi explains, Abraham should have lived one hundred eighty years, as his son Isaac did, but his life was cut short so that he would not see his grandson Esau scorn his religion. And why did Esau feel faint? Because he had been murdering people, which Rashi deduces from the mention of fainting and murder in Jeremiah 4:31. And what does the text mean when Esau says that he is in peril of death? According to Rashi, Esau asks Jacob what the birthright involves, and Jacob explains to him the obligation of the commandments, including the fact that the penalty for neglecting some of them is death, to which Esau responds, "If I am going to die through it, why should I desire it?" According to Rashi, then, Esau does not fear death from hunger but from the obligations of the commandments. Therefore he despises the birthright and sells it to Jacob.

Obviously Rashi's approach to this episode differs from any approach that modern critics might take, but within the contexts of medieval scriptural commentary and Jewish tradition, it makes perfect sense, and it helps to reinforce Jewish ideas about Jewish identity and obligation. Jacob neither steals the birthright nor cheats his brother. Rather, he accepts the obligations of the birthright even though those obligations can endanger him, just as the Jewish people accept the commandments and often suffer for that commitment.

Another appealing aspect of Rashi's commentary is his openness to multiple interpretations. Students of medieval commentaries know that both Jewish and Christian commentators frequently delighted in multiple interpretations of biblical passages, for they viewed the Bible as polysemous, as meaningful on a variety of different levels. Nonetheless, as we are about to see in the case of Nachmanides, commentators could also be doctrinaire, convinced not only that their interpretations were correct but that others were wrong. Rashi often offers a number of possible explanations, some of them drawn from the Talmud or the Midrash, and others from his teachers or from his own insights. His attitude, as he says in his comment on Genesis 33:20, is that "the words of the Torah ... may be given many different interpretations."

Occasionally, too, we can see Rashi struggle with an explanation; and we can even get a sense of the kind of person he was. In Genesis 43:11, the Hebrew word *batnim* appears, and Rashi says, "I do not know what these are, but in the definitions given in the Dictionary of R. Machir I have read that they are Pistachios [which he transliterates from the French]; I think that they are peaches." In the context of the passage, it matters little what *batnim* are, but Rashi cites one authority, then offers his own opinion without insisting on it. Rashi was a brilliant commentator, but he was also a human being. We can get a further sense of Rashi's humanness in one final example, this time not from his commentary but from a response he wrote to a question from a man who divorced his wife because she had developed a skin condition and he found her repulsive. Rashi says that the divorce is not justified, because the skin condition developed after they were married, but then he adds that the man is not behaving like a true Jew, since Jews are required to be kind to everyone and particularly to their spouses, and he concludes, "If that husband had set his mind on keeping his wife as much as he had set his mind on getting rid of her, her charm would have grown on him."[7] That is the kind of spirit that pervades the commentary of Rashi and that has helped to make him one of the heroes of medieval Judaism.

Another major commentator was Avraham ibn Ezra (1089–1164). Avraham ibn Ezra (not to be confused with Moshe or Moses ibn Ezra) was an accomplished poet who was born in Spain but spent the last two decades of his life traveling through Europe. His translator suggests that ibn Ezra left Spain because of that country's political and religious problems, because of his wife's death, because of his son's apostasy (his son Isaac is supposed to have converted to Islam and then back to Judaism), and because of his poverty, about which he wrote, "Were I a dealer in shrouds, no man would ever die ... Were I a seller of candles, the sun would never set."[8] Whatever the reason for his departure, ibn Ezra spent part of his time in exile writing a commentary on most of the Tanakh, a commentary that proved to be both influential and controversial. In his introduction to his commentary, he dismisses earlier commentators who misunderstand the text, who rely too heavily on Midrash, who reject Jewish traditions (the Karaites), and who "believe that the laws and statutes of the Torah are riddles" (Christians). He announces that he will join the company of those who try to understand the plain meaning of the text by relying heavily on an analysis of its grammar, and indeed, many of ibn Ezra's comments are grammatical in nature, though many are based also on tradition and on ibn Ezra's familiarity with current philosophical doctrines. At one point, for instance, he instructs his readers to ignore the teaching of Saadiah Gaon that man is superior to the angels, for "I have already explained to you in *The Book of Foundation* that all of his proofs are wrong" (25). Similarly, on Genesis 1:26, "Let us make man in our image," ibn Ezra cites and dismisses many earlier interpretations—about one he says, "Now this interpretation is absurd" (43)—and then presents a detailed grammatical examination of the verse, concluding with the talmudic dictum that the Torah speaks the language of man—that is, the Torah must use language that human beings can understand, must present its concepts in human terms—and therefore that the passage is an anthropomorphism (though he does not use that term). God, he says, does not have an "image," but "because man's soul is incorporeal and fills the body, which is a microcosm, in the same way that God fills the universe ... Scripture states, *in our image*" (46).

Obviously, ibn Ezra does not aim for, and certainly does not achieve, the concision of Rashi. Some of his comments go on for pages, and he shows the kind of argumentativeness that characterized so much twelfth-century thought, both Jewish and Christian. He is also rather daring in many of his comments. For example, both Rashi and Nachmanides, brilliant and critical thinkers though they were, operated on the principle that anything that was said by the ancient rabbis must have been true, and if something seemed peculiar, the problem was in their understanding and not in the rabbinic statement. Frequently, therefore, we see them struggling to make sense of a rabbinic statement. Ibn Ezra is not quite so reverent, though he surely had the greatest respect for the ancient sages. We can see his approach in his discussion of the Akedah, the Binding of Isaac. According to rabbinic tradition, Isaac was thirty-seven years old at the time of this episode: Sarah, we know, was ninety when he was born; and immediately after the Akedah, we read that she died at the age of one hundred twenty-seven. The rabbis attributed her death to shock at what had just happened and therefore calculated that Isaac was thirty-seven. Ibn Ezra comments, "Our sages, of blessed memory, say that Isaac was thirty-seven at the time of his binding. If this be a tradition, we will accept it. However, from a strictly logical point of view it is unacceptable" (224). While we might see this comment as making good logical sense, from the perspective of medieval Jewish tradition it is rather astounding. Ibn Ezra says that he accepts the tradition of the ancient rabbis, but he then logically dismisses it. Like his Christian contemporary Peter Abelard, he is willing to challenge accepted truths.

We can see ibn Ezra's daring even more clearly elsewhere. In Genesis 12:6, the text says, "The Canaanites were then in the land." Rashi understands this passage to mean that at that time in the story, the Canaanites were conquering the land from the descendants of Shem and were therefore living there. Ibn Ezra presents this interpretation as a possibility, but then he adds, "Should this interpretation be incorrect, then there is a secret meaning to the text. Let the one who understands it remain silent" (151). Ibn Ezra's words are puzzling, but apparently he implies that the passage means that the Canaanites were in the land at the time of Abraham but that they were no longer there at the time when Genesis 12:6 was written. Traditionally, of course, Genesis, along with the rest of the Torah, was written by Moses in the wilderness, when the Canaanites were indeed still in the land. If, therefore, the passage means that the Canaanites were there at the time of Abraham but not when the passage was written, then the passage must have been written much later, after the Israelite conquest of the land and thus long after the time of Moses. In short, ibn Ezra implies that Moses may not have written the entire Torah; but this possibility is so revolutionary, so counter to Jewish belief, that he dares not say it explicitly. Back in the twelfth century, he used a close reading of the text to engage in what we think of as modern textual criticism. It is no wonder that Nachmanides was so often critical of his commentary and that sixteenth-century talmudist Solomon Luria condemned it.[9]

Like Rashi, ibn Ezra addresses some of his commentary to refutations of Christian approaches. For instance, Christianity identified the serpent in the Garden of Eden with Satan, the devil, though the text of Genesis never alludes to such an identification. In fact, the Hebrew word that was later transliterated as *Satan* is not a proper name and simply means an accuser. Some Jewish texts, like the *Pirkei de Rabbi Eliezer,* said that Satan may have used the serpent to seduce Eve, but ibn Ezra rejects any such notion: "Others say that the serpent was in reality Satan. Now why don't they look at what Scripture states at the close of this chapter?" (65). And later in the same comment he adds, "Neither does an angel rebel against God" (66), clearly a response to Christian beliefs about Satan and the rebel angels as expressed by Augustine, for example, in Book XI of *The City of God.*

Similarly, ibn Ezra comments on the passage in Genesis 18 when three men appear to Abraham, "Behold, a few say that God is three men: He is one and He is three and they are inseparable. They forget that Scripture explicitly states, *And the two angels came to Sodom at even* [Genesis 19:1]," which shows that the three men were indeed separable" (189–90). Ibn Ezra here refers to the Christian doctrine of the Trinity, and his statement that "a few say" is particularly pointed, for European Christians often cited their numerical superiority to the Jews as proof of the correctness of their beliefs. Ibn Ezra, who had been in Muslim Spain and perhaps even in the Middle East, denies that numerical superiority at the same time that he denies the validity of Christian belief.

In another passage, which was later censored but which can be found in an early manuscript of the commentary, ibn Ezra refers to the origins of Christianity: "At first there were only a few people who believed in the man that was made into a god," and he mentions Constantine's role in making Christianity the official religion of the empire (271). The Middle Ages were not a time when ecumenicism was valued. Both Christians and Jews, as well as Muslims, believed that their religions were right and true and that others were therefore mistaken. We can see this sentiment again when ibn Ezra points to a mistranslation in Jerome's Latin translation of the Bible: "*She'olah* means down below, i.e., to the grave. Here the one who translated the Bible for those who err erred in translating *she'olah* as to hell" (353). Two points should be noted here. One is that ibn Ezra refers to Christians as "those who err." They are mistaken in their beliefs—not evil or perverse, as Christian comments on Jewish beliefs often concluded, but merely mistaken. And the second point is that somehow ibn Ezra was familiar with Jerome's translation. We do not know whether he knew Latin or whether he read the Vulgate translation, but this passage seems to indicate that he did both.

Ibn Ezra was clearly a great scholar. He had a thorough knowledge of Hebrew grammar, he knew the classic Hebrew texts (though he occasionally makes mistakes in referring to them—probably he had to rely on memory rather than on a reference library), and he had a great deal of secular knowledge as well. In discussing the rainbow that appeared after the Flood, he says, "If we would believe what the Greek scholars tell us, that the rainbow is produced by the sun's flames, then we must assume that after the flood God strengthened the sun's light" (125). Having grown up in Spain where the works of Greek authors had been translated into Arabic and Hebrew, ibn Ezra was familiar with many works that were just beginning to appear in the rest of Europe, often through the medium of Arabic and Hebrew translators.

The use of Greek is problematic. It is surprising, for instance, to find Rashi referring to a Greek word; in Genesis 35:8, Deborah is buried beneath an oak, which in Hebrew is *allon*. Rashi points out that *allon* in Greek means "another" and he derives a lesson from what he considers a multilingual pun. We may well wonder how Rashi knew anything about Greek. Presumably he found it in one of his classic Jewish sources, a work that was written when Greek was one of the languages used by Jews. In the case of ibn Ezra, his familiarity with the Greeks stemmed from his Spanish upbringing, and the same can be said about our third commentator, Rabbi Moses ben Nachman (1195–c.1270), known both by his acronym, Ramban, and by the Greek form of his name, Nachmanides (the son of Nachman).

Nachmanides was the major Jewish spokesman at the Disputation in Barcelona in 1263, and was also a major biblical commentator. While Rashi aimed at conciseness in his commentary and ibn Ezra was somewhat less concise, Nachmanides is absolutely prolix. His commentary on Genesis alone runs to over six hundred pages in the English translation. Nachmanides shows his familiarity with Greek thinkers from the very opening of his commentary. He opens by citing Rashi's comment that Genesis begins as it does to establish Jewish ownership of the Holy Land, and then he offers another possibility, that the Torah begins with the words "In the beginning God created" because "this is the root of faith, and he who does not believe in this and thinks the world was eternal denies the essential principle of the [Judaic] religion and has no Torah at all" (17). Rashi, in France, near the time of the Crusades, tried to indicate the Jewish right to the Promised Land, a concern shared by Nachmanides, who calls it "the choicest of places of the civilized world" (19); but Nachmanides has other interests as well. Living in Spain in the thirteenth century, he is more concerned with the effects that Greek, specifically Aristotelian, philosophy has had on religious thought. In his comment on "In the beginning" he counters the Aristotelian notion that the world had existed forever, that it had not been created and would not end. Therefore, he says, the Torah begins by saying that the world had indeed been created, by God, thereby establishing the basis of Jewish belief. Nachmanides was particularly concerned with this issue because many Jews were studying and adopting the Greek point of view and ultimately turning away from their Judaism.

Of course, Nachmanides' "proof" is only proof for those who accept the divine authority of the Torah, but his opening comments reflect the opposition between reason and revelation that had figured so importantly in the development of Christian scholasticism. Still, Nachmanides does not simply reject Greek thought. Instead, he reconciles it with biblical language, much as Christian theologians like Thomas Aquinas did. For instance, he explains that Hebrew has no word that indicates creation from absolute nothingness. We might say that an artist "creates" a painting or a chef "creates" a fine meal, but the artist and the chef do so by using pre-existing materials. When God created the world, Nachmanides says, He did so from absolute nothingness. But, Nachmanides continues, God did not create everything from that nothingness. God did not say, "Let there be lima beans" and there were lima beans. Instead, he says, God created "from total and absolute nothing a very thin substance devoid of corporeality but having a power of potency, fit to assume form" (23). That is, what God created from absolute nothingness was a single thing, primal matter, after which "He did not create anything [from nothingness], but he formed and made things with it" (23). This process may sound strange to us, but it would have been familiar to students of Greek thought, and in fact Nachmanides calls that primal matter by a Greek term, *hyly*; and then he explains that *hyly* is the same as the Hebrew *tohu*, which occurs in Genesis 1:2. Rashi says that *tohu* implies "astonishing," for the emptiness would have been astonishing, but Nachmanides provides a much more philosophical interpretation. God created *ex nihilo*, from nothingness, the primal matter, the *hyly* or the *tohu*, and from that he fashioned the rest of existence by giving to the primal matter form, represented by the Hebrew word *bohu*, for Genesis 1:2 says that the earth was *tohu va-vohu* (for phonetic reasons, the *b* of *bohu* becomes a *v* when *va*, and, is placed in front of it.) Here we can see the familiar Aristotelian concepts of matter and form as the basis of the phenomenal world, but Nachmanides gives those concepts a biblical basis:

> Now after having said that with one command God created at first the heavens and the earth and all their hosts, Scripture returns and explains that the earth after this creation was *tohu*, that is matter without

substance. It became *bohu* when he clothed it with form. Then [Scripture] explains that in this form was included the form of the four elements: fire, water, earth, and air. (25–26)

Nachmanides, then, accepts the biblical account of creation as absolutely true and accurate. He just does not accept a simplistic view of that biblical account. Instead, he makes sense of it by using the best tools available to him at that time, the Aristotelian notions of form and matter. But Nachmanides, who was a learned scholar, does not stop there, for he also incorporates into his account of creation ideas taken from Jewish mysticism. In this early part of his commentary, he refers to the *Sefer Yetzirah* (24), a very early work of Jewish mysticism, and to the Ten Emanations (21), a concept that developed in later Jewish mysticism.

In fact, Nachmanides' commentary is suffused with notions derived from Jewish mysticism, though they are often difficult to spot. Jewish mysticism was treated with a great deal of awe and was not opened to everyone. Thus, Nachmanides often alludes to mystical ideas without spelling them out. For instance, in commenting on the trees in the Garden of Eden, he says that "their secret is high and lofty" (86), but he never reveals what that secret is. That knowledge is reserved for initiates, those who are permitted to be familiar with mystical knowledge, and that knowledge is transmitted elsewhere, usually orally. Similarly, in discussing the serpent, he says that "all these things are twofold in meaning, the overt and the concealed in them both being true" (86), but he explains the overt and omits the concealed in his commentary. Underlying his whole commentary is another mystical tradition that he mentions in his introduction, "that the whole Torah is comprised of Names of the Holy One, blessed be He, and that the letters of the words separate themselves into Divine Names when divided in a different manner" (13).

Nachmanides' commentary, then, is an extraordinary combination of literal meanings (complemented by grammatical and etymological observations), philosophical discussions, and references to Jewish mystical traditions. He also, like Rashi and ibn Ezra, applies the words of the Torah to his own time. That Nachmanides was familiar with Christian religious beliefs is obvious from his conduct at the Barcelona Disputation, where he argued knowledgeably with his Christian opponents. He demonstrates that familiarity as well in his commentary. In discussing the wells that Isaac dug (Genesis 26:19–22), he reveals what he calls "a hidden matter" (334) that was relevant to his audience. In the biblical story, Isaac's herdsmen twice dig wells and find "living water," but other herdsmen quarrel with them, so Isaac names those wells *Esek* (Contention) and *Sitna* (Enmity). When he digs another well over which there is no quarrel, he calls it *Rehovoth* (Spacious). Nachmanides views this story as an allegorical foretelling of Jewish history. The first two wells represent the First and Second Temples, which were destroyed by Contention and Enmity. The third well, therefore, represents the Third Temple, whose construction will signify that the messiah has arrived, and "which will be speedily built in our days" (335). Nachmanides, it appears, had messianic expectations that he revealed in this passage. Furthermore, he implies another point when he mentions the well of living waters and refers to Jeremiah 17:13, where the fountain of living waters is identified with God. Therefore, he says, "*A well of living water* alludes to the House of God which the children of Isaac [the Jews] will build" (335). This Jewish messianic interpretation not only promises the Jews relief from the persecutions of the time, but it also challenges Christian interpretations of the passage which, based on John 4:10–15, viewed the well of living waters as a representation of Jesus. Nachmanides denies the validity of that view while simultaneously foretelling the coming of the true messiah.

Elsewhere, too, Nachmanides alludes to relations between Jews and Christians. He refers, for instance, to Jewish complicity in the takeover of ancient Israel by the Romans, since Jewish leaders sought alliances with their Roman counterparts. But Nachmanides does not use the name "Rome." Instead he refers to "Edom," which also was used to refer to Christianity, and he may well be warning his readers not to make alliances or establish close relationships with Christians. That view may conflict with modern ideas about getting along, but we must remember that in Nachmanides' time, a number of Christians used the knowledge they obtained from Jews to argue against Jewish beliefs. This interpretation is supported by another passage that comes shortly after. In explaining why Jacob divided up his camp in Genesis 32, Nachmanides explains:

> The intent of this is that Jacob knew that all his seed would not fall into Esau's hands. Therefore, in any case, one camp would be saved. This also implies that the children of Esau will not formulate a decree against us designed to obliterate our name entirely, but they will do evil to some of us in some of their countries. (398)

While he waited for and expected the messiah, who would gather the Jews together in their own country and bring an era of peace, he recognized that the dispersal of Jews in the Diaspora had certain advantages until the coming of the messiah, so that Jews who were persecuted in one area would find refuge in another. Little could he know how valuable this lesson would be two centuries later when the Jews were expelled from Spain.

Like his fellow commentators, Nachmanides regards the remarks made by the rabbis of the Talmud and the Midrashim as sacrosanct, but the commentaries of his near contemporaries incur criticism. In an introductory poem to his commentary, he praises Rashi extravagantly, even though he often disagrees with Rashi's comments. About ibn Ezra he says, "We shall have open rebuke and hidden love" (5). As Bernard Casper observes, the rebuke part is clear—at one point Nachmanides says, "Now I wonder who has blinded Abraham ibn Ezra's reasoning in this matter" (321)—but the love part is more difficult to discern.[10] We cannot know for certain why Nachmanides so frequently disparages ibn Ezra. Perhaps the latter's occasional errors or deviations from orthodox belief roused his successor's ire, or perhaps Nachmanides was signaling a preference for an Ashkenazic approach to biblical commentary. Despite Nachmanides' ire, though, Rashi, ibn Ezra, and Nachmanides himself are among the great medieval commentators.

Jewish and Christian Commentaries

There were, of course, other Jewish commentators as well, including members of the Kimhi family and Yehudah Abarbanel. In fact, there are Hebrew editions of the Tanakh, the *Mikraoth Gedoloth*, in which small portions of the biblical text on each page are surrounded by a variety of commentaries. But Christians also wrote extensive biblical commentaries, and it is instructive to look briefly at how the Jewish and Christian commentaries differed.

When we look at the commentaries from these two religious traditions, we can see another example of two groups who seemed to be engaged in the same enterprise but who interpreted that enterprise very differently. Even had they been using the same language, rather than Hebrew and Latin, their comments would for the most part have been mutually unintelligible. There were times, particularly in the twelfth century, when some Christian scholars consulted their Jewish counterparts in order to learn more about the literal meaning of the Bible, but the ideologies behind Jewish and Christian approaches differed so significantly that they might well have been commenting on different texts. For example, both traditions relied on fourfold levels of interpretation (though the Christian scheme is much better known than the Jewish one). The Jewish approach is known by the acronym PARDES, a Hebrew word (derived from Persian) that means "orchard" and came to be used to mean Paradise. As Casper explains, it stands for the following kinds of interpretation:

> P'shat—the simple literal meaning
> Remez—the hint that the words of Scripture refer to other meanings: when Moses raised his arms in battle against Amalek, it means that Israel prevailed as long as they looked toward heaven
> D'rash—the homiletical figurative meaning, as found often in the Midrash
> Sod—the secret allegorical meaning: in the Eden story, Adam equates with the power of thought, Eve equates with emotion, the Tree equates with intellect, and the serpent equates with lust[11]

We must note that the fourth level, Sod, was not as popular or as widely used as the other levels. It can be found in the ancient works of Philo of Alexandria and in the Jewish mystical writings of the Middle Ages.

The best statement of the Christian fourfold approach occurs in a letter attributed to Dante in which the author uses Psalm 114:1–2, describing the Exodus, to describe one literal and three allegorical levels:

1. Literal—the Exodus story describes how the Israelites left Egypt
2. Allegorical—the Exodus story signifies human redemption through Jesus
3. Tropological (or Moral)—the Exodus story signifies the movement of the soul from sin to grace
4. Anagogical—the Exodus story signifies the movement of the soul from the earthly to the heavenly world

Obviously these two schemes differ substantially. They agree on the literal level, though the Hebrew commentators paid far more attention to the literal level than did their Christian counterparts, for several reasons, among which are the following: 1) Christians regarded what they called the Old Testament as a foreshadowing of the New, so their focus tended to be on the latter, where they found the "fulfillment" of Scripture and the foundations of their belief. Jews regarded the Tanakh as their own particular history and as the foundation of their beliefs; 2) Christians regarded the many laws of the Old Testament as superseded. Jews regarded them as still active and worthy of close study; 3) Christians read the Bible in translations. Jews, reading the Tanakh in Hebrew and Aramaic, paid closer attention to the grammar, the etymology of words, and the literal meaning.

We can see these differences reflected throughout Jewish and Christian commentaries. In Psalm 1, for example, we can consider the commentaries of Augustine and Rashi. These two giants of their respective traditions lived many centuries apart, but their commentaries are among the most important in their traditions. Significantly, they differ on the meaning of the psalm's very first words. Rashi understands the Hebrew phrase *Ashrei ha-ish* to mean "The praises of a man" (though other Jewish commentators see them more traditionally as meaning "Happy is the man"), while Augustine relies on the Latin *Beatus vir*, which means "Blessed is the man." While these differences may not seem significant, what follows is significant indeed. Rashi says, "The praises of a man, and these are the praises of a man: that he did not follow, because since he did not follow, he did not stand, and since he did not stand, he did not sit." This is a single, literal restatement of the first verse: a man should be praised for not following the advice of the wicked, because if he does not listen to them, then he neither stands nor sits with them—he does not become accustomed to their wickedness. This comment contrasts markedly with that of Augustine: "'*Blessed is the man who has not walked in the counsel of the ungodly*'. The blessing applies to our Lord Jesus Christ … the Man of the Lord." This is a theological statement, and Augustine goes on to equate the "ungodly" with Adam; from that equation, he derives a new understanding of the series *walked* (or *followed*), *stood*, and *sat*: "Man walked in effect when he turned his back on God; he stood when he took pleasure in sin; he sat when, hardened in his own pride, he was incapable of retracing his steps unless He who had not walked in the counsel of the ungodly [Jesus] … came to deliver him" (Psalms 21).

Unlike Rashi's literal interpretation of the verse, Augustine's interpretation is highly allegorical. It is what we would call—though medieval Christians would not—"imposed allegory," for the words of the psalm never literally mention or even allude to Jesus. Augustine, on the basis of his belief that everything in the Old Testament foreshadows what is in the New, reads Jesus into the psalm. We can see a similar phenomenon in the well-known Psalm 23 (which for Augustine was Psalm 22). The psalm begins, "A song of David. The Lord is my Shepherd; I lack nothing." Rashi cites a talmudic dictum (Pesachim 117a) that wherever the text says "a song of David," David would play his instrument and the spirit of God would rest on him. Then Rashi adds that David trusts in God's protection: "In this desert where I am going, I am confident that I will lack nothing" (82). Once again, Rashi provides a straightforward literal interpretation. Augustine, however, again relying on the Latin translation, says, *"A Psalm for David himself.* It is the Church who addresses Christ. *The Lord feedeth me, and I shall want nothing.* Our Lord Jesus Christ is my shepherd; I shall lack nothing" (St. Augustine on *Psalms* 229). Again we can see that, from a twenty-first century perspective, Augustine is not interpreting the words of the text. Instead, he is making them fit into his preconceived theology.

These approaches that so largely characterize Jewish and Christian commentaries indicate why those communities had such difficulty communicating. They both claimed allegiance to the Bible, but not only did they define the Bible differently, they read it so differently that they might as well have been reading different books. There was, however, one book that both traditions read allegorically, the Song of Songs, which we examined briefly earlier. Scholars today may argue that this brief book is a collection of poems expressing love between a man and a woman, but ancient and medieval commentators, both Jewish and Christian, regarded it as an allegory. Both traditions regarded the book as supremely important—Rabbi Akiva says that all the *k'tuvim* (Writings), the third division of the Tanakh, are sacred, "but the *Song of Songs* is the most sacred" (Yadayim 3:5)—and they agreed that it should not be read literally. Jews read it as an allegory of God's love for Israel, while Christians read it as an allegory of Jesus' love for the Church, or occasionally as Jesus love for the individual soul.[12] These different approaches to allegory make individual comments particularly fascinating.

For instance, Song of Songs 4:2 is part of the praise of the beloved's beauty: "Your teeth are like a flock of shorn ewes." (This is probably not a sentence that a modern lover would use.) Rashi says that this line, like the surrounding lines, praises Israel in terms that are used to praise a beautiful woman. "Your teeth—are thin and white and arranged like wool and the order of a flock of ewes" (*Song* 42). Augustine, in an often mocked passage, says that the "teeth" are the saints:

> I contemplate the saints more pleasantly when I envisage them as the teeth of the Church cutting off men from their errors and transferring them to her body after their hardness has been softened as if by being bitten and chewed. I recognize them most pleasantly as shorn sheep having put aside the burdens of the world like so much fleece, and ascending from the washing, which is baptism. (*On Christian Doctrine* 39)

In the twelfth century, Honorius Augustodunensis interprets the teeth as the confessors and expositors of Scripture, who bite heretics.[13] Thus, even when both traditions read a text allegorically, they still read it very differently, and often their readings were aimed at each other.

It is both fascinating and instructive, then, to read and compare these Jewish and Christian commentaries, including the midrashim, which we have only barely touched on. These commentaries indicate the ways in which these communities perceived themselves in relation to their central texts, but they also show how profoundly they were influenced by the world around them. Nachmanides may have argued against the importance of Greek philosophy, but his commentary was clearly affected by that philosophy. The works of Rashi, and even more of Rashi's descendants the Tosafists, whom we met earlier, were products of the late-eleventh and twelfth centuries. The Jewish commentaries offer further evidence of the vitality of Jewish culture in those tumultuous centuries. There may have been tragedies in those centuries, but there was also tremendous creativity.

Medieval Hebrew Literature

Medieval Hebrew literature, both poetry and prose, provides a fascinating and difficult subject for both study and enjoyment. The difficulty of the subject takes several forms. First, we often do not know enough about the cultural context in which texts were produced, which limits our ability to understand as fully as possible the background of the literature. Also, understanding the texts often requires intimate familiarity with the Tanakh, with commentaries on the Tanakh, with the Talmud and the Midrash, and with the non-Jewish culture in whose midst the literature was created. And the literature is frequently written in difficult, highly ornamented Hebrew. Some medieval Jewish literature was composed in Aramaic, in Old Yiddish, in Ladino, and in Italian, among other languages, although Hebrew dominated, even though Hebrew was never a spoken, colloquial language during the Middle Ages. Instead, Hebrew was the language of prayer and study, and frequently of wonderful and deeply moving, imaginative literature. But Hebrew is a highly charged language, in the sense that it is difficult to say very much in Hebrew without using words that appear in the Tanakh, and the reader must therefore try to determine whether those words function as simple words or whether they constitute biblical allusions.

From its earliest existence, of course, Jewish culture has produced poetry, for example, the biblical songs of Moses and Miriam at the Red Sea, the song of Deborah, the entire book of Psalms, along with many other passages. When Jews in both the Diaspora and Israel began to develop the institution of the synagogue and to create the synagogue service, they naturally used many such biblical texts and created new poetical texts as prayers, but we must clarify what we mean by "poetical texts." We might be tempted to think of poetry as literature that goes halfway across the page, but, until recent times, poetic expression has tended to follow rules. In English, the most popular rules involve meter and rhyme, but much medieval English poetry, in both Old and Middle English, relied on alliterative patterns, and some poetry, like "Pearl" or "Sir Gawain and the Green Knight," combined rhyme, meter, and alliteration. Ancient Greek and Roman poetry was quantitative, which means that it depended on whether syllables were long or short according to the rules of those languages. Biblical poetry used yet another scheme. During the Middle Ages, Christian scholars, some of whom learned Hebrew, attempted to understand the rules of biblical poetry by imposing their knowledge of Latin poetry onto Hebrew verse, which was, of course, a fruitless enterprise. Even Jewish scholars and poets, influenced by the poetry of their non-Jewish contemporaries, failed to see the principles of biblical poetry, which employs a system of parallels, thoroughly described in James Kugel's *The Idea of Biblical Poetry*. We can illustrate the principle by looking briefly at Isaiah 1:2–3:

a) Hear, O heavens,
b) and give ear, O earth …
c) An ox knows its owner
d) an ass its master's crib:
e) Israel does not know,
f) my people takes no thought.

In these translated lines, which attempt to convey both the sense and structure of the Hebrew, we can see how the half-line b parallels and extends what is said in half-line a. The same is true in c-d and e-f, but we can also see that the whole line composed of c and d parallels the whole line of e and f, though in this case e-f does not extend but contrasts with c-d. The poetry contains neither rhyme nor meter, but it forms complex webs of lines and half-lines working with or against each other.

Medieval Hebrew poetry, however, does not preserve this scheme. Rather, it adopts and adapts other forms, just as medieval Latin poetry often abandoned the quantitative method and relied on meter and rhyme (O Fortuna/velut luna) or as Old English alliterative verse after the Norman Conquest and the development of Middle English was replaced by metrical verse, for instance, in the work of Chaucer.

Several other aspects of medieval Hebrew poetry require comment here. One is simple, though curious: medieval Hebrew poets were fond of "signing" their poems by building acrostics into them. This technique, which may strike us as odd, has biblical roots. Psalm 145, for instance, is an alphabetical acrostic in which each verse begins with a successive letter of the alphabet (with the letter *nun* omitted), and the longest psalm, 119, bases each stanza on a successive letter of the alphabet. The medieval poets often use alphabetical acrostics, but they also frequently use the first letter of each line to spell out their names or to offer some message. A particularly complex example is the Aramaic poem called *Akdamuth* by the eleventh-century Rabbi Meir ben Isaac. This poem, which is still recited in synagogues on the Festival of Shavuoth (Pentecost), begins with an alphabetical acrostic formed by the first letters of each couplet. After the last letter of the alphabet, the first letters of the lines spell out, in Hebrew, the words "Meir the son of Rabbi Isaac, may he be great in Torah and good deeds, amen. Be strong and courageous." Furthermore, and this brings us to another point about medieval Hebrew poetry, all ninety lines of this poem end with the same rhyme. Even if it were possible to end ninety English lines with the same sound (which it is not), we would regard such a poem as a monstrosity; but because Hebrew and Aramaic are constructed differently than English, poems with a single rhyme throughout were quite common. For example, because most Hebrew words in the feminine gender end with the sound –ah, many poems use that sound as their single rhyme.

Another introductory point is a bit more complex because it almost requires a knowledge of Hebrew. The simple fact is that medieval Hebrew poets, like poets everywhere, loved to play with words, and Hebrew allowed them to play in many ways. For instance, in one poem, Moshe ibn Ezra plays on the Hebrew root n-g-n (which has to do with music) and ends his poem with the words *kenagen ha-menagen*, "when the minstrel plays." Hebrew poetry is full of such word play, which is nearly impossible to render in English ("when the minstrel minstrelizes"?). And finally, this introduction must end with a warning: Israel Davidson's *Thesaurus of Medieval Hebrew Poetry,* which was published in 1925–1938, lists over 35,000 poems by over 2,800 poets, and more have been discovered in recent decades. Consequently, it is foolish to rely too heavily on generalizations about this body of poetry; what follows in this chapter is only the barest of introductions to a vast body of literature.

The Earlier Poetry[1]

The Bible contains a great deal of poetry. Jewish poetry also existed in non-Scriptural works, in the Talmud, and in writing that was contemporary with the Talmud, but medieval Jewish poetry proper begins with the creation of the *piyyut*. Yose ben Yose, Yannai, and Eleazar ben Kallir are among the earliest poets (*paytanim*). Although we do not have exact dates for these poets, scholars agree that they lived in the fifth through the seventh centuries in Palestine. Their poems were written for use in the synagogues and refer clearly to the weekly readings from the Torah, to the holidays, to life-cycle events (weddings and funerals, for example), and to Jewish history. One fascinating strand of *piyyutim*, recently investigated by Michael D. Schwartz and Joseph Yahalom, is the Avodah *piyyutim*. Avodah, which in Hebrew literally means "work," refers to the sacrificial service of the ancient Temple, and these Avodah *piyyutim* describe, often in great detail, specifically the sacrificial service that was performed by the High Priest on Yom Kippur. These Avodah poems were composed more than four hundred years after the destruction of the Temple in 70 C.E., but they recall with both fondness and deep sadness the details of the service as they are described in the Talmud. The fondness is based on the sense that in the time of the Temple, the High Priest and the people of Israel were able to fulfill the divine commandments precisely as they had been handed down. Of course, that historic nostalgia in many ways idealized the past, but such idealization would have come naturally to a people who were suffering under the indignities that Palestinian Jews had to endure. The sadness of these Avodah poems reflects a theme that runs through much medieval Hebrew poetry: the sense of loss, the sorrow that the Avodah service is no longer possible because the Temple has been destroyed, the sense that Israel has been and continues to be punished for its transgressions. These poems contrast past glory with present misery.

This theme dominates many other *piyyutim* as well. A poem by Eleazar ben Kallir that T. Carmi entitles "The Dialogue of Zion and God" (223), portrays Zion as a mother bewailing the fact that her husband has abandoned her, while the husband replies that he has not abandoned her, that he has been looking out for her from afar and that he will soon return. As Carmi's title indicates, the mother is Zion, mother of Israel, and the husband is God. This image, as we saw earlier, is based on the Song of Songs, as well as on many passages in the prophets. When Zion says that God "has not remembered my love as a bride," the poet refers to Jeremiah 2:2, and when God calls her "My dark one," the reference is to Song of Songs 1:5, but there are numerous other Scriptural references throughout the poem that the poet would have expected his audience to catch.

Many of Eleazar ben Kallir's *piyyutim* appear in modern prayer books. One, which is recited on the first day of Passover, is the prayer for dew.

During the winter months, the rainy season in Israel, prayers are said asking for sufficient rainfall. At Passover, in the spring, those prayers are replaced by very brief prayers for dew, but on Passover itself, this prayer is recited:

> Grant dew to favor thy land;
> Make us blessed with rejoicing,
> With plenty of grain and wine;
> Restore thy beloved land—with dew ...
>
> Let dew fall on the blessed land;
> Bless us with the gift of heaven;
> In the darkness let a light dawn
> For Israel who follows thee. (Birnbaum 634–36)

Here again is the theme of Israel's difficulties, but this time it is expressed not with sadness but with hope for future redemption, as in the same poet's prayer for rain that is recited on the festival of Succoth. We should also notice here the common notion that the land of Israel is considered special to God, that it is, in fact, God's land.

The origin of the *piyyutim* remains a mystery. One theory is that they originated under the Persians, who at various times forbad the recitation of the regular prayers. Jewish writers, therefore, created these poems as substitutes, and when the ban on prayers was lifted, the poems remained.[2] A more popular theory is that as the prayers became standardized, the cantors, the prayer leaders, created *piyyutim* to preserve the spontaneity of worship.[3] We cannot deny, however, that while the *piyyutim* reflect deep devotion, they also obviously allowed the cantors who composed them to show off, much as a cadenza allows the soloist in a concerto to show off. Unfortunately, we cannot recreate the music to which these poems were sung, but we can see from their elaborate word play and their often very technical references to the Tanakh, to the Talmud, and to other authorities that their authors were making a display of their erudition. These are learned poems that often display a surface level of meaning and a deeper level for those in the audience who were in the know. The number of surviving *piyyutim* indicates how popular they were, but the rabbis of the time, particularly those in Babylonia, opposed their use in the synagogue, partly because they found the poems unnecessary and disruptive and partly because the *piyyut* was a Palestinian invention and the Babylonian rabbis were interested in preserving their independence from Palestine.[4] Nevertheless, many of the *piyyutim* have been incorporated in the prayer book where they are accorded equal sanctity with the rest of the prayers.

As the Middle Ages progressed, however, and the rabbis in Babylonia became more authoritative, they too, began to compose poetry. Saadiah Gaon, the greatest of the geonim, wrote poems praising God and also poems that can be classified as *selichot*. That word comes from a root that means "pardon," and the word itself refers to penitential prayers. Not only are the ten days between Rosh Hashanah and Yom Kippur known as the Ten Days of Repentance, but during the days before Rosh Hashanah, it was (and still is) customary to recite such penitential prayers. Certain motifs appear quite naturally in these prayers: a sense of the speaker's sinfulness and unworthiness, sorrow at the suffering he is forced to endure, praise of God, hope for redemption, and pleading for God to manifest Himself in the world. While the speakers of the poem often sound like individuals, they actually represent the collective voice of Israel. These poems draw freely from the Tanakh—some may quote biblical lines occasionally, while others seem almost like pastiches of Scriptural verses. In either case, they are deeply moving.

One of the *selichot* attributed to Saadiah Gaon compares the present situation of the Jewish people to the situation after the destruction of the First Temple by Nebuchadnezzar:

> They smashed the Temple and looted their share …
> What *gazam* [a kind of locust] left over the *arbeh* [another kind of locust] devoured …
> What can I tell over? My sighs are so deep:
> My soul contends [against life], my communities grieve …
> We have been pillaged from generation to generation …
> O forceful One, awaken and rise to our judgment! (*Selichos* 473–5)

This poem, written almost nine hundred years after the destruction of the Second Temple and about fifteen hundred years after the destruction of the First Temple, regards those events as almost contemporary. Not only do they have contemporary relevance, as the Jewish people are in a situation analogous to those of their ancestors who experienced those traumatic events, but those events, and the current plight of Israel, all mark stages in the developing relationship between Israel and God. Furthermore, the references to Joel, to Job, and possibly to Psalms in the few quoted lines give biblical resonances to the poem. Everything that happens is therefore part of a divine plan. The poets neither deny nor rejoice in the suffering of Israel; there is no virtue to suffering. But despite the suffering, they maintain their faith. If Israel abandoned God when it worshipped the Golden Calf at Mount Sinai, or when it pursued other gods later on, it now faithfully accepts its punishment while longing for forgiveness, which will take the form of redemption, of restoration both to its homeland and to its proper relationship with God.

Poetry in Ashkenaz

These same themes are reflected over and over in medieval Hebrew poetry, for they represent an overarching ideology of medieval Jews; but there were also many variations on these themes as the historical situation changed. As the lives of the Jews became increasingly difficult over the centuries, their poetry reflected the worsening situation. A good example, still from a relatively early period, is a *selicha* (singular of *selichot*) by Rabbeinu Gershom Me'or ha-Golah, one of the rabbinical giants of the early-eleventh century. This poem is a double alphabetical acrostic—each set of two lines begins with a successive letter of the alphabet—and the last lines spell out the Hebrew name Gershom bar Yehudah. Rabbeinu Gershom was obviously a man of great faith, but he begins his poem with a direct challenge to God:

Where are all your great and awesome wonders,
That our fathers told us of …?

The poet describes the slavery in Egypt and the Babylonian Exile, both of which came to an end through divine power. But the Egyptian slavery lasted four hundred years, and the Babylonian Exile lasted seventy. The current exile has been going on for a millennium:

From one day to the next my pain increases,
Each day is worse than the one before.

Even though this poem is a *selicha*, a penitential poem, it is less a poem about repentance than it is a cry for redemption. Rabbeinu Gershom, of course, could not know what the future held, how much worse conditions would become even within a century of his death, but two lines in the poem foreshadow the coming problems. These lines, the couplet beginning with the Hebrew letter *samech*, have been corrupted, and there exist several versions of what they might have been. The following is a probable reading:

> The oppressive enemy is pushing Your precious one
> To exchange her Hope for a man-made faith.

These lines have been subjected to censorship because of a provocative word. In the second line, the Hebrew reads *"ba'amanath notzar,"* which Yaakov Lavon translates, quite accurately, as "man-made faith," but *notzar* also refers to Nazareth, to the Nazarene, and therefore to Jesus and Christianity. Consequently, the line could also be translated, "To exchange her Hope for a Christian faith," which would have been, at the very least, offensive in Rabbeinu Gershom's environment, where conversion to Christianity was encouraged and occasionally, even against Church teaching, coerced. In fact, Rabbeinu Gershom's own son converted to Christianity, probably as a result of coercion, and died before he could return to Judaism—if he could have done so at all, since abandoning one's conversion was a capital crime.

Rabbeinu Gershom's poem, then, is not a theoretical statement, nor is it a generic complaint about persecution. Rather, it reflects the anguish of one who has been directly affected by the evils that surround him. It can be no wonder that he pleads with God for respite, that, citing passages from Lamentations and Isaiah, he calls for vengeance on those who persecute Israel, and he concludes the poem:

> Build Your city as in days of old,
> Repair Your Altar [and the] Temple and Antechamber.
> There Judah and Israel, all of them shall serve You there,
> [And] Your Name will be great for all eternity. (*Selichos* 141–45)

Rabbeinu Gershom pleads with God for the rebuilding of Jerusalem and of the Temple, which means that he pleads for the coming of the messiah, since the Temple can only be rebuilt when the messiah comes.

What may strike us as remarkable about a poem like this—and there are many poems like this—is the profundity of the faith it expresses. Rabbeinu Gershom and the Jews as a whole could have brought an end to their suffering by giving in, by converting. Many Jews did so rather than give up their lives or endure such suffering, but most did not. They may have questioned God's plan, they may have informed God that it was time for the suffering to end, but, as this poem and many others indicate, they persevered. And worse was yet to come, as the Crusades loomed at the end of the century.

The faith of the Jews is expressed beautifully in a poem, probably from France near the time of the First Crusade, that still forms part of the Yom Kippur liturgy. The concluding stanza conveys the sense of the poem:

Like silver in the hands of a smith, who alloys or refines it, as he wishes
so are we in Your hands,
Healer of wounds. Oh, look to the covenant, do not heed the Accuser.
(Carmi 368)

Each stanza compares Israel to some material object (clay, stone, an axe)
and God to the master of that material (a potter, a mason, a blacksmith)
thereby illustrating and confirming God's absolute power over us. And
each stanza concludes with a plea that God remember the *b'rith*, the covenant that He made with Abraham and that has been confirmed through
the course of history, and furthermore that God not heed the claims of the
Accuser, the angel whose job it is to point out the wrongs that people have
committed, their failings. Thus, the anonymous poet acknowledges that
people have failed, have sinned, but he asks that their sins may be overlooked in light of the ancient relationship between Israel and God. The
poem, then, acknowledges sinfulness and appeals for God's grace.

But what came instead were the Crusades, with their death and
destruction. We looked earlier at the Crusade chronicles, with their
descriptions of the horrors that the people endured, but the poetry of
the time is perhaps even more horrifying. Many of the Crusade poems,
like the chronicles, rely on the story of the Akedah, the binding of Isaac.
In Genesis, of course, Abraham is prevented from sacrificing his son,
but in rabbinic literature we can find a variety of legends according to
which Isaac actually was killed and then revivified by God.[5] Thus, the
killing of children by their parents became an analogue, a modern
reenactment of the biblical story. An anonymous poem about the
slaughter in Mainz provides a good example.

The poem begins with the narrator speaking of his grief, wishing that
God would hear him, and describing the children, facing death at the
hands of the crusaders, singing out "Hear, O Israel, the Lord our God,
the Lord is one" (Deuteronomy 6:4), the verse that expresses the central
belief of Judaism and that a person is supposed to say before dying. The
importance of these first two stanzas, however, is that while Israel has
indeed heard about and believed in the unity of God, God must not have
heard their pleas, for if He had, such horrors could not have descended
on the people; and the poet goes on to describe those horrors:

Oh, how the children cried aloud! Trembling, they see their brothers
slaughtered; the mother binding her son, lest he profane the sacrifice by
shuddering; the father making the ritual blessing to sanctify the slaughter.

And then the poet expresses the confusion that must have beset the survivors who had witnessed such brutality and such evidence of faith. First, he turns from lamenting for the dead, who, in typical elegiac fashion, he imagines in the realm of eternal life, and he raises the issue of the sinfulness of Israel, who must have sinned terribly to have suffered such punishment. That sentiment may seem hackneyed at first, a kind of stereotypical response—"We must have done something to deserve this"—but then the poet shifts and reminds God of their faithfulness:

> O everlasting God, we seek refuge in the shadow of Your wings. We have been abandoned, alone and suffering, because we refused to bow our heads before the crucified one, a corpse trampled underfoot. (Carmi 372–3)

Such grief! Yes, he seems to say, we may have been sinful, but not so sinful as to deserve what happened. In fact, we have been faithful. We have not converted, nor have we followed other gods. How could You have let this happen? And surely it can be no surprise that he speaks so disparagingly of Christianity after what the crusaders had done. It can also be no surprise that he concludes his poem by asking God to avenge the slaughter, as His people continue to worship Him "in dread, night and day," by unifying His name, that is, by continuing to recite the Shema, the passage that declares God's unity.

It is difficult to find a logical thread in this poem (there was terrible slaughter, we must have sinned, but we did not sin, so avenge us), but of course logic is not an issue here. The event was so incomprehensible, as is every instance of human cruelty, and the poet tried to deal with it in the only terms he had. He could not abandon God, even if somewhere deep inside he worried that God had abandoned Israel. But to say that God had abandoned Israel was to accept the argument of the Christians, which he could never do. And so he has no answer but faith.

There are many such Crusade poems, a few of which appear in Carmi's anthology, but poems were written about other atrocities as well, comprising a large collection of martyrological poetry. In 1171, the Jewish community in Blois was accused of ritual murder, and many Jews were burned. Whereas the Crusade massacres had been carried out by mobs, often against the wishes of local religious and civic leaders, the mass-killing in Blois was instigated by the local count, who may have initially been trying to exact vengeance on his Jewish mistress. In one of his poems commemorating this event, Ephraim of Bonn speaks for all of Israel when he says:

All the peoples that laid me waste have regained their strength. But I, how long must I wait until the Messiah and the prophet Elijah restore my fortunes? May disaster strike all my evil neighbors! Woe upon them! They have earned their own disaster by destroying me. Is the Lord's arm so short that it cannot change my lot? Let Your words come true and we will pay homage to you in my city, Jerusalem. (Carmi 385)

Once again we see the same motifs: the tiny population of the Jews is at the mercy of its hostile neighbors, and God continues not to intervene. When will the messiah come and rescue the Jews, restoring them to their holy land? Similarly, in another poem about Blois, Baruch of Magenza (Mainz) writes:

You forbade the uncircumcised to offer You even rams. Then why did You hide Your face when they ravaged the holy people, the feeble Jews, who put their trust in You? ... Our skin is always ready for the sacrifice, so great is our trust in You. (Carmi 387)

The martyrs of Blois, having been burned at the stake, were indeed comparable to the burnt offerings in the ancient Temple; but, Baruch asks, if non-Jews were forbidden by divine command to bring animal sacrifices in the Temple, why were non-Jews allowed to sacrifice God's holy people? Baruch emphasizes that the Jews are willing to sacrifice themselves, thanks to their faith in God, but he questions why God would want or allow such a sacrifice. These poets, who were also scholars steeped in the study of the Torah and other holy writings, tried to understand the incomprehensible, to make sense of a world that appeared to deny their theology. In their poems we can see both faith and doubt simultaneously. Faith may always triumph in these poems, but the poets do not quietly accept the horrors that have been imposed on their people.

While the poems we have been examining are not well known except among devotees of medieval Hebrew poetry, there are two medieval compositions about martyrdom that are better known. One is a prose passage, *Av ha-Rachamim*, probably written at the time of the First Crusade and recited in synagogues on Sabbath mornings after the reading from the Torah. As we might expect from a liturgical passage, it emphasizes faith, calling on God to remember the martyrs and to avenge them. The desire for vengeance may not be the noblest emotion, but we can certainly understand why so many of these texts call for it. In many cases, the writers view vengeance as important for God, for if God does not avenge His people, He seems to concur in their suffering and justify their persecution. Thus the author of *Av ha-Rachamim* quotes Psalm 79:10, "Let the nations not say, 'Where is their God?'"

Yet another liturgical passage that continues to be used is the poem *Eleh Ezkerah*, "These I Remember," which is recited on Yom Kippur. Although we cannot be certain when this poem was written, it is clearly a medieval response to martyrdom, as it recounts the executions of ten leading rabbis in Roman times. Historically, the poem is quite inaccurate, since we know that these ten sages were not all executed at the same time, but by putting their stories together, the author, an otherwise unknown poet named Yehuda, whose name appears as an acrostic in the last stanza, creates a powerful statement about Jewish martyrdom.

One more touching poem about death should be mentioned, though it is not a story of martyrdom. One of the Ḥasidei Ashkenaz in the late-twelfth and early-thirteenth centuries was Eliezer bar Yehudah of Worms. One night while he was at home with his family and his students, two men broke into his house and killed his wife and two daughters and injured his son and some students. The civil authorities captured and punished the murderers, so this incident differs from those we have seen so far. Nevertheless, the profoundly devout Rabbi Eliezer wrote a heartbreaking poem in which he describes his wife as "modest and kind, sweet and wise." His thirteen-year-old daughter Bellet and six-year-old daughter Hannah are described as girls who study, pray, and learn their household duties. Clearly Rabbi Eliezer is devastated by their deaths, but he concludes:

> I put my trust in the Judge who has decreed my sentence; He has crushed me for my crimes. O Lord, the right is on Your side, the shame belongs to me. No matter how You treat me, I shall bless You and sing in Your honor; and I shall bow down before You. (Carmi 388)

The poem typifies the belief among the Ḥasidei Ashkenaz that human beings were meant to suffer, but that knowledge does not prevent our hearts from going out to the bereaved man.

Jewish martyrdom, however, did not concern only human beings. In 1242, after cartloads of the Talmud were burned in a public ceremony in Paris, Rabbi Meir of Rothenburg, who was a young man at the time, not yet the famous scholar he would become, wrote a moving lament for those burned books. In this poem, Rabbi Meir asks the burned parchment, as one might ask the souls of the deceased, to look out for the living, for those who yearn to return to the land of Israel. He recalls the giving of the Torah at Sinai, where there were thunder and lightning, while now the Torah is ablaze in the conflagration. Rabbi Meir's grief over the burned books is comparable to the grief we might have for someone who has died, for he acknowledges the centrality of those holy books in the life of Israel. After all, every evening one of the prayers tells us that "the words of Thy Torah ... are our life and the length of our days."[6] Hence, the burning of these books reminds him of the deaths of so many martyrs as he mourns, "bereaved and forlorn," dressed in sackcloth, unable to perceive the sun, the light, in the darkness that surrounds him.[7] But as always in these poems, Rabbi Meir looks hopefully to the future, when God will remember His marriage to Israel, will restore her to her lands, and the people will again be able to celebrate in happiness, and the darkness of their present existence will give way to the light of redemption.

This poetry from Ashkenaz seems unrelievedly gloomy, particularly in contrast to poetry from Andalusia, Muslim Spain. There are two major explanations for this situation. First, the Jews of Ashkenaz were less integrated into the surrounding society than the Jews of Andalusia. Andalusian Jews, at least those of the upper classes, were familiar with Arabic literature, adopting and adapting it to suit their needs. The Jews of Ashkenaz undoubtedly spoke the languages of their neighbors and possibly even read their literature, but that literature seems to have exercised little influence on them. Strangely enough, there is one Hebrew romance from the entire Middle Ages, *King Artus,* a story based on Arthurian legends and written in 1279. This fascinating short work illustrates the problem that Jews confronted in reading vernacular literature in Ashkenaz, for that literature was suffused with Christian concepts that had to be modified for Jewish audiences. For example, in Arthurian romances, many events occur on Pentecost, Easter, and Christmas. In *King Artus*, those Christian holidays are replaced by Jewish holidays. One of the central symbols of Arthurian romance is the Holy Grail, supposedly the cup that Jesus drank from at the Last Supper (or that caught his blood at the Crucifixion), hardly a symbol with which Jews could identify. In *King Artus*, it becomes a kind of communal charity bowl from which the poor are fed. Perhaps even more significantly, knighthood itself had become a Christian ideal. Jews may have had historical memories of warriors like Joshua and David, but there were no Jewish armies or military leaders in Ashkenaz. Ashkenzic Jews simply could not relate to the literature of their neighbors.

And a related reason for the morbidity of Ashkenazic Jewish literature is obviously the morbidity of the life that produced it. The simple fact is that life was, despite periods of respite, nasty, brutish, and short. Beginning particularly at the time of the Crusades, Jews frequently came under attack, so they were hardly likely to produce poetry that radiated sweetness and light. Rather, they mourned and they wondered when salvation would arrive. Or they prayed, attempting to understand their plight or to justify God's ways to themselves. Many of the prayers that are still used, particularly in Ashkenazic synagogues, originated in this troubling milieu, and we conclude our brief look at Ashkenazic literature by considering one of its sublime creations, a poetic prayer known by its first words, *U'nethanne Tokef,* which Carmi renders, "Now let us proclaim how majestic is the holiness of this day" (207). There is some debate over where and when this prayer was written, but it belongs here because of the legend associated with it, a legend told by Rabbi Ephraim of Bonn in the twelfth century. The legend says that the archbishop of Mainz often tried to convince Rabbi Amnon of Mainz to become a Christian, and Rabbi Amnon just as often refused. Once, however, perhaps under pressure from the archbishop, he said he would think about it. Immediately, he realized that he had made a dreadful mistake and he never returned to the archbishop, who soon had him arrested and tortured. On Rosh Hashanah, the New Year, the dying rabbi was carried into the synagogue, where he recited this poem and then died. According to the legend, he appeared shortly thereafter in a dream to Kalonymus ben Meshullam ben Kalonymus, to whom he dictated the poem. While this legend adds to the aura of the poem, some scholars date the poem a century or two earlier. Regardless, it is a powerful work that summarizes many Jewish beliefs about Rosh Hashanah and Yom Kippur, about sin and repentance and what happens to human beings in this world. Significantly, it is still recited on those holidays and constitutes one of the essential high points of the holiday service.

The poem depicts God as the judge and the witness for every person, determining the fate of each person for the coming year. Like sheep, everyone passes before God, who notes "who is to live and who is to die; who will come to the end of his time and who to an untimely end; who will perish by fire, and who by water; who by the sword, and who by wild beasts ..." Thus far the poem seems very deterministic in asserting that God's decrees, made on Rosh Hashanah and sealed on Yom Kippur, are inexorable, but then the poem adds a key line: "But penitence, charity, and prayer can avert the harsh decree" (207–9). God is a just judge, but God is also merciful, so that those three activities can persuade Him to change His mind. Those activities, of course, are always welcome, but particularly during the ten days between Rosh Hashanah and Yom Kippur. They hold out hope to human beings, who are naturally prone to sin, and they encourage people to make the world a better place.

The poem concludes by reminding us of how fragile we are, made of dust, our lives short and transient as a dream. In some ways the poem is quite simple—the vocabulary is not difficult, there are no acrostics, the imagery is traditional—and yet the poem itself offers a powerful statement about the frailty of human life and its simultaneous importance. Compared to God, human beings are insignificant, while at the same time, for human society to work, we have divine mandates for how we should behave. Some of us will live and others will die, some will flourish and others will suffer; and all we can do is our best. In an important sense, the Jews of Ashkenaz followed the teachings of this poem. Somehow they persevered.

The Poetry of Andalusia

In discussions of medieval Hebrew poetry, the focus is often on poetry written by Jews in Muslim Spain, and for good reason. That poetry, written under the influence of Arabic models and in a milieu that was not so oppressive as that of Ashkenaz, appeals much more immediately to modern readers. While Andalusian poetry contains many laments for the dead, for instance, the deceased tend to be friends or relatives of the poets rather than martyrs. The prayers of the Andalusian poets tend not to be as gloomy as those in Ashkenaz, and there is a far greater variety of genres in Andalusian poetry, including drinking songs, love poetry, military poetry, and philosophical verse. Andalusian poetry also contains far more word play than does its Ashkenazic cousin. And finally, Andalusian poetry may seem more interesting because we know a bit more about the poets than we do about their Ashkenazic counterparts.

Jewish life in Muslim Spain was generally not as oppressive as life in Ashkenaz. The Jews were dhimmis, second-class citizens, but what that status meant differed in different times and places. Sometimes it meant very little, but even when it meant more, Jews were usually more inte-grated into the general environment than they were elsewhere. They spoke Arabic, though they often wrote the language in Hebrew charac-ters, and they played important roles in a variety of Andalusian courts. Some of the greatest medieval Hebrew poets lived there during the tenth to twelfth centuries.

A fascination with words characterized Muslim courtly society. Even before the time of Mohammed, poetry played an important role in Ara-bic society, and the language of the *Qu'ran* deepened the reverence for Arabic. Muslim poets wrote about love and about wine, intricate worldly poems, like this stanza by the twelfth-century poet ibn Quzman:

> The talk goes on, the wine is drunk,
> I sing and she makes music.
> I ask of her—what one asks;
> she says "yes," and grants my wishes.
> Dawn is rising, the oppressor [the sun],
> why does it rise? (Lewis 74)

Not only is such poetry appealing, but the life it represents is appeal-ing as well. It reflects a life of pleasure, a life in which one can enjoy good things, a life verging on, and often crossing into, hedonism. Such a life appealed not only to the Muslim poets, to whom wine was theoreti-cally forbidden and who were supposed to follow strict laws regarding sexual activity, but to Jewish poets as well. And while the Jews also fol-lowed strict sexual laws, they had no prohibition against the moderate consumption of alcohol. Thus, a first reading of many Andalusian Hebrew poems makes them seem frivolous, if not actually sinful. As we will see, however, such immediate impressions may be mistaken, for scholars are still trying to determine how these poems should be read.

That statement may seem strange, since we are dealing with poems that are over seven hundred years old, but there is an explanation. Dur-ing, or more likely after, the lifetimes of these poets, their friends and successor gathered their works into collections called *diwans*, what we might think of as the *Collected Poems of* …, but these collections did not necessarily contain all of a poet's work. The works that the poets wrote for liturgical use would have been copied into prayer books, so the poet's *diwan* contained non-liturgical poems. Nineteenth-century critics gave these two kinds of poetry names such as "sacred verse" and "secular verse," but those terms are misleading, for, as I will argue, the so-called secular poems also have a religious dimension. "Liturgical" and "non-liturgical" verse would be more appropriate categories.[8]

After the *diwans* were collected, however, an interesting thing happened. Thanks in large part to the historical fate of Spanish Jewry, the *diwans* were often lost. Prayer books were preserved and recopied, so the poets' liturgical works were well known, but even when a *diwan* survived, the new cultural context in which the Jews found themselves meant that they no longer knew how to interpret those poems, which so often seemed to deal with a secular life that had now become foreign to the people. Consequently, large parts of this amazing poetic heritage were either forgotten or overlooked. Most of Yehuda Halevi's incredible poetry was first printed in 1840 and 1864, and most of Shmuel ha-Nagid's poetry did not appear until 1934, at a time that was hardly propitious for the study of Hebrew poetry.[9] The scholarly investigation of this poetry, therefore, is still relatively new, and basic disagreements about how to approach it have not been resolved. For example, some critics like to describe these poets as "courtier-rabbis," a term that others find troubling. The term implies a dual existence. On the one hand, these poets were experts on Jewish traditions, as we can see from their detailed, often obscure references in their poems to classic Jewish texts. On the other hand, they were so assimilated that they could disregard those texts, as well as Jewish laws and traditions, and take part in drinking parties and sexual trysts, including homosexual activity, often with young boys. Certainly, no one would argue that religious leaders are exempt from fleshly temptations, so it is possible that such activities took place. What is less likely, however, is that highly learned and religious men would write exquisite poetry in which they advertised their religious failings with such a sense of joy. Surely something else must be happening in those poems.

We in the twenty-first century, coming after the Romantic poets and after the philosophies of Descartes, Kant, and their successors, place a great deal of emphasis on the self, and we are inclined to think of poetry in Wordsworth's terms as "the spontaneous overflow of powerful emotion." Medieval poets, Jewish and non-Jewish, had no such notion. They regarded poetry as a craft, and a fine poem was a well-made object. We do, indeed, have stories about poets who created complex extemporaneous poems, but those poets were like Bach, who could improvise a six-part fugue: they were demonstrating their skill, their ability to manipulate words according to particular rules in order to craft a poem. This approach, incidentally, may help us to understand why so many poems contain acrostics, particularly using the poet's name; and it should also warn us not to identify the speaker of the poem, the "I," with the poet himself and not to regard the experiences related in the poem as reflecting the poet's own experiences.

With all of these warnings, then, we can begin to look at the poems, and it is appropriate that we begin with Dunash ben Labrat. Dunash, who lived in tenth-century Cordoba, was one of the creators of Andalusian Hebrew poetry, for he led the way in imitating Arabic poetry, in two ways. First, he introduced the use of Arabic genres and subjects in Hebrew verse, thereby laying the foundation for non-liturgical poetry. Second, he shaped the meter of Hebrew verse. We saw earlier that biblical verse employed elaborate parallelism, but parallelism was no longer used in poetry. Arabic poetry was quantitative, that is, it relied on patterns of long and short syllables, which it can do because Arabic vowels are understood to be long and short. Hebrew vowels, however, are not classed according to quantity, so that theoretically quantitative verse would not be possible in Hebrew; but Dunash devised a system in which the Hebrew vowels are assigned quantity, thereby creating the possibility of quantitative verse. Thus, in some modern editions of this poetry, we find at the beginnings of the poems an indication of the metrical scheme, for example (reading from right to left) ⁻⁻ ⁻⁻⁻ˇ ⁻⁻⁻ˇ. (In the English Renaissance, a number of poets, including Philip Sidney, tried to create English quantitative verse in imitation of the Latin poetry that they knew so well, but their efforts were unsuccessful, unlike those of the Andalusian poets who created a whole body of quantitative verse.)

In the following poem, Dunash also uses a theme that runs throughout Andalusian Hebrew poetry:

> He said: "Do not sleep! Drink old wine amidst myrrh and lilies, henna and aloes, in an orchard of pomegranates, palms, and vines, full of pleasant plants and tamarisks, to the hum of fountains and the throb of lutes.... There every tree is tall, branches are fair with fruit, and winged birds of every kind sing among the leaves. The doves moan melodiously, and the turtle-doves reply, cooing like reed pipes. There we shall drink among flower-beds fenced in by lilies, putting sorrow to rout with songs of praise. We shall eat sweets as we drink by the bowlful. We shall act like giants, drinking out huge goblets. And in the morning I shall rise to slaughter fat choice bulls and rams and calves. We shall anoint ourselves with fragrant oil and burn aloe incense. Oh, before doom overtakes us, let us enjoy ourselves in peace."

But I reproached him thus: "Silence! How dare you—when the Holy House, the footstool of God, is in the hands of the gentiles. You have spoken foolishly, you have chosen sloth, you have uttered nonsense, like the mockers and fools. You have forsaken the study of the Supreme God's law. Even as you rejoice, jackals run wild in Zion. Then how could we drink wine, how even raise our eyes—when we are loathed and abhorred, and less than nothing?" (Carmi 280)

This poem, as Raymond Scheindlin indicates, reflects the common Arabic (and Greek) practice of presenting an attractive idea and then attacking it, leading the reader to debate between the two sides.[10] In this poem, that format is more than a rhetorical device or an organizing principle. Rather, the poem raises real questions that confronted not only Dunash, but all the Jews of Andalusia. It recalls the legend behind why a Jewish groom breaks a glass at a wedding: according to a legend, the rabbi who was presiding over a wedding long ago became upset at the unrestrained rejoicing that he saw and broke a glass in order to remind the guests of the destruction of the Temple and of the sadness of their lives in exile. In this poem, Dunash presents both sides of the issue.

The first stanza presents the argument for pleasure in beautiful, seductive terms. Who would not want to spend time surrounded by tropical plants and birds, listening to music, feasting on delicacies? Life is short, after all, and we should enjoy ourselves. But then the answer comes: we cannot enjoy ourselves when the Temple stands in ruins, under the control of non-Jews, and the Jews live as strangers in a land not their own. We must ask which voice is right, and before we can answer that question, we must ask whose the voices are—"He said" and "I reproached him." They might be two separate people, or they might be two sides of one person: in either case, they reflect the bifurcated existence of the Jewish people and one of the dilemmas that confronts them. Should they assimilate, join in the life around them, and enjoy life to the extent that enjoyment is possible? Or should they maintain their separate identity in loyalty to God, to a temple destroyed a millennium earlier, and to a way of life that subjects them to loathing and scorn? These are questions that have always confronted the Jews in exile. Some have given in and assimilated, while others have struggled to preserve their identity, but the answers have not come easily for either side. As Scheindlin argues, both sides have merit.[11] The issue is never resolved. Probably, it can never be resolved, and each poet, each person, will have to struggle with it. The "I" of the poem says, "You have uttered nonsense," using the Hebrew word *hevel*, the "vanity" of Ecclesiastes 1:1, the "worthlessness" of Jeremiah 2:5: they "went after worthlessness and became worthless" (my translation). But how long can mourning continue? When will the exile end? How long can we wait? And is enjoyment in life really so worthless? The answers to these questions are neither easy nor self-evident, and the questions themselves reverberate throughout Andalusian poetry.

We can see them again in a poem by Shmuel ha-Nagid (Samuel the Prince), also known as Shmuel ibn Nagrela, who lived in the eleventh century. Shmuel is an almost mythic figure in Jewish history. He was a talmudist, a poet, a general, and an important leader in Cordoba. His poems cover a wide variety of genres: he wrote poems about his military campaigns, elegies, drinking songs, love songs, and many others, some of them quite long. One of his briefer poems restates Dunash's dilemma:

> Yours is the duty to make right your deeds
> And to give you reward will upon him [Him] lie.
> Do not spend (all) your days in his service
> But do a time for God and times for yourselves;
> Give no rest to wine in your nights!
> Put out the candle-light and lift up with your cups.
> Despise the voice of singers but make music with your jugs.
> And if in the grave there is no song, wine, or friend,—woe
> Fools, let this be the reward for your labors. (Weinberger 114)

At first glance, this poem seems to give sensible, if possibly blasphemous, advice: be righteous, but don't go overboard with religiosity; enjoy yourself with wine, with song, with good company. Enjoyment is not a bad thing, but what constitutes enjoyment? The poem says that we should give half the day to God and half to ourselves and then party all night, which means that we actually give only a quarter of our time to God. If, as the poem's opening tells us, God will give us our reward, then we must consider what that reward will be for offering God only a quarter of our time. And what does it even mean to offer God our time? If God suffuses our lives as we should allow Him to, we cannot turn that process on and off, which means that the advice the speaker is giving amounts again to worthlessness. After all, as the last line indicates, he is addressing fools. Such fools, seeking empty pleasures, will find their reward only in those pleasures. In short, the poem's actual advice is not to follow the advice it seems to offer, appealing though it may be. We cannot choose between God and the world, just as in Dunash's poem we could not resolve the claims of secular and religious views. Perhaps the secular and the religious cannot be separated.

On the other hand, we must not think of Shmuel and the other Hebrew poets as ascetics. Judaism is not a religion of asceticism. At every stage in the creation story, we hear that God approved of his work, that it was good, so we cannot simply dismiss it. As Shmuel tells us in another poem:

> There are five things that fill the heart
> With delight and drive away grief:
> A graceful form, a garden, wine, the ripple
> Of a stream and a poet, these awaken joy within me. (Weinberger 112)

All five of these elements appear frequently in the works of all the poets we are examining. What we cannot know for sure, however, is whether the poetry reflects the actual experiences of the poets or whether these elements constitute the traditional subjects of Arabic poetry and therefore supply the subject of Hebrew poetry as well. We might think of all the hundreds of Elizabethan love sonnets and wonder whether all of those sonneteers really had disastrous love affairs. More likely, unrequited love was just accepted as the major theme for sonnets, based on medieval traditions and especially on the works of Petrarch.

This explanation might also help us to understand the many poems like the following:

> I will be a ransom for the young lad who arose at night
> To the sound of the 'ud [a musical instrument] and the excellent flute players,
> Who saw a cup in my hand and said:
> "Drink the wine [literally "the blood of the grapes] from between my lips!"
> While the moon like the letter yod ['] was written
> Upon the garment of dawn with colors of gold. (Weinberger 106)

As is the case in much Andalusian poetry, we see at least the implications of a sexual relationship between the speaker and a young boy (or sometimes a young girl). Probably, the poets adopted this motif because it appeared so prominently in the Arabic models, though, as Norman Roth points out, in those models there is often overt sexual activity whereas in the Hebrew poems contact is limited to kissing.[12] Scheindlin suggests that the erotic aspects of the poem are subordinated to the striking concluding image, in which the moon, having the shape of *yod*, the smallest Hebrew letter, perhaps stands for God and the world to come, both of which are represented in Hebrew writing by that letter.[13] In any case, we should remember what Shmuel says in another short poem:

> He will incite you to evil with dream-like talk
> And with words of poetry he will urge you to deception.
> My son, not every dream comes true
> Neither are all the words of the poet veritable! (Weinberger 116)

In short, says this prolific poet, not all poetry is trustworthy, particularly not on its surface, a warning to us that we must be careful in our attempts to understand it.

Often these poems contain ambiguities that we cannot penetrate. At the same time, many of Shmuel's poems are quite clear:

> In the days when the young lads of Zion will be at home
> like the bright and shining sun on garden beds of spices
> They shall gaze upon the singing maidens with looks of love
> on eyes painted with the color of God's work ...
> I yearn for the prince's daughter who, in the nut garden
> placed her fawn by a lily to be gathered and planted.
> Behold the roaring lions who occupy it
> and prevent her from entering therein ...
> On seeing with my heart's eye my Holy of Holies a devastated heap
> and the foundation stone swallowed up among the rocks,
> with terror in my eyes I cried bitterly ... (Weinberger 54, with some punctuation changes)

Like his Ashkenazic brethren, Shmuel here laments the destruction of the Temple, his distance from Jerusalem, and the impossibility under present conditions of the Jews' return to their homeland, where young men and women should be leading happy, productive lives glorifying divine creation. Instead, the Temple still lies in ruins and the Jews are forbidden to return.

The poetry of Shmuel ha-Nagid, then, provides a panoramic view of his time. Its combination of secular and religious motifs, its humor, its use of standard themes, and its pathos all provide a sense of what life might have been like in his time. And beyond those factors, the poetry is beautiful in the Hebrew. Shmuel's skill with the language makes the reader smile with pleasure. For instance, the poem quoted above, "I will be a ransom," begins in the Hebrew *Ehi kopher le'opher kam be'layil.* The sounds of those first three words are memorable, and the language in the rest of the poem captures the sensuality that lies on the poem's surface. As we read these poems, we should remember again that Hebrew was not a spoken language for these poets or for their audience. This was the language of prayer and of study—and of poetry.

Shmuel ha-Nagid is the first of the four greatest Andalusian Hebrew poets. The others are Shlomo ibn Gabirol, Yehuda Halevi, and Moshe ibn Ezra. All four of these poets have become legendary as a result of stories about their lives (whether true or not), and two of them, ibn Gabirol and Yehuda Halevi, we will meet again in the next chapter when we look at Jewish philosophy, but they were all also poets of extraordinary ability.

Shlomo ibn Gabirol, another eleventh-century poet, is a tantalizing figure. What we know about him is typified by this story: in the middle of the nineteenth century, it was discovered that ibn Gabirol was the author of an Arabic philosophical work that had been translated into Latin and become known in Europe as the *Fons Vitae* (*The Fountain of Life*), attributed to "Avicebrol" or "Avicebron." For eight hundred years, his authorship of this work had been unknown. Similarly, much of what we think we know about him is questionable. Apparently, he served for a short time as a disciple of Shmuel, he suffered for much of his life from a terrible illness, he presents himself in his poetry as rather ugly (perhaps as a result of his illness), he is simultaneously deeply religious, arrogant, and impatient, and he died young—or possibly he did not. The evidence is contradictory. We can see some of these attributes in one of his more famous poems:

> I'm prince to the poem my slave,
> I'm harp to the court musicians,
> my song is a turban for viziers' heads,
> a crown for kings in their kingdoms:
> and here I've lived just sixteen years,
> and my heart is like eighty within them. (Cole 45)

If he was indeed sixteen when he wrote this poem, as was probably the case, we must marvel at both his skill and his arrogance. The feeling that he has such complete control over the poem, like a prince to a slave, is an extraordinary boast, but anyone can say that. What is more extraordinary is the truth of the boast. For instance, we may be inclined to regard the concluding lines as yet another sign of arrogance—I'm only sixteen but I'm as wise as a man of eighty—but actually these lines contain a talmudic reference. When one of the talmudic sages, Elazar ben Azariah, was made the head of the Sanhedrin at a very young age, he worried that he would not be taken seriously because of his youth, but overnight his hair turned gray, thereby giving him the aura of wisdom and authority. Ibn Gabirol, then, may be acknowledging his own powers, but he may also be attributing those powers to God, who works such miracles. In fact, the large number of ibn Gabirol's liturgical poems demonstrates profound piety and humility, as in the following:

> Before my being your mercy came through me,
> bringing existence to nothing to shape me.
> Who is it conceived of my form—and who
> cast it then in a kiln to create me?
> Who breathed soul inside me—and who
> opened the belly of hell and withdrew me?
> Who through youth brought me thus far?
> Who with wisdom and wonder endowed me?
> I'm clay cupped in your hands, it's true;
> it's you, I know, not I who made me.
> I'll confess my sin and will not say
> the serpent's ways, or evil seduced me.
> How could I hide my error from you when
> before my being your mercy came through me? (Cole 111)

In this deeply moving poem, ibn Gabirol combines Jeremiah ("Before I created you in the womb, I selected you"—1:5), Psalms, Jewish conceptions of sin and repentance, and medieval Neo-platonic and Aristotelian thought to create a preparatory exercise for prayer. Despite his illness, the poet thanks God for his creation, takes responsibility for his sins, and begs for forgiveness. There is no arrogance in this poem, which is still current a thousand years after its composition.

Another poem illustrates how these poems were used in the synagogue:

> At dawn I seek Thee
> my Rock and my Refuge
> I shall direct my prayer to Thee
> morning and evening.

Before Thy greatness
I stand affrighted
for Thine eye sees
all the thoughts of my heart.

What can the heart
and tongue achieve?
What strength has my soul
within my body?

The song of man
is pleasing to Thee.
Therefore I praise Thee
while still God's spirit is in me. (Lewis 183)

The word in the last line that means "spirit," *nishmath*, is the first word of an important prayer in the Sabbath and holiday morning service. Ibn Gabirol composed this poem as an introduction to that prayer, which does indeed consist of praises of God and which would be recited at or near dawn. The poem expresses the awe that the cantor would feel at addressing God and at representing the congregation before the Lord. But even a less overtly religious poem expresses ibn Gabirol's religious view of the world:

Winter with its ink of showers and rain
with its pen of lightning and palm of clouds
wrote a letter of purple and blue
over the beds of the garden

No artist in his cunning could measure
his work beside it—and so,
when earth longed for the sky
it embroidered the spread of its furrows like stars. (Cole 66)

The poem depicts the earth as the handiwork of a master poet and artist, who "wrote" and "embroidered" the beauties of nature. This poem delights in the natural world, emphasizing what we see over and over in the account of creation, that God saw that the world was good. At the same time, it implies an analogy between God and the poet, with the former "writing" and "embroidering" nature while the latter writes and ornaments poems. In this sense, the poem compares divine and earthly creation, the heavenly and earthly worlds, linking them together while still making a distinction between them. This relationship between the two worlds also characterizes ibn Gabirol's longest poem, the magisterial *Keter Malkhut*, "The Kingly Crown," which we will consider when we look at medieval Jewish philosophy.

The third of the great poets was Yehuda Halevi, possibly the most romantic figure of medieval Judaism. Halevi (eleventh-twelfth centuries) lived in the Christian part of Spain for some time, but eventually returned to Andalusia. He was a physician and philosopher—we will examine his *Kuzari* in the next chapter—but he is perhaps best known as a poet and as the person who left "golden age" Spain to journey to the land of Israel. According to legend, he arrived there after a difficult journey, and as he approached Jerusalem, he fell to his knees, only to be killed by an Arab horseman. The major problem with this romantic and appealing story is that it is not true. Halevi did indeed travel to Israel, where he died, but the circumstances of his death are unknown. He did, however, leave a poetic record of his journey, and the record has been augmented by discoveries in the Geniza. After the death of his wife in Spain, Halevi left his family and set out on the dangerous journey to Israel. He stopped for a time in Alexandria, where, the Geniza documents tell us, although he was regarded as a great celebrity, he still continued his journey to the Holy Land. His reasons for this pilgrimage are somewhat obscure, but probably, as is usually the case, he acted from a variety of motives. As his poems indicate, he believed deeply in the sanctity of the Holy Land and in its nearness to God. He frequently uses the image of windows or gates opening from Jerusalem, specifically from the Temple Mount, into Heaven. He was also undoubtedly greatly affected by the deteriorating situation of the Jews in Andalusia and became impatient with passively waiting for the arrival of the messiah and so decided to take an active role by making his pilgrimage. And he may well have been overcome by the death of his wife and felt a need to go somewhere else. We cannot know for certain. Nonetheless, his poetry reveals his deep devotion:

> My love, have you forgotten how you lay between my breasts
> Then why have you sold me forever to my enslavers?
> Did I not follow you through a barren land?
> Let Mount Seir and Mount Paran, Sinai and Sin be my witnesses!
> There my love was yours, and I was your delight ...
> Is there any savior but you? Any prisoner of hope but I?
> Give me your strength, for I shall give you my love! (Carmi 334)

The sensuality of this poem may seem surprising at first. It almost reads like a love poem, and in fact it is a love poem, but, based on the words of Jeremiah and the Song of Songs, it reflects the love of Israel for God. That love, for the moment, appears unrequited, as God seems to have abandoned Israel, who reminds Him of her faithfulness and who calls on important locales from the years of wandering in the wilderness as witnesses of that faithfulness. Then Israel reasserts her faithfulness, expressing love for God and hoping that her love will be returned.

The love in this poem seems simultaneously national and personal. The speaker is Israel, but the sentiments are also those of Yehuda Halevi, who, like so many of his compatriots, feels the heavy burden of the exile and worries that God has turned away from Israel forever. Another poem, directly related to his journey, conveys the same sense:

My heart is in the east, and I in the uttermost west—
How can I find savour in food? How shall it be sweet to me?
How shall I render my vows and my bonds, while yet
Zion lieth beneath the fetter of Edom, and I in Arab chains?
A light thing would it seem to me to leave all the good things of Spain—
Seeing how precious in mine eyes to behold the dust of the desolate
sanctuary. (Jehuda Halevi 1)

The speaker here feels the physical distance between Jerusalem at the eastern end of the Mediterranean and his position in Spain at the western end: he is separated from his homeland by almost the whole world. Similarly, Zion is held captive by Edom, that is, by the Christian world, which captured it during the Crusades, and he is bound by the Muslim world in which he lives. Not only do all the pleasures of Spain—and we know about those pleasures from so much of the Arabic and Hebrew poetry that was devoted to them—seem less enjoyable, but the speaker cannot fulfill his "vows and bonds." The Hebrew of that third line— "How shall I render my vows and my bonds" contains two significant references. The first word, *Echah*, is also the first word and the Hebrew title of the book of Lamentations, which depicts and laments the destruction of the Temple by the Babylonians and which is read every year on Tisha b'Av, the anniversary of that destruction. The Hebrew for "my vows and my bonds" is *nedarai ve'esarai*, words that recall the Kol Nidrei prayer that is recited at the very beginning of Yom Kippur. (In fact *nedarai* and *nidrei* come from the same root and look identical in the Hebrew.) Thus, those three words recall the destruction and the transgressions that led to that destruction, as well as the repentance for those transgressions. The speaker feels trapped in Spain as a result of historical circumstances, but he, along with Israel, repents and hopes to return from exile, even if the Temple is not yet rebuilt, even if the messiah has not yet come. Perhaps his journey toward Israel will even hasten the coming of the messiah and the rebuilding of the Temple. He would be content to see just the dust of the destroyed Temple and to be at that sacred spot. Even the dust and the ruins clearly outweigh all the pleasures of Spain. As he says in his famous "Ode to Zion," in which he recalls some of the famous places in the Holy Land:

> I would fall, with my face upon thine earth and take delight
> In thy stones and be tender to thy dust. (Jehuda Halevi 4)

Thus he dreams about the Temple rituals and he imagines himself in the Holy Land. Thinking of the sea and the sky, in biblical terms the waters above and the waters below, he writes:

> Then are they two seas bound up together;
> And between them is my heart, a third sea,
> Lifting up ever anew my waves of praise. (Jehuda Halevi 13)

Those two seas are united by the poet's heart. He, both as an individual and as the representative of Israel, brings them together and forms the bridge between God and the world, which means that he fulfills a prophetic role in the world. And where is the best place for prophecy? The Holy Land, of course,

> the land that is full of gates
> Toward which the gates of Heaven are open. (Jehuda Halevi 15)

He, and Israel, must return to their homeland, to the land that is closest to God, so that they can resume their ancient role as a "kingdom of priests" (Exodus 19:6). Too long they have lived in strange lands and accepted the cultures of those lands. In modern terms, they have assimilated. Now that situation must change:

> See now, yea see, my friend, and understand
> And turn aside from the lure of thorns and snares,
> And let not the wisdom of the Greeks beguile thee,
> Which hath no fruit but only flowers ... (Jehuda Halevi 16)

Here, as we will see more clearly in the next chapter, Halevi touches on an issue that was to split the Jewish world, the influence of Greek philosophy. Halevi was familiar with that philosophy, which had been translated into Arabic and which, during his lifetime, made its way into Christian Europe, but he, unlike Moshe Maimonides, rejected that philosophy, which attempted to explain the world in terms of logic. The philosophical approach is attractive, certainly. It has beautiful flowers, but it produces no fruit, nothing nourishing. Instead, it leads its adherents astray:

> Wherefore, then should I seek me out crooked ways,
> And forsake the mother of paths? (Jehuda Halevi 17)

Not only does Greek wisdom deceive, but it draws its adherents away from the true path, that is, the learning that characterizes Judaism. In short, Halevi has become dissatisfied with everything about Spain, so much so that he is willing to abandon his grown daughter and her family as well as all the comforts of his home and set out on a dangerous journey, moved by his religious zeal and by his understanding of Jewish history.

We have concentrated on this aspect of Halevi's poetry, but he wrote many other kinds of poetry as well, including prayers, lamentations, elegies, poems of praise, and beautiful love poems. For example, here is a poem that combines praise and ideas about love:

> The bridal pair stands amid the myrtles,
> Sending forth pure myrrh on every side.
> The myrtle desireth the sweetness of their fragrance,
> And spreadeth his wings like a cherub above them.
> The myrtle thinketh to cover their fragrance,
> But the sweetness of their spices overwhelmeth his scent. (Jehudah Halevi 53)

Halevi's poetry is exquisite. He used Hebrew masterfully and expressed a powerful set of emotions regardless of his subject. But Halevi was also clearly tormented. He virtually epitomizes what Ross Brann calls in the title of his book on Andalusian poetry *The Compunctious Poet*. Halevi was thoroughly immersed in his poetic milieu, which relied so heavily on Jewish adaptations of Arabic models, and yet he felt estranged from that milieu. Like so many others, poets and non-poets, he was faced with being a Jew in an alien culture. How could he reconcile the tensions created by the demands of those two cultures? Ultimately Halevi could not, and he set sail for Israel, but he was one of the few who did so. Most Jews, in both Ashkenaz and Sepharad, lived with those tensions and devised other methods of dealing with them, but we can see in their history, in their biblical commentaries, in their poetry, and elsewhere their efforts to remain Jewish despite the pressures of the culture around them, and the toll those efforts often took.

We can see the problem once again in the fourth of the great Andalusian poets, Moshe ibn Ezra (eleventh and twelfth centuries). Ibn Ezra was born in Muslim Spain and remained in Granada even after the Jews were attacked by the Almoravids in 1090. Some years later, however, he left Granada and spent his remaining years traveling through Christian Spain, writing poems that lamented his exile from his family. Like the other major poets, he was a master of Hebrew. For instance, he wrote a long series of poems like the following:

> Take for yourself flower beds as a couch
> And don't rest on shield and spear.
> The sound of the swallow, the crane, and the dove
> Will replace the sound of the lyre and cymbal. (Hebrew in *Moses ibn Ezra* 77; my translation)

In the Hebrew, the last words of each couplet are homonyms. In this poem, for instance, lines two and four both end with the word *tziltzal*, but in the former it means "spear" while in the latter it means "cymbal." Like so many of our poets, ibn Ezra loved such word play and was extremely good at it.

But many of his poems offer other difficulties related to some of the themes we have been examining. For instance:

> The garden wears a colored coat,
> The lawn has on embroidered robes,
> The trees are wearing checkered shifts,
> They show their wonders to every eye.
> And every bud renewed by spring
> Comes smiling forth to greet his lord.
> See! Before them marches a rose,
> Kingly, his throne above them borne.
> Freed of the leaves that had guarded him,
> No more to wear his prison clothes.
> Who will refuse to toast him there?
> Such a man his sin will bear. (Scheindlin, *Wine*, 35)

Raymond Scheindlin, one of the leading authorities on medieval Hebrew poetry, interprets this poem as a work that commands its readers to lead a life of hedonism. He views the rose as a king to whom the other components of the garden owe allegiance, which they can show by drinking a toast to him. Scheindlin therefore sees this poem as a wine poem, a popular form of the time.[14]

We could also see the poem quite differently, however. As Scheindlin points out, there are verbal echoes in the poem that refer to biblical figures such as Joseph, David, and Jehoiachin (a Judean king who was imprisoned and then released by the Babylonians). Those references alone might indicate that the poem is dealing with something more significant than hedonism. When ibn Ezra personifies the garden, with its coat of many colors, as well as the lawn and the trees, we can assume that the rose is also a personification, not simply of a king but of a particular king. And what king, other than Jehoiachin, has been imprisoned? Not a single human king but a kingly people, Israel. Once Israel is freed from its prison, the other nations will acknowledge its sovereignty, because that freedom will indicate that the messiah has arrived. According to this reading, the poem is much more serious and relies on themes that we have seen pervading medieval Hebrew poetry. Ibn Ezra equates Israel's current condition to being in prison, as does Todros ben Yehuda Abulafia over a hundred years later, in the thirteenth century:

Dear birds, fly to our friends,
Carry greetings from sufferers who sit immured in a dungeon. (Lewis 198)

But ibn Ezra holds out hope—all of nature and every nation will acknowledge Israel. Abulafia, who may himself have actually been in prison, is less hopeful, for he ends his poem by remarking that his guards bring no food, nor do ravens. Since ravens fed the prophet Elijah (Kings 17:4–6), thereby miraculously saving him, Abulafia is saying that a new miracle is needed to save Israel, but none seems forthcoming.

There are numerous other medieval Hebrew poets, but this brief survey indicates the beauty and complexity of their work, as well as its central concerns with issues that confronted people in their everyday lives. The poetry is often difficult to read in the Hebrew, both because of the poets' love of word play and because it makes so many references to biblical, talmudic, and midrashic literature. Even in translation, however, these poems are worth reading for their intrinsic beauty and for the picture they give us of the world that produced them.[15]

Prose

Not all of medieval literature was written in poetic form. There were also important prose works, such as *The Book of Delight* by Joseph ben Meir Zabara, but we conclude our brief look at medieval Hebrew literature by considering two startling works that employ what to us seems like an unusual prose style. These works are Yehuda Alharizi's *Book of Tahkemoni* and the *Mahberoth* (*The Notebooks*) of Immanuel ha-Romi, both written in a Hebrew adaptation of the Arabic *maqama*, rhymed prose with inserted poems. (The twentieth-century Israeli novelist S. Y. Agnon made use of this style as well.)

Yehudah Alharizi (1165–1225), if we can trust his introduction—and he is often too playful for us to trust him entirely—wrote his long book in response to an Arabic work, the *Maqamat* of Ibn Ali al-Hariri, which Alharizi had translated into Hebrew. The *Maqamat* is a virtuosic display of the powers of the Arabic language, and Alharizi apparently decided to demonstrate that Hebrew can be used even more virtuosically. The book is divided into fifty episodes, or "gates," which contain debates on a variety of topics, poetic contests, encounters with people at all levels of society, and a number of language tricks. For instance, one gate is written largely in archaic language, while another presents a passage in which every word contains a particular letter and then a passage in which that letter is never used (much as the twentieth-century French writer Georges Perec did when he wrote an entire novel without using the letter *e*). There is also something surreal about the *Book of Tahkemoni*, for virtually every gate is narrated by Heman the Ezrahite, and wherever he goes, he meets his friend Hever the Kenite, who is often in disguise. In some ways the *Book of Tahkemoni* recalls the fourteenth-century English poem *Piers Plowman*, in which characters appear and disappear with little regard for what we think of as reality.

Predictably, we can find in the *Book of Tahkemoni* references to themes that we have seen in the poetry, particularly to the exile of Israel. Gate Twenty-Eight, which focuses on Jerusalem, addresses this theme in detail. Gate Forty, a debate between the Sword and the Pen, has relevance for us now, as we can see in a brief excerpt that illustrates well the technique of rhymed prose:

> Then the Pen answered, saying, I am the prophet who dwells in Wisdom's tent, Jacob upright and excellent: he who clasps me tight grasps true delight. I bare recondite mystery and unknot secrecy, and to the wise

regale with hid or open tale. Through me spring the nation's laws, clipping Evil's claws. But for the Pen, story and wisdom and cunning were unknown to men. (304)

The *Book of Taḥkemoni* can be difficult to read—the rhymed prose occasionally becomes oppressive and Alharizi's references can be excessive—but David Segal's translation and notes help make the work accessible.

Immanuel ha-Romi (or Immanuel of Rome, 1265–1330, apparently known in his own time as Manoello Giudeo[16]) lived in Italy when conditions were relatively benign for the Italian Jews, except for incidents like the temporary expulsion of the Jews from Rome in 1321. Immanuel wrote biblical commentaries, a Hebrew grammar, and a number of Italian sonnets, but he is best known for the *Maḥberoth*, a long collection of poems bound together by prose narratives. His work is both highly satiric and erotic, and religious authorities warned against reading him, even though parts of the *Maḥberoth* reflect a deep religiosity. The *Maḥberoth* contains twenty-eight chapters, and we will consider the twenty-eighth, which is based, amazingly enough, on Dante's *Divine Comedy*. Parts of Immanuel's work seem like a parody of Dante, but it is difficult to be sure. For instance, when Immanuel encounters Isaiah, Jeremiah, Ezekiel, David, and Solomon in the afterlife, they are overjoyed to see him because they know him to be the only accurate commentator on their works. Is he making fun of Dante, who put himself in the company of Virgil, Horace, Homer, Ovid, and Lucan, or does he really believe that his commentary is superior to all others? We cannot know.

Immanuel is led through the afterlife by someone named Daniel, probably the biblical Daniel, whose name resembles Dante. Daniel is an appropriate guide for at least two reasons. One is the vision of the general resurrection in Daniel 12:2: "Many of those that sleep in the dust of the earth will awake, some to eternal life, others to reproaches, to everlasting abhorrence." The second reason is that Daniel is a book about exile—the action takes place in Babylonia—and Immanuel writes both as a Jew exiled from the Holy Land and as an Italian exiled from Rome.

Immanuel visits Tophet (Hell) and Eden (Heaven)—there is no Purgatory in Jewish belief—but his descriptions of those regions are neither as detailed nor as fraught with multiple significances as are Dante's. The seemingly haphazard organization of those regions and of the punishments and rewards they contain reflect the un-doctrinaire nature of Jewish thinking about life after death, as opposed to Dante's highly organized Thomistic views. Immanuel focuses on sins that involve hypocrisy, blasphemy, apostasy, witchcraft, and the denial of the doctrine of reward and punishment, as well as violations of sexual standards and excessive attachment to material things. Unlike Dante, Immanuel does not populate his place of punishment with his friends and enemies.

If Dante's heaven is a solemn and serene place where weighty philosophical and theological discussions take place with some regularity, Immanuel's Eden is quite different. Whatever serenity might have existed there is shattered when Immanuel enters and David, Ezekiel, Jeremiah, Isaiah, Solomon, Moses, and Joseph practically stumble over each other in their attempts to praise him. In a sense, Immanuel is only making explicit about himself what Dante implies about himself, but the effect is incongruous, as when we hear Isaiah say, "How my heart did rejoice when thou my text did expound! ... My words in the sight of others were as nought but to be passed by, until thou didst arise, and thy comment was the one agreeable to every eye ..." (75). No one ever accused Dante of excessive modesty either. Still, unlike Dante, Immanuel reserves a special area in Eden for the "righteous among the Gentiles."

Both the *Book of Tahkemoni* and the *Mahberoth* may seem somewhat strange to us, but in important ways all medieval literature is strange to us. To read Chaucer or Langland or Dante, we must learn to think medievally. To read Alharizi or Immanuel or any of the poets we considered, we must learn to read medievally and Jewishly. Doing so is a challenge, but the rewards are plentiful.

Philosophy and Kabbalah

It may seem odd to include philosophy and Kabbalah, Jewish mysticism, in the same chapter, but frequently those two traditions represent reactions to the same stimuli. In Eastern Europe in the eighteenth century, for instance, as a result of the Chmielnicki massacres of 1648, Judaism moved almost simultaneously in two directions: Haskalah and Ḥasidism. "Haskalah" means Enlightenment, and many Jews, in an attempt to enter "the modern world," turned to Western culture and to the rationalism that characterized so much eighteenth-century thought. Other Jews turned to the mystical and emotional world of Ḥasidism, a movement that emphasized religious fervor and joy and the diminution of the self. Similarly, we saw after the Crusade massacres the development of the Tosafists, rationalists in the tradition of Aristotle, who restored to talmudic study the application of stricter logic, and of the Ḥasidei Ashkenaz, the German Pietists, who, like the later Ḥasidim, rejected logic as a primary concern and promoted a somewhat different variety of religious fervor (that later influenced the development of the *Zohar*). This dichotomy, perhaps in a less blatant fashion, persisted through much of the Middle Ages. On the one hand we find thinkers who are commonly classified as medieval Jewish philosophers, while on the other hand we see traces of medieval Jewish mysticism that culminate in the production of the *Zohar*. Without minimizing the differences between philosophy and mysticism, or between the philosophers and their opponents, in their idealized forms philosophy and mysticism represent two routes to the same destination, the fulfillment of Judaism. Later medieval Jews fought bitterly over which route should be taken, but if we can stand back and view them from a distance, we will be able to discern their similarities as well as their differences.

All of the philosophers in the following pages lived in either Babylonia or Spain. Just as the Jews of Ashkenaz did not write much non-liturgical poetry, they seldom engaged in philosophical speculation. They had little contact with the Christian philosophers, who wrote in Latin, a language they did not understand, and they were more consumed with the problems of mere survival than were their Sephardic co-religionists. Even so, the works of these philosophers and kabbalists did become known in Ashkenaz.

Philosophy

Medieval philosophy, whether Jewish, Christian, or Muslim, differs significantly from modern philosophy. "Philosophy" itself means "love of wisdom," and we tend to think of philosophy as an impartial quest for the truth, whatever we might mean by "truth." Medieval philosophers, however, already knew the truth before they began philosophizing. That truth was the truth taught by their religions, which means, of course, that Jewish, Christian, and Muslim philosophers all based their thought on different versions of the truth; and their philosophies were, consequently, attempts to investigate those truths and often to persuade others of the validity of those truths. As Gordon Leff writes, medieval thinkers "sought to explain the natural and the human by reference to such tenets of faith as God, creation, the Incarnation, using philosophical and logical arguments to do so."[1] As his reference to the Incarnation indicates, Leff focuses on Christian philosophy. Jewish and Muslim philosophers naturally used philosophical and logical arguments to explore the tenets of their own faiths. Philosophers of all three faiths, however, were heavily influenced by the works of Aristotle, which had been translated into Arabic and preserved in Muslim culture and which were eventually translated from Arabic into Latin, often through the efforts of Jews. Thus, while Christian writers like Anselm of Canterbury (eleventh century) or Thomas Aquinas (thirteenth century) are better known to Western audiences, their work often depended on their Muslim and Jewish predecessors.

In all cases, however, faith remained primary. As Anselm explains in his *Proslogium*, his goal was not to persuade non-believers but to provide Christians with a rational basis for understanding their faith. Such, too, was the case with the Muslim and Jewish philosophers. Eventually, of course, philosophy went beyond this goal and began to question faith itself, which was what philosophy's opponents had always feared it would do, but the Jewish philosophers examined here set out not to challenge Judaism but to explore its beliefs and explain its rational basis. Whether a religion can be explained rationally is certainly a significant question, but these thinkers believed that, within particular limits, it could. As Gerson Cohen says about the Jewish philosophers, "Physics, logic, mathematics, astronomy, ethics, metaphysics, and even rhetoric, all of them in Arabic translations of, and commentaries on, the classical philosophers, were to be harmoniously blended with Bible and Talmud, midrash and the codes, liturgy and dogma."[2] A world of knowledge was opening up, thanks in large part to the ancient Greeks, and that world of knowledge entailed as well new ways of thinking. The goal of the medieval Jewish philosophers was to combine traditional Jewish thought with that new world and those new ways of thinking, proving thereby that Judaism was true and clarifying its doctrines, often in opposition to the beliefs of Christians and Muslims. As with Christian and Muslim thinkers, the conflict between faith and reason loomed large for the Jews, and that conflict will form the basis of our discussion.

Although there were earlier Jewish philosophers, like Isaac Israeli (850–c.932), the first Jewish philosopher of note was Saadiah Gaon (882–942). Saadiah made important contributions to many fields: he was a poet, but he also settled difficult calendrical problems, took a leading role in combating Karaite thought, prepared an early version of the prayer book, wrote biblical commentary and linguistic studies, and served as a gaon, that is, as the head of the academy in Sura in Babylonia. In his position as gaon, he put both his position and himself in some danger by standing firm on his principles in opposition to the more secular Jewish leaders. Remarkably, Saadiah had been born in Egypt and belonged to the Palestinian branch of Judaism. Thanks to his reputation as a scholar and leader, he was invited to head the Babylonian academy. Under Saadiah's influence, a number of Palestinian practices became integrated into Babylonian Judaism and then spread throughout the Jewish world.[3]

Saadiah's treatise, *Kitab al-Almanat wa'l-I'tiqadat, The Book of Beliefs and Opinions*, was written around the year 933 in Arabic, later translated into Hebrew by Judah ibn Tibbon (1120–c.1190). That it was written in Arabic was no accident. Yehuda Halevi's *Kuzari* and Maimonides' *Guide for the Perplexed* were also written in Arabic. One obvious reason is that their authors lived in Arabic-speaking lands, but all three authors were also masters of Hebrew. The poetry of Saadiah and Yehuda Halevi, as well as Maimonides' *Mishneh Torah,* are written in elegant Hebrew. If they were writing for Jewish audiences, why did they choose to write their philosophical works in Arabic? Obviously their audiences were fluent in Arabic, but more significantly, Arabic was the language of philosophy in the places where these authors lived, just as Latin was the language of philosophy in Ashkenaz; but while the Jews of Ashkenaz seldom knew Latin and were therefore excluded from that philosophical discourse, the Jews of the Middle East and Sepharad knew Arabic and therefore shared their neighbors' interest in philosophy.

Many people, however, opposed this interest in philosophy on the grounds that faith taught all that was necessary and that reason might well undermine faith. Nonetheless, many important thinkers tried to understand their faith through rational means, and it is often difficult for us to separate medieval philosophy from medieval theology. In fact, just as medievals would not have distinguished between astronomy and astrology, they probably could not have recognized the distinction that we make between philosophy and theology. This point is important because a prominent branch of Muslim thought, the *Kalam,* was precisely what we would call theology, and one branch of the *Kalam,* the *Mu'tazila,* employed a thoroughly rationalistic approach to the study of theology. While Saadiah, like Yehuda Halevi and Maimonides, took issue with *Kalam* beliefs, all three were profoundly influenced by the approach of the *Kalam* to questions of "beliefs and opinions."

To understand why this point is so vital, we must return to our earlier discussion of Judaism and of the Talmud in particular. Today we are accustomed to questions about belief, though such questions may be impossible to answer. For instance, if someone asks, "What do Christians believe about" any topic, the first response might well be, "Which kind of Christians?" Roman Catholicism, Greek Orthodoxy, Russian Orthodoxy, and all the branches of Protestantism may differ significantly on fundamental issues. Nonetheless, because belief is so basic to Christianity, each branch of Christianity can describe its belief system. But belief is not nearly so fundamental to Judaism, as we can see from the title of Menachem Kellner's book, *Must a Jew Believe Anything?* The obvious answer is that Jews do believe things. The one line from Deuteronomy 6:4 that we have cited so often, "Hear, O Israel! The Lord our God, the Lord is one," implies a number of beliefs: that the source of the line, the Torah, is the source of truth, that God exists, that God is one, and that God is the God of Israel. But traditional Jewish texts, like the Talmud and the Midrash, did not so much examine what lay behind such pronouncements—how do we know that the Torah is the source of truth? How can we prove that God exists? What does it mean to say that God is one?—as it examined the implications of those pronouncements. Of course the Torah is the source of truth, because God gave it to Moses on Mount Sinai, and therefore we must follow its rules. Of course God exists, even if He seems to have forgotten our plight at times, and so we must follow his rules. Of course God is one, and so we should not worship other gods, because they are by definition false, and therefore to worship them would be to abandon truth for falsity. And so the Talmud does not tell us what to believe. It tells us what to do. Often it tries to explain why the Torah makes particular demands— and often we can find our own explanations for those demands—but those demands are frequently mysterious. In Numbers 19, for instance, we find the law of the red heifer: the ashes of the red heifer are to be used for removing ritual uncleanness from people who have touched a corpse, but those who slaughter the heifer and come in contact with the ashes are thereby made unclean. The law seems incomprehensible. Similarly, Deuteronomy 22:10–11 offers a puzzle:

10. You shall not plow with an ox and an ass together.
11. You shall not wear cloth combining wool and linen.

We can understand why an ox and an ass should not be yoked together: such yoking could be harmful to one of the animals, and the Torah cares about the welfare of animals. But how can we understand why wool and linen should not be mixed together in a single garment? Some scholars see here a taboo against various kinds of mixtures; but even if those scholars are correct, they have not explained what lies behind the taboo. We would surely like to know and to understand, but even without knowledge and understanding, those laws are to be followed. Jewish texts throughout the Middle Ages, the commentaries and the codes, deal in minute detail with what the laws are and how they should be carried out, but Jewish philosophy (and its mystical counterpart) tries to explain what lies behind them. The philosophy may not try to explain individual laws, like the red heifer, but it attempts to examine the belief system that forms a basis for the laws.

Clearly the origin of Jewish philosophy lies outside of Judaism itself. Judaism, Christianity, and Islam all desired to prove their superiority. Each religion had its own version of Scripture, but those Scriptures were not conclusive. Christianity claimed that its Scripture had superseded the Jewish Scripture, and Islam claimed that its Scripture had superseded the Jewish and Christian versions. Furthermore, Jews rejected the New Testament and the Qu'ran, and Christians reinterpreted the Old Testament and rejected the Qu'ran, so none of the religions regarded the others' Scriptures as authoritative, which meant that they were not useful in argumentation. Argumentation required logical thought. Furthermore, both Christianity and Islam employed statements of belief, which Judaism lacked. As we will see, that situation changed during the medieval centuries, as Judaism adopted some of the modes of outside thought.

Saadiah's *Book of Beliefs and Opinions* investigates and elaborates on Jewish belief, by which he means "a notion that arises in the soul in regard to the actual character of anything that is apprehended" (14), though he is quick to point out that beliefs may be true or false.[4] Therefore, beliefs must be supported and proven, must be shown to be true. It would have been easy for Saadiah to use earlier writings to prove his points, but as Samuel Rosenblatt points out, Saadiah, though an expert in the Talmud, seldom cites that fundamental text.[5] Instead, he cites three bases of truth, "knowledge gained by [direct] observation ... the *intuition* of the intellect ... that knowledge which is inferred by logical necessity" (16). So far, then, Saadiah appears to be approaching the question of belief objectively, much as Descartes approaches his quest in the *Third Meditation*, but then Saadiah adds a fourth source of knowledge, "the validity of authentic tradition, by reason of the fact that it is based upon the knowledge of the senses as well as that of reason" (16), by which he means knowledge "which is furnished by authentic tradition and the books of prophetic revelation" (18). Furthermore, he adds, this fourth kind of knowledge confirms the other three.

To us, Saadiah's approach might seem peculiar, if not self-contradictory. Near the beginning of his treatise he describes human beings as "the species of rational beings" (7), which leads us to think that his arguments will be based entirely on logical thought, and yet shortly after that, he cites prophetic revelation as not only a source of human knowledge but as the most important source. We must realize, however, that Saadiah is neither naive nor self-contradictory. Instead, we are confronting one of the changes in thought that has occurred over the past thousand years. From Saadiah's perspective—a perspective shared by his Christian and Muslim contemporaries—Scripture did indeed constitute a rational source of knowledge. Scripture was, after all, the word of God and therefore constituted a direct source of truth, even if the text was often misunderstood or misinterpreted. For Saadiah and his contemporaries, *not* to regard Scripture as a rational source of understanding would have been considered irrational.

Several major problems for medieval Jewish thinkers revolved around the story of Creation, for Aristotle had taught that the universe was eternal and uncreated, while Genesis describes how the world came into being through divine action. As we saw in our discussion of biblical commentaries, Nachmanides in the thirteenth century, like many other thinkers, found a way of reconciling the Aristotelian and biblical approaches, though we might find that reconciliation unconvincing. Nachmanides accepted the biblical account of Creation and then demonstrated that the Greek account really implied and developed what Genesis said. Thus, the two sources of truth, the biblical and the Greek, did not contradict each other, if they were properly understood. But Nachmanides' position reflects developments during the three hundred years following Saadiah. Saadiah's position is rather different. Saadiah begins his examination of Creation by declaring:

> I say that our Lord, exalted be He, made it known to us that all things were created and that He had created them out of nothing. Thus Scripture says: *In the beginning God created the heaven and the earth* (Genesis 1:1). It says also: *I am the Lord that maketh all things; that stretched forth the heavens alone; that spread abroad the earth by Myself* (Isaiah 44:24). (40)

Saadiah's proof that the world was created at a particular time and that it was created by God is found in biblical statements. If the Torah says it, it is true, a point that would have sufficed for most people, but Saadiah goes further. Of course divine Creation is true, but Saadiah wants to know "whether it could be supported by reason as it had been verified by prophecy, and I found that it could be thus supported in many ways" (40–41). We know the truth from the Tanakh, he says. The nature of revelation, or prophecy, verifies that truth; but, he says, that truth can also be demonstrated through reason, which does not stand independent of prophecy but which supports prophecy. In other words, the truth, which is established by Scripture, is also rational, which means that the universe, too, is rational. Of course, that statement must make sense, because, according to Saadiah, human beings are "the species of rational beings" and were made in the image of God.

But even then, Saadiah's rational proof may strike us as odd. For instance, in his first proof that all things were created, he says (relying on the geocentric image of the universe that was current in his time):

> It is certain that heaven and earth are both finite, because the earth is in the center of the universe and the heaven revolves around it. It therefore follows, of necessity, that the force entering in them be finite, since it is impossible for an infinite force to reside in a finite body, for such a possibility is rejected by all that is known. Now, since the force that maintains these two is finite, it follows necessarily that they must have a beginning and an end. (41)

Because the heavens circle the earth in a definite pattern, both the heavens and the earth must be finite, that is, of limited power, and therefore they must have a beginning and an end. They cannot be eternal, as Aristotle argued, and therefore they must have been created. Saadiah pursues this line of thinking, examining the implications of his proof, but then he crowns his rational argument in support of the Scriptural account in what might strike us as a surprising fashion:

> I find that Scripture, too, testified to the fact that [the heavens and the earth] were both finite. It says, namely, *From one end of the earth even unto the other end of the earth* (Deuteronomy 13:8); and again: *From one end of heaven unto the other end of heaven* (Deuteronomy 4:32). (42)

If the earth has two ends and if heaven has two ends, then both entities are limited, that is, finite; and if both are finite, they must have come into existence at some time just as they will cease to exist at some time, under the direction of some infinite power, God.

We might want to argue, in twenty-first-century terms, that the notion of an expanding universe undercuts Saadiah's argument; more significant here is the way Saadiah argues. First he presents a position based on biblical texts: the world was created, as we read in Genesis and elsewhere, out of nothing. Then he offers rational proofs to support that position—in this case he offers four proofs, though we have only looked at one. He then concludes his discussion of each of those proofs by citing Scriptural passages that support them. In short, Scripture is supported by reason supported by Scripture, an arrangement that we might consider unsatisfactory in our quest for understanding but that worked well for Saadiah and his audience. Saadiah's goal is to examine and explain the beliefs of the Jewish people as they are derived from the Tanakh. He certainly recognizes the dangers of philosophical speculation, and he relies on the talmudic tradition that at one time, when scholars studied things thoroughly, knowledge was unified and without disagreements. Since the time of Hillel and Shammai in the first century, however, scholarship has declined, leading to misunderstandings and disagreements, a situation he tries to remedy in his work.

Saadiah, therefore, is very clear about his methodology. He cites a well-known talmudic warning against metaphysical speculation—"Whoever speculates about the following four matters would have been better off had he not been born; namely, 'What is below and what is above, what was before and what will be behind?'" (27, citing Hagigah 11b)—and then he explains that this warning refers not to metaphysical speculation in general but only to metaphysical speculation that is not based on biblical revelation, because such baseless speculation may easily go astray from the truth.

At one point, Saadiah says that he will offer proofs for his positions from the Tanakh, from history (by which he means biblical predictions of events that are supposed to take place), and from his own observations (315), while elsewhere he cites "rational arguments, Scripture, and tradition" (323). An interesting example of what he means by rational argument can be found when he discusses the always difficult problem of theodicy, the question of divine justice:

> Again we are confronted by the fact that God, the just, ordered the killing of the young children of the *Midianites* and the extermination of the young children *of the generation of the deluge.* We note also how He continually causes pain and even death to little babes. Logical necessity, therefore, demands that there exist after death a state in which they would obtain compensation for the pain suffered prior thereto … (330)

This passage occurs in Saadiah's chapter "Concerning Reward and Punishment in the World to Come," and it shows Saadiah's humanity in his recognition that there is something wrong in the suffering of children, even, we should note, Midianite children. Nonetheless, children do suffer. Therefore Saadiah constructs the following syllogism:

If God is just, and
if children suffer in this world,
then those children must be compensated after death.

Just as he cannot question whether children suffer, an obvious phenomenon, so he cannot question whether God is just, for him just as obvious a fact. Elsewhere he explains pain as a warning to human beings of the torments that the wicked will experience in the afterlife, though that notion would not explain away the suffering of children.

The point is not that Saadiah was, despite his protestations, irrational. Rather, he, like other medieval philosophers, was rational in terms different from ours. He and the others were so imbued with their religious outlook that they could not have conceived of seeing the world without it. We might be tempted to say that Saadiah is composing not Jewish philosophy but philosophy about Judaism, but for Saadiah there would have been no difference between the two locutions. Saadiah's major concerns are apparent in the topics he covers, such as the role of reason in Jewish belief, the creation of the world, the unity of God, aspects of divine justice, life after death, redemption, reward and punishment, and the proper conduct of life. Many of these concerns were also central to the *kalam*, but Saadiah gives them a distinctly Jewish slant, for his purpose is twofold: to explain Jewish beliefs and to refute the beliefs of others. These "others" consist of anyone who argues with the basic verities of Judaism, whether they be Jewish sectarians like the Karaites or proponents of other religions. What is most surprising about Saadiah's refutations of those "others" is his lack of vitriol. Unlike so many medieval writers of all faiths, he simply responds to their arguments without name-calling or insult.

For instance, Jewish sectarians claimed that various biblical prophecies concerning redemption referred to the Second Temple period, while Christians believed that they referred to the coming of the messiah. Among Saadiah's examples is the promise of peace in Isaiah 2:4: "Nation shall not take up sword against nation; they shall never again know war." Saadiah simply points out that war is still a part of daily life, and religious wars continue unabated. He argues with those who believe otherwise, against such clear evidence, but he does not denigrate them.

At the same time, Saadiah clearly believes that Judaism, as the only true religion, as God's gift to the Jewish people, will eventually triumph in the world, even if the lot of the Jews in his time was less than ideal. Thus, when he describes the time of the coming of the messiah in his treatise on redemption, he describes an earthly event in which the wicked will either be destroyed, will destroy each other, or will receive physical punishments. Those non-Jews who repent for their sins, however, will escape such punishments. Their reward will be that some will work for the Jews while the remainder will return to their countries and be submissive to Israel. Just as the universe was created for human beings, so all of mankind will revolve around the Jews. Such ethnocentrism was common in the medieval world.

While we may reject this extreme ethnocentrism in the modern world, at least in theory if not in practice, it is important that we understand what lay behind it. First, it reflects a historical reality in which the Jews, who believed they had received God's word and God's promise, were without a homeland and at the mercy of other nations, often suffering at their hands (though the suffering would get worse later). The promise of a triumph over these other nations helped the Jews cope with their situation. Secondly, this particular kind of ethnocentrism illustrates the centrality of Torah to Jewish life, as Saadiah illustrates.

It is no accident that Saadiah's last chapter, after his discussions of redemption, reward and punishment, and the afterlife, is entitled "Concerning How It Is Most Proper for Man to Conduct Himself in This World" (357). All of those other matters, subjects of metaphysical speculation, are important, but the culmination of the book, the point to which Saadiah has been leading his readers, concerns how we behave in the world, and the guide to how we behave is, of course, the Torah. Saadiah has definite ideas about redemption, the afterlife, and other speculative matters, but they all derive from and lead to Torah, just as his arguments so often begin and end with the Tanakh. The climax of *The Book of Beliefs and Opinions* comes very near the end, when Saadiah discusses what he calls the thirteen main activities of humankind, including such acts as eating and drinking, sexual activity, and learning, about all of which he makes sensible suggestions. In his discussion of worship, he notes that there are some people who believe that they should devote all of their time to worship, that is, to praising God, in the belief that if they do so, God will provide for their basic needs. Saadiah is too much a man of the world to adopt such a view. As he points out, one who worships without caring for bodily needs will soon die, and one who worships without reproducing will ensure the end of worship when he dies, so that exclusive devotion to worship will actually bring about the end of worship. And then Saadiah makes a vital statement that should seem familiar to us:

Furthermore, let me reveal what has eluded the advocates of this view; namely, that the service of God consists in [the fulfillment of] all the rational as well as the revealed precepts of the torah, as Scripture states: *And now, Israel, what doth the Lord thy God require of thee, but to fear the Lord thy God, … to keep the commandments of the Lord* (Deuteronomy 10:12, 13). (396)

After pages and pages of explanation, of rational argument, of refuting incorrect views, Saadiah brings his readers back to this basic point that underlies the Talmud and that is foundational for medieval Judaism: the most important activity that Jews can undertake is to fulfill as many of the commandments as possible, the moral ones and the ritual ones, the rational and revealed ones. Philosophy and metaphysics play a role in human thought, but performing the commandments is the service of God, and therefore performing the commandments constitutes the proper form of human conduct.

That conclusion may strike some readers as different from what they expect from philosophy, but medieval Jewish philosophy is often more "Jewish" than it is philosophical. It seeks understanding, but always within the framework of Jewish tradition. Different philosophers obviously handled the tension between philosophical inquiry and religious performance in different ways, and that tension occasionally caused terrible conflicts, but loyalty to the commandments remained a major aspect of medieval Jewish philosophy.

We can see this point in the philosophical career of Shlomo ibn Gabirol. While Saadiah's philosophical work was studied through the rest of the Middle Ages, ibn Gabirol's philosophical writings were virtually ignored by Jews; but these writings, which were translated at some time before 1150 from Arabic into Latin, were well-known in Christian Europe by the title *Fons Vitae, The Source of Life*. The author of this book was thought to be one Avicebron (or Avicebrol, among other variations on the name); and for seven hundred years, Avicebron was thought to have been a Muslim author. It was only in the nineteenth century that the work was discovered to have been written by ibn Gabirol. Oddly for a medieval philosophical work, the *Fons Vitae* makes no reference to any specific religious belief. Furthermore, the treatise is terribly confusing, so much so that no two commentators can agree about what it means.

But ibn Gabirol expresses his philosophy elsewhere, both more clearly and more in line with Jewish tradition, in his lengthy poem *Keter Malkhut, The Kingly* (or *Royal*) *Crown*. If the *Fons Vitae* was unknown to the Jewish community, *Keter Malkhut* was well-known indeed, even to the extent of being incorporated into the Yom Kippur service. Critics argue over the relationship between the poem and the philosophical treatise. Possibly the best conclusion is that of Julius Guttmann, who writes that the ideas expressed in the poem "are those of the metaphysical treatise, with the difference that the religious impulses which were only occasionally adumbrated in the *Fons Vitae* find full expression in the poem."[6]

The essential problem that concerns ibn Gabirol is the relationship between human beings and God. Neoplatonism reflects one aspect of that relationship, but there are many kinds of Neoplatonism. What they share (and this is a highly simplistic reduction of Neoplatonic thought) is a notion of a transcendent deity (or something like a deity), infinitely removed from human beings. Human beings long to be united with that deity, who is the source of all good. Because the world was created by the overflow of that goodness, human beings can achieve that unity by ascending through those emanations and ultimately become one with the deity. Such Neoplatonic thought obviously lends itself to mystical interpretations—Jewish mysticism, in fact, has a Neoplatonic basis. But ordinary Jewish belief, aside from Neoplatonism, also describes an utterly transcendent God, whose name cannot even be pronounced by ordinary mortals. At the same time, however, Judaism also believes in an intensely personal God, a God who appears in various ways to biblical characters, who speaks through prophets, and who cares deeply about his people Israel. We can see this dichotomy in the first two chapters of Genesis. Modern critics are undoubtedly correct in arguing that the two versions of the Creation story reflect two different traditions, but whoever put those stories together recognized that they reflect two apparently opposite but complementary views of God, the transcendent in chapter one and the immanent in chapter two. Ibn Gabirol's poem explores and develops those two views.

Keter Malkhut consists of forty stanzas of varying lengths, divided into three sections. The first section (stanzas 1–9) describes such attributes of God as His oneness, His existence, and His wisdom. The description of wisdom in stanza nine, with its discussion of the role of wisdom in Creation, leads to the second section (stanzas 10–32), in which the poet describes the created universe, beginning with the four elements and moving up through the heavenly sphere to the throne of God and to a contemplation of God's indescribable greatness. At this point, ibn Gabriol seems to have reached a Neoplatonic climax, a climb through the universe to a vision and identification with God, except for the last section, an extended confession of the poet's sinfulness and unworthiness and a plea for God's merciful judgment on him, motifs that make the poem appropriate for Yom Kippur. Suddenly the transcendent, glorious deity becomes personal and immanent, a being to whom the speaker can make a moving confession, presenting an occasionally terrifying view of himself and of human existence in general.

God's transcendence can be seen throughout parts one and two. In the second stanza, for instance, ibn Gabirol contemplates God's one-ness. Readers today may take that oneness for granted, but it was the subject of much speculation among medieval Jewish philosophers. It refers not only to the fact that there is only one God, rather than two or more, but also to God's absolute uniqueness and unity, an idea that is reflected in the Jewish tradition that one covers one's eyes and contemplatively draws out the statement, "Hear O Israel, the Lord our God, the Lord is one," in order to focus on that oneness. Thus ibn Gabirol says:

> You are One, and at the mystery of Your Oneness
> the wise of heart are struck drunk,
> for they know not what it is. (stanza 2)[7]

But if God is absolutely unique (that is, God's oneness is unlike what we usually think of as oneness) and transcendent, the Neoplatonic ques-tion concerns how God made the world, how multiplicity came into being. Ibn Gabirol addresses this issue in the ninth stanza, where he calls divine wisdom "the source of life" (*mekor ḥaim* in Hebrew, *fons vitae* in Latin!):

> Your are wise, more ancient than all primal things
> And wisdom was the nurseling at Your side ...
> You are wise, and from Your wisdom You have
> set apart Your appointed purpose
> like a craftsman and an artist. (stanza 9)

The Hebrew word for "nurseling," *amon*, also means "workman" or "artist." And what does "wisdom" mean? In the Wisdom literature of the Bible, such as Proverbs, Wisdom is equated with Torah: thus Wisdom

> is a tree of life to those who grasp her,
> And whoever holds on to her is happy.
> The Lord founded the earth by wisdom ... (Proverbs 3:18–19)

From such passages, the ancient rabbis deduced that the Torah pre-existed, and actually served as a blueprint, for Creation. Furthermore, the word translated in stanza 9 as "purpose" (*ḥefetz*) can be translated as "will." Thus, God's Will arises from the Torah, which God created as a blueprint for Creation, and that Will created "being from Nothingness" (stanza 9).

All of this Neoplatonic theory seems very confusing, but the result is that ibn Gabirol can maintain a distinction between God and the corporeal world while simultaneously explaining, at least to his own satisfaction, how God could create the corporeal world. Then in the second section of the poem he can take us from the four basic elements of the universe up through the Ptolemaic spheres that were believed to constitute the cosmos—the spheres of the moon, Mercury, Venus, the sun, Mars, Jupiter, Saturn, the realm of the fixed stars, all the way to the throne of God's glory—a journey that comes centuries before Dante's journey to God in the *Paradiso*. But whereas Dante ends his poem with the vision of God (though we know that he returns to earth to write the *Comedy*), ibn Gabirol adds the third section of his poem, which begins:

> O God, I am ashamed and confounded
> To stand before Thee ... (stanza 33)

What follows is an extended confession and self-condemnation, a plea for God's help, and a request for more time to prepare for death, to repent.

In the third section, ibn Gabirol adapts a number of earlier prayers, addressing God both as an individual and as a representative of human kind. Strikingly, he tells God:

> For if Thou shouldst pursue my iniquity,
> I will flee from Thee to Thy self,
> And I will shelter myself from Thy wrath in Thy shadow ... (stanza 38)

He will take refuge from the stern justice of the transcendent God of Creation in the mercies of the personal deity. Part of his plea is that God should "open my heart to Thy law" (stanza 39), for "in me are no good deeds," since he lacks "righteousness ... piety ... prayer ... innocence ... justice" (stanza 40). So what he needs, in the tradition of the talmudic rabbis and of Saadiah, is a return to Torah, the ability to carry out its commandments, because the Torah is the basis of Creation, and by conforming to its dictates he can be reconciled to God in both God's transcendent and immanent aspects. As is so often the case in medieval Jewish philosophy, Torah is at the center. The *Fons Vitae* is a medieval philosophical text; the *Keter Malkhut* gives that philosophy a Jewish context.

Another far longer work that attained popularity was *The Book of Direction to the Duties of the Heart*, by an eleventh-century Spanish-Jewish judge named Baḥya ibn Paquda. Ibn Paquda's goal in his work is to bring together what he calls the external and internal duties. "Religion itself is divided into two parts. One is the knowledge of the external duties of the body and its members; the other is the internal knowledge of the secret duties of the heart" (87).[8] The external duties are the rituals, while among these "secret duties" are the belief in one God, obedience to God, and awareness of the wonders of the world as a means of attaining knowledge of God, all of which form the basis for the ritual duties. Thus, the theme to which ibn Paquda continually returns is "that the duties of the members are of no avail to us unless our hearts choose to do them and our souls desire their performance" (89). Without internal motivation, the external duties, important though they may be as divine commandments, have no value. Carrying out the internal duties makes the external duties meaningful. The focus of Jewish study had always been on the correct fulfillment of the rituals; but if the internal duties were always implied, they were seldom discussed in detail. Ibn Paquda discusses them. Although he tells us that his book belongs "to the field of metaphysics" (102), its ultimate goal is to influence human behavior. He wants to show people how to worship God, not just through prayer but through their approach to everyday activities, an approach that requires love and dedication.

Of course, we can argue that ibn Paquda overstates his case, that intentionality was always fundamental to carrying out the commandments. Nevertheless, we can also recognize that performing the commandments can become routine, that people do them without thinking about them, that people recite prayer or perform rituals mechanically, and ibn Paquda reminds his audience how important intentionality is. Ibn Paquda's point seems simple in many ways, and yet it ultimately requires much of human beings. For instance, like all medieval Jewish writers, ibn Paquda believes deeply in a doctrine of divine reward and punishment. After all, the Torah declares that God will reward those who follow His commandments and punish those who do not. And yet ibn Paquda argues repeatedly that human beings should not behave in particular ways in order to gain reward or avoid punishment. He frequently cites the statement of Antigonos of Socho in *Pirkei Avot* that we should not be like servants who serve in order to get a reward. Instead, we should serve without any thought of reward, simply because our duty is to serve. Such an attitude reflects a higher level of internal duty.

Ibn Paquda is sometimes referred to as a mystic or an ascetic, but those terms are misleading. Bahya's "mysticism" has nothing to do with achieving a spiritual unity with God, and his asceticism amounts to little more than following the strictures of the Torah. What has endeared him to so many readers throughout the centuries—and he has been more popular with ordinary readers than some of his more scholarly colleagues—is his own sincerity as he calls on readers to be, themselves, sincere as they carry out the laws of the Torah.

The fifteenth-century scholar Joseph Albo takes a quite different approach to the performance of the commandments. In his commentary on Deuteronomy 10:12 (the passage that we saw Saadiah stress), "What doth the Lord thy God require of thee, but to fear the Lord thy God?" he emphasizes the difficulties of fearing the Lord properly. Such fear, he says, cannot be achieved easily. Therefore, God gave Israel the commandments, "because by keeping the commandments of the Torah one may achieve the human purpose which we should attain by great labor and enormous effort through fear and love and God's service with all one's heart and soul." As Nehama Leibowitz says, fulfilling the commandments "will gradually lead us to the higher plane of fear."[9] Once again, however, we must notice that whether the teachings of the Torah are approached through love or through fear (or through both together), those teachings, those commandments, are absolutely central to medieval Jewish thought.

This discussion of medieval Jewish philosophy concludes with necessarily brief examinations of two giants, Yehuda Halevi and Moshe (Moses) Maimonides, both of whom are revered in Jewish history, even though they held many opposite views. Yehuda Halevi, whom we met earlier as one of the greatest of Hebrew poets, has been a beloved and romanticized figure. Maimonides, on the other hand, has been not so much loved as respected. Not only are there few romantic aspects to his reputation, but he was the cause of major upheavals in Jewish life, and yet he appears as the second Moses in the motto "from Moses to Moses there was no one like Moses." For many years, a portrait purported to be that of Maimonides (which it is not) has decorated the front cover of children's Hebrew notebooks, thereby making him a symbol of Jewish learning. But we will begin with Yehuda Halevi.

Yehuda Halevi, the great poet, also wrote the *Kuzari*, a work that was composed in Arabic and then translated into Hebrew. The *Kuzari* lays out a coherent view of Judaism in a world that Halevi knew was bound to end, the world of Spanish Jewry. Although that world would survive for several more centuries, Halevi recognized that the Jews would be the ultimate losers in the struggle between the Muslims and the Christians. That foresight helps to explain the real name of the book we call the *Kuzari*: *Kitab al-Radd wa-'l-Dalil fi 'l-Din all-Dhalil, The Book of Argument and Proof in Defense of the Despised Faith.*[10] The *Kuzari* is Halevi's defense of a religion that was despised by the adherents of the two religions that claimed it as an ancestor. To some degree he uses current traditions in philosophy as part of his defense, but ultimately he rejects that philosophy in favor of revelation.

The title *Kuzari* derives from the Khazars, a central Asian people who several centuries before Halevi's time had converted to Judaism. The Jewish diplomat ḥasdai ibn Shapruth had written letters to the king of the Khazars, and it is easy to understand why the Khazars became legendary among the Jews: the idea of a Jewish kingdom, with a Jewish king, must have seemed reassuring to a people who so strongly felt their exile and their alienation from the societies around them. The *Kuzari* opens with the declaration, "I was asked to state what arguments and replies I could bring to bear against the attacks of philosophers and followers of other religions, and also against [Jewish] sectarians who attacked the rest of Israel" (35).[11] Halevi presents here the sense of persecution that Jews must have felt, as well as his view of philosophy as equivalent to another persecuting religion, that is, a belief system that, like Christianity, Islam, and the Karaites, attacked the beliefs of the Jews. Here we return to the vexed question of whether Judaism is a system based on belief, a question that Halevi will try to answer while he struggles with the problem that the only way he can defend Judaism is by countering its beliefs to the beliefs of its attackers. He accomplishes this seemingly contradictory task by recalling the story of the king of the Khazars and inventing a dialogue that constitutes the rest of his treatise. According to Halevi, the king of the Khazars, before his conversion, had a dream in which an angel seemed to tell him, " 'Thy way of thinking is indeed pleasing to the Creator, but not thy way of acting' " (35). Because the king seeks to please his Creator, he invites several people to advise him about how to respond. His first advisor is a philosopher, who explains that there is no such thing as a personal God, that the world has existed forever, and that the king should attempt to become like the Active Intellect without concern for the outward manifestations of religious belief in either words or deeds. The king immediately rejects this advice, which, despite its rejection of a personal God, still relies heavily on belief rather than on action, thus confirming Halevi's earlier assertion that philosophy is actually another form of religion. Furthermore, the king adds, philosophers never receive prophetic visions, thus proving that they are really quite distant from divine truth.

The king then consults Christian and Muslim scholars. (Jews, he says, are so few and so disliked that they are not worth consulting!) The Christian scholar presents a summary of Christian beliefs. Considering the antagonism among these religions, Halevi's presentation of Christian beliefs is surprisingly fair, though he does refer to the Christian notion that God turned his wrath on the Jews despite Jesus' own statement defending the Torah, "Do not think that I am come to destroy the law" (Matthew 5:17), a statement that must have seemed very strange to Jews, who saw that Christians did not follow the law as Judaism understood it. The king rejects these Christian beliefs as illogical and turns to the Muslim scholar, whose words he also rejects, denying that any proof exists that the *Qu'ran* is divinely inspired.

Finally, by process of elimination, he turns to a Jewish scholar, and his dialogue with the Rabbi constitutes the rest of the treatise. That dialogue clarifies Halevi's view of Judaism and explains why, in Halevi's view, the king was correct in rejecting philosophy, Christianity, and Islam. We must remember that in the king's original dream, he was told, "Thy way of thinking is indeed pleasing to the Creator, but not thy way of acting." The first three scholars he interviews, however, all focus on matters of belief or thought, not on action. The king wants to know how to act, what to do. In the course of his discussion with the Jew, he learns that "man cannot approach God except by means of deeds commanded by him" (111), that is, by following the commandments in the Torah, which, according to Jewish tradition, was given to the Jews by God at Mount Sinai in the presence of over a million witnesses. (And according to another tradition, the souls of all Jews, including those unborn, were present at Mount Sinai.) Thus, those laws, those controls over human action, constitute Judaism. Given by God to the Jews, the law will teach the king how to act.

Of course, the validity of the Torah seems to constitute more the subject of belief than of action, as the Rabbi clearly says at the beginning of his argument: "I believe in the God of Abraham, Isaac and Israel, who led the children of Israel out of Egypt with signs and miracles; who fed them in the desert ... who sent Moses with His law ..." (44). Even so, the fact that so many people witnessed the giving of the Torah makes that gift a fact rather than a belief, and if the Torah was indeed a divine gift, then what it tells us, both the stories about the patriarchs and matriarchs, for instance, and the laws, is simply factual rather than the subject of belief. Hence, according to Halevi, Judaism is the only system that does not rely on mere belief and that simultaneously tells us what actions are pleasing to God.

Significantly, the Rabbi divides the laws into the rational and the ritual. We have already seen in the Tanakh, in the Talmud, in Saadiah, in ibn Gabirol, and in Bahya the centrality of the laws for the Jewish religion. Now Halevi makes explicit what is implicit in their discussions, that "the divine law cannot become complete till the social and rational laws are perfected. The rational law demands justice and recognition of God's bounty. What has he, who fails in this respect, to do with offerings, Sabbath, circumcision ...? These are, however, the ordinations especially given to Israel as a corollary to the rational laws" (112). Halevi here makes the point that the biblical prophets make over and over, that ritual law without social justice is an abomination:

Though you pray at length,
I will not listen.
Your hands are stained with crime ... (Isaiah 1:15)

This essential concept is important to Halevi for reasons beyond its inherent rightness, for behind much of what Halevi says is the idea that the Jews are a holy and exclusive people. Both Christianity and Islam sought converts. Judaism generally did not. In fact, during the Middle Ages, converting to Judaism was considered a capital crime in both Ashkenaz and Sepharad, so that converts were rather scarce, though there were some. Halevi's notion is that Jews are born Jews, that there is, in modern terms, a "Jewish gene." Consequently, even though the king does convert to Judaism, he can never be fully Jewish. (Whether his offspring could be, since they would be born into Judaism, is a question that Halevi does not address.)

Judaism, in Halevi's conception, was never meant to be universal. We saw the same point in Saadiah, when he spoke of how the other nations would exist after the redemption. Several times in the *Kuzari*, both the king and the Rabbi refer to God's "secret plan" for Israel. Late in the book, the Rabbi describes that secret plan in oblique terms. It should

be compared to the wisdom hidden in the seed which falls into the ground, where it undergoes an external transformation to earth, water, and dirt, without leaving a trace for him who looks down upon it. It is, however, the seed itself which transforms earth and water into its own substance.... In the same manner the law of Moses transforms each one who honestly follows it.... The nations merely serve to introduce and pave the way for the expected Messiah, who is the fruition, and they will all become His fruit. Then, if they acknowledge Him, they will become one tree. (226–27)

His point in this confusing passage seems to be that Israel, which follows the laws of Moses, is like the seed that falls into the earth and transforms the earth and water into a tree. Israel, then, has the power, like the seed, to transform the elements in which it finds itself into a tree "capable of bearing the Divine Influence," that is, Israel will bring forth the messiah, whom all the nations will then acknowledge. Here the Rabbi develops a point that he made earlier, using another analogy, when he compared Israel to the heart and the other nations to the other organs (109). The heart is central to the operation of the body, but it is also most susceptible to disease. Furthermore, after his seed analogy, the Rabbi launches into a long discussion of *Sefer Yetzirah, The Book of Creation.*

Sefer Yetzirah was an early work—its date of authorship is unknown, but in the Middle Ages it was attributed to the patriarch Abraham—that presented the Hebrew language as having mystical properties that served as the foundations of Creation. After all, God had created the world through language, and the language He used was Hebrew. Not only did *Sefer Yetzirah* see mystical and magical possibilities in Hebrew words and even in individual Hebrew letters, but later commentators on the book (including Saadiah Gaon) developed those possibilities. But while many writers delighted in these mystical and magical elements, they also felt that they were dealing with knowledge that needed to be kept hidden, as we will see when we discuss the *Zohar*, so that passages are often very obscure. For example, Halevi mentions the parts of an animal that could be used as sacrifices in the Temple and notes that the heart, the brain, the lungs, and the diaphragm are not among them. "This is a most profound secret, the lifting of which is prohibited" (232–33). Much of his discussion of *Sefer Yetzirah* is like this comment. Nevertheless, his use of *Sefer Yetzirah* emphasizes the uniqueness of the Hebrew language and therefore of the people who use that language. It also points to elaborate correspondences between microcosmic and macrocosmic levels of existence, thereby establishing the centrality of Israel in the divine scheme of creation.

Allied to this centrality is the role of the land of Israel in both Judaism and world history. Early in the *Kuzari*, the Rabbi refers to the importance of the Holy Land by citing rabbinic sayings and rulings. For instance, if a woman refuses to accompany her husband to Israel, he can divorce her without financial compensation; and if a man refuses to go to Israel with his wife, he must divorce her and pay the compensation (98). When the king chastises the Rabbi for not being in Israel himself, the Rabbi confesses his failing, and later we learn that he has, like Halevi, decided to move there. As he tells the king, "Jerusalem can only be rebuilt when Israel yearns for it to such an extent that they embrace her stones and dust" (295). The rebuilding of Jerusalem, with its implied rebuilding of the Temple, has clear messianic overtones. Just as Israel is special, so the land of Israel is special (as we saw, too, in Halevi's poetry). If the people of Israel would return to Israel rather than simply yearning to return to it, the messianic age would arrive. Halevi's controversial point is that Jews should not wait idly or passively for the coming of the messiah but that they have a role to play in that dramatic event. Hence the Rabbi plans a journey to Israel, and Halevi himself made the trip.

Halevi, then, stresses the role of Israel in the history of the world, and in doing so he rejects current philosophical preoccupations. In discussing the prophets, he proclaims, "Had the Greek philosophers seen them when they prophesied and performed miracles, they would have acknowledged them, and sought by speculative means to discover how to achieve such things" (210–11). While his contemporaries are besotted with philosophy, he implies, the philosophers themselves would have envied and tried to emulate the prophets. How much more, then, should they be the subject of Jewish study! But Halevi also adapts Greek thought to Judaism. A wonderful example is Halevi's description of the pious man, the sage, who completely controls his mental and physical passions and who does not seek power: "He is fit to rule, because if he were the prince of a country he would be as just as he is to his body and soul" (137). He would arrange his people as Moses arranged the children of Israel at Mount Sinai. He could empty his mind of all worldly thought, calling up in his mind images of biblical scenes. He prays with total devotion: "Prayer is for his soul what nourishment is for his body" (139). He obeys the commandments and does pious works. He is, in short, Halevi's Judaic depiction of Plato's philosopher-king, the person who so masters himself that he can rise above transitory worldly appearances and see the transcendent realities that are truly important. But whereas Plato's philosopher-king is an idea that has never existed, Halevi knows that according to Jewish tradition, there have been many sages who achieved the ideal. The sages of the Talmud were so regarded. Some readers might regard Halevi himself as such a sage. In a letter found in the Geniza, he is described by someone who knew him as "the quintessence and embodiment of our country, our refuge and leader, the illustrious scholar."[12] Nevertheless, the designation of the Jewish philosopher-king might more appropriately be applied to the extraordinary thinker who followed Halevi in the later twelfth century, Moses Maimonides.

Maimonides is like Dante, Beethoven, or Einstein: he is one of the giants of human thought, so much so that we can never feel that we fully grasp the totality of his accomplishments. Those accomplishments are even more startling in light of the facts of his life. Since he is so well known for his attempt to show the harmony between Greek philosophy and Judaism, it is fitting that he is known as Maimonides, which is a Greek form that means "son of Maimon." His Hebrew name, Moshe ben Maimon, means Moshe the son of Maimon, but in Jewish history, Maimonides is best known as the Rambam, which is an acronym for Rabbi Moshe ben Maimon. ("Rambam," incidentally, should not be confused with "Ramban," the acronym of Nachmanides.) Maimonides was born in Cordova in about 1135, but after the arrival of the Almohades in 1148, his family fled to southern Spain and then to North Africa, where, again because of the Almohades, they were forced to hide their religious practices. After a visit to Israel, Maimonides moved to a city near Cairo called Fostat, where, thanks to the support of his merchant brother David, he had time to study and write. When David drowned on one of his journeys, however, Maimonides was not only devastated at his loss, but he also became responsible for his family. He became a physician, but he remained devoted to his studies and later became the leader of Egyptian Jewry. In a famous letter, he describes his busy days treating patients (among whom was the sultan), seeing petitioners, and trying to pursue his studies. He died in 1204.

Maimonides wrote many works, including a commentary on the Mishnah when he was in his early twenties, a number of medical treatises, and many letters. Among those letters are some public letters, the most famous of which was his letter to the Jews of Yemen. When the Jewish community in Yemen was subjected to conversionary pressures, its leaders wrote to Maimonides for advice. The fact that Maimonides was only thirty years old at the time indicates the extent of his renown.

Maimonides' response was so consoling and helpful that he became for centuries a revered figure for Yemenite Jews. In our discussion, though, we will focus on two of Maimonides' most famous works, the *Mishneh Torah* and the *Moreh Nevukim, The Guide for the Perplexed.*

These two works are often viewed as belonging to different realms, the religious and the philosophical. *The Guide for the Perplexed* is almost always mentioned in histories of medieval philosophy, the *Mishneh Torah* almost never. Similarly, students of halakhah use the *Mishneh Torah* as a basic text but tend to avoid the *Guide*. In both cases, a division is made between the major concerns of the two works, between halakhah and philosophy. Isadore Twersky argues, "A major part of Maimonides' achievement, and its historical significance, is the integration of both."[13] Focusing on one and excluding the other creates a distorted view of Maimonides' thought.

In order to understand the *Mishneh Torah*, which was completed around 1180,[14] we must recall some details about the Talmud. The earlier part of the Talmud, the Mishnah, was compiled from oral records and put into written form under the direction of Rabbi Yehuda ha-Nasi in about 200, largely because of fears that the oral traditions might be forgotten. Written in Hebrew, the Mishnah was organized in six "orders," which were themselves divided into sixty-three tractates. During the next several centuries, rabbinic discussion continued, resulting in the compilation of the Gemara, which is far longer than the Mishnah. Furthermore, while the Mishnah employs a clear organizing principle, the Gemara does not: discussions are filled with digressions, with odd turns, and with startling associative logical leaps. These discussions always return to the central point, but the organization of that point is not always clear, and often the halakhic decisions are not so clear either. Thus, Talmud study was difficult and potentially confusing, added to which was the use of Aramaic as the language of the Gemara, a language that was no longer well known among Jews.

Among the differences between Ashkenazic and Sephardic Jews in Maimonides' time was their reaction to this situation. Ashkenazic Jews continued and even intensified the talmudic debates, as we saw in the case of the Tosafists. Sephardic Jews, on the other hand, tried to organize the confusion by creating codes of the laws. One of the most famous such codes before Maimonides was the eleventh-century *Halakhoth* of Rabbi Isaac Alfonsi, whose very title indicates that it is a listing of the laws, the halakhoth. But Alfonsi's code points to another complication. The Torah contains, according to tradition, six hundred thirteen commandments. No one could possibly obey all the commandments, not because there are so many but because, for instance, some apply only to men and some only to women. In addition, many of the laws apply only to people living in the land of Israel or only to activities pertaining to the Temple, which no longer existed. Thus, while everyone acknowledged that there were six hundred thirteen commandments, many of them seemed more theoretical than practical. Given the intricacies of the practical commandments, earlier codes and commentaries focused on them and omitted the more theoretical commandments.

Maimonides recognized that this practice was problematic; that it, along with the difficulties inherent in Talmud study, it could easily lead to those theoretical laws being forgotten. And even the practical laws were difficult to learn unless one was immersed in the study of the Talmud and of related texts. Therefore, he says, he studied all of the relevant texts so that he could address

> the forbidden and the permitted, the impure and the pure, and the remainder of the Torah's laws, all in clear and concise terms, so that the entire Oral Law could be organized in each person's mouth without questions or objections.
>
> Instead of [arguments], this one claiming such and another such, [this text will allow for] clear and correct statements based on the judgments that result from all the texts and explanations ... from the days of [Moses] until the present. [This will make it possible] for all the laws to be revealed to both those of lesser stature and those of greater stature, regarding every single [commandment] ...
>
> To summarize: [The intent of this text is] that a person will not need another text at all with regard to any Jewish law. Rather, this text will be a compilation of the entire Oral Law ...[15]

The scope of Maimonides' project is breathtaking. He created a complete code of all the commandments in clear Hebrew, not only a list of the six hundred thirteen biblical commandments, but also all of the rabbinic elucidations of those commandments—not just that no work should be performed on the Sabbath, but all the regulations defining work and clarifying what is and is not permitted. Furthermore, in most un-talmudic style, he did not list his sources and he did not engage in discussions of how these laws were finalized, which was very much a concern of the Tosafists.

It is difficult for us to realize how daring this plan was. Judaism had been established through a chain of tradition, with each generation revering the ones that came before and examining the argumentation that led those earlier generations to arrive at their rulings. Now Maimonides planned to omit that argumentation (though he certainly retained the reverence). Since many of the laws were still subject to dispute—since such dispute was at the heart of the Talmud itself—he was setting himself up as the judge and final arbiter of Jewish law. His goal was to rescue talmudic law by making it available to everyone, but the audacity of his undertaking created many opponents, who wanted to know what his sources were and what gave him the right to make such decisions.

A modern edition of the *Mishneh Torah*, in small print, with commentary, contains hundreds of pages, so it clearly is a comprehensive collection of laws, but it is also, as Twersky insists, a philosophical statement. Of course, any law code, like the Constitution of the United States, is based, whether explicitly or implicitly, on philosophical views and expresses the philosophy of its authors or compilers, but the *Mishneh Torah* goes beyond that kind of philosophy as well. Its basic point, of course, is that these laws are of divine origin and therefore must be followed. Thus, when Maimonides lists the six hundred thirteen commandments at the beginning of the *Mishneh Torah*, he does not list them in the order of their occurrence in the Torah. He begins with the commandment to believe in the existence of God, who created the world. The second commandment is to believe in His unity, and the third is to love Him. From there he moves on to commandments that require external human action. Thus, he starts with belief, moves to an internal action—love, complicated by the question of how a person can be commanded to love something—and then to external actions that confirm that the first three commandments are being carried out, for one who neither believes in one God nor loves God is unlikely to obey the rest.

But Maimonides' philosophy in the *Mishneh Torah* goes even further. For instance, his decision to include *all* the laws, not just the currently practical ones, demonstrates an important aspect of his thought. Maimonides worried that the laws might be forgotten, but if laws can no longer be obeyed, why should they not be forgotten? We might argue that simply preserving the past is a worthwhile endeavor, as people today strive to record and preserve languages that are dead or dying, and such an argument can be persuasive. Maimonides, however, does not make that argument. He preserves those laws for at least two other reasons: first because the Jews would be restored to their own land and those laws would then be in effect again, and second because Maimonides believed that every law exists to teach at least one of three lessons: "a) establishment of civilized society—principles of social utility and justice; b) development of the ethical personality—principles of goodness and love of fellow man; or c) intellectual perfection—true knowledge and experience of God."[16] Each of the laws and all of their ramifications, then, lead to the improvement of individual human beings and of the society in which they live. In a letter to Rabbi Hasdai ha-Levi, Maimonides wrote that "the entire Torah is actually a code of ethics designed to safeguard the human soul. Consequently, every *mitzvah* [commandment] has a reason and a purpose," even if sometimes they are not disclosed.[17]

This point is implied throughout the *Mishneh Torah* and expressed overtly in the *Guide of the Perplexed*. This long, difficult work was written to help those who were perplexed by the apparent contradictions between Aristotelian philosophy and the teaching of religion, a problem that occupied Jews, Christians, and Muslims through much of the Middle Ages. Maimonides uses some fascinating techniques to explore the problem in Jewish terms. It seems unlikely, as Herbert Davidson has shown, that Maimonides actually had first-hand experience with much of Aristotle's work, but he knew Aristotle through the Arabic Aristotelians who had been writing about the Greeks.[18] Nevertheless, he held Aristotle and other philosophers in high esteem as thinkers who tried to understand the universe. Not surprisingly, then, he included the ancient rabbis in the company of such philosophers. If the rabbis were philosophers, then the Judaism they expounded was philosophy, which means not only that it achieved an exalted status in the world but also that it was an organized and coherent system of thought. Furthermore, that system of thought commented on the thought of the philosophical schools, as we can see in this comment on Job:

> The opinion of *Job* is in keeping with the opinion of Aristotle; the opinion of *Eliphaz* is in keeping with the opinion of our Law; the opinion of *Bildad* is in keeping with the doctrine of the Mu'tazila; the opinion of *Zophar* is in keeping with the doctrine of the Ash'ariyya. (494)[19]

If the sages were philosophers, then they can and should be discussed in the context of and in the terms of philosophy.

But of course Jewish "philosophy" is based on the Tanakh, which must be properly understood, so Maimonides clarifies how we should read that text. Through much of Book I, he focuses on the anthropomorphic aspects of the Tanakh, those passages that describe God in human terms, as having emotions or bodily limbs, as speaking or standing or sitting. Maimonides is especially concerned that we recognize that all such passages are figurative, that they are written to accommodate human beings' limited understanding, and that they do not literally describe God, who is so far beyond our normal understanding that we cannot begin to grasp the nature of His existence. For example, in Lamentations 5:19 we read, "But You, O Lord, are enthroned forever." Maimonides explains that "a sitting individual is in a state of the most perfect stability and steadiness" and therefore "this term is used figuratively to denote all steady, stable, and changeless states" (37). God, being incorporeal, neither sits nor stands, but God is steady, stable, and changeless.

Clearly, then, Maimonides is not engaged in philosophy as we usually think of it, though philosophy textbooks treat him as a philosopher by focusing on the more "philosophical" passages in the treatise. Maimonides, however, is expounding a philosophy of Judaism, in the context of his philosophical environment. In fact, he frequently contends that he must hide many things, citing Jewish traditions about esoteric knowledge. He discusses the *Account of the Beginning* (*ma'aseh bereshith*) and the *Account of the Chariot* (*ma'aseh merkavah*, referring to the vision of Ezekiel 1), which he identifies with natural science and with theology; but he knows that these are also the subject of metaphysical and mystical speculation, areas in which he does not enter. Perhaps these are areas that, as Davidson says, Maimonides would have considered "daft," but we certainly get the feeling that Maimonides feels he cannot reveal all that he knows about them.[20]

A major concern for Maimonides is the nature of prophecy, for prophecy is the system through which we learn the truth. Over and over, Maimonides cites Moses as the epitome of the prophet, the man who came closest to a full confrontation with and understanding of God. Therefore, the Torah, traditionally written through the agency of Moses, expresses that truth. Our problem is that, through historical accident, we have forgotten how to read that Torah fully. And what is prophecy? It is "an overflow overflowing from God, may He be cherished and honored, through the intermediation of the Active Intellect, toward the rational faculty in the first place and thereafter toward the imaginative faculty. This is the highest degree of man and the ultimate term of perfection that exists for his species ..." (369). Prophecy, he says, is revelation, but goes first to the rational faculty, to reason, and then to the imaginative faculty. Thus, when he discusses a point in Job, he says, "See how these notions came to me through something similar to prophetic revelation" (488). Maimonides is not calling himself a prophet here, but he acknowledges the "shock of recognition" when an idea strikes him, when he has a sudden insight. Then his reason can work on it, but first it must come from somewhere.

In this brief discussion, perhaps Maimonides' complexity has become apparent. Not only are his ideas difficult in themselves, but his attempt to bring together Judaism and twelfth-century Arabic Aristotelianism can be confusing. His insistence that religion can be discussed in rational terms, however, is important, as is his constant emphasis on the value of the human intellect. The development of that intellect, through study, contemplation, and the carrying out of the commandments, was central to his thought.

Maimonides did have one more profound effect on the developments of Judaism. We have seen other Jewish philosophers focus on Jewish beliefs. So, too, did Maimonides, but as usual, in a more thorough fashion than did others. Maimonides came up with what are often called the thirteen principles of faith, thirteen principles that he says form the basis of Judaism, including belief in God, belief in the oneness of God, belief in the incorporeality of God, belief that the Torah came from God, and belief in the messianic era. As Menachem Kellner argues, many of these principles refer directly to controversies of the twelfth century.[21] Interestingly, Maimonides' contemporaries did not always find this list convincing. Many wondered how he came up with thirteen. Why not three? Or one? In short, Maimonides' principles of faith were not immediately accepted. At the same time, in light of the challenges posed by Christian and Muslim principles of faith, it was convenient to have a Jewish list as well; and though other scholars constructed their own lists, Maimonides' remained the most popular. When prayer books started to be printed, the printers often included Maimonides' list, thereby giving it even more legitimacy. The list was even turned into a poem, "Yigdal," which is regularly sung in synagogue services. Even so, we should remember that Maimonides' list is Maimonides' list, and with all due reverence to Maimonides, it was as much the printers as anyone else who made the list seem normative.[22]

Maimonides' positions presented several difficulties to his contemporaries. By focusing on the role of the human intellect in salvation, he lessened the role of God in human affairs.[23] Although he stressed the requirement that people love God, his image of God stresses the transcendent rather than the immanent aspects of the deity. Furthermore, his view that the commandments were often highly symbolic was seen as undermining Jewish practice. After all, if the commandments are only symbolic and lack intrinsic meaning, people might be less inclined to follow them. Undoubtedly this criticism of Maimonides was prompted not so much by Maimonides himself as by some of his readers, who went further in this direction than he did and actually abandoned the commandments. Maimonides' works were considered so threatening that numerous rabbis—we might call them anti-rationalists—tried to forbid the reading of those works. In addition, the growing number of kabbalists dismissed Maimonides' thought. The anti-rationalists and the kabbalists, of course, were opposed by Maimonides' supporters, with each group attacking the others. Some, like Nachmanides, who had kabbalistic leanings, disagreed with much that Maimonides said but still defended him and gave the controversy a civil tone. Others did not. At various times and in various places, particularly in southern France, bans were pronounced against his works. In 1305, a century after his death, a rabbinical ban was issued that forbade the study of metaphysics or of Greek philosophy before the age of twenty-five and excommunicated anyone who interpreted the Tanakh allegorically, saying, for instance, that Abraham and Sarah represent matter and form or that the sons of Jacob represent the constellations and who thereby weakened the observance of the commandments.[24]

This Maimonidean conflict, in fact, had very serious consequences. The controversy became so heated that non-Jewish authorities became involved, though it is not clear which side in the controversy invited their interference. As these authorities looked into the issue, they became aware of the importance of the Talmud in Jewish life and began to investigate that text, leading to increased persecution of the Jews on the basis of their talmudic learning. Another consequence was that some educated Jews, who knew Maimonides' works and regarded the commandments as symbolic, converted much more easily under the threat of persecution than did less educated Jews, who maintained the commandments out of faith, as Joseph ben Shem Tov ibn Shem Tov claimed: "the rationalism of the *Guide of the Perplexed* discouraged Jews from martyring themselves for their faith and hence contributed to the mass conversions to Christianity in Spain during and after the anti-Jewish riots of 1391."[25] Even if his view is correct, the fault lay more with interpretations of Maimonides than with Maimonides himself. Nonetheless, the accusation was serious indeed and led to the mistaken idea that while the *Mishneh Torah* belonged to the world of religion, the *Guide of the Perplexed* belonged to the world of philosophy and that there was for Maimonides a difference between those two worlds.

Kabbalah

Maimonidean rationalism was far from the only influence on Jewish thought in the twelfth and thirteenth centuries. Another difficult and controversial current of thought at that time involved Kabbalah. The word "kabbalah" itself simply means "tradition," but the kabbalistic tradition is very complex. Kabbalah has come to mean Jewish mysticism, of which there are several strands, but it is important to understand that Kabbalah never stood apart from Judaism. It was—and is—another school of Jewish thought, and the medieval kabbalists were devout followers of the commandments, even if they interpreted the commandments through their own world view. In doing so, they did nothing different than Maimonides, Halevi, or the rabbis of the Talmud had done.

In Jewish tradition, mysticism refers to secret knowledge about God and the universe. Sources of that secret knowledge appear already in the Tanakh, particularly in the story of Creation and in the theophanies of Isaiah (chapter 6) and Ezekiel (chapter 1). The Creation story gave rise to *ma'aseh bereshith,* and the theophany of Ezekiel, combined to some degree with that of Isaiah, gave rise to *ma'aseh merkavah,* both of which are alluded to in the Talmud. Although the Talmud contains many references to these matters, it treats them as secret and almost dangerous topics, as is illustrated by the story of the four great rabbis who ascended to Paradise. Of the four, three came to bad ends: Ben Azzai saw Paradise and died; Ben Zoma saw and went mad; Elisha ben Abuyah became an apostate (and was known afterwards as *Acher,* the other); only Rabbi Akiva departed in peace (Hagigah 14b). So dangerous was this subject that it was only to be taught to a small audience, one person at a time, and that person had to be male, over forty, and married. Because these strictures were followed so closely, we do not know for certain what constituted this hidden knowledge, though we do have, from the talmudic centuries and after, Jewish hymns and other writings that rely on the traditions of Gnosticism. Gnosticism, from the Greek *gnosis,* knowledge, claimed to be a secret kind of knowledge, known only to a relative few, and it was based on an absolute division between the spiritual and material worlds—the former being good and the latter unalterably evil. Early Christianity had to confront Gnosticism because it denied that the divine could come into contact with the material and not be forever defiled, and we can see Christianity responding to this challenge at the beginning of the Gospel According to John. Jewish Gnosticism was not so radical, but it did exist.

Apparently this tradition of hidden knowledge continued through the early part of the Middle Ages, though again, its existence as an oral tradition means that we know little about it. In the twelfth and especially the thirteenth centuries, it began to flourish. Scholars are very much divided over many aspects of kabbalism: why it flourished when it did, how authentic the traditions were, precisely what those traditions meant, and other problems. Nachmanides, in his biblical commentaries, referred to secret knowledge about the Tanakh that he could not convey in writing. Maimonides, too, makes such a claim in the *Guide*, though we might well doubt that these two thinkers were referring to the same kind of knowledge. Kabbalistic trends developed in Provence during this period (though the Ḥasidei Ashkenaz had promoted mystical ideas in Germany in the eleventh to the thirteenth centuries). But in the very late-thirteenth century, the central work of the kabbalistic tradition, the *Zohar*, appeared in Castile.

Like so much about Kabbalah, the *Zohar* is a work fraught with problems. It claims to be an ancient work, from the second century, that was found and made public by Moshe de Leon, but clearly it was written in the late-thirteenth and early-fourteenth centuries by the same Moshe de Leon, perhaps with the help of others. It is written almost entirely in a somewhat artificial dialect of Aramaic, which is amazing when we remember that Aramaic was the language of the Talmud but had not been spoken for centuries. It is written as a kind of commentary on much of the Torah, though it focuses on Shimon ben Yoḥai, a second-century sage, and his circle of disciples.

Gershom Scholem, one of the giants of scholarship in the twentieth century, believed that kabbalistic thought was influenced by Gnosticism and Neoplatonism, which were adapted to a Jewish viewpoint. Moshe Idel, following Scholem, argues that in the ancient world, Jewish thought entered Gnosticism, which meant that many centuries later, Jews who encountered Gnosticism found elements in it that were already compatible with their views.[26] In either case, kabbalistic thought was clearly influenced by the *Sefer Yetzirah*, *The Book of Creation*, which we encountered earlier. This early work (its date, as we saw earlier, is not known for certain) presented the Hebrew alphabet as the language of Creation and the numbers as having mystical or magical powers. The numbers from one to ten are particularly important because the *Sefer Yetzirah* refers to them as *sefiroth*, which means "countings" but which became transformed in the later tradition to mean divine emanations. *Sefer Yetzirah* and another work, the *Bahir*, along with oral traditions, exercised tremendous influence on the *Zohar*. Yet another possible influence on the development of Kabbalah was the Albigensian heresy, a flowering of Gnostic thought in the south of France in the late-twelfth and early-thirteenth centuries. Some scholars argue that the Jews of southern France may have been influenced by the Albigensians. The Albigensians were annihilated by the Church and the monarchy, but aspects of their thought might well have lived on in Jewish mysticism.

The *Zohar* is a tremendously confusing book, so much so that it often seems to mean whatever the reader wants it to mean. Arthur Green offers a helpful introduction to the text in his *Guide to the Zohar*.[27] The *Zohar* deals with matters that we have not seen as major concerns in our study of medieval Judaism, concerns such as the nature of God and an interest in cosmic rather than earthly matters. The *Zohar*'s cosmology is based on the *sefiroth*, that term which in the *Sefer Yetzirah* referred to numbers but which developed into "a complex and dynamic structure of divine powers," or, more Neoplatonically, "stages or rungs in the self-manifestation of the Deity."[28] Part of the problem that the *Zohar* tries to solve is the question of how God, with his unique Oneness (an odd but accurate phrase) created a world full of multiplicity. The *sefiroth*, or emanations, attempt to answer this question. The ten *sefiroth* are often portrayed as follows:

Keter (Crown)

Binah (Understanding)   Ḥokhmah (Wisdom)

G'vurah (Power)   Ḥesed (Love)

Tifereth (Beauty)

Hod (Splendor)   Netzaḥ (Endurance)

Y'sod (Foundation)

Malkhuth (Kingdom)

The relationships among these ten emanations, each of which operates on multiple levels of symbolism, are complex indeed, involving abstract concepts, parts of the body, biblical figures, and sexual motifs (which derive in part from the allegorical reading of the Song of Songs). *Malkhuth* is also identified as the *Shekhinah*, the indwelling of God in the world, a female principle that is to be united to the male principle which is represented by the transcendent deity. Furthermore, the kabbalists "claimed that *Shekhinah* is the community of Israel.... Poised precisely at the border between the divine and the lower worlds, she is at once the this-worldly presentiment of God and a heavenly embodiment of Israel."[29] Here is how the *Zohar* describes one small aspect of the *sefiroth*:

> When Concealed of all Concealed verged on being revealed, it produced at first a single point, which ascended to become thought. Within, it drew all drawings, graved all engravings, carving within the concealed holy lamp a graving of one hidden design, holy of holies, a deep structure emerging from thought, called מי(*Mi*), *Who*, origin of structure. Existent and non-existent, deep and hidden, called by no name but *Who*.[30]

This passage, as Daniel Matt's commentary indicates, describes the early history of the *sephiroth* as they were conceived in God's "mind" and as they emanated from each other.

Just this tiny bit of kabbalistic vocabulary indicates the difficulties of understanding it. Nevertheless, kabbalistic thought, occasionally in more simplistic constructions, became quite popular. One theory is that Kabbalah was composed or gained popularity in reaction to the development of Jewish philosophy. As we saw, Jewish philosophy, especially as presented by Maimonides, relied almost entirely on a rational approach to religious questions, but rationalism and religion are not natural companions. More probably, philosophy and Kabbalah both developed as reactions to situations we have observed: the growing threat of the non-Jewish world, the development of Christian and Islamic thought, increasing questions about the validity of revealed religion, and other factors. Both sought to offer deeper explanations of Jewish thought and practice, and both employed the centrality of the Torah and its commandments for the Jewish people.

In the nineteenth century, scholars of Judaism largely dismissed Kabbalah as a subject for serious study. Being rationalists, they preferred philosophical approaches. That preference, however, misrepresented the history of philosophical and kabbalistic thought, for the kabbalistic far exceeded the philosophical in popularity for many centuries. Of course, most people did not read the *Zohar* or any other of the more sophisticated kabbalistic writings. Their knowledge was based on more simplistic accounts that occasionally made greater use, for instance, of the angelology and demonology that are found in the *Zohar* and that tended to lapse into superstition. Still, kabbalistic beliefs—that there is more to the world than we can understand rationally, that there are mystical resonances to everything in the world, that somehow the elements of this lower world reflect the elements of the upper world—helped to sustain the

Jews through their difficult history. At times like 1492, at the expulsion from Spain, more people found greater consolation in Kabbalah than in Maimonides, which helps to explain why Kabbalah became so popular at that time. Traces of kabbalistic thought can even be found in modern prayer books, thanks in large part to the influence of Hasidism. Beginning with Gershom Scholem in the twentieth century, scholarly attention has begun to consider the Kabbalah far more carefully, but there are still many aspects that we do not understand. One point that is quite clear about both philosophy and Kabbalah, however, is that neither presented an alternative to Judaism. They were both expressions of deep religiosity.

Epilogue

In popular usage, the word "medieval" is often taken to mean "backwards" or "primitive." Similarly, Jewish history is often thought of as a series of persecutions and disasters. I hope that this book has helped to dispel both notions. Certainly there was brutal, primitive behavior during the Middle Ages, as there has been in every age. No century exceeded the twentieth in brutality, and the twenty-first is not off to a promising start. And Jewish history certainly has its share of disasters and persecutions, but it also has its glories. Whatever happened during the Middle Ages, Judaism not only survived but it transformed itself, defined itself, created poetry and philosophy, and paved the way for its continued existence in the modern world. We must never forget the evils, but if we remember only the evils, we can have no understanding of or appreciation for what Jewish life really meant.

Jews had no kings in the Middle Ages, no equivalent to Charlemagne or Richard the Lionhearted, nor did they have knights, either real, like the Black Prince, or fictional, like the knights of the Round Table. Nor did they have queens like Eleanor of Aquitaine. They did have great religious leaders, poets, commentators, philosophers, and kabbalists. But mostly they had ordinary people who lived their religion to the best of their ability, often in the face of great oppression. Most of them resisted the temptation to become apostates, despite pressures that we can barely imagine. They longed for a return to their homeland, but while they waited, they created a culture whose influence we can see in modern Judaism. They persevered—and they transcended mere perseverance. Many died unnatural deaths, but as a people they survived and triumphed. Their story deserves retelling, and I can only hope that I have done it justice.

Appendix 1: Chronology

Jewish		Christian and Muslim	
c.50–135	Rabbi Akiva	46–57	Journeys of Paul
68–73	Great Revolt against Rome		
70	Destruction of Second Temple		
132–135	Bar Kohba Rebellion	c.160–220	Tertullian
Late 2nd–early 3rd centuries	Yehuda ha-Nasi		
c.200	Mishnah completed	c.342–c.420	St. Jerome
		354–430	St. Augustine
c.500	Gemara completed	c.540–604	Gregory the Great
		c.570–632	Mohammed
		622	Hegira of Mohammed
		711	Muslim conquest of Spain
		742–814	Charlemagne
c.875	Death of Amram ben Sheshna Gaon	779–840	Agobard of Lyons
882–942	Saadiah ben Yosef Gaon		
10th century	Menahem ben Jacob ibn Saruq		
c.906–1006	Sherirah ben Hanina Gaon		
c.915–c.970	Hasdai ibn Shapruth		
939–1038	Hai ben Sherira Gaon		
c. 960–1028	Gershom ben Yehuda Me-or ha-Golah		

Mid-10th century	Dunash ben Laprat		
993–c.1055	Shmuel ha-Nagid		
1013–1103	Yitzhak ben Ya'akov Alfasi (Rif)c.		
1020–c.1057	Shlomo ibn Gabirol		
1040–1105	Rashi		
c.1055–c.1135	Moshe ibn Ezra		
		1056	Almoravides arrive in Spain
c.1075–1141	Yehuda Halevi	1062–c.1140	Petrus Alfonsi
c.1080–c.1174	Shmuel ben Meir (Rashbam)		
1089–1164	Abraham ibn Ezra		
		1095	Beginning of First Crusade
Late 11th century	Bahya ben Yosef ibn Paquda		
12th century	Yitzhak ben Mordecai (Rivam)		
1100–1171	Jacob ben Meir Tam		
c.1105–c.1170	Yosef Kimhi		
c.1110–1180	Abraham ibn Daud		
c.1120–c.1190	Yehuda ben Shaul ibn Tibbon		
c.1125–1198	Avraham of Posquières (Rabad)		
c. 1135–1204	Moshe Maimonides	1135	Almohades arrive in Spain
c.1150–1217	Yehudah ben Shmuel he-Hasid		
		1157–1199	Richard I (England)
		1160–1216	Innocent III
c.1160–c.1235	David Kimhi		
c.1160–c.1230	Shmuel ben Yehuda ibn Tibbon		
c.1165–c.1230	Eleazar ben Yehuda of Worms (Ha-Rokeah)		
1170–1235	Yehuda ben Shlomo al-Harizi	1165–1223	Philip II Augustus (France)
		c.1181–1226	St. Francis of Assisi
1190	Mass suicide at York		
d. 1190	Yom Tov of Joigny		
1194–1270	Moses Nahmanides		
Late 12th century	Benjamin of Tudela		
13th century	Ya'akov ben Abba Anatoli		
13th century	Moses of Coucy		

c. 1215–1293	Meir ben Baruch of Rothenburg	1214–1270	Louis IX (France)
		1215	Fourth Lateran Council
		1215	Magna Carta
		c.1225–1274	Thomas Aquinas
c.1235–c.1310	Shlomo ben Avraham Adret (Rashba)		
c.1240–1305	Moshe ben Shem Tov de Leon		
1242	Burning of Talmud in Paris		
1247–c.1298	Todros ben Yehuda ha-Levi Abulafia		
		1254–1324	Marco Polo
c.1261–1328	Immanuel ben Shlomo ha-Romi		
		1265–1321	Dante
1290	Expulsion of Jews from England		
1326–1408	Yitzhak ben Sheshet Perfet (Ribash)		
		1348	Plague in Europe
c.1380–c.1441	Shem Tov ibn Shem Tov		
1391	Anti-Jewish riots in Spain		
c.1412	Death of Hasdai Crescas		
15th century	Shem Tov ibn Shem Tov		
c.1450–c.1516	Ovadiah Bertorino		
1492	Expulsion from Spain		

Appendix 2: Names in Hebrew and English

Throughout the text, I have used the Hebrew forms of names for medieval figures, but many of them are better known by the English translations of their names. For the convenience of readers, here is a list of both the Hebrew and English versions of the names.

Hebrew Name	English Name
R. Avraham ben David (Rabad)	R. Abraham ben David
Avraham ibn Daud	Abraham ibn Daud
Avraham ibn Ezra	Abraham ibn Ezra
Immanuel ha-Romi	Immanuel of Rome
Moshe ben Maimon (Rambam)	Moses Maimonides
R. Moshe ben Nachman (Nachmanides)	R. Moses ben Nachman
Moshe ibn Ezra	Moses ibn Ezra
Moshe of Coucy	Moses of Coucy
R. Shlomo ben Adreth	R. Solomon ben Adreth
Shlomo ben Yitzhak (Rashi)	Solomon ben Isaac
Shlomo ibn Gabirol	Solomon ibn Gabirol
Todros ben Yehuda Abulafia	Todros ben Judah Abulafia
Ya'akov Anatoli	Jacob Anatoli
R. Ya'akov Tam (Rabbeinu Tam)	R. Jacob Tam
Yehuda Alharizi	Judah Alharizi
Yehuda ha-Levi	Judah ha-Levi
R. Yehuda ha-Nasi	R. Judah the Prince
Yosef ibn Shem Tov	Joseph ibn Shem Tov
Yosef Kimhi	Joseph Kimhi
R. Yitzhak ben Sheshet Perfet	R. Isaac ben Sheshet Perfet
R. Yitzhak ben Ya'akov Alfasi	R. Isaac ben Jacob Alfasi
Rabbeinu Yitzhak (Rivam)	Rabbeinu Isaac

Notes

Preface

1. Herrin, *Formation of Christendom*, 9.
2. Colish, *Medieval Foundations*, 149.
3. Baron, *History and Jewish Historians*, 96.

Chapter 1

1. Baron, *Social and Religious History*, III 5,7.
2. Cohen, *Beginnings of Jewishness*, 78–79; and Cohen notes that that "way of life is not defined."
3. Ibid. 105–06.
4. Steinsaltz, *We Jews* 43; Boyarin, *Border Lines*, 8.
5. 1) Kellner, *Must a Jew Believe*, 45; 2) Steinsaltz, *We Jews* 48; 3) Kugel, *On Being a Jew*, 6; 4) Neusner, *Mishnah,* xxix.
6. Marcus, *Jew in the Medieval World*, 34.
7. Einbinder, *Beautiful Death*, 170, citing Ephraim Urbach, *Ba'alei ha-tosafot.* Jerusalem: Mosad Bialik, 1955: 386. "Tefillin," phylacteries, will be explained shortly.
8. Grayzel, *Church and the Jews*, 127.
9. Baer, *Jews in Christian Spain,* I.4.
10. J. Marcus, *Jew in the Medieval World*, 397.

Chapter 2

1. Grayzel, *Church and the Jews*, 241.
2. Kehati, *Shabbat*, 1.

3. Agus, *Rabbi Meir*, 22.

4. In Freehof, *Responsa Literature*, 10–11.

5. Shiffman, *From Text to Tradition*, 192.

6. See Brody, *Geonim of Babylonia*, 161.

7. Ibid. 4.

8. Cited in Rabinowitz, *Social Life*, 218.

9. For a full discussion of this story and its tragic aftermath, see Daniel Gordis, *God Was Not in the Fire*, 198–202.

10. Bokser, *Post-Mishnaic Judaism*, 462.

11. Rubenstein, *Culture of the Babylonian Talmud*, 33.

12. Ibid. 33.

13. Neusner, *How the Talmud Works*, 28.

14. Brody, *Geonim of Babylonia*, 333.

15. Kraemer, *The Intended Reader*, 133.

16. Many of the medieval rabbis whom we will encounter are known by the acronyms of their Hebrew names. Thus "Rif" is derived from the initials of Rabbi Yitzhak Fasi and "Rashi" from Rabbi Shlomo ben Yitzhak.

17. See I. Marcus, "History, Story and Collective Memory."

18. Spiegel, "On Medieval Hebrew Poetry," 856.

19. G. Cohen, *The Book of Tradition*, xliii.

20. Brody, *Geonim of Babylonia*, 85ff.

21. Frank, "Karaite Ritual," 249.

22. Goitein, *Mediterranean Society*, V. 363.

23. Reif "Centennial Assessment," 22.

24. Nemoy, *Karaite Anthology*, xvi.

25. Bloomfield, *Piers Plowman*, 37.

26. Grossman, *Pious and Rebellious*, 1.

27. Rabinowitz, *Social Life*, 7, 90.

Chapter 3

1. Quoted in Scheil, *Footsteps of Israel*, 196.

2. Katz, *Exclusiveness*, 4.

3. Baron, *Social and Religious History*, 5:85.

4. Kellner, *Must a Jew Believe*, 13 n2.

5. Chazan, *Fashioning Jewish Identity*, 248.

6. Wilken, *John Chrysostom*, 124, 126, quoting Chrysostom's Homilies against the Jews.

7. Parkes, *Antisemitism*, 64.

8. Brown, *World of Late Antiquity*, 82.

9. Ibid. 143.

10. Baker, *Image of Man*, 82.

11. Seiferth, *Synagogue and Church*, 35.

12. Markus, *Gregory the Great*, 77; J. Marcus, *Jew in the Medieval World*, 113.

13. Markus, *Gregory the Great*, 78.

14. Baron, *Social and Religious History*, 3:31.

15. Grayzel, *Church and the Jews*, 93.

16. Ibid. 103.

17. Ibid. 105, 107.

18. Rubin, *Gentile Tales*, 15.

19. Saperstein, *Jewish Preaching*, 177.

20. Baer, *Jews in Christian Spain*, I:14.

21. Kellner, *Must a Jew Believe*, 32 n.11.

22. See Langmuir, *Toward a Definition* and Abulafia, *Christians and Jews*.

23. Berger, *Jewish-Christian Debate*, 4.

24. Quoted in Chazan, *Fashioning Jewish Identity*, 263.

25. Quoted in Southern, *St. Anselm*, 51.

26. Dahan, *Christian Polemic*, 107–08.

27. Quoted in Seifert, *Synagogue and Church*, 17.

28. Abulafia, *Christians and Jews*, 98.

29. Van Engen, "Ralph of Flaix," 159.

30. Abulafia, *Christians and Jews*, 106; Chazan, "From the First Crusade," 49; Berger, "The Attitude of St. Bernard," 106.

31. Grayzel and Stow, *Church and the Jews*, 273.

32. Grayzel, *Church and the Jews*, 251.

33. Ibid. 241.

34. Dahan, *Christian Polemic*, 34.

35. Toaff, *Love, Work, and Death*, 111.

36. See Stow, *Alienated Minority*, 76–77.

37. Blumenkranz, "Roman Church," 89.

38. Berger, "Gilbert Crispin," 34.

39. Stow, *Alienated Minority*, 77.

40. Jordan, "Last Tormentor," 25.

41. Twersky, *Rabad*, 21.

42. Roth, *History of the Jews in England*, 9.

43. Menache, "Faith," 354–55.

44. Rubin, *Gentile Tales*, 27, 87, 99.

45. Grayzel and Stow, *Church and the Jews*, 116, 123–24.

46. Stow, *Alienated Minority*, 218.

47. Jordan, *French Monarchy*, 76.

48. Stow, *Alienated Minority*, 220–21; Baron, *Social and Religious History*, IV:205.

49. J. Marcus, *Jew in the Medieval World*, 43.

50. Toaff, *Love, Work, and Death*, 50.

51. Roth, "Italy," 107–8.

52. Cahn, "Expulsion of the Jews," 103.

53. Blumenkranz, "Roman," 82.

54. Finkel, *Responsa Anthology*, 19.

55. Rubin, *Gentile Tales*, 89.

56. Stacey, "Conversion of Jews," 267; Grossman, *Pious and Rebellious*, 205.

57. Stacey, "Conversion of Jews," 267.

58. Stow, *Alienated Minority*, 66.

59. J. Marcus, *Jew in the Medieval World*, 143.

60. J. Cohen, "Mentality of the Medieval Jewish Apostate," 22.

61. See Lasker, "Jewish Critique," 121–2.

62. Berger, *Nizzahon Vetus*, 25.

63. Abulafia, *Christians and Jews*, 70.

64. Berger, *Nizzahon Vetus*, 29–30. Chazan discusses the passages on Matthew in *Milhamot HaShem* in *Fashioning Jewish Identity*.

65. Chazan, *Fashioning Jewish Identity*, 307.

66. These points are discussed in Daniel Lasker's *Jewish Philosophical Polemics*.

67. Firestone, "Jewish Culture," 282–83.

68. Lewis, *Jews of Islam*, 13.

69. Runciman, *History of the Crusades*, 21.

70. Lewis, *Jews of Islam*, 14.

71. Ibid. 33.

72. Epstein, *Responsa of Rabbi Solomon ben Adreth*, 7ff.

73. J. Marcus, *Jew in the Medieval World*, 397; Lewis, *Jews of Islam*, 90.

74. Firestone, "Jewish Culture," 290, 294.

75. Ashtor, *Jews of Moslem Spain*, III.117, 72.

76. Ibid. 226.

77. Gampel, "Letter to a Wayward Teacher," 391–92.

78. Scheindlin, "Merchants and Intellectuals," 323.

79. Cohen, *Under Crescent and Cross*, 165.

80. Gampel, "Letter to a Wayward Teacher," 397.

81. Goitein, *Mediterranean Society*, II.302–3; Lewis, *Jews of Islam*, 99.

82. Gampel, "Letter to a Wayward Teacher," 422.

Chapter 4

1. Saperstein, *Jewish Preaching*, 176.

2. J. Marcus, *Jew in the Medieval World*, 3ff.

3. Ibid. 20.

4. Loewe, *Ibn Gabirol*, 4.

5. Stow, *Alienated Minority*, 50.

6. Baron, *Social and Religious History*, III.45–6, 127.

7. Stow, *Alienated Minority*, 53.

8. Irshai, "Confronting a Christian Empire," 203.

9. Brown, *World of Late Antiquity*, 174.

10. Runciman, *History of the Crusades*, 10–12.

11. Brody, *Geonim of Babylonia*, 105–106.

12. Gil, *History of Palestine*, 181.

13. Brody, *Geonim of Babylonia*, 117ff.

14. Ibid. 35–6.

15. Baron, *Social and Religious History*, V.22.

16. Rubenstein, *Culture of the Babylonian Talmud*, 158.

17. Hoffman, *Canonization of the Synagogue Service*, 91.

18. Brody, *Geonim of Babylonia*, 11.

19. Baron, *Social and Religious History*, V.60–1; Brody, *Geonim of Babylonia*, 132.

20. It has become convenient in our time to think of European Jews as Ashkenazim and Jews who originated in the East as Sephardim, but that distinction is too simple. Sephardim literally refers to Jews from the Iberian Peninsula (*Sepharad* means Spain), but after the expulsion from Spain in 1492, many of the Sephardim fled to countries in the Middle East and the Jews of those countries became identified with the Sephardim. (see Fine, *Judaism in Practice*, 11–13).

21. Reif, "Centennial Assessment," 27.

22. Stow, *Alienated Minority*, 150.

23. Toaff, *Love, Work, and Death*, 67–8; Stow, *Alienated Minority*, 240.

24. Golb, *Jews in Medieval Normandy*, 15.

25. Seiferth, *Synagogue and Church*, 54; Schwarzfuchs, "France and Germany," 135; Glick, *Abraham's Heirs*, 53–6.

26. Schwarzfuchs, "France under the Early Capets," 145.

27. Chazan, *Medieval Jewry in Northern France*, 12.

28. Runciman, *History of the Crusades*, ix.

29. Ibid. 136.

30. Peters, *First Crusade*, 101.

31. Ibid. 102–3.

32. Baron, *Social and Religious History*, IV.104.

33. Chazan, "From the First Crusade to the Second," 46–7; J. Cohen, "A 1096 Complex?" 12–13.

34. Van Engen, "Introduction," 3.

35. Runciman, *History of the Crusades*, 141.

36. Gil, *History of Palestine*, 827–8.

37. Asbridge, *First Crusade*, 319, 322.

38. Runciman, *History of the Crusades*, 134.

39. Stow, *Alienated Minority*, 106.

40. Shepkaru, "To Die for God," 340–41.

41. J. Marcus, *Jew in the Medieval World*, 129.

42. Einbinder, *Beautiful Death*, 28.

43. Chazan, *Medieval Jewry in Northern France*, 37; Einbinder, *Beautiful Death*, 48.

44. J. Marcus, *Jew in the Medieval World*, 24.

45. Jordan, *French Monarchy*, 4; Chazan, *Medieval Jewry in Northern France*, 65.
46. Jordan, *French Monarchy*, 90.
47. Chazan, *Medieval Jewry in Northern France*, 123.
48. Ibid. 132–3.
49. Jordan, *French Monarchy*, 118.
50. Chazan, *Medieval Jewry in Northern France*, 180ff.
51. Jordan, *French Monarchy*, 208, 233, 240.
52. Ibid. 243–4; Grayzel, *Church and the Jews*, 96.
53. Menache, "Faith, Myth, and Politics," 371.
54. Roth, "Jews of Oxford," 51; Lipman 67.
55. Stacey, "Jews and Christians," 343–4.
56. Heng, "Romance of England," 147.
57. Stacey, "Conversion of Jews," 270.
58. Ibid. 277.
59. J. Marcus, *Jew in the Medieval World*, 125.
60. Roth, *History of the Jews in England*, 22–4.
61. Stacey, "Jews and Christians," 347.
62. See J. Marcus, *Jews in the Medieval World*, 131–6.
63. Stacey, "Conversion of Jews," 282–3; Jordan, *French Monarchy*, 147.
64. Menache, "Faith, Myth, and Politics," 360–1.
65. Baer, *History of the Jews in Christian Spain*, I.37–8.
66. Ibid. 76.
67. Ibid. 76.
68. Assis, *Golden Age of Aragonese Jewry*, 51.
69. Baer, *History of the Jews in Christian Spain*, II.13ff.
70. Assis, *Golden Age of Aragonese Jewry*, 9; Baer, *History of the Jews in Christian Spain*, II.112.
71. Baer, Ibid. II.95ff.
72. Ibid. 104–5.
73. Ibid. 133.
74. Ibid. 281.
75. J. Cohen, *Friars and the Jews*, 15–6.
76. Assis, *Golden Age of Aragonese Jewry*, 54; Baer, *History of the Jews in Christian Spain*, II.174ff.
77. Baer, Ibid. II.167ff.

Chapter 5

1. Goitein, *Mediterranean Society*, I.1–2.
2. Goitein, *Letters*, 7.
3. Goitein, *Mediterranean Society*, V. 6.
4. Baskin, "Dolce of Worms," 430.
5. Toaff, *Love, Work, and Death*, 32, 7, 11.

6. Baumgarten, *Mothers and Children*, chapter 4.
7. Toaff, *Love, Work, and Death*, 54–5.
8. Katz, *Exclusiveness*, 59.
9. Goitein, *Letters*, 17–18.
10. Saperstein, *Jewish Preaching*, 113.
11. In Smalley, *Study of the Bible*, 78.
12. Karnafogel, *Jewish Education*, 62.
13. In Twersky, *Rabad*, 33.
14. I. Marcus, *Rituals of Childhood*, 16.
15. Reif, *Judaism and Hebrew Prayer*, 153.
16. Langer, "Revisiting Early Rabbinic Liturgy," 152.
17. Hoffman, *Canonization of the Synagogue Service*, 3–4.
18. Reif, *Judaism and Hebrew Prayer*, 57, 102.
19. Ibid. 135, 187.
20. Hoffman, *Canonization of the Synagogue Service*, 11ff.
21. Nulman, *Encyclopedia of Jewish Prayer*, 38.
22. Hoffman, *Canonization of the Synagogue Service*, 101.
23. Nulman, *Encyclopedia of Jewish Prayer*, passim.
24. I. Marcus, *Piety and Society*, 1.
25. Fine, "Introduction," 17.
26. I. Marcus, *Piety and Society*, 25.
27. Katz, *Exclusiveness*, 93, 95; Stow, *Alienated Minority*, 133–4.
28. I. Marcus, *Piety and Society*, 1.
29. Karnafogel, *Jewish Education*, 75.
30. Perlmutter, *Tools for Tosafos*, 12, 33.
31. Karnafogel, *Jewish Education*, 69–70.
32. I. Marcus, *Piety and Society*, 112.
33. Freehof, *Responsa Literature*, 42.
34. Agus, *Meir of Rothenburg*, 61–7.
35. Ibid. 22.
36. Ibid. 17.
37. Ibid. 243.
38. Finkel, *Responsa Anthology*, 31.
39. Ibid. 33.
40. Kellner, *Must a Jew Believe*, 7.
41. Shepkaru, "To Die for God," 327ff.
42. Goitein, *Mediterranean Society*, V.410–12.
43. Ibid. 402.
44. G. Cohen, *Book of Tradition*, 263.
45. Goitein, *Mediterranean Society*, V. 391.
46. Saperstein, *Jewish Preaching*, 182.
47. Grossman, *Pious and Rebellious*, xiii.
48. Ibid. 174, 129.

49. Agus, *Meir of Rothenburg*, 326.
50. Baumgarten, *Mothers and Children*, 40.
51. Fine, "Introduction," 27.
52. Hoffman, "The Role of Women," 112–13.
53. Baskin, "Women and Ritual Immersion," 138; Finkel, *Responsa Anthology*, 16.
54. Stow, *Alienated Minority*, 131.
55. Grossman, *Pious and Rebellious*, 155.
56. Ibid. 178; Baumgarten, *Mothers and Children*, 187.
57. Kramer, "Women Speak for Themselves," 185.
58. Baskin, "Dolce of Worms," 431; Kramer, "Women Speak for Themselves," 186–7.
59. Grossman, *Pious and Rebellious*, 27, 105.
60. Ibid. 98.
61. Goitein, *Letters,* 221f.
62. Grossman, *Pious and Rebellious*, 40.
63. Reif, "Centennial Assessment," 23.
64. Grossman, *Pious and Rebellious*, 164.
65. Baumgarten, *Mothers and Children*, 44.
66. Einbinder, *Beautiful Death*, 10.
67. Baumgarten, *Mothers and Children*, 8.

Chapter 6

1. Bland, "Defending, Enjoying," 281ff.
2. Agus, *Meir of Rothenburg*, 266.
3. Agus, "Rashi," 221.
4. Pearl, *Rashi*, 10.
5. Ibid. 48.
6. Signer, "God's Love for Israel," 134.
7. J. Marcus, *Jews in the Medieval World*, 303.
8. Strickman, "Forward," x.
9. Ibid. xx.
10. Casper, *Introduction to Jewish Bible Commentary*, 86–7.
11. Ibid. 34–5.
12. Matter, *Voice of My Beloved*, 166.
13. Ibid. 72.

Chapter 7

1. In order to give as broad a sense as possible of these poems, I will quote from a variety of translations. After each quotation, the name of the translator and the page number will appear in parentheses.

2. Petuchowski, *Theology and Poetry,* 13.

3. Stern, "New Directions," 106, following E. Fleischer, *Shirat hakodesh ha'ivrit biyemei habeinayim.* Jerusalem: Keter, 1975.

4. Hoffman, *Canonization of the Synagogue Service,* 66–7.

5. See Shalom Spiegel, *The Last Trial.*

6. Birnbaum, *Daily Prayer Book,* 192.

7. Rosenfeld, *Tisha B'av,* 161–2.

8. Raphael Loewe (54–5) prefers "liturgical" and "social."

9. Spiegel, "On Medieval Hebrew Poetry," 884.

10. Scheindlin, *Wine, Women, and Death,* 43.

11. Ibid. 44.

12. N. Roth, "Deal Gently," 23–4.

13. Scheindlin, *Wine, Women, and Death,* 70–1.

14. Ibid. 37–9.

15. For translations, see the bibliography under each poet's name as well as the entries for Carmi, Lewis, and Scheindlin. All of the translators approach their task with different ideas about translation, and they all produce good translations according to their individual criteria.

16. Alfie, "Immanuel of Rome," 313.

Chapter 8

1. Leff, *Medieval Thought,* 11.

2. G. Cohen, *Book of Tradition,* xix–xx.

3. Brody, *Geonim of Babylonia,* 122.

4. All references are to Saadiah Gaon. *The Book of Beliefs and Opinions.* Trans. Samuel Rosenblatt. New Haven: Yale University Press, 1948.

5. Rosenblatt, "Introduction."

6. Guttmann, *Philosophies of Judaism,* 101.

7. Unless otherwise noted, all passages from the poem are from *Selected Religious Poems of Solomon ibn Gabirol,* trans. Israel Zangwill, with the important difference that I have, for the sake of bringing out the personal character of the poem, changed every "Thou" to "You," every "Thy" or "Thine" to "Your." The translation by Peter Cole presents the poem very well in more contemporary language.

8. All quotations by ibn Paquda are from *The Book of Direction to the Duties of the Heart,* trans. Menahem Mansoor.

9. Leibowitz, *Studies in Devarim,* 101; quoting from Albo's *Sefer ha-ikkarim.*

10. Guttmann, *Philosophies of Judaism,* 137.

11. All quotation from the *Kuzari* are from *The Kuzari: An Argument for the Faith of Israel,* trans Hartwig Hirschfeld.

12. Goitein, *Mediterranean Society,* V. 289.

13. Twersky, *Introduction to the Mishneh Torah,* 96.

14. Ibid. 518.

15. *Mishneh Torah,* 1:32.

16. Twersky, *Introduction to the Mishneh Torah,* 388, citing *Guide of the Perplexed* III.27.

17. *Letters of Maimonides,* 106.

18. Davidson, *Moses Maimonides,* 121.

19. All quotations from the *Guide* are from *Guide of the Perplexed,* trans. Shlomo Pines.

20. Davidson, *Moses Maimonides,* 308.

21. See Menachem Kellner's *Must a Jew Believe Anything?*

22. Davidson, *Moses Maimonides,* 158.

23. Ibid. 377.

24. Baer, *Jews in Christian Spain,* I.301-2; Davidson, *Moses Maimonides,* 409.

25. Baer, *Jews in Christian Spain,* II.138; Davidson, *Moses Maimonides,* 415.

26. See Scholem, *On the Kabbalah and Its Symbolism.*

27. The *Guide* is published both as a separate volume and as the introduction to the first volume of Daniel Matt's translation of the *Zohar.*

28. Idel, *Kabbalah,* 112; Green, *Guide,* 35.

29. Green, *Guide,* 51. Green's chapter on the *sefiroth* is particularly helpful.

30. *Zohar,* 8 (1:20).

Bibliography

Abulafia, Anna Sapir. *Christians and Jews in the Twelfth-Century Renaissance*. London: Routledge, 1995.

Agus, I. A. "Rabbinic Scholarship in Northern Europe." In *The Dark Ages: Jews in Christian Europe, 711–1096*. Ed. Cecil Roth and I. H. Levine: 189–209. New Brunswick: Rutgers University Press, 1966.

———. "Rashi and his School." In *The Dark Ages: Jews in Christian Europe, 711–1096*. Ed. Cecil Roth and I. H. Levine: 210–48. New Brunswick: Rutgers University Press, 1966.

Agus, Irving A. *Rabbi Meir of Rothenburg*. Philadelphia: Jewish Publication Society, 1947.

Alfie, Fabian. "Immanuel of Rome, Alias Manoello Guideo: The Poetics of Jewish Identity in Fourteenth-Century Italy." *Italica* 75 (1998): 307–29.

Alharizi, Judah. *The Book of Taḥkemoni: Jewish Tales from Medieval Spain*. Trans. David Simha Segal. Oxford: Littman Library of Jewish Civilization, 2001.

Asbridge, Thomas. *The First Crusade: A New History*. Oxford: Oxford University Press, 2004.

Ashtor, Eliyahu. *The Jews of Moslem Spain*. 3 vols. Trans. Aaron Klein and Jenny Machlowitz Klein. Philadelphia: Jewish Publication Society, 1973.

Assis, Yom Tov. *The Golden Age of Aragonese Jewry: Community and Society in the Crown of Aragon, 1213–1327*. Portland, OR: Vallentine Mitchell & Co., 1997.

Augustine. *The City of God against the Pagans*. Vol. VI. Trans. William Chase Greene. Cambridge, MA: Harvard University Press, 1960.

———. *On Christian Doctrine*. Trans. D. W. Robertson, Jr. New York: Liberal Arts Press, 1958.

———. *St. Augustine on Psalms*. Trans. Dame Scholastica Hebgin and Dame Felicitas Corrigan. Westminster, MD: Newman Press, 1960.

Avodah: An Anthology of Ancient Poetry for Yom Kippur. Ed. and trans. Michael D. Swartz and Joseph Yahalom. University Park, PA: Pennsylvania State University, 2005.

Baer, Yitzhak. *A History of the Jews in Christian Spain,* 2 vols. Trans. Louis Schoffman. Philadelphia: Jewish Publication Society, 1961.

Baker, Herschel. *The Image of Man.* Cambridge, MA: Harvard University Press, 1947.

Baron, Salo W. *History and Jewish Historians.* Philadelphia: Jewish Publication Society, 1964.

———. *A Social and Religious History of the Jews,* 18 vols., 2d ed. Philadelphia: Jewish Publication Society, 1957.

Baskin, Judith R. "Dolce of Worms: The Lives and Deaths of an Exemplary Medieval Jewish Woman and her Daughters." In *Judaism in Practice: From the Middle Ages through the Early Modern Period.* Ed. Lawrence Fine: 429–37. Princeton: Princeton University Press, 2001.

———. "Women and Ritual Immersion in Medieval Ashkenaz: The Sexual Politics of Piety." In *Judaism in Practice: From the Middle Ages through the Early Modern Period.* Ed. Lawrence Fine: 131–42. Princeton: Princeton University Press, 2001.

Baumgarten, Elisheva. *Mothers and Children: Jewish Family Life in Medieval Europe.* Princeton: Princeton University Press, 2004.

Benjamin of Tudela. *The Itinerary of Benjamin of Tudela: Travels in the Middle Ages.* Trans. Marcus Nathan Adler. Intros. by Michael Signer, Marcus Nathan Adler, A. Asher. Malibu, CA: Joseph Simon/Pangloss Press, 1987.

Berakhot. Trans. Maurice Simon. London: Soncino, 1960.

Berger, David. "The Attitude of St. Bernard of Clairvaux toward the Jews." *Proceedings of the American Academy for Jewish Research* 40 (1974).

———. "Gilbert Crispin, Alan of Lille, and Jacob ben Reuben: A Study in the Transmission of Medieval Polemic." *Speculum* 49 (1974): 34–47.

———. *The Jewish-Christian Debate in the High Middle Ages: A Critical Edition of the Nizzahon Vetus.* Philadelphia: Jewish Publication Society, 1979.

Biale, David, ed. *Cultures of the Jews: A New History.* New York: Schocken, 2002.

Birnbaum, Philip. *Daily Prayer Book.* New York: Hebrew Publishing Company, 1949.

Bland, Kalman. "Defending, Enjoying, and Regulating the Visual." In *Judaism in Practice: From the Middle Ages through the Early Modern Period.* Ed. Lawrence Fine: 281–97. Princeton: Princeton University Press, 2001.

Bloomfield, Morton W. *Piers Plowman as a Fourteenth-Century Apocalypse.* New Brunswick: Rutgers University Press, 1962.

Blumenkranz, B. "The Roman Church and the Jews." In *The Dark Ages: Jews in Christian Europe, 711–1096.* Ed. Cecil Roth and I. H. Levine: 69–99. New Brunswick: Rutgers University Press, 1966.

Bokser, Baruch M. *Post-Mishnaic Judaism in Transition: Samuel on Berakhot and the Beginnings of Gemara*. Chico, CA: Scholars Press, 1980.

Boyarin, Daniel. *Border Lines: The Partition of Judaeo-Christianity*. Philadelphia: University of Pennsylvania Press, 2004.

Brann, Ross. *The Compunctious Poet: Cultural Ambiguity and Hebrew Poetry in Muslim Spain*. Baltimore: Johns Hopkins University Press, 1991.

Brody, Robert. *The Geonim of Babylonia and the Shaping of Medieval Jewish Culture*. New Haven: Yale University Press, 1998.

Brown, Peter. *The World of Late Antiquity, A. D. 150–750*. New York: W. W. Norton, 1971.

Cahn, Walter. "The Expulsion of the Jews as History and Allegory in Painting and Sculpture of the Twelfth and Thirteenth Centuries." In *Jews and Christians in Twelfth-Century Europe*. Ed. Michael A. Signer and John Van Engen: 94–109. Notre Dame: University of Notre Dame Press, 2001.

Carmi, T., ed. *The Penguin Book of Hebrew Verse*. New York: Penguin Books, 1981.

Casper, Bernard M. *An Introduction to Jewish Bible Commentary*. New York: Thomas Yoseloff, 1960.

Castle, Dovid. *Living with the Sages. Vol. I. Rashi and the Tosafists*. Jerusalem: Feldheim, 1996.

Chazan, Robert. "The Barcelona 'Disputation' of 1263: Christian Missionizing and Jewish Response." *Speculum* 52 (1977): 824–42.

———. *Fashioning Jewish Identity in Medieval Western Christendom*. Cambridge: Cambridge University Press, 2004.

———. "From the First Crusade to the Second: Evolving Perceptions of the Christian-Jewish Conflict." In *Jews and Christians in Twelfth-Century Europe*. Ed. Michael A. Signer and John Van Engen: 46–62. Notre Dame: University of Notre Dame Press, 2001.

———. *Medieval Jewry in Northern France: A Political and Social History*. Baltimore: Johns Hopkins University, 1973.

Chilton, Bruce. *Rabbi Paul: An Intellectual Biography*. New York: Doubleday, 2004.

Chrétien de Troyes. *Perceval: The Story of the Grail*. Trans. Burton Raffel. New Haven: Yale University Press, 1999.

Chronicle of Ahimaaz. Trans. Marcus Salzman. 1924; reprint New York: AMS, 1961.

Cohen, Arthur. *The Myth of the Judeo-Christian Tradition and Other Dissenting Essays*. New York: Schocken, 1971.

Cohen, Gerson, D., ed. and trans. *The Book of Tradition (Sefer Ha-Qabbalah)* by Abraham Ibn Daud. Philadelphia: Jewish Publication Society, 1967.

Cohen, Jeremy. "A 1096 Complex? Constructing the First Crusade in Jewish Historical Memory, Medieval and Modern." In *Jews and Christians in Twelfth-Century Europe*. Ed. Michael A. Signer and John Van Engen: 9–26. Notre Dame: University of Notre Dame Press, 2001.

————. *The Friars and the Jews: The Evolution of Medieval Anti-Judaism.* Ithaca: Cornell University Press, 1982.

————. "The Mentality of the Medieval Jewish Apostate: Peter Alfonsi, Herman of Cologne, and Pablo Christiani." In *Jewish Apostasy in the Modern World.* Ed. Todd M. Endelman: 35–41. New York: Holmes and Meier, 1987.

Cohen, Mark R. *Under Crescent and Cross: The Jews in the Middle Ages.* Princeton: Princeton Unversity Press, 1994.

Cohen, Shaye J. D. *The Beginnings of Jewishness: Boundaries, Varieties, Uncertainties.* Berkeley: University of California Press, 1999.

————. "The Destruction: From Scripture to Midrash." *Prooftexts* 2 (1982): 18–39.

————. "The Significance of Yavneh: Pharisees, Rabbis, and the End of Jewish Sectarianism." *Hebrew Union College Annual* 55 (1984): 27–53.

Colish, Marcia L. *Medieval Foundations of the Western Intellectual Tradition, 400–1400.* New Haven: Yale University press, 1997.

Commentarius Cantabrigiensis in Epistolas Pauli e Schola Petri Abaelardi. Ed. A. Landgraf. South Bend: University of Notre Dame Press, 1937.

Dahan, Gilbert. *The Christian Polemic against the Jews.* Trans. Jody Gladding. Notre Dame: University of Notre Dame Press, 1998.

Davidson, Herbert A. *Moses Maimonides: The Man and His Works.* New York: Oxford University Press, 2004.

De Lange, Nicholas, ed. *Hebrew Scholarship and the Medieval World.* Cambridge: Cambridge University Press, 2001.

————. "Hebrew scholarship in Byzantium." In *Hebrew Scholarship and the Medieval World.* Ed. Nicholas de Lange: 23–37. Cambridge: Cambridge University Press, 2001.

Eidelberg, Shlomo, ed. and trans. *The Jews and the Crusaders: The Hebrew Chronicles of the First and Second Crusades.* Madison: University of Wisconsin Press, 1977.

Einbinder, Susan L. *Beautiful Death: Jewish Poetry and Martyrdom in Medieval France.* Princeton: Princeton University Press, 2002.

Epstein, Isidore. *The Responsa of Rabbi Simon b. Ẓemaḥ Duran.* New York: Ktav, 1930.

————. *The "Responsa" of Rabbi Solomon ben Adreth of Barcelona (1235–1310).* New York: Ktav, 1925.

Fathers According to Rabbi Nathan. Trans. Judah Goldin. 1955; reprint New York: Schocken, 1974.

Fenton, Paul B. "Jewish-Muslim Relations in the Medieval Mediterranean Area." In *The Cambridge Genizah Collections: Their Contents and Significance.* Ed. Stefan C. Reif. Cambridge: Cambridge University Press, 2002.

Fine, Lawrence, ed. *Judaism in Practice: From the Middle Ages through the Early Modern Period.* Princeton: Princeton University Press, 2001.

Finkel, Avraham Yaakov. *The Responsa Anthology.* Northvale, NJ: Jason Aronson, 1990.

Firestone, Reuven. "Jewish Culture in the Formative Period of Islam." In *Cultures of the Jews*. Ed. David Biale: 267–302. New York: Schocken, 2002.

Frank, Daniel. "Karaite Ritual." In *Judaism in Practice: From the Middle Ages through the Early Modern Period*. Ed. Lawrence Fine: 248–64. Princeton: Princeton University Press, 2001.

Freehof, Solomon. *The Responsa Literature* and *A Treasury of Responsa* (two volumes in one). New York: Ktav, 1973.

Gampel, Benjamin R. "A Letter to a Wayward Teacher: The Transformations of Sephardic Culture in Christian Iberia." In *Cultures of the Jews*. Ed. David Biale: 389–447. New York: Schocken, 2002.

Genesis Rabbah. Trans. Rabbi Dr. H. Freedman and Maurice Simon. In *The Midrash Rabbah*. Ed. H. Freedman and Maurice Simon. London: Soncino, 1977.

Gil, Moshe. *A History of Palestine, 634–1099*. Trans. Ethel Broido. Cambridge: Cambridge University Press, 1992.

Glick, Leonard B. *Abraham's Heirs: Jews and Christians in Medieval Europe*. Syracuse: Syracuse University Press, 1999.

Goitein, S. D. *Letters of Medieval Jewish Traders*. Princeton: Princeton University Press, 1973.

———. *A Medieval Society: The Jewish Communities of the Arab World as Portrayed in the Documents of the Cairo Geniza*. 5 vols. Berkeley: University of California Press, 1967–1988.

Golb, Norman. *The Jews in Medieval Normandy: A Social and Intellectual History*. Cambridge: Cambridge University Press, 1998.

Goldin, Judah. "The Period of the Talmud (135 B.C.E.–1035 C.E.). In *The Jews: Their History, Culture, and Religion*. Vol. 1. Ed. Louis Finkelstein: 115–215. New York: Jewish Publication Society, 1960.

Gordis, Daniel. *God Was not in the Fire*. New York: Simon & Schuster, 1995.

Grayzel, Solomon. *The Church and the Jews in the XIIIth Century*. Philadelphia: Dropsie College, 1933.

———. "The Confessions of a Medieval Jewish Convert." *Historia Judaica* 17 (1955): 89–120.

Grayzel, Solomon and Kenneth R. Stow. *The Church and the Jews in the XIIIth Century, 1254–1314*. Vol. 2. New York: Jewish Theological Seminary and Detroit: Wayne State University Press, 1989.

Green, Arthur. *A Guide to the Zohar*. Stanford: Stanford University Press, 2004.

Grossman, Avraham. *Pious and Rebellious: Jewish Women in Medieval Europe*. Trans. Jonathan Chipman. Waltham, MA: Brandeis University Press, 2004.

Guttmann, Julius. *Philosophies of Judaism*. Trans. David W. Silverman. New York: Holt, Rinehart and Winston, 1964.

Halevi, Judah. *The Kuzari: An Argument for the Faith of Israel*. Trans Hartwig Hirschfeld. Introduction Henry Slominsky. New York: Schocken, 1964.

Halevi, Jehudah. *Selected Poems of Jehudah Halevi*. Trans. Nina Salaman. Ed. Heinrich Brody. Philadelphia: Jewish Publication Society, 1924.

HaNagid, Shmuel. *Selected Poems of Shmuel HaNagid.* Trans. Peter Cole. Princeton: Princeton University Press, 1996.

Heng, Geraldine. "The Romance of England: *Richard Coer De Lyon*, Saracens, Jews and the Politics of Race and Nation." In *The Postcolonial Middle Ages.* Ed. Jeffrey Jerome Cohen: 135–71. New York: St. Martin's Press, 2000.

Herman-Judah. *Short Account of His Own Conversion.* In *Conversion and Text: The Cases of Augustine of Hippo, Herman-Judah, and Constantine Tsatsos.* Trans. Karl F. Morrison. Charlottesville: University of Virginia Press, 1992.

Herrin, Judith. *The Formation of Christendom.* Princeton: Princeton University Press, 1989.

Hoffman, Lawrence A. *The Canonization of the Synagogue Service.* Notre Dame: University of Notre Dame Press, 1979.

———. "The Role of Women at Rituals of their Infant Children." In *Judaism in Practice: From the Middle Ages through the Early Modern Period.* Ed. Lawrence Fine: 99–114. Princeton: Princeton University Press, 2001.

Horace. *Satires, Epistles, and Ars Poetica.* Trans. H. Rushton Fairclough. Cambridge, MA: Harvard University Press, 1926.

Ibn Ezra, Abraham. *Ibn Ezra's Commentary on the Pentateuch: Genesis.* Trans. H. Norman Strickman and Arthur M. Silver. New York: Menorah Publishing, 1988.

Ibn Ezra, Moses. *Selected Poems of Moses ibn Ezra.* Trans. Solomon Solis-Cohen. Ed. Heinrich Brody. Philadelphia: Jewish Publication Society, 1934.

Ibn Gabirol, Solomon. *Selected Poems of Solomon ibn Gabirol.* Trans. Peter Cole. Princeton: Princeton University Press, 2001.

———. *Selected Religious Poems of Solomon ibn Gabirol.* Trans. Israel Zangwill. Philadelphia: Jewish Publication Society, 1924.

Ibn Paquda, Bahya. *The Book of Direction to the Duties of the Heart.* Trans. Menahem Mansoor. London: Routledge & Kegan Paul, 1973.

Idel, Moshe. *Kabbalah: New Perspectives.* New Haven: Yale University Press, 1988.

Immanuel of Rome. *Tophet and Eden.* Trans. Herman Gollancz. London: University of London Press, 1921.

Irshai, Oded. "Confronting a Christian Empire: Jewish Culture in the World of Byzantium." In *Cultures of the Jews.* Ed. David Biale: 181–221. New York: Schocken, 2002.

Jerome. *Select Letters of St. Jerome.* Trans. F. A. Wright. Cambridge, MA: Harvard University Press, 1933.

Jordan, William Chester. *The French Monarchy and the Jews.* Philadelphia: University of Pennsylvania Press, 1989.

———. "The Last Tormentor of Christ: An Image of the Jew in Ancient and Medieval Exegesis, Art, and Drama." *Jewish Quarterly Review* 58 (1987): 21–47.

Juvenal and Persius. Trans. G. G. Ramsay. Cambridge, MA: Harvard University Press, 1918.

Kanarfogel, Ephraim. *Jewish Education and Society in the High Middle Ages*. Detroit: Wayne State University Press, 1992.

Kaplan, Mordecai M. *Judaism as a Civilization*. Enlarged edition. New York: Reconstructionist Press, 1957.

Katz, Jacob. *Exclusiveness and Tolerance: Studies in Jewish-Gentile Relations in Medieval and Modern Times*. Oxford: Oxford University Press, 1961.

Kellner, Menachem. *Must a Jew Believe Anything?* London: Littman Library of Jewish Civilization, 1999.

King Artus: A Hebrew Arthurian Romance of 1279. Ed. and trans. Curt Leviant. New York: Ktav, 1969.

Koran. Trans. N. J. Dawood. Hammondsworth: Penguin, 1956.

Koran Interpreted. Trans. Arthur J. Arberry. New York: Macmillan, 1955.

Kraemer, David. "Composition and Meaning in the Bavli." *Prooftexts* 8 (1988): 271–91.

———. "The Intended Reader as a Key to Interpreting the Bavli." *Prooftexts* 13 (1993): 125–40.

———. *The Mind of the Talmud: An Intellectual History of the Bavli*. Oxford: Oxford University Press, 1990.

Kramer, Joel L. "Women Speak for Themselves." In *The Cambridge Genizah Collections: Their Contents and Significance*. Ed. Stefan C. Reif. Cambridge: Cambridge University Press, 2002.

Kugel, James. *The Idea of Biblical Poetry: Parallelism and Its History*. New Haven: Yale University Press, 1981.

———. *On Being a Jew*. Johns Hopkins University Press, 1990.

Lamentations Rabbah. Trans. A. Cohen. In *The Midrash Rabbah*. Ed. H. Freedman and Maurice Simon. London: Soncino, 1973.

Langer, Ruth. "Revisiting Early Rabbinic Liturgy: The Recent Contributions of Ezra Fleisher." *Prooftexts* 19 (1999): 179–94.

Langland, William. *Piers Plowman: The B Version*. Ed. George Kane and E. Talbot Donaldson. London: The Athlone Press, 1975.

———. *Piers Plowman by William Langland: An Edition of the C-text*. Ed. Derek Pearsall. Berkeley: University of California Press.

Langmuir, Gavin. *Toward a Definition of Antisemitism*. Berkeley: University of California Press, 1996.

Lasker, Daniel. "The Jewish Critique of Christianity under Islam in the Middle Ages." *Proceedings of the American Academy for Jewish Research* 57 (1990–91): 121–53.

———. *Jewish Philosophical Polemics against Christianity in the Middle Ages*. New York: Ktav, 1977.

Lavon, Yaakov, trans. *The Complete Art Scroll Selichos: Ashkenaz*. Ed. R. Avie Gold. Brooklyn: Mesorah, 1992.

Leff, Gordon. *Medieval Thought: St. Augustine to Ockham*. Hammondsworth: Penguin Books, 1958.

Leibowitz, Nehama. *Studies in Devarim (Deuteronomy)*. Trans. and adapted, Aryeh Newman. Jerusalem: Maor Wallach, nd.

Lewis, Bernard. *The Jews of Islam*. Princeton: Princeton University Press, 1984.

———, trans. *Music of a Distant Drum: Classical Arabic, Persian, Turkish, and Hebrew Poems*. Princeton: Princeton University Press, 2001.

Lipman, Vivian D. *The Jews of Medieval Norwich*. London: Jewish Historical Society of England, 1967.

Lipton, Sara. *Images of Intolerance: The Representation of Jews and Judaism in the Bible Moralisé*. Berkeley: University of California Press, 1999.

Loewe, Raphael. *Ibn Gabirol*. New York: Grove Weidenfeld, 1989.

Maimonides, Moses. *The Guide of the Perplexed*. Trans. Shlomo Pines. Chicago: University of Chicago Press, 1963.

———. *Introduction to the Talmud*. Trans. Zvi L. Lampel. New York: Judaica Press, 1975.

———. *Letters of Maimonides*. Trans. Leon D. Stitskin. New York: Yeshiva University Press, 1977.

———. *A Maimonides Reader*. Ed. Isadore Twersky. Springfield, NJ: Behrman House, 1972.

———. *Mishneh Torah*. Trans. Rabbi Eliyahu Touger. Jerusalem: Moznaim: 1989.

Malter, Henry. *Saadiah Gaon: His Life and Works*. Philadelphia: Jewish Publication Society, 1942.

Marcus, Ivan G. "The Dynamics of Jewish Renaissance and Renewal in the Twelfth Century." In *Jews and Christians in Twelfth-Century Europe*. Ed. Michael A. Signer and John Van Engen: 27–45. Notre Dame: University of Notre Dame Press, 2001.

———. "From Politics to Martyrdom: Shifting Paradigms in the Hebrew Narratives of the 1096 Crusade Riots." *Prooftexts* 2 (1982): 40–52.

———. "History, Story and Collective Memory: Narrativity in Early Ashkenazic Culture." *Prooftexts* 10 (1990): 365–88.

———. "Jews and Christians Imagining Each Other in Medieval Europe." *Prooftexts* 15 (1995): 209–26.

———. *Piety and Society: The Jewish Pietists of Medieval Germany*. Leiden: E. J. Brill, 1981.

———. *Rituals of Childhood: Jewish Acculturation in Medieval Europe*. New Haven: Yale University Press, 1996.

Marcus, Jacob. *The Jew in the Medieval World. A Source Book: 315–1791*. 1938. Reprint, New York: Atheneum, 1975.

Markus, R. A. *Gregory the Great and His World*. Cambridge: Cambridge University Press, 1997.

Matter, E. Ann. *The Voice of My Beloved: The Song of Songs in Western Medieval Christianity*. Philadelphia: University of Pennsylvania Press, 1990.

McFarlane, K. B. *John Wycliffe and the Beginnings of English Nonconformity*. London: English University Press, 1952.

Meir of Rothenburg. "O Law that has been consumed by fire." In *Tisha B'Av Compendium*. Trans. Rev. Abraham Rosenfeld: 161–2. New York: The Judaica Press, 1989.

Menache, Sophia. "Faith, Myth, and Politics in the Stereotype of the Jews and their Expulsion from England and France." *Jewish Quarterly Review* 75 (1985): 351–74.

Mishnah: A New Translation. Trans. Jacob Neusner. New Haven: Yale University Press, 1988.

Nachmanides. *Commentary on the Torah: Genesis*. Trans. C. Chavel. 1971. Reprint, New York: Shilo, 1999.

———. *The Disputation at Barcelona*. Trans. Charles B. Chavel. New York: Shilo, 1983.

Nemoy, Leon. *Karaite Anthology: Excerpts from the Early Literature*. New Haven: Yale University Press, 1952.

Neusner, Jacob. "Defining Judaism." In *The Blackwell Companion to Judaism*. Ed. Jacob Neusner and Alan J. Avery-Peck. Malden, MA: Blackwell, 2000.

———. *How the Talmud Works and Why the Talmud Won*. Kalamazoo, MI: Medieval Institute Publications, 1996.

———, ed. *The Mishnah: A New Translation*. New Haven: Yale University Press, 1988.

——— and Alan J. Avery-Peck, eds. *The Blackwell Companion to Judaism*. Malden, MA: Blackwell, 2000.

Newman, Paul, B. *Daily Life in the Middle Ages*. Jefferson, NC: McFarland & Co., 2001.

Nulman, Macy. *The Encyclopedia of Jewish Prayer*. Northvale, NJ: Jason Aronson, 1993.

Pagis, Dan. "Trends in the Study of Medieval Hebrew Literature." *AJS Review* 4 (1979): 125–41.

Parkes, James. *Antisemitism*. Chicago: Quadrangle Books, 1963.

Perlmutter, Haim. *Tools for Tosafos*. Southfield, MI: Targum, 1996.

Peters, Edward, ed. *The First Crusade: The Chronicle of Fulcher of Chartres and Other Source Materials*. Philadelphia: University of Pennsylvania Press, 1971.

Petuchowski, Jakob J. *Theology and Poetry: Studies in the Medieval Piyyut*. London: Routledge & Kegan Paul, 1978.

Pirkei Avot. In *The ArtScroll Siddur*. Trans. Nosson Scherman: 545–87. New York: Mesorah: 1984.

Rabinowitz, L. *The Social Life of the Jews of Northern France in the XII-XIV Centuries*. 2^d ed. 1938. Reprint, New York: Hermon Press, 1972.

Rashi. Commentary on Pentateuch. In *Pentateuch with Targum Onkelos, Haphtaroth and Rashi's Commentary*. Trans. Rev. M. Rosenbaum and Dr. A. M. Silberman. New York: Hebrew Publishing Co., nd.

———. Commentary on Psalms. In *Psalms: Translation of Text, Rashi and Commentary*. Trans. Rabbi A. J. Rosenberg. New York: Judaica Press, 1991.

———. Commentary on Song of Songs. In *The Song of Songs: A New English Translation*. Trans. Rabbi A. J. Rosenberg. New York: Judaica Press, 1992.

Reed, Annette Yoshiko. *Fallen Angels and the History of Judaism and Christianity: The Reception of Enochic Literature*. Cambridge: Cambridge University Press, 2005.

Reif, Stefan C., ed. *The Cambridge Genizah Collections: Their Contents and Significance*. Cambridge: Cambridge University Press, 2002.

———. "A Centennial Assessment of Genizah Studies." In *The Cambridge Genizah Collections: Their Contents and Significance*. Cambridge: Cambridge University Press, 2002.

———. *Judaism and Hebrew Prayer: New Perspectives on Jewish Liturgical History*. Cambridge: Cambridge University Press, 1993.

Richardson, H. G. *The English Jewry under Angevin Kings*. London: Methuen, 1960.

Rosenblatt, Samuel. "Introduction." In Saadiah Gaon, *The Book of Beliefs and Opinions*. New Haven: Yale University Press, 1948.

Rosenfeld, Rabbi Abraham. *Tisha B'av Compendium: Tephilot and Kinot*. New York: Judaica Press, 1989.

Roth, Cecil, ed. *The Dark Ages: Jews in Christian Europe, 711–1096*. New Brunswick: Rutgers University Press, 1966.

———. *A History of the Jews in England*, 3rd edition. Oxford: Clarendon Press, 1964.

———. "Italy." In *The Dark Ages: Jews in Christian Europe, 711–1096*. New Brunswick: Rutgers University Press, 1966.

Roth, Norman. "'Deal Gently with the Young Man': Love of Boys in Medieval Hebrew Poetry of Spain." *Speculum* 57 (1982): 20–51.

Rubenstein, Jeffrey L. *The Culture of the Babylonian Talmud*. Baltimore: Johns Hopkins University Press, 2003.

Rubin, Miri. *Gentile Tales: The Narrative Assault on Late Medieval Jews*. Philadelphia: University of Pennsylvania Press, 2004.

Runciman, Steven. *A History of the Crusades. Vol. 1: The First Crusade*. 1951. Reprint, New York: Harper & Row, 1964.

Saadiah Gaon. *The Book of Beliefs and Opinions*. Trans. Samuel Rosenblatt. New Haven: Yale University Press, 1948.

Saperstein, Marc. *Jewish Preaching 1200–1800: An Anthology*. New Haven: Yale University Press, 1989.

Scheil, Andrew P. *The Footsteps of Israel: Understanding Jews in Anglo-Saxon England*. Ann Arbor: University of Michigan Press, 2004.

Scheindlin, Raymond. "Communal Prayer and Liturgical Poetry." In *Judaism in Practice: From the Middle Ages through the Early Modern Period*. Ed. Lawrence Fine, 39–51. Princeton: Princeton University Press, 2001.

———. *The Gazelle: Medieval Hebrew Poems on God, Israel, and the Soul*. New York: Oxford University Press, 1991.

———. "Merchants and Intellectuals, Rabbis and Poets: Judeo-Arabic Culture in the Golden Age of Islam." In *Cultures of the Jews: A New History*. Ed. David Biale: 315–86. New York: Schocken, 2002.

————. *Wine, Women, and Death: Medieval Hebrew Poems on the Good Life*. New York: Oxford University Press, 1986.

Schiffman, Lawrence. *From Text to Tradition: A History of Second Temple and Rabbinic Judaism*. Hoboken: Ktav, 1991.

Schirmann, Jefim. "The Function of the Hebrew Poet in Medieval Spain." *Jewish Social Studies* 16 (1954): 235–52.

Scholem, Gershom. *Origins of the Kabbalah*. Ed. R. Zwi Werblowsky. Trans. Allan Arkush. New York: Jewish Publication Society, 1987.

Schwarzfuchs, S. "France and Germany under the Carolingians. In *The Dark Ages: Jews in Christian Europe, 711–1096*. Ed. Cecil Roth: 122–42. New Brunswick: Rutgers University Press, 1966.

————. "France under the Early Capets." *The Dark Ages: Jews in Christian Europe, 711–1096*. Ed. Cecil Roth: 143–61. New Brunswick: Rutgers University Press, 1966.

Seiferth, Wolfgang S. *Synagogue and Church in the Middle Ages: Two Symbols in Art and Literature*. Trans. Lee Chadeayne and Paul Gottwald. New York: Frederick Ungar, 1970.

Shabbat. Ed. Rabbi Pinhas Kehati. Trans. Edward Levin. Jerusalem: Eliner Library, 1994.

Shepkaru, Shmuel. "To Die for God: Martyr's Heaven in Hebrew and Latin Crusade Narratives." *Speculum* 77 (2002): 311–41.

Signer, Michael A. "God's Love for Israel: Apologetic and Hermeneutical Strategies in Twelfth-Century Biblical Exegesis. In *Jews and Christians in Twelfth-Century Europe*. Ed. Michael A. Signer and John Van Engen, 123–49. Notre Dame: University of Notre Dame Press, 2001.

————. "King/Messiah: Rashi's Exegesis of Psalm 2." *Prooftexts* 3 (1983): 273–8.

———— and John Van Engen, eds. *Jews and Christians in Twelfth-Century Europe*. Notre Dame: University of Notre Dame Press, 2001.

Smalley, Beryl. *The Study of the Bible in the Middle Ages*. South Bend: University of Notre Dame Press, 1964.

South English Legendary. Ed. Charlotte D'Evelyn and Anna J. Mill. London: Oxford University Press, 1951–2.

Southern, R. W. *St. Anselm and his Biographer*. Cambridge: Cambridge University Press, 1963.

Spiegel, Shalom. *The Last Trial*. Trans. Judah Goldin. New York: Schocken: 1969.

————. "On Medieval Hebrew Poetry." In *The Jews: Their History, Culture, and Religion. Vol 1*. Ed. Louis Finkelstein: 854–92. New York: Jewish Publication Society, 1960.

Stacey, Robert. "The Conversion of Jews to Christianity in Thirteenth-Century England." *Speculum* 67 (1992): 263–83.

————. "Jews and Christians in Twelfth-Century England: Some Dynamics of a Changing Relationship." In *Jews and Christians in Twelfth-Century Europe*. Ed.

Michael A. Signer and John Van Engen: 340–54. Notre Dame: University of Notre Dame Press, 2001.

Steinsaltz, Adin. *The Talmud: A Reference Guide.* Trans. Israel V. Berman. New York: Random House, 1989.

———. *We Jews: Who Are We and What Should We Do?* Trans. Yehuda Hanegbi and Rebecca Toueg. San Francisco: Jossey-Bass, 2005.

Stern, David. "New Directions in Medieval Hebrew Poetry." *Prooftexts* 1 (1981): 104–15.

Stow, Kenneth R. *Alienated Minority: The Jews of Medieval Latin Europe.* Cambridge, MA: Harvard University Press, 1992.

Strickman, H. "Forward." In *Ibn Ezra's Commentary on the Pentateuch: Genesis.* Trans. H. Norman Strickman and Arthur M. Silver. New York: Menorah Publishing, 1988.

Tacitus. *The Histories.* Trans. Clifford H. Moore. Cambridge, MA: Harvard University Press, 1931.

Toaff, Ariel. *Love, Work, and Death: Jewish Life in Medieval Umbria.* Trans. Judith Landry. Portland, OR: Vallentine, Mitchell & Co., 1996.

Tomasch, Sylvia. "Postcolonial Chaucer and the Virtual Jew." In *The Postcolonial Middle Ages.* Ed. Jeffrey Jerome Cohen: 243–60. New York: St. Martin's Press, 2000.

Townley Plays. Ed. George England. London: Oxford University Press, 1897.

Twersky, Isadore. *Introduction to the Code of Maimonides (Mishneh Torah).* New Haven: Yale University Press, 1980.

———. *Rabad of Posquières: A Twelfth-Century Talmudist.* Rev. ed. Philadelphia: Jewish Publication Society, 1980.

Van Engen, John. "Introduction: Jews and Christians Together in the Twelfth Century." In *Jews and Christians in Twelfth-Century Europe.* Ed. Michael A. Signer and John Van Engen: 1–8. Notre Dame: University of Notre Dame Press, 2001.

———. "Ralph of Flaix: The Book of Leviticus Interpreted as Christian Community." In *Jews and Christians in Twelfth-Century Europe.* Ed. Michael A. Signer and John Van Engen: 150–70. Notre Dame: University of Notre Dame Press, 2001.

Van Steenberghen, Fernand. *Aristotle in the West: The Origins of Latin Aristotelianism.* Trans. Leonard Johnston. Louvain: E. Nauwelaerts, 1955.

Weinberger, Leon J., ed. and trans. *Jewish Prince in Moslem Spain: Selected Poems of Samuel ibn Nagrela.* University of Alabama Press, 1973.

Wilken, Robert L. *John Chrysostom and the Jews: Rhetoric and Reality in the Late Fourth Century.* Berkeley: University of California Press, 1983.

Yuval, Israel J. *Two Nations in Your Womb: Perceptions of Jews and Christians in Late Antiquity and the Middle Ages.* Trans. Barbara Harshav and Jonathan Chipman. Berkeley: University of California Press, 2006.

Zohar, Vol 1. Trans. Daniel C. Matt. Stanford: Stanford University Press, 2004.

Index

About the Author

THEODORE L. STEINBERG is Distinguished Professor of English at SUNY Fredonia and the author of over thirty articles and four books, including *Reading the Middle Ages* (2003).